Japan's First Student Radicals

Harvard East Asian Series 70

The East Asian Research Center at Harvard University administers research projects designed to further scholarly understanding of China, Japan, Korea, Vietnam, and adjacent areas.

Japan's First Student Radicals

Henry DeWitt Smith, II

Harvard University Press
Cambridge, Massachusetts
1972

cB

Contents

Tables

Charts

Preface

Drama dictates that this story begin near the end, on January 18, 1969. Throughout that day, beginning shortly after dawn and lasting on into the next afternoon, thousands of Japanese riot police laid seige to several buildings on the campus of Tokyo University in an effort to evict the masked and helmeted student radicals who had occupied the university campus for over six months. This epic exchange of rocks, firebombs, and tear gas, now commemorated on the Japanese left as the "1.18 Incident," proved the climax of the turbulent student movement of the late 1960s and occasioned much comment both in Japan and abroad.

On the same day and on the same campus, however, no more than three hundred yards from the center of the raging battle, occurred an event wholly neglected by journalists but of striking historical interest. Some sixty men, most in their mid-sixties, had gathered in the alumni club to reminisce about their own days as left-wing student activists in the 1920s. Coming together for the first time since their graduation from Tokyo Imperial University over three decades before, these men—now prominent politicians, journalists, writers, and businessmen—were commemorating the fiftieth anniversary of the founding in December 1918 of the Shinjinkai (New Man Society), the leading prewar left-wing student group. Wholly coincidental to the more newsworthy activities nearby, this reunion of the former Shinjinkai membership was a dramatic indication of the long history of student radicalism in modern Japan.

Striking as this coincidence may have been, it would be misleading to conclude that the historical significance of the Shinjinkai, the group which this book will treat in the greatest detail, lies purely in the newsworthiness of its postwar successors. While such continuity is certainly of interest, I would prefer to deal with it in the manner of a postscript and to see the student movement of the period between the world wars as a phenomenon of great importance in itself, marking off a new era in the development both of the concerns of the young and of social protest in modern Japan. The changes which the prewar student movement effected in the structure of the entire left-wing movement will be dealt with in the final chapter; some preliminary observations are in order, however, on the broad patterns of generational concern in Japan leading up to the beginnings of the student movement in 1918.

The unusually rapid pace of modernization in Japan since the Meiji Restoration of 1868 has naturally caused a continuing pattern of generational dislocation. The evolving crises of "youth" (by which term I refer to that small minority of the young at a given time who are educated, articulate, and concerned with broad national issues) in modern Japan can be understood only by reference to certain basic intellectual assumptions inherited from the Tokugawa period (1600–1868). These assumptions were transmitted in the traditions of the elite warrior-official samurai class and began with the notion that all men have a determined place in society. While there is a certain tension between the Confucian ideal that a man's "place" be determined by his abilities and the long-established Japanese tendency to ascribe rank by birth, it is nevertheless accepted that some men will naturally emerge to lead the rest: the youth with whom we are here concerned considered themselves, often unconsciously, part of this natural ruling elite. A further assumption of the Tokugawa Confucian heritage was that political behavior is basically a matter of ethics and that the right to govern thus falls to the ethically pure—again, a category to which the young are quick to assign themselves. A third assumption is that the ethical behavior of those who rule is closely related to the study of basic principles. This meant that students, those engaged in full-time study, were almost by definition concerned with politics.

Upon these basic assumptions, broadly Confucian in origin, was imposed the historical situation of the systematic adoption of Western models to achieve rapid economic development and military prepared-ness. The resultant tensions which were thrust upon all Japanese intellectuals, and the young in particular, may be broadly classed as two: those deriving from the "Westernness" of the process and those deriving from its "modernity." The earliest strains were largely of the former sort, relating to the problem of cultural identity, and have been provocatively analyzed by Kenneth Pyle in *The New Generation in Meiji Japan*. This generation was "new" relative to the "old men of Meiji" who had engineered the revolutionary reforms of the Restor-ation; specifically, they were "the first generation of Japanese to attend the new Western-oriented schools of higher learning." [1] Reaching maturity in the decade before the Sino-Japanese War of 1894–95, this generation struggled with the fundamental problem of national identity and of the proper use to be made of the Japanese heritage in the process of modernization.

The two opposing sides of the "new generation" of Meiji Japan, the Westernizers of the Min'yūsha and the traditionalists of the Seikyōsha, had in common a preoccupation with the integrity of Japan as a nation vis-à-vis other nations; "everywhere in Meiji Japan," one writer has observed, "one is struck by the stress on dedication and responsibility to what is described as the national interest." [2] Success for youth in late nineteenth century Japan was measured against potential contribution to the success of the nation in its struggle for international security and recognition. State service, thus, was the highest ideal for Meiji students, an ideal strongly reinforced by Con-fucian precedent. This rather exclusive concern for national interest meant on the one hand a tendency to gloss over social and economic divisions *within* the nation and on the other a reluctance to indulge in self-centered philosophizing. The sights of Meiji students were set high and wide, giving their ambitions a certain heroic cast.

A major shift from this Meiji pattern of the nation-centered youth began to occur around the turn of the century and was apparent by the death of the Emperor Meiji in 1912. Of the two major historical

1. Kenneth B. Pyle, *The New Generation in Meiji Japan—Problems of Cultural Identity, 1885–1895* (Stanford, 1969), p. 3.
2. Marius B. Jansen, "Changing Japanese Attitudes Toward Modernization," in Marius B. Jansen, ed., *Changing Japanese Attitudes Toward Modernization* (Prince-ton, 1965), p. 67.

developments which effected this shift, perhaps the more important was a series of dramatic diplomatic successes which released Japan from the sense of foreign threat that had done much to mold the nationalism of the earlier "new generation." Revision of the unequal treaties, military victory first over China and then over tsarist Russia, alliance on equal terms with Great Britain, and entrance into the imperialist club of nations with the acquisition of Formosa and Korea: in the course of ten-odd years, the enduring Meiji goals of national independence, military might, and international respect had been achieved beyond all doubt.

A second major determinant in attitudes among the young was a basic transition in the character of state education, from the variegated, open, and largely Western emphases of the early decades of Meiji to a pattern of highly uniform indoctrination in the official myths of imperial Japan. At the same time, discipline and the enforcement of standard behavior (the requirement of uniforms for students in higher education was one example) became increasingly effective, and one finds a gradual shift away from the diversity and rowdiness of the early Meiji student population. For Japanese educated under the new uniform state system, which was in full operation by about 1905, national identity presented no immediate crisis, for it was built into the educational curriculum. The fact of nationalism by indoctrination meant that adolescent rebellion would most typically be in opposition to the state rather than in support of it. It meant at the same time that a reemergence of a perceived threat to national integrity, of the sort which was to occur in the 1930s, might trigger the deep nationalist responses that had been conditioned in the period of compulsory education.

These changes in Japan's place in the world and in the educational system were reflected in the emergence of a wholly new image of Japanese youth in the decade between the war with Russia in 1904–05 and the First World War. This might be seen as a "middle generation" between the "new generation of Meiji Japan" and the generation of students with which this book is concerned. This middle generation is usually seen as engaged in negative retreat from the heroic, outgoing nationalism of the earlier generation. From a focus on the "nation" emerges a stress on the "self," whether in the form of the selfish acquisition of wealth (the "success youth" or *seikō seinen*) or of existentialist despair ("the anguishing youth" or *hammon seinen*).[3] Symbolic of the new pattern was the suicide of First Higher School student Fujimura Misao, who in 1903 leapt from the Kegon Falls at Nikkō after carving some nihilistic verses in a nearby tree.[4] One scholar sees a general shift from the "political youth" of mid-Meiji to the "literary youth" of the early twentieth century.[5] Maruyama Masao speaks contemptuously of "the retreatism of the youth of this new era," susceptible either to a "feeling of dull and nihilistic boredom" or to a "vulgar and light-hearted" pursuit of material success.

Perhaps the most revealing analysis of this middle generation was made by Tokutomi Sôhō, the key spokesman for the earlier "new generation of Meiji", in his 1916 *Taishō no seinen to teikoku no zento* (Taishō youth and the future of the empire). Distressed by the selfish concerns of the "Taishō youth" (after the Taishō period, 1912–1926), Soho made an analogy to the fortunes of a merchant family. The Restoration leaders were like the founders of the enterprise, which had finally succeeded under the second generation, corresponding to that of Soho himself. But it was typically the third generation in merchant families, Soho pointed out, that saw a decline in fortunes of the house, since these "rich master's sons" (*kanemochi no wakadanna*) were soft and spoiled, having no knowledge of the hardships of the two generations before them. The "Taishō youth" were thus the *kanemochi no wakadanna* of modern Japan, taking for granted the national prestige for which their Meiji predecessors had struggled; they were like those born atop a mountain, who enjoy the view but fail to realize how hard it was for their parents to reach the summit.[6]

---

3. Masao Maruyama, "Patterns of Individuation and the Case of Japan: A Conceptual Scheme," in Jansen, ed., *Changing Japanese Attitudes Toward Modernization*, pp. 508–509. This typology of youth was outlined in Tokutomi Iichirō (Sohō), *Taishō no seinen to teikoku no zento* (Min'yūsha, 1916), pp. 8–26, where in addition to the "success youth" and the "anguishing youth" he describes a "model youth" (*mohan seinen*), a "debauched youth" (*chindeki seinen*), and a "nondescript youth" (*mushoku seinen*).

4. Karasawa Tomitarō, *Gakusei no rekishi—Gakusei seikatsu no shakaishiteki kōsatsu* (Sōbunsha, 1955), p. 74.

5. Uchida Yoshihiko and Shiota Shōbei, "Chishiki seinen no sho-ruikei," in Chikuma shobō, ed., *Kindai Nihon shisō shi kōza*, 8 vols., (editor, 1959–61), IV, 268–270.

6. Tokutomi, pp. 5–8.

It would be a mistake, however, to see in these images of the middle generation of the period 1905–1918 merely a negative reaction to the heroic nationalism of Meiji youth. In longer perspective than was possible for Tokutomi in 1916, one may rather detect a *positive* attitude, in the sense of a preliminary grappling with the second class of tensions, those related less to the problem of "Westernness" than to that of "modernity." It was in this period that Japan began to emerge as a modern nation on a truly quantitative scale, as the economy took on the characteristics of modern-style growth. With economic growth came all the tensions of dislocation, isolation, and alienation which are imposed by industrialization and its resultant population shifts and urbanization. The reactions of the middle generation were in effect the first responses to the complexities and ambiguities of modern life, a confused but honest groping in the absence of the settled single standard of national integrity which had sustained the previous generation. It would be fairer to protray this generation as "self-concerned" rather than "selfish," as seeking within the individual a standard which the nation no longer provided.

The middle generation led directly into the generation with which this book is concerned. The pivot in the change was the First World War, for a number of reasons which will be made clear in the course of the narrative. In general terms, however, the change was produced by Japan's continued modern-style growth. The rapid development of the capitalist system, for example, especially in its primary concern for a high growth rate rather than equal distribution of prosperity, created a wide variety of new social tensions to which students were particularly quick to respond. The mushrooming growth of communications—publishing, transportation, radio—meant a broader awareness of what was happening throughout the country. The rapid expansion of the urban complexes and the corresponding stagnation of the rural sector meant a weakening of the solidarity of old family patterns and a search for new forms of association.

These various trends, in conjunction with specific events after 1918, led to the emergence of a new type of "social youth", who in the conventional analysis is seen as escaping from the self-centered anguishing of his "literary youth" predecessor and replacing "self" with "society." [7] The concern was now with domestic strife rather than national integrity or personal melancholy. The preoccupation of this new post-World War I generation with social problems and their political solution did not mean, of course, that the earlier dilemmas of young Japanese had been resolved: rather they had been overlaid with a crisis which in the historical circumstances seemed more pressing. The problem of cultural identity with which the "new generation of Meiji" had grappled was to be revived in far less heroic guise in the 1930s, and many young Japanese were to turn again to a single-minded pre-occupation with the fate of the nation. The problem of individual fulfillment and religious seeking which had characterized the "middle generation" likewise never disappeared: it simply became a recessive trait during the interwar period.

I have attempted to describe and analyze the organized activities of this generation of "social youth" in the 1920s in the left-wing student movement, while emphasizing the continuities of the movement in terms both of the Meiji heritage and of the post-World War II legacy. I have focused on the Shinjinkai at Tokyo Imperial University, both because it was the largest and most prestigious of the many prewar student groups and because its activities, covering the full range of left-wing student activism, serve as a microcosm of the entire student movement. The Shinjinkai itself was dissolved, along with all other legal left-wing campus groups, in the late 1920s, and I have treated the problem of student activism in the 1930s only in hasty outline. This superficial treatment stems largely from my conviction that the focus of student concerns was then no longer represented by the communist movement, which survived only in a state of barren secrecy. It was only when history took a further critical shift in 1945 that the left-wing student movement again became a central generational motif.

I have at no point attempted to delineate the many interesting comparisons which can be made between the Japanese student movement in the 1920s and student movements in other countries, both before

7. Uchida and Shiota, pp. 271–272. This section on the "social youth" was written by Shiota and deals specifically with the Shinjinkai and the Kensetsusha Dōmei.

and after World War II, feeling that the primary interest in the history of the Shinjinkai lies in its role within the Japanese context rather than in the typology of student movements. It might merely be suggested that a comparison with the Chinese student movement provides one of the most striking contrasts in terms of the role played by nationalism, which was as much a weakness to the student radicals in Japan as it was a strength to their Chinese counterparts. Those interested in the comparative approach to student movements will find much provocative material in recent scholarship on the subject.[8]

Acknowledgment is due to many institutions and persons encountered in the course of my research. I am grateful to the Academic Establishment—in my case, the Stanford Center for Japanese Studies, Harvard University, the United States Office of Education, and the Foreign Area Fellowship Program—for more-than-adequate facilities and funds. Professor Albert Craig of Harvard University offered much incisive advice as a thesis adviser, and Gail Bernstein, Tetsuo Najita, Kate and Yoshiyuki Nakai, and Patricia Golden Steinhoff, among others, were kind enough to read the manuscript and provide constructive criticism. The list of benefactors in Japan is long, and I can only single out a few. Professor Ishida Takeshi of the Institute of Social Science at Tokyo University kindly arranged for me to use the name and facilities of his institute. Professor Banno Junji, Mrs. Ishida Reiko, and Miss Ishii Yōko served as patient tutors, while Mr. Ariyama Teruo and Miss Imai Noriko provided valuable assistance in scanning periodicals for information on the student movement. Mr. Oguro Kazuo of the Institute of Social Science shared with me his expertise on prewar government materials. Mr. Watanabe Etsuji, formerly of the All-Japan Federation of Labor (Dōmei), was unsparingly generous with his time, his own library, and his knowledge of the Japanese left. Finally and above all, I am deeply indebted to the former members of the Shinjinkai, and in particular to Mr. Ishidō Kiyotomo. All those members whom I approached were, with only rare exceptions, willing to spend long hours discussing their personal past and to offer me unstint-

8. For a bibliography of this material, see Philip G. Altbach, *A Select Bibliography on Students, Politics, and Higher Education*, rev. ed. (Cambridge, Mass., 1970).

ing hospitality. Their failing memories may have often blurred the image of events long past, but their unfailing passion and integrity as human beings made the causes of their student days far more understandable to one of a very different time and culture.

Japan's First Student Radicals

1 | The Prewar Japanese University System

Student radicals like to think of themselves as free agents, independent critics who stand apart from established institutions and see the flaws and tensions to which those enmeshed in the institutions are blind. To the extent that students are occupational transients with no lasting responsibilities, this is true. And yet students, despite their denials, are the prisoners of the schools they attend: campus political activism depends as much upon the nature of the educational system and its role in society as upon a critical fusion of youthful idealism with burning causes. The school not only molds student attitudes and thus, unwittingly, prepares the way for radical behavior but also provides a base of organization without which students would be powerless to exert political pressure. To understand both the roots and the scope of student radicalism in prewar Japan, it is necessary first to consider the structure of the Japanese university system and the ways in which its unique traditions worked to create an environment highly hospitable to a political student movement.

The prewar university was the pinnacle of the modern Japanese system of education, which emerged in the three decades following the Meiji Restoration of 1868, and which by the early years of the twentieth century was complete in basic structure.[1] Since the system was constructed by a process of accretion, it was so complex—until at last simplified by post-World War II reforms—as to defy simple description. The broad formula was a little education for the many and a

1. For a more detailed description of the prewar educational system in English, see Herbert Passin, *Society and Education in Japan* (New York, 1965), chap. 5.

great deal of education for the few, with intermediary levels to provide the technical skills necessary for manning a rapidly industrializing modern state. The system may be seen as an elaborate network organized vertically into four broad levels and horizontally into a number of multiplying channels (sometimes referred to as "tracks," "streams," or "pipelines"); these are depicted in Chart 1. Each shift from one level to another was determined almost exclusively by competitive examinations, which substantially decreased the number of students and forced each of the survivors to make a critical choice among a variety of channels.

The lowest level was primary, consisting of a single channel, the elementary school, compulsory and coeducational for four years from 1886 and extended to six years in 1907, by which time 97 percent of all school-age children were in attendance.[2] Graduation from elementary school was the end of formal education for the majority of prewar Japanese, but those with the necessary intelligence, ambition, social acceptability, and financial resources could move on to the secondary level. Here they were faced with the first stage of division into separate channels, which were three in number.[3] Of minor importance was a low-level program of vocational training, terminal in two to three years. Much more heavily attended was a "higher elementary school," which provided an additional three years of preparatory training and led to a further stage of division into high-level vocational training or a course of normal education to provide teachers for the elementary schools. The third post-primary option was a "middle school" which was almost exclusively preparatory for the third, or college, level and normally consisted of five years. It was this channel alone which led to the higher reaches of the educational system.[4]

The elementary and secondary levels offered minimal potential for

2. Naka Arata, *Meiji no kyōiku* (Shibundō, 1967), p. 274.

3. Here and in the following statistics, I have omitted female students, who in higher education were few in number and dedicated largely to such studies as home-making, music, and literature. The few who had any interest in politics played only a very minor role in the student movement. See Chapter 6 at note 43.

4. It was possible, after 1919, to enter higher school after only four years of middle school, but only the brightest students were able to do so, generally about one fourth of the total. There did exist a number of minor alternative routes, which however accounted for only a tiny percentage of the total students in higher education. Entrance to the higher schools in particular was almost impossible without completing middle school.

student radicalism. The vast majority of the schools were part of the public educational system and under the control of government authorities. As such, they were highly dispersed geographically, offering no single large concentrations of students which might encourage a

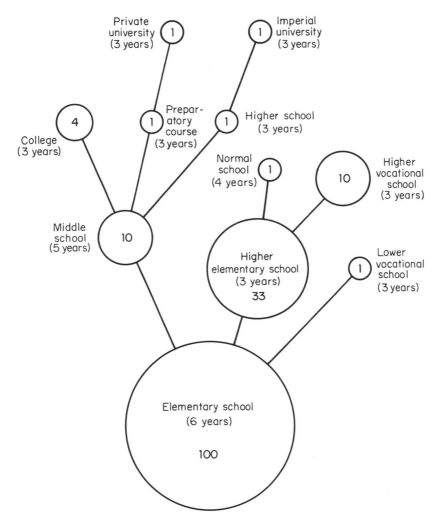

Chart 1. Educational channels in prewar Japan [a]

[a] This chart applies only to males. Numerals within each circle indicate the approximate number of students to enter each type of school out of one hundred elementary school graduates in 1920. These have been calculated from statistics in Mombushō, ed., *Gakusei hachijūnen shi* (1954), pp. 1042–1067.

mass student movement. Even more important, the rigidity of the curriculum, the stress on orthodoxy, and the intensity of competition all
combined to stifle any critical attitudes which might be brewing in an
individual's mind. Rowdiness and disobedience were scarcely unknown
in schools at the secondary level, to be sure, but such activity was
rarely politically inspired.

The only students to continue past the secondary level were those
in middle school. At the end of five years of intensive preparation
came the examinations which formed the tightest bottleneck in the
entire system of education, far more competitive on the whole than
those which had been taken first to enter the secondary level. After
years of grueling study under an inelastic curriculum which stressed
rote memorization far more than critical analysis, almost one half of
the students found themselves unable to continue their education. For
the remainder, the next step again called for a choice among different
channels, all, as before, mutually exclusive. The choice to be made
involved two dimensions, that of a three-year terminal "college" program versus a six-year "university" program, and that of a private institution versus a state or public institution. The "college" course of
three years (occasionally more) covered a wide and complex variety of
institutions, but all had in common an emphasis on technical and
professional training which would make employment possible immediately after graduation. On the whole, the state and public colleges
prepared for technical professions such as medicine, dentistry, forestry,
agriculture, and engineering, while the private colleges (many of which
were affiliated with a private university under the status of *semmombu,*
or "specialty divisions") catered more to the training of middle-level
clerical talent for government and industry, often in night school programs. Most colleges were legally classified as *semmon gakkō* or "specialty schools."

THE IMPERIAL UNIVERSITY

Both the state and the private university programs were divided into
two levels, a three-year preparatory course of the "general education"
variety followed by three years of professional training. But where the
private universities carried out both these levels on the same campus,

with an organizational distinction between "preparatory course" (*yoka*) and "main course" (*honka*), the state system was organized into two completely independent institutions, the preparatory "higher school" (*kōtō gakkō*) and an "imperial university" for professional training. Although the two were integrated in the sense that almost all higher school graduates entered an imperial university, they were separate in geographical location and in administration and hence deserve separate consideration.

The imperial university in prewar Japan was a distinctly modern institution, and like other modern institutions in that country emerged in its fully developed form as a unique blend of Japanese precedents, Western models, and some genuine innovations by the Meiji statesmen.[5] The direct premodern antecedents of the imperial university system were some small government-sponsored centers which were more in the nature of research agencies than educational institutions. The most important of these, known in late Tokugawa as the Kaiseijo, was devoted to the study of Western learning. Closed in the turmoil of the Restoration, the Kaiseijo was revived by the Meiji government, which altered the name to the Kaisei School (Kaisei Gakkō) and established it as the official state institution for Western studies. For the following two decades, the school underwent a series of changes in name and organization, but on the whole remained a small institution for the training of an elite handful of men versed in Western learning. It is crucial to note the thoroughly Western nature of the university, closely according with its origins: the teachers were mostly foreigners, with Japanese serving only in the capacity of assistants, and it was normal for lectures to be given in the language of the professor. By virtue of their small numbers—for the twenty years following the Restoration, the annual graduating classes were rarely over one hundred— the students were a confident and ambitious elite, virtually guaranteed of secure government positions on graduation.

This early Meiji university—called the University South School (Daigaku Nankō) from 1871, the Tokyo Kaisei School (Tōkyō Kaisei Gakkō) from 1874, and Tokyo University (Tōkyō Daigaku) from 1877

5. The most detailed account of the prehistory of the imperial university system is in Tōkyō teikoku daigaku, ed., *Tōkyō teikoku daigaku gojūnen shi,* 2 vols (editor, 1932), I, 5–448.

—underwent the most critical change with the Imperial University Ordinance of 1886.[6] By this reform, the university, which until that time had been a fairly independent institution left to develop in its own haphazard way, was molded into a critical piece of machinery for the Prussian-style state constructed in a series of reforms culminating in the Meiji Constitution of 1889.[7] Essentially an amalgam of its original function as an institute for the assimilation of useful Western knowledge and of the Prussian-inspired concept of the university as a tool of state policy, the new Imperial University was to be the model for all university education, both public and private, until 1945. The notion of the Imperial University's usefulness to the state was clearly articulated in the opening article of the ordinance: "The Imperial University has as its purpose the teaching of those arts and sciences essential to the state, and the research of unexplored areas of learning." [8]

The original Imperial University in Tokyo was organized into five faculties (technically called "colleges" until 1918) of Law, Medicine, Engineering, Letters, and Science, to which were later added Agriculture (1890) and Economics (1919). In 1897, a second imperial university was established in Kyoto, and from this point the official titles for the imperial universities were preceded by place names as a means of distinction. A third generation of imperial universities followed a decade later with the founding of Tohoku Imperial in 1907 and Kyushu Imperial in 1910. These four universities were the heart of the imperial university system in prewar Japan, although passing notice must be made of the addition of five more with Hokkaido in 1918, Osaka in 1931, Nagoya in 1939, and two in the overseas colonies of Korea and Taiwan in the 1920s. Also within the state university system, but denied the title of imperial university, were a number of single-faculty schools of commerce, technology, and medicine. These institutions,

6. Two other elements went into the Meiji university; one was a medical school, descended from a pre-Restoration government medical office, and the other was the Confucian Academy (Shōheikō), originally founded in 1630. The medical school was at one point known as the "University, East School" (Daigaku tōkō), as distinguished from the "South School." Both of these two alternate lineages, however, were secondary, and the Western learning mainstream dominated the imperial university system from the start.

7. Ōkubo Toshiaki, *Nihon no daigaku* (Sōgensha, 1943), pp. 301–314.

8. Tōkyō teikoku daigaku, ed., *Tōkyō teikoku daigaku gojūnen shi*, I, 934.

however, as well as all the lesser imperial universities, were devoted to technical education to the exclusion of the liberal arts, and hence had minor potential for student radicalism.

The lofty status of Tokyo Imperial University (and its later sister institutions in a hierarchy determined roughly by order of founding) has never been challenged. This status was assured in the early years by such formal advantages as exemption from the difficult civil service examinations for graduates of the Faculty of Law. Yet far more important than such legal mechanisms (which have largely disappeared) has been the tacit acceptance of Tokyo Imperial University (now Tokyo University) by all segments of Japanese society as the sanctioned incubator for the ruling elite. This prestige has been greatest for graduates of the Faculty of Law (a "Tokyo University within Tokyo University")[9] because of the tremendous preference afforded them since Meiji in the state civil service. But since the turn of the century, Tokyo University graduates have become preeminent in *every* field, including private enterprise. Not only are they preferred for initial jobs but once hired they are promoted more rapidly—not because of superior ability (although this is often the case) but merely because of the label of "Tōdai," the popular abbreviation for Tokyo University. Since such preference has been strongest in the national bureaucracy, a vicious circle has been generated whereby those having the authority to reform the situation are loath to close off the very channels by which they themselves have risen to power.

Japan's modern elite has thus been structured by a curious mix of achievement and ascription. Social origins are (at least in theory) unrelated to one's entrance into the elite pipeline of education, which is governed purely by competitive examination. But once entrance into the preferred course is achieved, one's rise is governed almost totally by ascription, by the mere label of the school attended. In a general sense, then, the hierarchy of social classes which determined a man's future at birth in traditional society was replaced in the Meiji era by a hierarchy of educational institutions which determined one's future during adolescence. What remained unchanged was the conviction throughout the great part of society that certain people were destined

9. Shimizu Hideo, *Tōkyō daigaku hōgakubu* (Kōdansha, 1965), p. 20.

to stand out above others and that this natural elite would lead society. This concept was given specific rationalization during the Tokugawa period by the Confucian notion that leadership in society is a task reserved for a select few of superior virtue and intellect. In traditional China, the means for selecting this elite had been the examination system, whereas Tokugawa Japan had an elite by birth (although these respective ideals were enough abused in reality to make the two systems less contrasting than one might imagine).

The Meiji state shifted Japan to the ideal of an examination-selected elite, but the basic vision of a natural elite remained. The students of Tokyo Imperial University in the twentieth century would of course be reluctant to admit a "Confucian" content to their image of their own role in society, for their orientation was largely Western. Yet beneath the Western rhetoric, they were very much the heirs of the Tokugawa samurai. This consciousness, unarticulated as it may have been, gave the imperial universities a high potential for student radicalism. Sure that their position indicated a special responsibility to society and the power to change the injustices they perceived, these students would naturally be the leaders of any mass student movement.

THE HIGHER SCHOOL

The higher school, a three-year college-level institution which prepared students for the imperial universities, was a unique institution in prewar Japan and of considerable importance in creating an educational environment conducive to student radicalism. In the original scheme of Inoue Kowashi (Minister of Education, 1893–94), as set forth in the Higher School Ordinance of 1894, this institution was assigned the dual purpose of providing a college-level terminal education and of preparing for the imperial university. Inoue had actually first proposed that the new type of school be included under the appellation "university," but in the end relented from fear of jealous anger on the part of the Imperial University at being forced to share its prestigious title. Thus the euphemism "higher school" (*kōtō gakkō*) was adopted.[10] In practice, Inoue's dual scheme for the higher school did not materialize, and its function was reduced exclusively to the prepa-

10. Ōkubo, p. 360.

ration for admission to the imperial universities.[11] The size of the higher school network was consciously coordinated to ensure that virtually every graduate was assured admission to some imperial university, provided that he be prepared to make some concessions in regard to the faculty chosen (medicine, for example, was fairly competitive, and letters was a sure bet).[12]

The number of higher schools grew with the imperial university system itself. Before 1918 they were eight, identified by number in order of founding, and varying among them slightly in prestige, depending largely on seniority and contiguity to imperial universities. Hence the oldest (First Higher in Tokyo, Second Higher in Sendai, and Third Higher in Kyoto) were the most prestigious and consequently the most difficult to enter. Over a period of a decade from 1919, the number of higher schools was quadrupled in coordination with the expansion of the imperial university system in the same years. The majority of these new schools—which were named after their location rather than by numbers—were state-run, although recognition was granted to four *private* higher schools in the Tokyo and Osaka urban areas, which tended to cater to the sons of the well-to-do.

The unique atmosphere of higher school education has been well preserved in nostalgic memoirs of the several generations of Japan's modern elite which attended them. The educational function was conceived to be that of a broad liberal training in preparation for the narrowly professional bent of the imperial university. The curriculum was more flexible than that of the lower levels, and pressure far less. Instruction in the classical Japanese and Chinese traditions was of only minor importance, in contrast to the dominance of comparable pursuits (Greek and Latin) in the elite Western universities of the same era. Foreign (that is, Western) language bulked large in the curriculum, accounting for over one third of the total hours of instruction. This assured that the higher school students were on the whole competent to read English and one other foreign language, abilities

11. For a detailed account of the development of the higher school, see Kaigo Tokiomi, ed., *Inoue Kowashi no kyōiku seisaku* (Tōkyō daigaku shuppankai, 1968), pp. 405–464.

12. During the 1920s, however, a significant degree of competition for entrance to imperial universities developed, although it remained true that a place could almost always be found for a student willing to compromise; the overseas imperial universities in Taiwan and Korea were especially popular in this respect.

which would give them access to the untranslated bulk of Western socialist literature when their interests turned in that direction.

The tone of higher school life before the war was one of freedom and irresponsibility. The majority of higher schools were located in provincial towns and undisturbed by the confusion of modern metropolitan life. Most of the schools had a system of compulsory dormitory lodging, which served as a melting pot where the broad spectrum of family background, social status, and regional dialect was narrowed by the students' common conviction of their own superiority and common allegiance to the institution which brought them together. On most higher school campuses, students were in control of dormitory life in a system of "self-government" (jichi) which provided the precedent for later student demands for greater control over university life.[13]

Rowdiness in the higher schools was common and on the whole tolerated. The emphasis of the entire higher school program was on individual fulfillment as human beings, an emphasis best suggested by the pervasive use of the word seishun. Unlike the corresponding English "adolescence," this term suggests not a confused and painful period of emergence into adulthood, but rather the prime of youth, a time for unfettered self-expression, pure enjoyment, and a certain carefree irresponsibility. Thus one finds a typical stress on literary activities, on the cultivation of lasting friendships, and on quiet meditation. One recent eulogizer of the prewar higher school spirit sees in it "the energy and sentimentality of youth, as well as a certain decadence. Whether relaxing or studying, on the whole there was a certain gut-level feeling of 'living life to the hilt.'"[14]

The open, easy-going, sentimental ethos of the higher school terminated abruptly in the transition to the imperial university, and it was in this very transition that the most powerful psychological encouragement to student radicalism was afforded. Entrance into the university meant confrontation with the real world, an emergence from the protected dormitories of the higher school into the dirty boarding houses of the city (few university students lived in dormitories in prewar Japan). In many cases, the transition was from provincial town to the

13. The origins of the dormitory system and its unique character are described in Karasawa, Gakusei no rekishi, pp. 80–94.

14. Ōgiya Shōzō, ed., Ā gyokuhai ni hana ukete—Waga kyūsei kōkō jidai (Yūki shobō, 1967), p. 2.

metropolis, an unsettling shift from the ordered security of traditional Japan to the politically charged and untidy confusion of the modern city. The content of education likewise changed abruptly from a broad, liberal orientation to a highly technical curriculum of professional training. Higher school graduation was a farewell to *seishun,* with its hedonism and irresponsibility. The higher school–imperial university shift represented the confluence in the psychology of Japan's modern elite of the warm, meandering country stream of *seishun* with the chill rushing torrent of adult responsibility. It was the intensity of this shift that created a psychological mood highly conducive to political activism.

The old imperial university was comparable in tone to the professional graduate schools in the American educational system today: it was businesslike and unemotional. The higher school, by contrast, was comparable to the American undergraduate college; it was the place where lasting friendships were formed and where "school spirit" was a vital force, demanding an allegiance in later years unequaled by the professional school. In a sense, one former Shinjinkai member has noted, there was really no such thing as a "Tokyo University student"; the university was merely "an assembly of groups that extended on from the higher schools." [15] The real basis of the "school cliques" (*gakubatsu*) among the prewar-educated elite was thus less the university than the higher school. The strength of cliquism on the basis of higher school bonds was to exert a strong influence on the organizational patterns of the student movement at imperial universities, where political activism was in most cases the outgrowth of higher school attitudes and associations.

THE PRIVATE UNIVERSITY

Private higher education in prewar Japan was of totally different origin from the state system and—at least in the early stages of development—outrightly antagonistic to it. This antagonism was reinforced by consistent discrimination within the state bureaucracy against the graduates of private universities, regardless of the quality of education

15. Kawamura Matasuke in Nomura Masao, *Hōsō fūunroku,* 2 vols., (Asahi shimbun sha, 1966), II, 206.

offered. Private universities were not even allowed the legal classification of "university" (*daigaku*)—although they did in fact use the term —until the University Ordinance of 1918. This is not to say, however, that private universities were without pride or excellence, for many of them merely turned to supply professions other than the state bureaucracy. It was in this way that Keiō University came to provide many recruits for the business world and that Waseda sent many graduates into journalism.

In terms of the potential for student radicalism, the private universities offered as a compensation for the bureaucratic elitism of the imperial universities a kind of "outsider elitism," a sense of haughty contempt for established lineages of authority in government which naturally encouraged rebellious attitudes among the students. At the same time, however, private university students tended to be more urbane and less prone to the naive enthusiasm which underlay the political activity of their more rustic contemporaries at the imperial universities. This difference occurred largely because the great majority of private universities were located in the two megalopoles of Tokyo and Kyoto–Osaka, conducted the full six years of the preparatory-professional course on a single urban campus, and catered to a greater extent than state universities to the sons of the urban elite.

Of the wide variety of private universities in prewar Japan, some were more susceptible than others to political activity. The degree of susceptibility may best be described according to the three major types of private schools founded in the Meiji era.

Western learning schools were the successors of the *shijuku* or "private academies" of the Tokugawa period. With the Meiji Restoration and the sudden demand for increased education in Western arts, the private academies grew and multiplied, so that by 1874 there were 74 private schools specializing in the teaching of foreign learning versus only 17 such public institutions.[16] Most of the private academies were eventually to collapse under economic and political pressure as the vogue for things Western tapered off in mid-Meiji, but one of the few to survive, the present Keiō University, went on to become one of the most prestigious of all private universities. The stability of Keiō, how-

16. Ikazaki Akio and Usuda Noboru, *Shigaku no rekishi* (Shin Nihon shuppan sha, 1967), p. 37.

ever, was won only by establishing a firm tradition of supplying leaders for private business, a tradition which over the years has given Keiō a staid and conservative demean and has worked consistently to discourage political radicalism. It is for this reason that Keiō, despite its prestige, has always played a minor role in the history of the Japanese student movement.

Religious schools were the most numerous among prewar private universities, although most were so small that the overall enrollment was negligible in comparison with the secular universities. Some were founded as educational projects of native Buddhist sects, while others were first established by Christian missionaries. The potential for student political activity at such universities was ambiguous. Their small size and otherworldly orientation tended to work against political activity, but the social concerns of certain sects (more often Christian than Buddhist) could encourage radicalism. Thus, for example, students at Dōshisha University, a Christian school in Kyoto, played a prominent role in the Kansai student movement in the 1920s; it must be noted, however, that Dōshisha was the product of Japanese Christian radicals rather than benevolent foreign missionaries, a difference which remains apparent today in a distinctive Dōshisha blend of evangelism and political activism. On the whole, the religious universities before the war (especially the Buddhist ones) were from their size and from religious considerations barred from playing a major role in the left-wing student movement.

Law schools. As the Meiji state assumed its mature form in the second decade after the Restoration, a demand developed for men trained in law and politics which could not be met by the limited facilities of the imperial university (at that time only a single school in Tokyo). It was this demand that encouraged the emergence of a number of schools which placed primary emphasis on training in law and aimed at staffing the middle levels of both government and business. From this small group of private "law schools" emerged most of the major private universities in modern Japan: Waseda, Nihon, Chūō, Meiji, and Hōsei, all of which are located in Tokyo. These schools were founded not only independently of government aid and encouragement, but often in a spirit of positive opposition to the Meiji establishment. Launched in the period of the "movement for freedom and people's rights" (jiyū minken undō), the law schools tended to define their educational role by reference to the slogans of that movement. Most obvious in this respect was Waseda, founded in 1882 by Ōkuma Shigenobu the year after he left the Meiji government and only a few months after the formation of his new opposition political party, the Kaishintō. The founding spirit of the school was well expressed at the opening ceremonies when one of the speakers cried, "I expect to see from the Tokyo Semmon Gakkō [the early name of Waseda] the emergence not of these clever types who give in to authority and seek only their own security, but rather of virtuous men who will ever seek to devote themselves truly to the people." [17]

The development of these "law schools" in the several decades after their founding showed two distinct patterns. All but Waseda quickly lost any spirit of "outsider" independence from the political establishment and followed a pattern of compromise and adaptation so as to conform as closely as possible to the state model set by the imperial universities. Although not legally under the supervision of the Ministry of Education, the majority of the private universities docilely followed the educational guidelines set down by the state and rapidly forfeited all earlier opportunities to create a vital tradition of independent private higher education.[18] This pattern of compromise stemmed basically from financial instability; unblessed by the generous subsidies granted the imperial universities, the private schools could sustain themselves only by making education more efficient, which normally involved reducing the quality and increasing the scale. All the private universities of law-school origins thus grew at a very rapid pace in the 1920s, but at the price of operating principles which far more suited factories than schools. Because of the need for funds, these schools tended on the whole to accept the bulk of applicants (whether they had room for them or not), so that competition for entrance was far less than the imperial universities or than Keiō and Waseda.[19] This situation remains true today.

17. Ozaki Shirō, Waseda daigaku (Bungei shunjū sha, 1953), p. 26. The speaker was journalist Narushima Ryūhoku.
18. Nagai Michio, Nihon no daigaku (Chūō kōron sha, 1965), p. 42.
19. In the period 1920–1930, the average entrance rate (number admitted out of 100 applicants) was 13 for the higher schools, while that for Waseda and Keiō

Waseda alone of the law-school type of private university has managed since its founding to maintain a tradition of academic excellence and independent spirit in spite of the handicap of financial weakness under which all private universities suffer. It is thus easy to understand why Waseda was the only private university before the war to play a dominant role in the student movement: its prestige and excellence assured the students of a necessary degree of elitist self-confidence, its size guaranteed an effective base for organization, and its strongly independent spirit provided a hospitable intellectual climate. To be sure, Waseda throughout the 1920s effected many compromises which worked to undermine its spirit of independence, making the usual alliance with the zaibatsu without which private education in Japan would collapse and hesitating to oppose state measures of educational control.[20] Still, the "Waseda spirit" which earned it the reputation of the "Campus of Freedom" remained strong enough throughout the prewar period to guarantee its students a place of radical leadership second only to Tokyo Imperial.

SIZE AND DISTRIBUTION OF THE UNIVERSITY POPULATION

Two further elements of the structure of the prewar Japanese university system are relevant to the setting of student activism: the rapid growth of the total university population in the 1920s and its increasing concentration in the great urban centers. These quantitative factors introduced a variety of strains into the life of Japanese university students after 1918 which created a setting that guaranteed some kind of student unrest. When these various structural elements combined with the pressing social and political issues of the period, the result was a steady growth of student activism which will be traced in detail in the following chapters.

After the founding of all the major lineages of university education in early and mid-Meiji, the first two decades of the twentieth century

---

preparatory courses was identical at 22; other private university preparatory courses varied widely from year to year but tended to average between 50 and 70. Entrance rate statistics are given in the *Mombushō nempō*.

20. Kikukawa Tadao, *Gakusei shakai undō shi*, rev. ed. (Kaiguchi shoten, 1947), p. 398.

were a period of consolidation and only moderate growth. From 1918, however, the system of higher education entered a period in which it was to expand at a rate almost triple that of the preceding years. The University Ordinance of 1918 may be taken as the starting gun for this period of expansion, although the real reasons lay in Japan's steady economic growth in the early twentieth century and the demands which had been created for more skilled technicians and administrators. This ordinance was one of a series of reforms made in accord with the recommendations of the Special Council on Education (Rinji kyōiku kaigi), which was set up in September 1917 to devise methods for improving the entire system of education. The key provisions of the University Ordinance recognized private universities on the same basis as the imperial universities and authorized the upgrading of certain state technical colleges to single-faculty universities. At the same time, the council's recommendation for a greatly expanded network of higher schools was adopted, a program which necessarily entailed a concomitant expansion of the imperial university facilities. Throughout the early 1920s, thus, there was a great blossoming of higher education, both state and private, which slowed down in the late twenties to a period of only modest growth in the 1930s. Table 1 indicates the rate of increase for students in higher education in this period.

This expansion set in motion a number of forces working to irritate students, encourage hostility to established authority, and thus in a negative way to stir political rebellion. In the first place, expansion was accomplished (except in the case of the higher schools) not by creating more schools but simply by upgrading and expanding existing institutions, almost all of which had been in operation since the nineteenth century. This often led, especially in private universities, to cutting corners on the quality of education by neglecting to provide enough additional teachers and facilities to accommodate the new students. The quality of teaching and of student life was adversely affected and student discontent was heightened. Furthermore, the swelling of the numbers of university students, especially in Tokyo where the bulk of higher education was concentrated, made university life far more impersonal than before. The Meiji student population was comparatively tight-knit, so that students felt integrated enough to consider open political rebellion a distasteful alternative. By the late

1920s, however, a student at any of the imperial universities or major secular private universities in Japan was one in thousands and much more likely to turn to a tightly organized political movement in an effort to express his dissatisfaction.

Table 1. Increase of students in higher education,
1914–1938

Year	Total number of students	Four-year increment (percentages in parentheses)
1914	53,814	
		11,366 (21)
1918	65,180	
		32,957 (51)
1922	98,137	
		46,065 (47)
1926	144,202	
		35,997 (25)
1930	180,199	
		4,058 (2)
1934	184,257	
		12,350 (6)
1938	196,607	

Source: Mombushō, ed., Gakusei hachijūnen shi, pp. 1058–1063. This figure includes male students in colleges (semmon gakkō), higher schools, and universities.

A further adverse consequence of university expansion in the 1920s was a growing rate of unemployment among graduating students. The expansion plan had been devised in a period of unprecedented economic boom and was premised on the continuation of general prosperity. The 1920s turned out to be a decade of depression, however, and the economy was unable to absorb all the university-trained talent that was being prepared for it. This maladjustment was to create by the late 1920s a critical problem of "intellectual unemployment," all the more serious because of the promise of worldly success on which the entire system of higher education was predicated and which gave it its great stability. It was, in other words, the unique way in which university education in modern Japan came to be equated with success that worked to produce the two most powerful encouragements of student radicalism: the elitism of the students at the most prestigious universities and their frustration should the promise of success be unfulfilled.[21]

The final structural characteristic of the prewar Japanese system of higher education which worked to encourage and facilitate student radicalism was a high degree of concentration in urban areas and especially in the capital of Tokyo. In Japan, where the building of a university system was closely integrated with the process of modern urbanization, the older tendency in Europe and America to locate universities in isolated and tranquil rural towns was almost wholly absent (the only exceptions were a few small religious universities).[22] The oldest and largest universities in Japan were located at the time of their founding on the edges of the major cities, and as the cities themselves grew, the universities were drawn into the vortex of metropolitan turmoil.

A breakdown of the Japanese student population at the college and university level by city in 1934—the year which saw the last noticeable left-wing student activity before the war—shows that the two megalopoles accounted for over three quarters of the total (out of 166,594 students, Tokyo–Yokohama had 57 per cent and Kyoto–Osaka–Kobe 18 per cent).[23] Of the remaining one quarter, most were in college-level technical schools and small religious institutions which offered little political stimulus. Not only was the university population concentrated in urban areas, but within those areas a small number of schools accounted for the bulk of the students. The two major im-

21. Takeuchi Yoshimi has pointed out the contrast of the social role of Japanese higher education with that of modern China, where there is no guaranteed linkage between university and employment. Quoted in Sumiya Etsuji, Takakuwa Suehide, and Ogura Jōji, *Nihon gakusei shakai undō shi* (Kyoto: Dōshisha daigaku shuppan bu, 1953), p. 66, n. 8.

22. Nagai Michio in Asahi jānaru, ed., *Daigaku no niwa*, 2 vols. (Kōbunsha, 1964), II, 289. It is interesting that attempts have been made in the postwar period to relocate certain universities in rural settings (Tokyo University of Education is the most publicized example), but these have been met with strong resistance from students and faculty and have provided a major issue in the student movement of the 1960s.

23. These figures are for all male students in colleges (*semmon gakkō*), universities, and higher normal schools, and are derived from statistics in Naikaku tōkeikyoku, ed., *Nihon teikoku tōkei nenkan* vol. 56 (1937), and Mombushō, ed., *Nihon teikoku Mombushō nempō* vol. 62 (1934).

perial universities in Tokyo and Kyoto were dominant both in breadth and in numbers. Each had seven different faculties, covering the entire spectrum of professional training, whereas all other universities, both state and private, were limited to a much smaller range. In 1934, Tokyo Imperial had a total of 8,050 students and Kyoto 5,565, together accounting for over one third of the entire university-level student population. Next to the two imperial universities were the great secular private universities of Tokyo: Keiō, Waseda, Meiji, Chūō, Nihon, and Hōsei. While less than half as large as Tokyo Imperial at the university level, each of these schools had both a preparatory college (*yoka*) and an attached three-year terminal college program (*semmombu*) which substantially swelled their total enrollment. These seven large universities in the capital and their accompanying preparatory and college programs thus accounted for 63 per cent of the total post-secondary student population in Tokyo and 36 per cent of that in the entire country.

This high concentration of the Japanese student population in a small number of large universities in Tokyo and somewhat lesser number in Kansai, with the rest scattered throughout the country, had important implications for the student movement. In the first place, the urban environment itself, with its confusion and accelerated pace of life, tended naturally to encourage a radicalism among youth yearning for a more rational and clear-cut moral ordering of society. The high concentration of all political and intellectual life in the capital was further encouragement: being in immediate contact with the machinery of national politics, Tokyo students naturally felt in a conveniently close position to exert political pressure. This situation is not unlike that in France and is in distinct contrast to the case of the United States, where the political capital is of minor importance as a university town.

The concentration of the Tokyo student population into a small number of universities meant that communication was greatly eased. All the seven major schools listed above except Keiō (of small radical potential anyway) were located within a manageably small area to the north and west of the center of Tokyo and hence offered a tempting prospect of organizing a large amount of students with minimal legwork. In the 1920s a handful of students with a mimeograph machine, a dozen reams of cheap paper, and a knack for dodging the police could broadcast their message to the prime segment of the Japanese student population in a single day. This compactness and ease of communication were to prove of great importance in sustaining the prewar student radicals in the face of ever-increasing suppression.

Mention must finally be made of the potential importance of the provincial centers of higher education, which consisted almost entirely of state-run higher schools and technical colleges. While each of these schools was relatively small, the average enrollment being under seven hundred, they were of importance by reason of their wide distribution, which was in marked contrast to the concentration of the majority in the center. Every prefecture in prewar Japan had one or the other of these types of school (occasionally both), generally located in the provincial capital. This provided a ready-made network for the *expansion* of a radical student movement from the center to the provinces. The middle and normal schools at the secondary level, while far more difficult to radicalize, were likewise evenly distributed throughout the country and might also be considered part of this network. These isolated centers could never themselves initiate or even sustain a radical student movement, but they nevertheless provided ideal channels for instigating brief and limited campaigns in the provinces which the leaders from the center were to find of considerable use. In this way the dualism in the distribution of the educational system, with a high concentration of the majority in two metropolitan areas and a correspondingly high dispersal of the minority throughout provincial Japan, worked from both directions to facilitate an effective nationwide student movement.

2 | The Roots of the Modern Student Movement

The founding of the Shinjinkai (New Man Society) in 1918 at Tokyo Imperial University demands recognition as the inception of the modern Japanese "student movement" only if that term is taken to indicate sustained, articulate, organized political activity. Student "activism," however, in the sense of any spontaneous protest for a given cause (political or otherwise), may be traced far back into the Meiji roots of modern Japanese education. The many documented student uprisings in Meiji Japan failed, for lack of sustained organization, to qualify as a true "movement"; yet they were critical in providing the college and university campuses with a tradition of audacity on the part of students and tolerance on the part of educators. This Meiji heritage, rudimentary though it was, helps explain the rapid growth of the student movement in the 1920s.

ROWS AND STRIKES

The three basic styles of student activism in the Meiji period were, in ascending order of sophistication, student rows, school strikes, and political protests. The student row was the oldest as well as the crudest form, having its roots in the samurai schools of Tokugawa era, where a heavy stress on military training fostered pugnacious student attitudes and frequent fights. Even after the military emphasis in higher education disappeared in early Meiji, bellicosity survived. Both educators and society as a whole exhibited a high degree of tolerance for student rowdiness, perhaps less from awe of students than in the age-old conviction that boys will be boys.

Accounts of Meiji student life abound with brawls, pranks, and riots. One classic chronicle is Natsume Sōseki's *Botchan,* which depicts the mischief of students at a provincial middle school at the time of the Russo-Japanese War. The novel is climaxed by an all-out fray between middle and normal school students, in the course of which several teachers are pummeled.[1] Such outbreaks were common in the higher schools as well, so much in fact that a number of institutional forms for student rowdiness emerged. Such were the *makanai seibatsu* (attack on the cook), a dining hall riot in protest against unpalatable food, or the *sutōmu* (from English "storm"), a curious ritual in which higher school dormitory students would arise on signal in the dark of night and parade about with torches, shouting, fighting, breaking windows, and overturning furniture. The plentiful lore of life in the old higher schools suggests that such incidents were commonplace.[2]

Such undirected violence is in itself of only slight relevance to student political activity. It was most pronounced among the more immature students, in middle and higher schools, and rare at universities, except for occasional riots fired by dunkenness (a major problem among Meiji students) rather than playfulness. Rowdiness was not a uniquely Japanese phenomenon, as any account of American boarding school or college life in the same era will prove, nor did it survive as a strong tradition into the twentieth century. By the 1930s, notes one chronicler of student life, the practice of the higher school *sutōmu* had all but disappeared: students no longer rioted for the mere sake of rioting.[3] This Meiji heritage of casual student violence worked to create an atmosphere in the schools which was hospitable to more organized forms of rebellion. As the student political movement emerged in its highly organized form in the 1920s, it may in a sense have come to replace aimless violence as the primary mode for the overt expression of student passions, thus accounting for the gradual decrease in campus rioting.

1. Natsume Sōseki, *Botchan,* Mori Yasotarō, trans. (Kinshōdō, 1948), pp. 235–40.
2. Karasawa, *Gakusei no rekishi,* pp. 92–93, 105.
3. *Ibid.,* p. 159. It should be added that occasional instances of the *sutōmu* may still be found in Japan.

Of greater interest than pranks and riots in the heritage of Meiji student activism were organized student protests against actions by school administrators. Such protests differed from rowdiness both in the issues, which involved serious grievances rather than whimsical excuses, and in the techniques, which relied not on physical violence but on coercion by means of a coordinated student strike. Known generically as *gakkō sōdō* (school disturbances), these protests in some cases were settled short of an actual strike, but even then the *threat* of a strike was focal. The very term for school strike in the Meiji era, *dōmei kyūkō,* in its similarity to the word for a labor strike (*dōmei higyō*) reflects the calculated, coercive dimension to the *gakkō sōdō* which went far beyond mere rowdiness. At the same time, however, the "school disturbances" fell short of the standards of organized political radicalism which were to emerge in the 1920s in three ways.

In the first place, the issues were seldom ideological, centering rather on specific student complaints. The classic grievance was disciplinary action taken by school authorities and considered unjust by the students, whose demand was typically the rescinding of the punishment and the dismissal of the principal. Another common focus of dispute was personnel, with students organizing either to protest the dismissal of a popular teacher or to force the dismissal of an incompetent one. Other problems which formed grounds for student strikes were dormitory regulations (especially curfew rules), dining hall food, or curriculum changes.

Second, the disputes were with few exceptions limited to a single campus, a natural result of the specific, concrete nature of the issues. Contact among student activists at different schools was minimal, for they had no common ideology to bind them together, nor indeed would such alliances be of any use in situations where the only enemy was the school administration on a particular compus. In most school disturbances, the Ministry of Education was cast not in the role of villain, but rather of neutral mediator, working out a solution to satisfy both students and administration. The solution typically reached was the transfer of the principal or offending faculty member to a different school and token disciplinary action for the student strike leaders (either short-term suspension or simple reprimand).

A third distinguishing feature of Meiji student strikes was a high frequency at middle and normal schools in the provinces. A chronology of the Japanese left-wing movement in the Meiji twenties (1887–1896), for example, records a total of twenty-five *gakkō sōdō* prominent enough to appear in the national press.[4] Of these, ten were in middle schools, eight in normal schools, and the remainder scattered among higher schools (three), commercial schools (three), and private schools (one). The incidents were geographically spread throughout provincial Japan, occurring in twenty different prefectures; only a single incident was to be found in the capital of Tokyo, and none in Kyoto or Osaka. This concentration at the secondary level of the educational system was in part due to the dominance in numbers of those schools but was also related to the relatively greater importance of discipline—and hence disputes relating to discipline—in middle and normal schools.

Although the origins of the school strike are not clear, the phenomenon is at least as old as the modern school system itself, and its prevalence throughout the Meiji era is suggested by the frequency of control directives issued by the Ministry of Education. The first such reaction was apparently in 1893, when Minister of Education Inoue Kowashi issued a directive demanding strict controls in the face of any student demands for the resignation or transfer of school personnel.[5] Official concern, however, failed to moderate student activism, as confirmed by a succession of similar edicts by the ministry in 1894, 1896, 1902, and 1909, in each case decrying a recent increase in the number of *gakkō sōdō* and demanding stricter control and severer punishments for offending students.[6] In 1897, Uchimura Kanzō lamented that *"gakkō sōdō* are sweeping Japan like an epidemic, and almost no prefectural middle or normal school is without a serious problem." [7] In 1909, a newspaper report listed fifty-two such incidents over a five-year period, noting that fully twenty-three had occurred in the preceding three months.[8]

In the period 1909–10, educational authorities took extensive mea-

---

4. Morooka Sukeyuki, "Meiji nijūnendai no shakai undō nempyō," *Nihonshi kenkyū* no. 25 (September 1955), pp. 40–60.

5. *Ibid.*, p. 56.

6. *Ibid.*, pp. 57, 60; Meiji hennen shi hensankai, ed., *Shimbun shūsei Meiji hennen shi*, 15 vols., limited second edition (Rinsensha, 1940–41), XII, 434, and XIV, 16.

7. Tamaki Motoi, *Nihon gakusei shi* (San'ichi shobō, 1961), p. 70.

8. Sumiya *et al.*, *Nihon gakusei shakai undō shi*, p. 54.

sures to curb school disturbances, and although some temporary success may have resulted, the *gakkō sōdō* was already too deeply entrenched in the traditions of student life to be eradicated, and incidents continued at a regular pace through the 1910s. In some cases, the phenomenon spread to the universities as well.[9] The most spectacular of these was the Waseda Incident of 1917, in which a student protest against the construction of a statue of Countess Ōkuma triggered an explosion of diverse issues and factions that led to open student violence in the fall of 1917. This dispute was in the classic pattern of the *gakkō sōdō*, being limited to a single campus and fomented by non-ideological issues. It was thus fundamentally different from the genuinely political movement which was welling up among other students in the same period.[10]

Despite the nonideological character of traditional *gakkō sōdō*, the transition from middle school strike to university political movement was not so difficult. Through the Meiji tradition, Japanese students came to be convinced that they had the right to a voice in school administration, and experience showed such techniques as strikes and demonstrations to be effective guarantees of that right. A veteran of a *gakkō sōdō* at the secondary level could, stimulated by the heightened political consciousness that comes with age, turns naturally to a more politically oriented style of activism upon reaching the university. The sixteen-year-old middle schooler who managed to force the resignation of a provincial school principal might, as a twenty-year-old law student in Tokyo, turn his sights to more lofty symbols of authority, even to the entire political establishment.

Such a pattern of development may in fact be found in the two central figures in the birth of the modern Japanese student movement, Asō Hisashi and Akamatsu Katsumaro. Asō had been suspended from middle school in Ōita prefecture for involvement in a student strike in

9. The earliest documented instance of a university strike is that at Keiō in early 1888; see Konno Washichi, "Nihon saisho no gakusei sutoraiki," *Jimbutsu ōrai*, 10.4 (April 1965), 42–49.

10. Another major university "disturbance" occurred several years later, at Meiji University in 1923, over the dismissal of two popular teachers. Here again, there was no connection with the left-wing political student movement. For detailed coverage of both the Waseda and Meiji incidents, see the *Tōkyō asahi shimbun*. Accounts of the Waseda Incident may also be found throughout the writings of the novelist Ozaki Shirō; the best is *Waseda daigaku*, pp. 75–138.

1906,[11] while Akamatsu was expelled from the Tokuyama Middle School as the ringleader in a similar strike in 1911.[12] These men went on to Third Higher School in Kyoto and then to the Faculty of Law at Tokyo Imperial University; by 1918, when they joined to launch the Shinjinkai, both were confirmed socialists. Few would disagree that the activist temperaments of both men were given early encouragement by their common middle school strike experience.

MEIJI POLITICAL PROTESTS

Student activism before 1918 was by no means limited to spontaneous rowdyism and school strikes aimed at specific campus grievances: ample evidence of student involvement in national political movements may also be found. While this activity never reached the stage of self-perpetuating intermural organization that is characteristic of a genuine student movement, it offered persuasive precedents. In distinct contrast to the other two types of activism, which were in large degree limited to provincial middle and normal schools, political involvement was almost entirely confined to university students in Tokyo.

Meiji student political activism was largely concentrated in the *jiyū minken* movement of the early 1880s and in the socialist movement in the period around the Russo-Japanese War of 1904–05. In the *jiyū minken* movement, Tokyo University, as the only university level institution in the capital at the time, formed the center of student sympathy. In early 1881, at the instigation of the politician Ono Azusa, several Tokyo University students formed a political study group, the Ōtokai, with the aim of participating in the liberal political movement. This student group, led by Takada Sanae, a year later became the nucleus of Ōkuma Shigenobu's political party, the Kaishintō, and many of its members went on to become leading party politicians.[13] Also in 1882, a Tokyo University medical student, Katagiri Michiya, became an officer in the Young Liberal Party (Seinen Jiyūtō), a youth

11. Asō Hisashi, *Dakuryū ni oyogu* (Shinkōsha, 1923), pp. 98–112. This is a fine account of the classic oust-the-principal type of school strike.
12. Noguchi Yoshiaki, *Musan undō sō-tōshi den* (Shakai shisō kenkyūjo, 1931), p. 5.
13. Tamaki, pp. 45–46.

group affiliated with Itagaki Taisuke's Liberal Party.[14] It is reported that many Tokyo University students joined the various opposition political parties in these years.[15]

Two decades later, after a period of relative quiescence, students rallied to the second major opposition political cause in Meiji Japan, the socialist movement. With the founding of the private "law school" universities in the intervening years, the student population of Tokyo was now much larger and more politically acute. In December 1901 a crowd of one thousand students from several different universities made an expedition to the Ashio Copper Mine in Tochigi prefecture north of Tokyo to conduct an on-the-spot survey of the alleged poisoning by mining wastes, which became one of the great causes of the socialist movement.[16] Two years later students provided a major element of support when the weekly *Heimin shimbun* (Commoners' news) began publication as the first full-fledged organ of the Japanese socialists, launching a vociferous campaign in opposition to the impending war with Russia. The *Heimin shimbun* reported that the Waseda Social Studies Association (Waseda Shakai Gakkai) was founded on November 22, 1903, and shortly after decided to accept only committed socialists as members. This group, with a membership of about thirty, held monthly lectures on socialism and conducted an active antiwar campaign on the Waseda campus during 1904.[17]

The Waseda group seems to have soon disappeared, doubtless with the graduation of its founders, but general student interest in socialism remained high. In February 1906 the first Japanese Socialist Party (Nihon Shakaitō) was formed, and many students were among its members. A Tokyo Metropolitan Police Bureau report of the same year claimed that of an estimated 14,000 socialists in Tokyo, fully 7,500 were students. If correct, this would mean that the majority of all uni-

14. Tanaka Sōgorō, *Shiryō Nihon shakai undō shi*, 2 vols. (Tōzai shuppan sha, 1947–48), I, 148.
15. Takakuwa Suehide, *Nihon gakusei shakai undō shi* (Aoki shoten, 1955), p. 301.
16. Takakuwa, p. 30.
17. Rōdō undō shi kenkyūkai, ed., *Shūkan, Heimin shimbun*, Meiji shakai shugi shiryōshū, 20 vols. (Meiji bunken shiryō kankōkai, 1962), supp. vol. III, p. 28. The last meeting of the group reported in the *Heimin shimbun* was held on November 19, 1904. See *ibid.*, supp. vol. IV, p. 459.

versity students in Tokyo were "socialists." However exaggerated, these figures suggest substantial participation by students in the Meiji socialist movement.[18]

The Meiji government was, needless to say, inhospitable to student involvement in political protest movements, and, as in the case of the *gakkō sōdō*, issued periodic warnings against such activity, demanding school authorities to take strict disciplinary measures. This hostile government attitude, which was to remain unchanged until 1945, was clearly delineated in the Law on Gatherings (Shūkai Jōrei) of 1880, Article Seven of which prohibited teachers and students of both public and private schools from attending political meetings or joining political associations, subject to a fine.[19] Students rarely heeded this law, however, as is reflected by the frequency of successive administrative edicts by the Ministry of Education, which strove to define more clearly the limits of acceptable political activity and mobilized the disciplinary apparatus of the schools themselves as a means of control. In 1883, following the discovery of Tokyo University student participation in the liberal party movement, the Ministry of Education issued a notice restricting, ironically, student participation at "scholarly lectures"— presumably to prevent political groups from using "scholarship" as a pretext for agitation. Similar pronouncements were issued in 1885 and 1889. During the period of student involvement in the socialist movement, the ministry came forth with still further admonitions, in 1902 and 1906.[20]

The Meiji heritage of student activism dictated future directions both for the students themselves and for the educators and bureaucrats whom they opposed. The three styles of student activism provided all the techniques and forms of a true student movement except numbers and persistence, both of which would emerge from the forces at work in the Japanese universities in the early 1920s. The educators, on the

18. Tanaka, *Shiryō Nihon shakai undō shi*, II, 31.

19. For the text of the law, see Midoro Masaichi, ed., *Meiji Taishō shi 1: Genron hen* (Asahi shimbun sha, 1930), pp. 95–97. The provision on students was carried through in later revisions of the law, first in the Law on Gatherings and Political Associations (Shūkai oyobi seisha hō) of July 25, 1890, and then in the Peace Police Law (Chian keisatsu hō) of March 10, 1900, which remained in force until the end of the Pacific War.

20. Tanaka, *Shiryō Nihon shakai undō shi*, I, 148, 169, 350; Morooka, p. 45; and Takakuwa, p. 42.

other hand, were firmly set on a negative course of commitment to strict control of the student left. The ineffectiveness of the Meiji control system, which was tantamount to outright tolerance, merely heightened the frustration of the authorities and convinced them that solutions lay with further negative prohibitions rather than with a modicum of positive understanding.

THE TAISHŌ FERMENT

Given a favorable institutional environment and the Meiji precedents for student activism, all that remained to touch off a durable and organized student political movement was the proper set of issues and ideas that would fire young minds and stir students to create their own organization, founded not on specific grievances but upon broad concepts of political and social reform. These crystallizing ideas and issues all came together in the year 1918, a turning point in the history of modern Japan as well as the modern West, to inspire a vigorous and variegated movement for the reform of existing institutions. It was within a complex tapestry of social and intellectual ferment that the initial strands of the modern Japanese student movement were woven.

World War I itself was a major element in this ferment. On a purely material level, the war had placed Japan in the advantageous position of a belligerent with minor fighting responsibilities and a major opportunity to profit economically, both from the war-related orders of her allies and from the trade vacuum in Asia caused by the preoccupation of the European colonial powers. Japan was thus launched on an economic boom with its predictable consequences of rapid inflation, lagging wage increases, and resultant upsurge in labor unrest and popular discontent over the unequal distribution of the fruits of prosperity.

This discontent was reflected in a rapid increase in labor union organization and in wage disputes. Until 1915, the Yūaikai (Friendly Society), a labor organization founded in 1912 on the principles of cooperation between labor and management and of mutual aid among the laborers themselves, was virtually the only active labor group in Japan. But as the war boom progressed and the price-wage gap stirred the working class to action, the part-Christian, part-Confucian persuasion of the Yūaikai began to give way to more belligerent attitudes; at the same time, a number of radical independent unions were formed. The total number of unions in Japan rose rapidly, from four in 1915 to fourteen two years later, and then to 71 in 1919.[21] Labor disputes spiraled upward, reaching a peak in a prolonged period of strikes in mid-1919.

An even more ominous symptom of popular discontent was the outbreak of nationwide rioting in the summer of 1918 over the soaring price of rice. Touched off by defiant women stevedores in a fishing village on the Sea of Japan, the riots quickly spread, fanned by the summer heat and by detailed reports in the city newspapers. Rioting spread from the provinces into the urban areas, where the warehouses of great rice merchants were attacked and burned. Over a period of two months, unrest and disputes flared up among urban laborers, mine workers, and tenant farmers under the stimulus of the rice riots, and in the end the Terauchi government was forced to resign, giving way to Japan's first true party cabinet under Hara Kei. In many ways, the rice riots provided the most crucial single stimulus to the broad and uncoordinated movement known by later historians as the "Taishō Democracy Movement." The rice riots demonstrated to many politicians, labor leaders, and intellectuals the power of a mass movement based on popular discontent. Students were especially affected: Hatano Kanae, for example, relates being much stirred by the riots, which he witnessed in Nagoya during summer vacation of his second year at Tokyo Imperial. Later the same year, Hatano was one of the first students to join the Shinjinkai.[22]

World War I also had profound intellectual repercussions. The rhetoric of Wilsonian Democracy, which viewed the conflict as the "war to end all wars," fought to "make the world safe for democracy," struck sympathetic chords among intellectuals in Japan. Students in particular were stirred by this idealism, with its stress on pacifism, self-determination, and openness, which set much of the tone for the early student movement. A wholly different ideological heritage of the war years was the 1917 Bolshevik Revolution. The Russian Revolution

21. Sōdōmei gojūnen shi kankō iinkai, ed., *Sōdōmei gojūnen shi,* 3 vols. (editor, 1964–68), I, 47.
22. Hatano interview.

was at the time of its outbreak interpreted by most Japanese intellectuals as menacing or ephemeral, but scarcely encouraging; nevertheless, the ideological repercussions of this event were in the long run to have a far more profound effect on Japanese radical thought, and consequently on the student movement, than the fleeting intoxication with Wilsonian democracy.

The liberalizing stimulus of World War I worked to encourage the "Taishō Democracy" movement for the reform of existing institutions. Behind this movement lay a small group of influential professors and journalists who provided the sophisticated theoretical underpinnings of specific demands. While these "Taishō democrats" professed a strong commitment to social and economic reforms, it was largely to specific alterations of the structure of representative government that they addressed their polemical and theoretical talents. Although they tended to emphasize universal suffrage to the point that it appeared a panacea, they called at the same time for the elimination of genro power, the institution of party cabinets responsible to the Diet, and limitation of the authority of the House of Peers and Privy Council. The influence of the Taishō democrats stemmed in large measure from the prestige which many of them enjoyed as university professors, especially those from the imperial universities in Tokyo and Kyoto: the very authority accorded such professors by the state ironically allowed for a wide margin of heretical thinking concerning the state itself.

Unorthodox interpretations of political and social theory among imperial university professors were no novelty by 1918. Professor Wadagaki Kenzō was discussing socialism in Imperial University lectures as early as 1888, although the majority of reform-minded professors fully accepted the capitalist system. More typical of the Meiji professoriate's unorthodoxy was perhaps the Social Policy Association (Shakai Seisaku Gakkai), founded in 1896 by a group of professors, who, frankly imitating the social reformism of the German Verein für Sozialpolitik (after which they named their group), advocated reforms of the economic system to achieve more harmonious relations between labor and capital.[23] In the field of constitutional law, Minobe Tatsukichi, an unassuming professor at Tokyo Imperial, attracted attention for his

23. Takano Iwasaburō, "Shakai seisaku gakkai sōritsu no koro," *Teikoku daigaku shimbun,* no. 607 (November 4, 1935), p. 7.

unorthodox interpretation of the location of sovereignty in the Japanese state. Minobe's "organ theory" provoked a dispute with his rival Uesugi Shinkichi which by 1912 had "assumed the proportions of a bitter feud." [24]

The novelty of the Taishō democrats lay not in their mild unorthodoxy, which had substantial precedent, but in the extensive use of journalism to propound their views. Whereas the members of the Social Policy Association and other early reform advocates had put forth their ideas in scholarly periodicals and abstruse theoretical tomes, Taishō democrats like Yoshino Sakuzō and Ōyama Ikuo preferred to utilize more popular media, such as the progressive monthlies *Chūō kōron* (The central review) and *Chūgai* (Home and abroad), the influential daily newspaper *Ōsaka asahi shimbun,* and a variety of lesser political and religious organs. For the first time, the dissident views of university professors were becoming widely popular through the distribution achieved by such publications. Japanese journalism had, of course, always tended to be critical of the political establishment, but now the authority of the university behind these attacks provided a new dimension of effectiveness.

University liberals were by no means the only progressive intellectuals in the period of Taishō Democracy; in the background lurked an isolated group of more radical thinkers, the veterans of the Meiji socialist movement. The execution in January 1911 of Kōtoku Shūsui and eleven others convicted of plotting to assassinate the emperor had driven the socialist movement underground into its "winter age." Those dogged enough to survive suppression and disappointment began tempered journalistic efforts as early as 1912, and by 1918, when a thaw in the government control policy began, five major veterans of the Meiji socialist movement remained active.[25] Although their activity was contemporary with that of the Taishō democrats, they were separated by an enormous gulf of respectability and influence. Kyoto Imperial professor Kawakami Hajime, writing his serialized *Bimbō monogatari* (Tales of the poor) in the *Ōsaka asahi shimbun* in 1916,

---

24. Frank O. Miller, *Minobe Tatsukichi: Interpreter of Constitutionalism in Japan* (Berkeley, 1965), p. 28.

25. These were Arahata Kanson, Ōsugi Sakae, Sakai Toshihiko, Takabatake Motoyuki, and Yamakawa Hitoshi; most other radical socialists in this period were followers of one of these five.

could stir the conscience of every intellectual in western Japan, but the anarchist Ōsugi Sakae in the same year could reach only a minute audience in his tiny monthly *Kindai shisō* (Modern thought), which collapsed after three of the first four issues were banned.

These veteran socialists were seen not only as outsiders with no respectable status within the fixed institutions of Japanese society, but as dangerous renegades. The Ministry of the Interior classified them as "persons requiring special surveillance, Class A" and watched their moves with an elaborate spy apparatus. In the eyes of their potential adherents—such as university students—the memory of Kōtoku made many chary of too close an association. Still, the force of character, undaunted convictions, and experience of these men—although the average age of the leading five was only thirty-seven, they were old as revolutionaries go—assured that in time, given a modicum of freedom, they would be a source of inspiration for the young. But even though students did eventually come to admire the radicalism of the Meiji veterans, the gap of respectability was never to be closed. So telling was the prestige of the university that these strong-willed outsiders were destined ultimately to be excluded from the ranks of the left wing itself.

Within the cross-currents of intellectual ferment at the end of World War I may be fitted four organizational lineages which developed in concert and coalesced in late 1918 in the founding of the Shinjinkai. Two of these were predicated on concrete formulas for social and political reform ("university extension" and "student-laborer contact"), while the other two were simply small cliques of young intellectuals with few specific blueprints for reform but an inexhaustible supply of enthusiasm.

UNIVERSITY EXTENSION

The Japanese university system was in its origins dedicated to the service of the state and not of society. Throughout the Meiji era, the sole function of the university was seen as the production of technicians who would advance the fortunes of the Japanese nation, but not necessarily of the Japanese masses. The curriculum of the imperial universities and most private universities was thus dedicated to the techniques of statecraft; little attention was paid to study of the causes and cures of broad social ills. The students themselves were, in the stereotype of Meiji literature, devoted singlemindedly to *risshin shusse*, fame and success, which normally meant high political or bureaucratic office. Personal advancement took precedence over social service.

By the end of Meiji, however, a perceptible change was underway as the new "Taishō youth" began to emerge, less concerned with his own success than with the problems of society. Or at least so the stereotype goes; in fact, the Taishō youth may merely have been reflecting his diminished chances for fame and success as the ranks of the elite swelled. In early Taishō, a change in the employment pattern of imperial university graduates occurred, with a shift away from government posts towards companies, banks, newspapers, teaching, and a variety of lesser professions.[26] This trend meant that students as a whole were less under the spell of the state as the key to all success and that they were more willing to consider both ideas and careers which did not bear the stamp of state orthodoxy. This broadening of perspective was leading more and more students to demand a greater degree of coordination between the university and society as a whole; to use a recent American idiom, they were seeking "relevant" roles for the university in society.

This concept of the relevance of the university to society was a natural extension of Confucian concepts of the relationship of learning to state policy which held sway in the Tokugawa period. The imperial university professor was in many ways the successor of the Confucian teacher, or *jusha,* serving in a similar mixture of capacities as moralist, educator, bureaucrat, and transmitter of culture (although where the *jusha* was an authority on Chinese culture, the university professor now transmitted Western culture). The professors in Taishō Japan were to an extent merely fulfilling the social role handed down from the Confucian teachers as "constant critic of the life of the times, a living conscience for the age," when they began to speak out on the relevance of scholarship to the great social issues of the day.[27]

26. Karasawa, pp. 162–63.
27. John W. Hall, "The Confucian Teacher in Tokugawa Japan," in David S. Nivison and Arthur F. Wright, eds., *Confucianism in Action* (Stanford, 1959), pp. 268–301.

The clearest expression among university professors of the proper approach to the links between university and society emerged in the concept of "university extension" proposed by Yoshino Sakuzō, the Tokyo Imperial University professor of politics who was the foremost theoretician of Taishō Democracy and the patron of the early Shinjinkai. Yoshino took the phrase "university extension" from the British adult education movement with which he presumably became acquainted during his brief stay in England in 1913. Upon his return to Japan shortly after, Yoshino discussed means of implementing this concept with Sasaki Sōichi, a professor of politics at Kyoto Imperial University whom Yoshino had first met in Berlin, where they became close friends. The project upon which they decided—the publication of a magazine dealing with current social and political issues in a popular style—made it clear that their concept of "university extension" differed greatly from the English model. Rather than striving to make the privileged educational facilities of the university more accessible to all classes through tutorial programs and lectures, Yoshino and Sasaki envisioned a far more didactic mission, whereby university intellectuals would preach the message of social reform to society at large—from a distance.

Bringing together a group of several other intellectuals, most of them linked as Tokyo Imperial University and Second Higher School classmates, Yoshino and Sasaki founded the University Extension Society (Daigaku Fukyūkai), which in June 1915 began the publication of a semi-monthly magazine entitled *Kokumin kōdan* (The popular lectern).[28] In this magazine appeared articles by talented and progressive young university professors who were in accord with Yoshino's concept of encouraging academic figures to speak out on the problems of society as a whole. It was in *Kokumin kōdan* that Yoshino first propounded the theory of *mimponshugi,* his own version of "democracy," which in further elaborations in *Chūō korōn* was to win for him the

28. For details on this magazine, see Kaji Ryūichi, "Mimponshugi zengo," in Ōkōchi Kazuo and Takahashi Seiichirō, eds., *Rōdō seisaku to sono haikei* (Nihon keizai shimbun sha, 1949), pp. 41–58, and Kaji Ryūichi, "Mimponshugi to Daigaku fukyūkai," *Kōsen rempō,* no. 14 (January 1, 1967), p. 3. Kaji, however, consistently refers to the magazine as *"Kokumin kōza,"* an error which has been corrected in a recent secondary study by Ōta Masao, "Taishōki ni okeru demokurashii yakugo kō," *Kirisutokyō shakai mondai kenkyū,* no. 13 (March 1968), pp. 39, 47.

tag of "the apostle of democracy." Kawakami Hajime, then a professor of economics at Kyoto Imperial University and later to become Japan's most celebrated Marxist economist, was typical of the young liberals who wrote for *Kokumin kōdan*.

Kokumin kōdan was discontinued for financial reasons in September 1915 after only six issues, but the concept which it had launched was pursued in other popular intellectual journals. The work of the University Extension Society itself was carried on by a younger generation with the inauguration in January 1917 of *Daigaku hyōron* (The university review) by a number of young Christian students at Tokyo Imperial University.[29] The magazine was organized and financed by Hoshishima Nirō, at the time a third-year law student whose substantial personal wealth enabled him to become a publisher at a young age. Hoshishima had become close to Yoshino through his membership in the Hongō YMCA, of which the professor was an active leader and director from 1917.

The opening declaration of *Daigaku hyōron* defined its task as promoting the obligation of the Japanese university to "enlighten the people and criticize the culture," and as forging "a link between society and the university," echoing the rhetoric of *Kokumin kōdan*.[30] In content, *Daigaku hyōron* closely resembled the popular *Chūō kōron*, although its circulation and influence were substantially less. Aimed at an intellectual audience, *Daigaku hyōron* featured articles on current political and social problems by many of the famous liberal professors of the day and as such played a positive role in the spread of Taishō Democracy.[31] Many of the writers were Christians, as were all of the student editors, reflecting the importance of Japanese Christians (especially Unitarians, who accounted for most of the *Daigaku hyōron* staff) in the liberalism of this period.

The concept of "university extension" which lay behind both *Kokumin kōdan* and *Daigaku hyōron* was rooted in the assumption

29. For a detailed study of this magazine, see Ōta Masao, "Hoshishima Nirō to *Daigaku hyōron*," *Kirisutokyō shakai mondai kenkyū*, no. 11 (March 1967), pp. 116–168.

30. Ōta, "Hoshishima Nirō to *Daigaku hyōron*," p. 132. The English subtitle of the magazine from July 1917 until December 1919 was "The University Extension."

31. For an analysis of the role of *Daigaku hyōron* in the spread of Taishō Democracy, see Ōta Masao, "Taishō demokurashii undō to Daigaku hyōron sha gurūpu," *Dōshisha hōgaku*, no. 102 (October 1967), pp. 21–51.

that the university and the intellectuals who staffed it were blessed with a superior understanding of social problems and that they had only to voice their opinions to effect reform. It was a movement not to bring the universities into closer touch with the realities of society but rather to make more of society aware of the ideas of intellectuals through the device of popular journalism. The approach was thoroughly didactic and thoroughly intellectual. This type of thinking was to have a profound influence on the attitudes of the early student radicals by way of close organizational ties between *Daigaku hyōron* and the Shinjinkai. Asō Hisashi's novel *Reimei* suggests that the Shinjinkai founders had originally hoped to convert *Daigaku hyōron* into the organ of the Shinjinkai itself.[32] Hoshishima was apparently reluctant to give up his own magazine (although he did in fact do so not long afterwards to run for the Diet) but willingly agreed to finance the first Shinjinkai organ, *Democracy,* and to provide the editor of *Daigaku hyōron,* Nobusada Takitarō, as its legal publisher. It is no coincidence that *Democracy* in many ways resembled *Daigaku hyōron,* the major difference being that the articles were written by students rather than professors.

The "university extension" concept instilled in the early Shinjinkai members a conviction that evangelism and enlightenment were valid means of effecting social and political reform. In retrospect, this assumption seems naive, and university intellectuals were eventually to awaken to the reality that direct contact between the university and society were of greater importance than preaching from above. Thus several years later a kind of "university extension" much truer to the English model was to appear in the university settlement movement. Yet traces of the didacticism which lay behind *Kokumin kōdan* are by no means purged from the attitudes of Japanese intellectuals today, even though Marxism has replaced democracy as their basic creed.

THE RŌGAKKAI MODEL

While Yoshino and other such senior intellectuals were attempting to "extend" their own university-bred ideas of society and politics to a wider audience, a younger group of intellectuals in the Yūaikai in

32. Asō Hisashi, *Reimei* (Shinkōsha, 1924), pp. 71, 121.

Kyoto and Tokyo had gone one step further; rather than addressing the people from above, they were striving to enter "into the people" and develop close contact with the working classes. In Tokyo, the most influential were three young men who had all begun working for the Yūaikai while still university students in 1914. In contrast with the *Daigaku hyōron* group, these men were all from private universities: Nosaka Sanzō from Keiō, Hisatome Kōzō from Waseda, and Sakai Kisaku from Nihon. They all entered the Yūaikai on a full-time basis upon graduation, and together with a parallel trio of young Yūaikai officials of working-class origin they launched a movement in opposition to the moderate conciliatory tendencies which had dominated the union since its founding in 1912.[33]

By the spring of 1917, at the Fifth Annual Congress of the Yūaikai, all these men had managed to locate themselves in high posts within the union, in a position to compete with the old-guard leadership. One of the major concerns of the "young intellectual" group was to foster a more efficient dialogue between the intellectual and laborer elements within the Yūaikai. Specifically, they envisioned some sort of framework which would bring together students and young laborers, who would be bound together in the spirit of youth and could successfully unite the education of the one and the class consciousness of the other to strengthen and expand the labor movement. This idea was implemented in late 1917 with the creation of the Rōgakkai (Worker-Student Society).

The Rōgakkai was founded in early December 1917, following the success of a Yūaikai-sponsored "joint worker-student rally" at which both laborers and students gave speeches. Yūaikai president Suzuki Bunji became the head of the group, Waseda professor Kitazawa Shinjirō the vice-president, and students from various Tokyo universities served as officers together with the three "young intellectuals." Despite auspicious beginnings, the Rōgakkai did not enjoy great success in bringing university students in contact with young workers and seems to have served primarily as an informal social group for workers alone.[34] But whatever the success of the Rōgakkai as an organization,

33. Matsuo Takayoshi, *Taishō demokurashii no kenkyū* (Aoki shoten, 1966), pp. 175, 184.

34. There are no records of Rōgakkai activity in Tokyo after July 1918 when the group was reported to have changed its name to the Social Problems Study

the precedent of student involvement in the labor movement had been well established by the activities of Nosaka and other private university students.

Similar student involvement in Yūaikai activity was to be found in Kyoto, which was to provide a further source of inspiration for the Shinjinkai students.[35] In Kyoto the situation was somewhat different from that of Tokyo in that the local Yūaikai organization was considerably more radical and more intellectual, peculiarities that stemmed from the leadership by the skilled weavers of the Nishijin district. Organized under bosses who encouraged their political interests, these traditional artisans were radical not from economic oppression but from intellectual curiosity, elitist pride of profession, and leisure time to spare for union organization. While this Kyoto radicalism was to prove short-lived, it did serve to attract several young student-intellectuals into the Yūaikai organization there. A further contrast with the Tokyo situation was the participation of a number of imperial university students in the Kyoto Yūaikai together with those from private schools (Dōshisha was the most conspicuous of the latter). This head start of the imperial university students in the Kyoto area may be explained by the traditionally greater liberalism of Kyoto Imperial and by the specific influence of the young professor Kawakami Hajime.

The central figure in the Kyoto Yūaikai was Takayama Gizō, who had been elected president of the local branch in 1917 while still a second-year student at Kyoto Imperial University. Also important was Furuichi Haruhiko, who was a year below Takayama at the university but had begun his contacts with the labor movement much earlier, as a middle-school student in Tokyo. These two men, together with a number of younger Dōshisha and Kyoto Imperial students, performed much the same function as the "young intellectual" group in Tokyo, setting a precedent for student participation in and leadership of the burgeoning labor movement.

The Rōgakkai concept was also attempted in Kyoto when in the fall

---

Group (Shakai mondai kenkyūkai) in the face of complaints from the police. See *ibid.,* pp. 197–198.

35. A detailed and reliable secondary account of the activities of Kyoto students in the labor movement in this period may be found in Watanabe Tōru, ed., *Kyōto chihō rōdō undō shi,* rev. ed. (Kyoto: Kyōto chihō rōdō undō shi hensankai, 1968), pt. 2 (pp. 61–308), which was written by Matsuo Takayoshi.

of 1918 a group of the same name (normally distinguished from the already inactive Tokyo organization by the term "Kyoto Rōgakkai") was founded under the leadership of Takayama and composed largely of Kyoto Imperial University law students. Whereas the Tokyo Rōgakkai evolved in the direction of a workers' social group, the Kyoto version took the opposite course, becoming a purely student group devoted to the study of socialism and labor problems. Although the label was the same, the interpretation of the term *rōgaku* (lit., "labor-study") differed, meaning, "worker and student" in Tokyo and "the study of labor" in Kyoto. The Kyoto Rōgakkai became the center of the Kyoto student movement in the period of the early Shinjinkai, although it was far less active than its Tokyo counterparts, devoting itself mainly to quiet study sessions under the leadership of Kawakami.[36] But whatever the differences in the forms of Rōgakkai organization in Tokyo and Kyoto, the basic model of student involvement in the labor movement was firmly established by the fall of 1918 and was to be a persuasive example for the students of the Shinjinkai to follow in their drive to enter "into the people."

Asō Hisashi and His Clique

A small clique of recent graduates of Tokyo Imperial University emerged in the course of 1918 around the person of Asō Hisashi, who was then a cub reporter of the *Tōkyō nichinichi shimbun* (the predecessor of the present *Mainichi shimbun*). This group was to play a major role in determining the direction of the early Japanese student movement, which began with the founding of the Shinjinkai in December of that year.[37] At the core of the Asō clique was a group of

36. For Rōgakkai activities, see Horie Muraichi, ed., *Kaisō no Kawakami Hajime* (Sekai hyōron sha, 1948), pp. 173–221; Nagasue Eiichi, ed., *Mizutani Chōzaburō den* (Minshu shakaitō hombu kyōsenkyoku, 1963), pp. 21–37; and Kikukawa, *Gakusei shakai undō shi*, pp. 35–37, 113, 209.

37. Asō's famous "autobiographical novel" *Reimei*, written in early 1924, is the most detailed source of information on the activities of the Asō clique in 1918–19, but must be used with caution, since the line between fact and fiction is hazy (as the author himself warns in the preface). The book's usefulness is further impaired by the use of initials in place of most proper names; these initials (many of which are obvious) have been deciphered in the postwar edition (Kaiguchi shoten, 1947), but with numerous errors. I have attempted wherever possible to provide other sources to corroborate the *Reimei* account.

three who had been close friends ever since they were classmates at Third Higher School in Kyoto. While at higher school, these three— Asō, Yamana Yoshitsuru, and Tanahashi Kotora—had been the leading members in a debating group called the Jūōkai, taking a keen interest in the political parties and actively participating in the movement to "protect the constitution" which brought down the Katsura government in early 1913.[38] While students at Tokyo Imperial University from 1913 to 1917, they drifted apart and were involved in no conspicuous political activity, but following graduation their long-standing mutual interest in society and politics was stimulated anew by the events of 1917–18, and they began meeting with increasing frequency.

It was through the activities and interests of Asō, whose native political instincts and excitable personality made him the natural leader of the group, that others were added to the Third Higher core in 1918. One such was Okanoe Morimichi, who came in contact with Asō through their common interest in things Russian. Asō had been a dedicated Russophile ever since developing a consuming interest in Tolstoy while a middle-school student.[39] He had gone on to read all the translations of Russian novels available and was especially fond of Turgenev, finding in the *narodniki* of *Virgin Soil* his model for intellectuals entering into the people. The Bolshevik Revolution in October 1917, which took place shortly after Asō's graduation and entrance into the *Tōkyō nichinichi,* had caused him tremendous excitement. In January 1918 Asō wrote a seven-part article in the *Tōkyō nichinichi* entitled "From Peter to Lenin," in which he enthusiastically portrayed the Bolsheviks as the final crystallization of the primordial Russian character, with which he felt well acquainted through his reading.

Asō's article was apparently the link that brought him together with Okanoe,[40] who since his graduation from the university in 1916 had been employed as a researcher at the East Asian Economic Research

38. For the activities of the Jūōkai, see Asō, *Dakuryū ni oyogu,* pp. 291–292, 342–353, 369–374, and Andō Katsuichirō, ed., *Daisan kōtō gakkō benrombu bushi* (Daisan kōtō gakkō benrombu, 1935), pp. 94–123. Kishii Jurō was a fourth member of the Third Higher core of Asō's clique and later joined the Shinjinkai, but was absent during most of 1918 serving a one-year term in the army. Kishii interview.

39. Asō, *Dakuryū ni oyogu,* pp. 118–119, 267–269, and *passim.*

40. Asō, *Reimei,* pp. 20–22.

Bureau (Tōa Keizai Chōsa Kyoku) in Tokyo. Because of its connection with the South Manchurian Railway Company, this organization enjoyed substantial government support and was able to amass many materials on recent events in Russia.[41] Okanoe's access to this material, and an affection for things Russian which fully equalled Asō's, made them natural friends. Okanoe, who normally went under the pen name of Kuroda Reiji (from "Kropotkin" and "Lenin") was a genuine eccentric, a master of several languages, ranging from Russian to Malay, who expressed his contempt of traditional Japanese ways by eating potatoes and wearing Russian worker's garb.[42] It was through Okanoe that Sano Manabu, a fellow researcher at the East Asian Research Bureau, was also introduced to the Asō clique. Sano was likewise interested in the recent developments in Russia, and it was the combination of his and Okanoe's scholarly talents with Asō's enthusiasm that produced a book entitled *Kagekiha* (The Bolsheviks), which was written jointly by the three and published in June 1919, becoming the earliest complete introduction to the Russian Revolution to appear in Japan.[43]

Asō's other interest was in the Japanese labor movement, an interest stemming from his infatuation with the Turgenev-inspired ideal of entering "into the people." Since his graduation, Asō had closely followed developments within the Yūaikai and became acquainted with Nosaka Sanzō, who was also drawn into the Asō clique, even though he was not a graduate of Tokyo Imperial University and thus somewhat of an outsider.[44] It is possible that Asō and his Third Higher friends attended some of the meetings of the Rōgakkai, which Nosaka had helped organize in late 1917, but until the fall of 1918 the interest of Asō and the others in the Yūaikai remained passive.[45] In the mean-

41. Kaji Ryūichi, "Sano Manabu to sono jidai," *Kokoro,* 6.8 (August 1953), 50–51.

42. Kaji Ryūichi, *Rekishi o tsukuru hitobito* (Ōyaesu shuppan K. K., 1948), p. 125; Asō, *Reimei,* pp. 15–16.

43. The book was published by Min'yūsha under the pseudonyms of "Asayama Kaisuke" (Asō), "Kuroda Reiji" (Okanoe), and "Katashima Shin" (Sano).

44. Nosaka's association with the Shinjinkai was brief, since he left for Europe in July 1919. Nosaka, a central figure in the postwar Communist Party, denies his membership in the Shinjinkai; personal correspondence, October 18, 1967.

45. This suggestion is made by Matsuo, *Taishō demokurashii no kenkyū,* p. 198. Tanahashi Kotora in an interview recalled attending a single Rōgakkai meeting; it is doubtful, however, that any of Asō's group attended regularly.

time, Tanahashi was employed in the Ministry of Justice and the well-to-do Yamana was for the most part idle.

The rice riots in the summer of 1918 provided the stimulus needed to bring together all these young men into a coherent group and to crystallize their welling impulse to enter "into the people." The group began meeting regularly that fall at Asō's house for study and discussion.[46] At some of these meetings, Okanoe attempted to teach the Russian language (although apparently with little success). At another of the gatherings, Sano Manabu gave a scholarly lecture on the significance of the Communist Manifesto. Soon the talking led to action, as one by one the members of the group became involved in the labor movement. In September, Tanahashi entered the Tokyo Yūaikai to replace Nosaka, who was scheduled to travel to Europe the following summer. In about November, Yamana moved to a small house in the working-class district of Tsukishima to conduct a survey of laborer health and hygienic conditions which had been commissioned by the government. Tanahashi also went to live in Tsukishima shortly after, as did Sano, who, however, kept his job at the research bureau. Asō himself was the last to go, quitting his newspaper job and entering the Yūaikai in June 1919.

One reason for Asō's delayed entrance into the Yūaikai was his preoccupation in this period with the exciting ferment which was underway in the academic world. Critical to Asō's involvement in this activity was his close association with Yoshino Sakuzō, whom he had come to know while a student at Tokyo Imperial University and remained close to after graduation. In the fall of 1918, Yoshino became the center of attention in the Japanese intellectual world in his famous debate with the members of the Rōninkai (Society of Rōnin), a right-wing group descended from the Kokuryūkai (Amur River Soci-

46. Asō, *Reimei,* p. 94 and *passim,* refers to this group as the "Suiyōkai" (Wednesday club), while Akamatsu Katsumaro, "Shinjinkai no rekishiteki ashiato," *Kaizō,* 10.6 (June 1928), 69, gives "Mokuyōkai" (Thursday club); both terms have their adherents among secondary writers. In fact, however, it is doubtful that the group had any formal name at all at the time. Tanahashi Kotora's personal diary for the period lists eight meetings of the group from September 1918 through January 1919 (five on Thursday, two Saturday, and one Wednesday) but refers to it simply as a *"dōshi no kai"* or *"dōjinkai"* (roughly, "the gang"). (Tanahashi interview.) Asō doubtless devised the name later to give the group an identity, while Akamatsu's version may have been a confusion of the characters *sui* and *moku.*

ety). This confrontation was set off by an article which Yoshino had written in the November issue of *Chūō kōron*, entitled "A Rejection of the Social Suppression of Freedom of Speech," in which he denounced the Rōninkai for its use of bullying and threats in forcing the dismissal of liberal elements on the *Ōsaka asahi shimbun* editorial staff in late September.[47] Yoshino's accusation that the Rōninkai was harming the national interest while hiding behind patriotic slogans infuriated its members and led them—unwisely—to accept Yoshino's proposal for a public debate.[48]

The debate was held November 23 at the Nammei Club in the Kanda district of Tokyo before a packed crowd of students and workers which flowed out into the street, where Yūaikai president Suzuki, a close friend of Yoshino, relayed the gist of the proceedings within in a booming voice. The majority of the crowd strongly supported Yoshino, and it is scarcely surprising that tradition has accorded the professor a spectacular victory over his opponents. The excitement generated by this "debate for democracy," not only among the young students and laborers who attended it but among liberal intellectuals in general, can scarcely be exaggerated, and it may fairly be interpreted as the event which launched the Taishō Democracy movement into full swing.

Asō served as Yoshino's bodyguard during the debate and in his autobiographical novel *Reimei* has provided one of the most graphic descriptions of the event.[49] In the wake of the debate, Asō struck on the idea of utilizing the excitement which had been generated to launch an organized movement among academic liberals, and to this end he worked to bring together Yoshino with Fukuda Tokuzō, a prominent economist from Tokyo Higher School of Commerce.[50] The two men agreed to unite in the cause of "democracy," and in early December a meeting was held between them, each accompanied by his

47. For the details of this incident, see Asahi shimbun, Ōsaka honsha, Shashi henshūshitsu, ed., *Murayama Ryūhei den* (Asahi shimbun sha, 1953), pp. 505–535.
48. Tanaka Sōgorō, *Yoshino Sakuzō* (Miraisha, 1958), pp. 222–223.
49. Asō, *Reimei,* pp. 212–227.
50. Fukuda's academic career was unique in its fluctuation between a state and a private university. He was a professor at Higher Commerce (Tokyo University of Commerce from 1920, and Hitotsubashi University today) from 1900 to 1904 and 1919 to 1930, and at Keiō University from 1905 to 1911 and 1912 to 1918. Hence he drew colleagues from both schools into the Reimeikai. See Keiō Gijuku, ed., *Keiō Gijuku hyakunen shi,* 5 vols. (editor, 1962), V, 67–73.

for the English "speech" and "debate." [55] In the period after the Russo-Japanese War, student debating became a fad, encouraged by the efforts of Noma Seiji in the publication of *Yūben* (Eloquence) from 1910 as the first magazine of what was to become the great Kōdansha publishing empire. Noma himself had been one of the prime movers in the founding of the Midorikai Debating Club in November 1909 when he was an administrative official at Tokyo Imperial University.[56] Throughout late Meiji and early Taishō, student debating clubs served as the primary vehicle for student political interest, as in the case of Asō Hisashi's Third Higher School group. Far from radical, however, these debating clubs tended to be implicitly committed to a parliamentary system of government, as evidenced by the great popularity in this period of student Mock Diets.[57]

In the fall of 1918, Yoshino Sakuzō was the president (in effect, faculty adviser) of the Midorikai Debating Club and as such responsible for appointing the student directors (*gakusei iin*), one from each of the eight higher schools. Those appointed for the new academic year in September were six in number, since there were no available representatives from Fifth or Sixth Higher: Miyazaki Ryūsuke (First), Suzuki Yoshio (Second), Akamatsu Katsumaro (Third), Nonaka Tetsuya (Fourth), Ishiwatari Haruo (Seventh), and Fukuda Keijirō (Eighth).[58] The first major event in the club calendar that year was a joint oratorical meet with their counterparts at Kyoto Imperial University, an annual event which had been inaugurated two years earlier by none other than Asō Hisashi when he was a student.[59]

55. For the origins and early development of school debating in Japan, see Miyazaka Tetsubumi, "Meiji jidai ni okeru kagai enzetsu tōron katsudō ni tsuite no ichi kōsatsu," in Ishikawa Ken hakushi kanreki kinen rombunshū hensan iinkai, ed., *Kyōiku no shiteki tenkai* (Kōdansha, 1952), pp. 409–427.

56. Seiji Noma, *Noma of Japan: The Nine Magazines of Kodansha* (New York, 1934), pp. 128–130.

57. Mock Diets apparently began in the late 1880s under the stimulation of preparations for the convocation of the Imperial Diet in 1890. At Waseda, the Mock Diet became an annual event in 1888; see Waseda daigaku arubamu kankōkai, ed., *Waseda daigaku arubamu* (editor, 1963), p. 57. After a period of decline, Mock Diets were again revived in the 1910s; see, for example, Andō, ed., *Daisan kōtō gakkō benrombu bushi*, p. 119.

58. Miyazaki Ryūsuke, "Shinjinkai to wakaki hi no Katsumaro-kun," *Nihon oyobi Nihonjin*, 7.2 (March 1956), 43.

59. Asō Hisashi denki kankō iinkai, ed., *Asō Hisashi den* (editor, 1958), p. 50, gives this fact on the hearsay of a former classmate of Asō.

In Kyoto a number of students and recent graduates from the imperial university there, such as Takayama and Furuichi, were deeply involved in the labor movement and hence one step ahead of the Tokyo students who arrived for the joint debate in late October. It is no coincidence that these Kyoto radicals were also, much like Asō and his group, deeply involved in student debating and hence were on hand to welcome the Tokyo delegation upon its arrival.[60] The political atmosphere at the time was intensified by such startling events of the past several months as the rice riots and the Rōninkai attack on the *Ōsaka asahi shimbun.* All these circumstances combined to generate among the young university students a sense of excitement and anticipation which was well conveyed by the themes they chose for speeches at the oratorical meet the night of October 27. Miyazaki spoke on "The Crisis of the Japanese People" and Akamatsu on "How We Shall Advance," while Taman Kiyoomi, a Kyoto classmate of Takayama and Furuichi, contended that "Youth Must Rebuild the Nation." [61]

Much talk was exchanged among the Tokyo and Kyoto debaters, and in the process of the discussion three of the Tokyo Imperial delegation found that their ideas were much in accord. Consideration of the social and family background of each of these three students reveals that a consensus on the need for social and political reform was not unexpected.

Akamatsu Katsumaro was the son of a Buddhist priest who had forfeited an inherited position of great influence in the religious hierarchy in Kyoto to devote himself to charitable works in Yamaguchi prefecture, setting up orphanages, developing programs for the rehabilitation of ex-convicts, and taking an active concern for the outcasts of west Japan.[62] Shortly before he died in 1921, he asked his son Katsumaro not to worry about a funeral or gravestone but only to "strive to reform the present irrational society and build a new world in which

60. Takayama, Furuichi, and Taman Kiyoomi had, in fact, created a major incident for their political interests as student debaters in March 1917 at Kyoto Imperial. It was this incident which led Takayama and his classmates into labor union activity. For a detailed account, see Watanabe, ed., *Kyōto chihō rōdō undō shi,* pp. 81–83.
61. Ibid., p. 99.
62. The best source for Akamatsu's early life is Noguchi, pp. 4–6.

all can live together." [63] Katsumaro was not the only one to follow his father's advice: his younger sister Tsuneko became a prominent leader in the women's labor movement and a postwar Diet member for the Japanese Socialist Party, .while his younger brother Iomaro was a prized disciple of Kawakami Hajime's at Kyoto Imperial University in the early 1920s. Akamatsu had been active in student debating at Third Higher and on entering Tokyo Imperial University became a close follower of Yoshino Sakuzō, whose daughter Akiko he was later to marry. Akamatsu was a forceful personality, gregarious, cheerful, and voluble, with a slight stammer which added an enhancing charm to his powerful ability to persuade. He was to be the single most dominant figure in the early Shinjinkai.

Miyazaki Ryūsuke, like Akamatsu, came from an activist family. His father Tōten (Torazō) was famous as Sun Yat-sen's leading Japanese sponsor and himself from a family of radicals: the best known of Ryūsuke's uncles was Miyazaki Tamizō, who devoted much of his life to espousing a single-tax scheme.[64] Ryūsuke inherited a generous amount of the spirit of adventure from his father, through whom he was in contact with China in a number of ways, traveling to a family home in Shanghai every summer. It was through his father that he became closely acquainted with Yoshino Sakuzō, who shared a deep concern for the future of China, having served for three years as tutor to the son of Yüan Shih-kai prior to his study in Europe. Although not of the same intellectual caliber as Akamatsu, Miyazaki was a fiery and romantic activist, both in appearance and speech. Miyazaki had enlisted himself in the cause of reform as early as the fall of 1917, when, as a first-year university student, he set up a "current affairs study group" (jikyoku kōkyūkai) which sponsored lectures on the university campus by such noted liberal politicians as Ozaki Yukio and Inukai Tsuyoshi.[65]

Ishiwatari Haruo offered a very different type of background from

63. [Hōsei daigaku] Ōhara shakai mondai kenkyūjo, ed., Shinjinkai kikanshi: Demokurashii, Senku, Dōhō, Narōdo (Hōsei daigaku shuppankyoku, 1969), p. 478.

64. For Miyazaki Tōten's activities, see Marius Jansen, The Japanese and Sun Yat-sen (Cambridge, Mass., 1954). For other information on Miyazaki's background, see Noguchi, pp. 273–275.

65. Miyazaki Ryusuke interview. Miyazaki has a photograph taken at one such lecture in about late 1917 showing Ozaki, Yoshino, Hoshishima, Miyazaki and his younger brother Shinsaku, and ten other students and laborers.

either of the others, being born of the traditionally outcast eta class in Tokyo's Asakusa district.[66] By concealing his origins, Ishiwatari had managed to rise to the prestigious heights of the imperial university but presumably retained an acute consciousness of the social injustice of the caste system from which he had escaped. Yet at the same time, Ishiwatari's background doubtless inhibited his radicalism, for fear of blackmail should the truth be discovered. Few in the Shinjinkai knew the truth of his origins, although one former member claims that it was such a discovery that led to Ishiwatari's eventual disappearance from the group. He wrote several articles in the Shinjinkai magazine under the pen name Sumida Haruo (after the River Sumida, which runs through the shitamachi district where he was born) but passed from prominence shortly after. A quiet type with the somber "look of a warrior," he had none of the charm or flamboyance of his two fellow activists.[67]

Led by their backgrounds to take a keen interest in social and political reform, the three Debating Club members on the train back to Tokyo discussed the possibility of organizing a group to pursue the spirit of reform which had emerged so vividly in the encounter with the Kyoto debaters.[68] After returning to Tokyo, the three continued to discuss their ideas, but the catalyst which finally drove them to action was the Yoshino–Rōninkai debate. An initial plan to turn the Debating Club itself in radical directions was abandoned from the opposition of conservative elements, and it was agreed in a series of meetings in late November and early December, in a grubby student restaurant named the Hachinoki, to organize a wholly new group, which would bear the appropriate name of New Man Society.[69]

A poster was prepared to recruit members "to form a group for the

66. This fact is now known among a number of former Shinjinkai members, but rarely voiced; the only documentary evidence I have found is a single veiled sentence by Ōya Sōichi: "Ishiwatari was from a special status (tokushu na mibun no de) which has occupied a special place in the history of the liberation movement in Japan." Ōya Sōichi, Ōya Sōichi no hon 4: Nihonteki chūseishin (Sankei shimbun shuppankyoku, 1967), p. 178.

67. Miwa Jusō denki kankōkai, ed., Miwa Jusō no shōgai, p. 182.

68. Kikukawa, Gakusei shakai undō shi, pp. 33–34, quotes a conversation which supposedly took place on this train trip, but this in all likelihood is a product of the author's imagination.

69. Miyazaki, "Shinjinkai to wakaki hi no Katsumaro-kun," p. 43. Taira Teizō, in Miwa Jusō denki kankōkai, ed., Miwa Jusō no shōgai, p. 176, gives an

discussion of socialism, anarchism, and so forth," and sometime in the first week of December 1918 about a dozen students met at the Hachinoki to launch the Shinjinkai.[70] Within the next few weeks, an agreement was made with Asō Hisashi, who through his close contacts with Yoshino was in touch with the students, to bring his own clique into the Shinjinkai, setting a precedent of joint student-alumni membership. Thus the inchoate intellectual ferment among the young in 1918 was harnessed by organization, and in mid-January 1919 after the students' return from New Year's vacation, the Shinjinkai began its activity in earnest, soon followed by similar groups in other Tokyo universities.

---

undocumented account of this period which Miyazaki claims is completely garbled. (Miyazaki interview.) The name "Shinjinkai" was, according to Miyazaki, a natural choice, and not the proposal of any individual.

70. The exact founding date of the Shinjinkai is not known. Akamatsu, in "Shinjinkai no rekishiteki ashiato," p. 68, explains that "the birth of the Shinjinkai was brought about in such a very simple atmosphere, with no splendid formality like a 'founding ceremony,' that the founding date is not precise." Corroboration is provided by the first issue of the Shinjinkai magazine, which gives simply "early (jōjun) December" as a founding date (Shinjinkai kikanshi, p. 18). Asō Hisashi denki kankō iinkai, ed., Asō Hisashi den, p. 107, gives an exact date of December 5, which has been followed in other secondary works but which must be discarded for lack of any evidence. A Ministry of the Interior report on left-wing groups in 1921 likewise provides an exact date (December 15), which must similarly be dismissed as unreliable; see Shakai bunko, ed., Taishōki shisō dantai shisatsunin hōkoku (Kashiwa shobō, 1965), p. 31.

3 | The Early Shinjinkai, 1918-1921

The Shinjinkai was born of a mood rather than a program, of an amorphous rhetoric rather than a set of ideological dogma. The group's initial statement of purpose, drafted by Akamatsu Katsumaro, reads:

I. We will work for and seek to advance the new trend towards the liberation of mankind which is a universal cultural force.

II. We will engage ourselves in the movement for the rational reform of contemporary Japan.[1]

This ill-defined, rhetorical approach was by no means peculiar to the Shinjinkai but in fact characterized all the intellectual and student groups formed in the same period. The Reimeikai, for example, declared itself committed to "strive for the stabilization and enrichment of the life of the Japanese people in conformity with the new trends of the postwar world," while the Waseda Minjin Dōmeikai (People's League), founded shortly after the Shinjinkai, noted that "the tide of the new age is marching irresistibly in the direction of total democratization, bringing into harmony national sensitivities and class consciousness." [2]

Such a "mood" is best presented not by logical analysis but by a casual journey through its imagery. Within the rhetoric of the early Shinjinkai, these images were central:

1. *Shinjinkai kikanshi,* p. 18.
2. *Ibid.*

New. The very name of the group, New Man Society, reflects the prominence of this element, which is reiterated time and again in the imagery of the coming of spring, of new buds sprouting, of flowers blossoming, of the cultivation of virgin soil. The term "pioneer" capsulized the Shinjinkai sense of newness, as seen in the decision announced in the June 1919 issue of *Democracy* to change the magazine's name to *Senku* (Pioneer). The following issue of the magazine suggested the source of inspiration for this theme in a partial translation of Walt Whitman's "Pioneers! O Pioneers!" (from *Leaves of Grass*), of which they took care to select those stanzas most appropriate to their own mood, such as:

> All the past we leave behind,
> We debouch upon a newer mightier world, varied world
> Fresh and strong the world we seize, world of labor and the march,
> Pioneers! O Pioneers! [3]

Bright. The image of brightness pervades the rhetoric of the Shinjinkai and may also be found in the names of similar intellectual groups, such as the Reimeikai (Dawn Society), or the Waseda student group Gyōminkai (Dawn of the People Society). Such imagery conveyed the tremendous optimism of this "dawn period," as Asō Hisashi was later to characterize it; the first verse of the official Shinjinkai song, composed by Akamatsu for the first anniversary celebration, is almost blinding in its rhetoric:

> Lo, the hope for the dawn of civilization
> Shines forth with a red glow,
> And in the eyes of all mankind
> Is burning like a flame.[4]

Total. Pioneers, the Shinjinkai members felt, must totally reshape "old" reality, renewing everything handed down from the past. Akamatsu in "The True Spirit of the Liberation Movement," a central statement of early Shinjinkai thinking, insisted that "The systems making up Japanese culture, which has been built on faulty founda-

3. *Ibid.*, p. 93.
4. *Ibid.*, p. 144.

tions, form a single harmoniously organized structure . . . The fighters in the camp of liberation should not aim at simply the economic system, or the social system, or the political system, or foreign relations, but should make their target each and every aspect of the culture which has risen from irrational foundations. They must pledge themselves to the reform of all things which might stand in the way of the just progress of mankind, leaving no stone unturned." [5]

Universal. The Shinjinkai members would have agreed with an American observer who wrote in 1923 of trends among youth after World War I that "unrest is worldwide. The sparks of idealism struck by allied statesmen before and immediately following the armistice kindled a flame which has swept to the remotest corners of the earth." [6] Beginning with the Russian Revolution, the Japanese students drew inspiration from every sign of ferment which they could detect in other countries and felt themselves bound up in a surging tide of universal dimensions. This feeling gave to the Shinjinkai a spirit of internationalism which was most clear in their hospitality to the nationalist movements of Korean and Chinese students. One Korean student at Tokyo Imperial, Kim Chun-yŏn, was taken in as a member, and in the wake of the suppression of the Korean nationalist uprisings in March 1919 (the Samil Movement) the Shinjinkai magazine pledged its support to the Korean people (although never going so far as to advocate independence of Japanese rule).[7]

Ties with Chinese students were especially close, thanks to the many contacts of Miyazaki Ryusūke and Yoshino Sakuzō. Through Yoshino's efforts, a delegation of student leaders of the May Fourth movement from Peking University spent about three weeks traveling in Japan in the spring of 1920, meeting and talking with liberal students and intellectuals.[8] The Shinjinkai, which entertained the group at a banquet

5. *Ibid.*, p. 84.

6. Stanley High, ed., *The Revolt of Youth* (New York, 1923), p. 32. This book also has an interesting chapter on Japanese students by an American missionary, pp. 191–203.

7. See *Shinjinkai kikanshi*, pp. 23–24, for two articles in the April issue of *Democracy*. These articles were probably responsible for the banning of this issue. For Kim's ties with the Shinjinkai, see Kim Chun-yŏn, *Na ŭi kil*, 2nd ed. (Seoul, 1967), pp. 7–8.

8. For a detailed secondary account of the visit, see Matsuo, *Taishō demokurashii no kenkyū*, pp. 297–303.

in Tokyo, was enthusiastic over such proof of the international scope of their movement: "We rejoice in joining hands with courageous people, no matter what nationality, who are pressing forward on the tide of universal reform. It is an event of deep significance for the advancement of the trend of reform both in Japan and China, indeed in the entire Orient, when the progressive youths of both countries come together in one place and achieve a full and open understanding." [9]

Popular. The orientation of the early Shinjinkai students was "popular" in two senses. On the one hand, they were committed to all the political demands of Taishō Democracy and to universal suffrage in particular, as seen in their enthusiastic participation in the suffragist demonstrations of early 1919 and 1920.[10] But beyond this support of a more popular system of representative government was an emotional tendency to deify the "people" as the repository of all that is honest, natural, and pure. Their model for this romantic populism was the Russian *narodnik* with whom they had become infatuated through the novels of Turgenev. They were further inspired by a poem of Ishikawa Takuboku entitled "After a fruitless argument," which was carried in the second issue of *Democracy* and probably served as an inspiration later to rename the magazine *Narod* (Russian for "people"). The young students' impatience to join hands with the people was well reflected in the second stanza of Takuboku's poem:

We know what it is we want:
We know what the people want
And we know what's to be done.
Yes, we know more than the young Russians of fifty years ago.
Yet, even so, not one of us clenches his fist,
Crashes it on the table
And shouts V'NAROD! [11]

9. *Shinjinkai kikanshi*, p. 285.
10. For a secondary analysis of the Shinjinkai attitudes towards universal suffrage, see Kanda Bunjin, "Gakusei no shakai shugi undō kikanshi," *Shisō*, no. 464 (February 1963), pp. 121–122.
11. *Shinjinkai kikanshi*, p. 35. The translation is from Goeffrey Bownas and Anthony Thwaite, trans., *The Penguin Book of Japanese Verse* (Baltimore, 1964), p. 182.

Young. The early Shinjinkai members were insistent upon their qualifications as "youth" rather than as students. This insistence stemmed not from a "generation gap" type of failure to communicate with elders which is popularly ascribed to student movements but more from a cult of the quality of youth itself, its energy and idealism. The "Publication Statement" in the first issue of the magazine concluded with this eloquent pronouncement on the role of youth: "As we face the dawn, who, then, should take charge of the reform of Japan today? How about the privileged classes who now occupy the positions of national leadership? How about the educated classes, the bureaucrats, the military, the party politicians, the capitalists, the university professors? Their lack of qualification has been too eloquently proved by their behavior both now and in the past. Their record clearly shows too much wickedness, vulgarity, and lack of principle to win the confidence of the masses. We have already given up hope in the ruling class. In times like these, the drive for reform must come from youth itself, youth whose conscience is pure, whose intellect keen, whose spirit afire. The blood of youth is untainted, the standpoint of youth is impartial, the ideals of youth are lofty. Has not the day come for youth to rise up as one?" [12]

Natural. Like all romantics, the Shinjinkai members saw in nature their ideal of perfection, and frequently contrasted the injustices of human society with the balance of the natural world. One member described stopping by the Chikuma River in Nagano prefecture during a lecture tour to the provinces: "As we peered far below through the trunks of the high, aged pines, the Chikuma flowed by in its azure depths, casting white spray against the cliffs. Looking downriver, we saw the chain of the Japan Alps towering high in a shroud of purplish haze. In nearby fields the wheat was green with a new-dyed freshness. The skylarks were singing brightly. Nature was wise, she was free. Yet what a contrast that man, beside such nature, should be driven by foul desires. After our week of campaigning, we were deeply impressed by the pure, eternal form of nature, ever untainted." [13]

It followed that if the evils in human society were unnatural, the task of correcting them was natural. The students' frequent use of

12. *Shinjinkai kikanshi*, p. 4. The author is Akamatsu.
13. *Ibid.*, p. 309. The author is Shimmei Masamichi.

words like "tide" and "trend" suggests their conviction that a natural, predetermined force was pressing in the direction of a just society. This tremendous optimism, later to be denounced by a more cynical generation of students as the heresy of "revolution-around-the-corner-ism" (*kakumei zen'ya shugi*), was well expressed by Asō in *Reimei:* "Before them lay the single goal of the ideal human society. If only they were to stretch out their hands, yes, just stretch out their hands, they could reach it. Before them lay revolution: they had only to shout out, yes, only to shout out, and they would be answered, revolution would be theirs." [14]

Humanistic. An editorial in the first issue of the Shinjinkai magazine declared "neo-humanism" to be the creed of the group, putting forth the formula of "rising above matter through matter": "These young philosophers are pure humanists in the sense that they desire to bring into this world the spirit of love and peace. Yet they are not of the sort, like the old religionists and those who rely on ancestral virtue, to compromise with 'these degenerate times' and strive to purify it with empty sermonizing and submissive morals. They seek rather, through strength and conviction, to eradicate the system of materialistic competition which stands in the way of the spirit of love and peace, and to liberate mankind from this state of materialistic struggle." [15]

Despite the talk of "material means," it is clear that the "humanism" of the Shinjinkai was distinctly religious in its stress on nonmaterial ends. This passage suggests a specific rejection of both Confucian tendencies to "rely on ancestral virtue" (*itokushugi*) and of Buddhistic accommodationism and quietism ("these degenerate times" [*daraku seru gense*] is a Buddhist term). Although not specified, a distinctly Christian tone pervades this passage and in fact much of the rhetoric of the early Shinjinkai. Many of the members had at one time been lured by Christianity, including founders Akamatsu and Miyazaki, and although most were quick to reject formal professions of faith, the stress on an active "spirit of love and peace" persisted. One of the clearest indications of the "humanistic" tone to the early Shinjinkai was in Akamatsu's interpretation of Marx, who is portrayed as some-

14. Asō, *Reimei* (postwar edition), p. 160. The clauses containing "revolution" were censored in the prewar edition, p. 362.
15. *Shinjinkai kikanshi*, p. 3.

thing of a Christ figure: "The basic drive of our reform movement is an ardent humanitarian spirit which, on a foundation of matter, strives to build a shining kingdom of true goodness and beauty which will rise above matter. While we do not believe in the whole of Marx's material view of history, yet we are deeply moved by the example of his moral life, he who sacrificed everything and died a martyr for the great cause of human emancipation." [16]

The Shinjinkai "mood" was the product of the pressure of the events of the day, of sheer novelty as the first important student group organized not for specific grievances but on the basis of ideological commitment. As such, the mood was bound to disappear or at least metamorphose into a different mood as the organization outstripped the temporal limitations of "newness" and "youth." This early spirit of the Shinjinkai at its founding was sustained for a period of approximately one year before it began to erode in the spring of 1920. The two major factors in sustaining the founding mood throughout 1919 were on the one hand the progress of the left-wing movement in general and on the other the intimacy of the group fostered by communal living.

The year 1919 was probably the last truly encouraging time which the Japanese left was to experience until the end of the Pacific War. Intellectuals and students had banded together in a number of enthusiastic new groups along the lines of the Shinjinkai and Reimeikai and were energetically spreading the good word in lectures and articles. A host of durable new journals appeared in the first half of 1919 which were to increase vastly the influence of the left-wing press in Japan. Now the newsstands offered a choice previously unimaginable; among the commercially based liberal magazines, the classic *Chūō kōron* was supplemented by *Kaizō* (Reform) in April and *Kaihō* (Liberation) in June. Kyoto professor Kawakami Hajime began his personal *Shakai mondai kenkyū* (Studies in social problems) in January, and the liberal journalists excluded from the *Ōsaka asahi shimbun* launched *Warera* (We) a month later. The Reimeikai published its monthly lectures as the *Reimei kōenshū*, while the Shinjinkai's first magazine, *Democracy*, went for eight issues from March to December.

The labor movement showed a parallel surge, responding to con-

16. *Ibid.*, p. 85.

ciliatory moves on the part of management in the wake of the dis-
quieting rice riots the year before with a new aggressiveness, making
the summer of 1919 an even more traumatic one for employers than
the preceding. The months of July through October alone saw over
three hundred strikes, more than the total of the preceding several
years.[17] This activity was naturally accompanied by a great increase
in the number and size of labor unions, and the Yūaikai, which remained the major national federation, took on an increasingly radical
tone as the younger leaders like Asō Hisashi managed to shut out the
old Christian moderates.

Also important to sustaining the excited confidence of the Shinjinkai
in its first year was the communal life of most of the membership at the
huge thirteen-room mansion in the outskirts of Tokyo which had belonged to the Chinese revolutionary leader Huang Hsing.[18] Miyazaki
Ryūsuke's father, Tōten, who had been close to Huang in the heyday
of the T'ung-meng hui, served as custodian of the house after Huang's
death in 1916 and gladly assented to the Shinjinkai request to make it
their headquarters. The house served much the same function as
Takayama Gizō's large family house in the outskirts of Kyoto in the
same period, as a gathering place for radical intellectuals, young and
old. Among the senior luminaries known to have paid visits to the
Shinjinkai house in Takada-mura (near the present Mejiro Station)
were Kagawa Toyohiko, Morito Tatsuo, Ōsugi Sakae, Kondō Kenji,
Vassily Eroshenko, and Kushida Tamizō.[19]

The Huang mansion served as the Shinjinkai headquarters for just
over one year beginning April 1919. For the first two months Asō,
with his wife, lived in as the senior member and was succeeded that
summer by Sano Manabu, who until then had been living in Tsukishima. Both these men, from their close involvement with the labor
movement at the time, did much to focus the group's enthusiasm; they
also left a large library, which provided a stockpile for early Shinjinkai

17. Aoki Kōji, comp., *Nihon rōdō undō shi nempyō*, 4 vols., (Shinseisha,
1968–   ), I, 224–276.
18. For a description of the mansion, see Asō, *Reimei*, pp. 340–347.
19. *Shinjinkai kikanshi*, pp. 259, 280, 337. Eroshenko (1891–1952) was a blind
Russian poet and Esperanto advocate who spent several years in Japan, enjoying
great popularity in left-wing circles until his deportation in 1921. For the role
of Takayama's Kyoto house, see Watanabe, ed., *Kyoto chihō rōdō undō shi*, p. 121.

research and translation efforts.[20] Something of the unifying mood in the Takada-mura headquarters is caught in the reminiscences of Hayashi Kaname: "Seen from the outside, life in the mansion was highly unordered . . . There was scarcely any time for the leisurely reading of books, for quiet thinking, for orderly discussions . . . Since we were living together, a unanimity of mood (*kibunteki itchi*) easily developed, and theoretical discussions tended to be conducted in an offhand, haphazard way . . . I found that social theory was taken in not through the head in the form of theory, but rather absorbed through the skin by way of the atmosphere around me." [21]

The Shinjinkai left the Huang mansion in May 1920 following the expulsion of Miyazaki Ryūsuke as a member because of his relations with the poetess Itō Byakuren.[22] Thereafter, the central Shinjinkai leaders continued to live together, in the tradition of the *gasshuku* or "communal lodging" which was popular among students with common interests. But the later Shinjinkai *gasshuku* tended to include only a very small proportion of the membership and hence could not serve to give the entire group the same "unanimity of mood" which it earlier enjoyed.[23]

ATTITUDES TOWARD THE UNIVERSITY

Unlike most student movements, the early Shinjinkai showed very little concern for—and in some cases even a positive aversion to—the university from which it sprang. Neither the problems nor the organizational advantages of the campus had much lure for these prophets of the "new thought," who declared in their founding statement that

20. Asō, *Reimei*, p. 400.

21. Hayashi Kaname, "Shinjinkai no koro," in Tōkyō daigaku kyōdō kumiai shuppan bu, ed., *Rekishi o tsukuru gakusei-tachi*, 2nd ed. (editor, 1948), pp. 170–171.

22. For an account of this famous incident, see Miyazaki Ryūsuke, "Yanagihara Byakuren to no hanseiki," *Bungei shunjū*, 45.6 (June 1967), 220–230. The objections to the Byakuren affair by the other members stemmed from her noble birth and her marriage to Kyushu coal magnate Itō Denzaemon. In later years, following her elopement with Miyazaki, she was to disprove this ascription of bourgeois character.

23. In July 1920 a new permanent headquarters was set up at Komagome Kami-Fujimae-chō, which was maintained until the reorganization of the Shinjinkai late the following year. In March 1921 five members were listed as living in the headquarters; *Shinjinkai kikanshi*, p. 412.

"It is truly like thunder in a clear sky that such a group espousing the new thought should emerge from the campus of the Tokyo Imperial University Faculty of Law, which heretofore has to. all appearances been a school for training the lackeys of the bureaucracy and zaibatsu. We are a group of youths who have wholly transcended class-bound ideas and the workings of social favoritism . . . We aim to dissociate ourselves from university-oriented ideas (*gakkō-teki kannen*) and to bring together like-minded people merely as a pure youth group, opening the doors to all classes." [24] It was of course in line with the spirit in which the Shinjinkai was founded that they should stress their own qualifications not as students, but as *youth*.

The disenchantment of students with the university was reflected first of all at the educational level, where it was by no means limited to the politically conscious. Since the university in prewar Japan was primarily an institution for the training of professional men, the curriculum tended on the whole to be technical and uninspiring. All teaching was done by the lecture system, after the German model, and interplay between student and professor was minimal. While there were, of course, close personal ties between a professor and his small but select group of disciples, classroom sessions by contrast were coldly formal and tedious.[25] Many professors merely mumbled through the lecture notes which they had used without revision for many years, giving rise to the students' contemptuous charge of "one set of notes to last thirty years" (*ichi nōto sanjūnen*).[26]

Sheer boredom, then, was the reaction of many students to the university curriculum, although there were always a few professors whose lectures were stimulating and well-attended, men like Yoshino at Tokyo Imperial and Kawakami at Kyoto. Among the members of the Shinjinkai the most common response to a curriculum which they found boring and irrelevant was avoidance. Rather than demonstrate for more meaningful courses or censure teachers for their incompetence, radical university students before the war by and large took the alternative of simply refusing to attend classes. This option was facilitated by a lack of rigor in the academic requirements of the university.

24. *Shinjinkai kikanshi*, p. 18.
25. Sumiya, *Kenkyūshitsu uchisoto*, p. 150.
26. Kikukawa, *Gakusei shakai undō shi*, p. 16, quoting Yoshino Sakuzō as reported in the *Teikoku daigaku shimbun*, no. 5.

Examinations were given annually in the last month of the academic year (July until 1919, March thereafter) and were extremely difficult to fail, given the normally high intelligence of university students and a few days to prepare. Expulsion from the university for "delinquence in studies" (*gakugyō fushin*) was virtually unknown: Tokyo Imperial University records fifteen such cases in the ten-year period 1922–1931, out of a total of 2,063 dropouts for all reasons.[27]

Among the Shinjinkai members, a few of the more scholarly oriented did take their studies seriously, although in most cases it was within the framework not of the barren lecture system but of close personal ties with a single professor. The majority of Shinjinkai members, however, and all the more active ones, spent almost none of their time in the classroom, appearing only for the examinations. In fact, hardly a memoir of former student activists exists which does not at some point mention, in near boastful tones, the general failure of the students to attend lectures. Yet such a rejection of the university curriculum did not mean a lack of interest in study, for in fact a great amount of the energy expended by Japanese student radicals has always been devoted to the study of material not covered in the classroom. Especially in the later Shinjinkai, through the systematic development of the "study group," the radical students evolved an anti-curriculum, as we shall see, even more demanding than the orthodox one of the university itself.

If the radical students had little use for the university as an educational institution, what of its social dimension? The university, after all, presented a physical situation in which a large number of students were closely integrated by common friendships and activities and offered an ideal situation for the mobilization of an effective political movement. Here one finds a critical contrast between the early and later Shinjinkai: while radical students in the period after 1923 were to devote considerable attention to utilizing the social structure of the campus for their own ends, such a possibility appears never to have occurred to the early Shinjinkai. Three reasons for this distinctive feature of the years 1919–1922 may be suggested. In the first place, extracurricular activities, the most logical vehicle for on-campus organization, were, with the exception of athletics, still underdeveloped. Fur-

27. These statistics are provided annually in Mombushō, ed., *Nihon teikoku Mombushō nempō*, sections on Tokyo Imperial University.

thermore, the Shinjinkai, in the naive enthusiasm of its first years, had no interest in organization of any kind, nor in expanding the size of the group beyond its basic core of some twenty intimate members. Since the group was elite and manageable, there was no need for officers, committees, or precise allotment of duties.[28] Finally, the participation of alumni, with their variety of professional interests, tended to draw the focus of the group away from the campus and towards the left-wing movement at large.

The Shinjinkai members also took a dim view of the university's overall role in the political structure and dismissed the notion that the university as such might serve as an instrument of radical social and political reform. This attitude was related to the Shinjinkai demand for "total reform," and the conviction that the very foundations of Japanese culture must be built anew, a task for which the university, resting upon those faulty foundations, offered little assistance. This attitude was brought out most clearly in the Shinjinkai response to the Morito Incident, the first major case of a professor's dismissal from an imperial university for left-wing political views. The occasion of the incident was "Kropotkin's Anarchist Communism as a Social Ideal," an article written by Assistant Professor Morito Tatsuo in the first issue of *Keizaigaku kenkyū* (Economic studies), the organ of the newly independent Faculty of Economics at Tokyo Imperial University.[29] Although Kropotkin's thought was the topic of a number of pieces by Morito and other intellectuals both before and after the article appeared in January 1920, this particular occasion was inflated into a major incident through the agitation of the Kōkoku Dōshikai (Brotherhood for National Support), a group of right-wing students under Professor Uesugi Shinkichi.[30] Forced to take action on the issue, the Faculty of Economics voted on January 13 to suspend Morito, and

28. Hayashi Kaname, "Shinjinkai no koro," p. 170.
29. The English translation of the title was provided on the back cover of the magazine itself; the Japanese was "Kuropotokin no shakai shisō no kenkyū" (Studies in Kropotkin's social thought). For details on the Morito incident, see Minobe Ryōkichi, *Kumon suru demokurashii* (Bungei shunjū sha, 1959), pp. 9–34; Sakisaka Itsurō, ed., *Arashi no naka no hyakunen* (Keisō shobō, 1952), pp. 155–170; Sakisaka Itsurō, *Nagare ni kōshite* (Kōdansha, 1964), pp. 95–103; and Kikukawa, *Gakusei shakai undō shi*, pp. 95–101.
30. Morito's article stirred up such interest in Kropotkin that the magazine *Kaizō* alone featured twelve articles on Kropotkin in special sections of the magazine in the March and May issues of 1920. None of these were even banned, much less their authors prosecuted.

the following day he was indicted for seditious writings under the Newspaper Law.

The incident immediately became a *cause célèbre* both among university students and in the intellectual community as a whole. Large campus rallies were held by the students of the faculties of law and economics. Liberal intellectuals arose as one to defend Morito; the Reimeikai emerged from almost four months of inactivity to hold a rally of support, and the Bunka Gakkai (Cultural Society), a similar group, sponsored a mass lecture meet that was supported by some two hundred progressive groups. The major liberal periodicals—*Chūō kōron, Kaizō, Kaihō,* and *Warera*—were filled with articles by aroused academics analyzing the legal, political, and moral implications of Morito's suspension and indictment and censuring both the Faculty of Economics and the government for their actions.

The Shinjinkai might well have been expected to join in this protest not only because of the proximity of the dispute, but because Morito himself was a major academic patron of the radical students, having been one of four featured speakers in the Shinjinkai's first anniversary lecture series only a few weeks before his suspension from the university. And yet the Shinjinkai was largely uninvolved in the protest movement. Not a single Shinjinkai member helped organize the student protest rallies on the university campus, which were in the hands of much less radical students.[31] This noninvolvement stemmed less from a lack of sympathy for Morito, whose cause they strongly supported, than from acute disillusionment with the university itself, especially in view of the sobering fact that Morito had been suspended by the vote of his fellow professors. "A university composed of such professors," wrote Yamazaki Kazuo in the March 1920 issue of *Senku,* "is of absolutely no use except to scholar-lackeys of a capitalist economic system." In the same issue, Miwa Jusō found the student rallies in defense of Morito equally depressing in their moderation and quibbling over the wording of resolutions. Finally, in the following issue, the Shinjinkai, in line with its founding statement that rejected preoccupation with "university-like ideas," flatly stated: "This group will from now on follow the general policy of not becoming deeply involved

31. Sakisaka, *Nagare ni kōshite,* pp. 101–102, lists some of these students, including himself.

in movements which are purely for the sake of freedom of speech or freedom of thought. Intellectuals should understand that we have united for the cause of reforming those social conditions which permit the existence of such a useless system [as the university]." [32]

One problem which cannot go unmentioned is the possibility that the members of the Shinjinkai were hypocritical in their attitudes towards the university, being content to take advantage of the very privileges which they denounced in their founding statement as "social favoritism." They promised to "open the doors to all classes," and yet in fact membership in the Shinjinkai was exclusively limited to students in the Law Faculty of Tokyo Imperial University. (The "membership" offered to workers, described below, was clearly of a second-class variety.) They denied their concern with such issues as academic freedom, and yet took full advantage of that very freedom in using the extra-territorial sanctuary of the university campus to hold their meetings in peace while similar gatherings of extra-mural socialists would be immediately dissolved by the police. And finally, not a single member of the early Shinjinkai withdrew from the university as a gesture in defiance of its elitism: all graduated on schedule and thus availed themselves of the label *Akamon-de,* a graduate of Tokyo Imperial University, which would assure them respect and preference the rest of their lives.

Such doubts remain open to dispute. Some would argue that an unjust institution can be more easily toppled from within than from without; yet the Shinjinkai never hoped to destroy the university. Others would de-emphasize the political implications of attending a university; which demands no explicit acceptance of a specific ideological creed. But whatever the arguments, the problem of the student radicals' response to the elitism built into the Japanese educational system is a central problem in assessing the broader implications of the student movement.

THE EVANGELISTIC IMPULSE

Most of the organized activity of the early Shinjinkai was devoted to publicizing, by spoken and written word, the progressive causes which

32. *Shinjinkai kikanshi,* pp. 216, 220, 233.

the members espoused. They conceived of their mission less in terms of instituting specific programs or of forging a strong organization than merely a spreading of good news. This naive optimism survived for three full years, despite signs in the final months of the magazine that the evangelistic impulse was wearing thin. Such an approach to social reform followed closely in the pattern set by the academic liberals such as Yoshino Sakuzō of "university extension" in the sense of leaving the confines of the university to preach the message of reform to the people. The Shinjinkai carried on the same lofty approach.

The major organ of Shinjinkai was its magazine.[33] Such a student magazine was by no means new in Japan, for literary-minded youth had already established a tradition of the *dōjin zasshi* (Japan's "little magazines"), which has played such an important role in modern Japanese literature. The Shinjinkai magazine represents perhaps the earliest effort of students, however, to turn this tradition to political ends. The Shinjinkai magazine went through a number of title changes owing to the vagaries of political pressures and personnel changes. The duration of the magazine was: *Democracy*, eight issues from March through December 1919; *Senku*, seven issues from February to August 1920; *Dōhō* (Brothers), eight issues from October 1920 to May 1921; and *Narod*, nine issues from July 1921 to April 1922.[34]

Of these four versions, all were basically of the same type, with the exception of *Dōhō*. They were for the most part aimed at an intellectual audience, largely students in the universities, and featured a varied

33. Another important journalistic effort of the Shinjinkai members, although not strictly speaking a project of the group itself, was in connection with the magazine *Kaihō*, which had been launched by Omoya Sōkichi, the general manager of Daitōkaku, a prosperous Osaka publishing firm and publisher of the *Reimei kōenshū*. Omoya had originally hoped to win Reimeikai sponsorship for this magazine (see Asō, *Reimei*, p. 365), but failed and turned to the Shinjinkai members for assistance. Akamatsu became the first editor of *Kaihō* from the time of his graduation in 1919; other Shinjinkai members involved in the writing and editing of *Kaihō* in 1919 were Sano, Kaji Ryūichi, Yamazaki, Miyazaki, Akamatsu, and Asō. Shinjinkai ties with Omoya were further tightened when Daitōkaku became the publisher of the magazine *Senku* (*Democracy* had been financed by Hoshishima Nirō, who however gave up his support to enter party politics and ran for the Diet in early 1920). It appears that a serious dispute developed between Omoya and the Shinjinkai, however, leading in the spring of 1920 to a complete break of the Shinjinkai with both *Kaihō* and Daitōkaku (see *Shinjinkai kikanshi*, p. 233). The Shinjinkai publisher after April, 1920, was Shūeikaku.

34. The Shinjinkai magazines have been reprinted in a single volume as [Hōsei daigaku] Ōhara shakai mondai kenkyūjo, *Shinjinkai kikanshi*.

fare of scholarly analysis, translation, commentary on current affairs, news of members, and occasional short stories or poetry. *Dōhō*, by contrast, was oriented far more to a laborer audience in the "branches" of the Shinjinkai and placed emphasis on polemic articles aimed at arousing the workers. It was also considerably smaller than the other three, although the Shinjinkai magazine was on the whole of very modest proportions, reaching a maximum of forty-eight pages in *Senku*.

The influence of the magazine, given a circulation which probably did not exceed five hundred, was impressive.[35] The correspondence columns of the magazine, especially after 1920, carried a number of letters from workers in provincial areas who were clearly devoted readers and who in some cases began their own organizations under its stimulus. The total number of rural readers was probably small, however, and the preponderance of Shinjinkai influence was among students. Certainly radical students at other universities such as Waseda or Kyoto Imperial were regular readers of the magazine, and in the absence of any intercollegiate political federation, the Shinjinkai publication served as a means of communicating new ideas to students in other schools. A number of provincial higher school students were also mentioned as readers of the magazine.[36]

One persistent problem which confronted the magazine project was government censorship and suppression. Like all legal publications, the Shinjinkai magazine was required to register under the Newspaper Law and place a substantial deposit in bond, being thereafter subject to censorship and possible suppression for violation of the terms of the law. Out of a total of thirty-two issues of the Shinjinkai magazine, at least eleven were banned from the newsstands, although in the majority of cases this measure had little effect, since it was taken after all issues had been distributed to subscribers.[37]

35. The second issue of *Democracy* boasted that the first issue had "sold out" five thousand copies (*Shinjinkai kikanshi*, p. 42), but Miyazaki Ryūsuke (who was at the time doing most of the work of editing the magazine) stated in an interview that this was a fanciful exaggeration.

36. One such group was in Sendai; see *Shinjinkai kikanshi*, p. 38. Some of these higher school students went on later to join the Shinjinkai, such as Okada Sōji from Matsumoto Higher.

37. The only case in which most of the issues were seized was the second issue of *Democracy*, of which only one copy has survived, in Miyazaki's personal collection. For an account of the seizure of this issue, see Asō, *Reimei*, pp. 329–337.

More successful than suppression of the magazine itself was the prosecution of individual Shinjinkai members for offending articles, which occurred on three separate occasions. In December 1919 Miyazaki Ryūsuke was fined fifty yen for an article, "The Negation of Politics and the New Culture," in the July issue of *Democracy*. In October 1920 Yamazaki Kazuo was fined two hundred yen as editor of the July 1920 issue of *Senku*, which contained a translation of the IWW song, "Workers, Unite." Finally, in 1922 one hundred yen fines were levied on Chiba Yūjirō as editor and on Kuruma Kyō as author for an article entitled "Friend or Enemy" in the December 1921 issue of *Narod*. In every case, the students were defended by such leading liberal lawyers as Katayama Tetsu and Hoshishima Nirō, but to no avail.[38] Fines of the order of one hundred yen ($50) were substantial, especially for students, and placed a considerable strain on the Shinjinkai finances.

The Shinjinkai satisfied its evangelical impulse to publicize the good word of social reform not only through the written word but through the spoken as well, as would be expected of a group which originated in the university debating club. In the early Shinjinkai, there were three formats for oratorical publicity: open meetings on campus, provincial speaking tours, and academic lectures.

Open meetings on campus, generally known as *senden enzetsukai* or "publicity speech meetings," were most frequent after 1919, when the Shinjinkai had gathered enough members to allow an expansion of activities beyond the magazine alone. The meetings were normally held once a month in one of the large classrooms of the Faculty of Law and were generally well attended, with crowds as large as three hundred, including not only university students from all over Tokyo, but middle school and girls' school students, and occasionally laborers affiliated with the Shinjinkai branches.[39] Usually three or four Shinjinkai members would lecture for a half-hour each, and frequently a guest speaker was featured as an added attraction. Among such guests

38. For these incidents, see *Shinjinkai kikanshi*, pp. 181, 380, 558; Ōhara shakai mondai kenkyūjo, *Nihon rōdō nenkan*, 4 (1923), 171; and Katayama Tetsu, *Kaiko to tembō* (Fukumura shuppan, 1967), pp. 73–74. In the Yamazaki case, the offending translation was actually by Shimmei Masamichi, but Yamazaki claimed authorship to protect Shimmei and hence was actually fined one hundred yen each on two counts, one as editor and one as author. Yamazaki interview.

39. See, for example, *Shinjinkai kikanshi*, pp. 38, 207.

were the radical journalist Ōba Kakō, the anarchist Ishikawa Sanshirō, the Kobe Christian labor leader Kagawa Toyohiko, and university professors Abe Jirō, Yoshino Sakuzō, and Ōyama Ikuo.

Provincial speaking tours, or *yūzei*, likewise came into prominence only after the first year of Shinjinkai activity, although one foray to Kyoto and Nagoya was made in April 1919 in an unsuccessful attempt to organize Shinjinkai branches there.[40] By far the most important of the speaking tours was made in April 1920. Over a space of nine days, a delegation of seven Shinjinkai members traveled throughout Nagano prefecture, giving a total of seven talks in towns ranging from the prefectural capital of Nagano City to the tiny village of Nagase. In each place, they made contact with local liberal groups, most frequently journalists and schoolteachers, who warmly greeted the students from the prestigious imperial university. While the crowds which gathered ranged only from one to two hundred, they tended to include the most prominent of the provincial intelligentsia, and provoked favorable responses in an area known for its liberal traditions. Something of the enthusiasm and evangelical fervor of the trip may be sensed in the lengthy report in the Shinjinkai magazine at the conclusion of the tour, in which one member wrote: "We are truly like an army returning triumphantly from victory, though we need not weep and feel downcast, as might a conscience-ridden general, for we have taken no lives. Just as young buds come forth when spring returns to Shinano, in the face of bitter cold, unfavorable terrain, and cruel surroundings, so must the seeds which we have sown sprout forth, flower, and then bear fruit. We must pursue our pilgrimage until new buds sprout in fresh greenness on every piece of ground." [41]

The Nagano speaking tour was the peak of Shinjinkai influence in the provinces, for from mid-1920, with the beginning of the postwar depression and a reintensification in police control of the socialist movement, the provincial activists were the first to feel the brunt of suppression. During New Year's vacation in January 1921 a group of four traveled to Hokkaido, but spent most of their time in private

40. For an account of the trip, see *ibid.*, p. 78. Mention is made of the founding of the "Kyoto Shinjinkai," which however is never mentioned again and probably had no real organizational existence, being merely a gesture of solidarity between the Shinjinkai and the Kyoto Rōgakkai.

41. *Ibid.*, p. 308.

meetings with workers and local liberals rather than attempting to hold public meetings which would be subject to police surveillance.[42] The last recorded case of an organized Shinjinkai speaking tour was in April 1921, when three members accompanied the liberal journalist Hasegawa Nyozekan to Yamagata prefecture to give a series of three public meetings, again attracting crowds of about two hundred.[43]

Academic lectures in Tokyo were the third major format for Shinjinkai-sponsored oratorical activity. Termed *kōenkai,* these were given not by student members but by prominent academic liberals under Shinjinkai auspices. The earliest public activities of the Shinjinkai were of this sort. In late January 1919 Waseda professor Ōyama Ikuo spoke in a Faculty of Law classroom on "The Consciousness of a New Man" and drew a crowd of four hundred. This was followed a month later with the novelist Arishima Takeo, who then enjoyed wide popularity among Japanese students, speaking "On My Own Art." [44] Then in December 1919, to celebrate the first anniversary of the group, the Shinjinkai Academic Lectures (Shinjinkai Gakujutsu Kōenkai) were inaugurated. The first series was held over a period of three days from December 7, featuring Kushida Tamizo, Ōyama, Yoshino, and Morito Tatsuo. The event was such an unqualified success that the lectures were revised and published in book form the following year. The second in the series was held in late October 1920, and the speakers were Kitazawa Shinjirō, Murobuse Kōshin, Arishima Takeo, and Hasegawa Nyozekan. Again the lectures were published as a book.[45]

The sponsorship of these lectures, which featured the most popular liberal professors, writers, and journalists of the day (socialists were conspicuously absent), and the publication in book form later, were notable achievements of the Shinjinkai in publicizing the message of Taishō Democracy among intellectuals. When all the Shinjinkai publicity efforts—the magazine, lectures, and rallies—are totaled up, it would seem that this single small student group commanded an au-

42. For an account, see *ibid.,* p. 403.
43. *Ibid.,* p. 427.
44. *Ibid.,* p. 38.
45. A third in the series was scheduled for December 10, 1921, but aborted. For details on the series, see *ibid.,* pp. 181, 380, 526. The two book versions were Kushida Tamizō *et al., Minshū bunka no kichō—Daiikkai Shinjinkai gakujutsu kōenshū* (Shūeikaku, 1920) and Hasegawa Nyozekan *et al., Shinshakai e no sho-shisō —Dainikai Shinjinkai gakujutsu kōenshū* (Shūeikaku, 1921).

dience which in numbers was probably no more than a few thousand, but which included the most distinguished intellectuals in Japan.

THE IMPORT OF ISMS

Unified in a spirit of enthusiasm and confidence, the Shinjinkai neither had nor found necessary a specific ideological commitment. Rather they turned for inspiration to a wide variety of political writings, the single common feature of which was Western origin. Hayashi Kaname has described the confusion of isms in the early Shinjinkai as "an age in which all kinds of radical thought were whirling about together, not merely political democracy and bolshevism, but also social democracy, syndicalism, IWW thought, guild socialism, anarchism, Fabianism, and national socialism were all blooming at once, like spring flowers in the north country, presenting a beautiful scene of many colors." [46] A graphic illustration of these "many colors" was the succession of Western thinkers whose portraits appeared on the front covers of *Democracy,* a motley assortment including Rousseau, Tolstoy, Marx, Kropotkin, Abraham Lincoln, Rosa Luxemburg, and Lazarus Zamenhof, the Russian inventor of Esperanto.

To stress the Western origin of the most conspicuous influences in the early Shinjinkai is not to say that these influences were "foreign" to the students. The elite course within the Japanese educational system was, after all, Western not only in structure but in much of its content as well. Foreign language instruction began in middle school and was given great emphasis in higher school as the most important single criterion for entrance to the university, by which time every student had a reading competence in at least two foreign languages (usually English and German).[47] The majority of professors in the universities had studied in Europe or America and organized their instruction along Western lines. For the Japanese university student, much of his education had been "Western," to be sure, but only occidental conceit would assume such learning to be "foreign" or "strange" in twentieth-century Japan. A Japanese university student in the

46. Hayashi Kaname, "Shinjinkai no koro," p. 173.
47. The only other foreign language in which higher school students were instructed was French; the languages of such neighboring countries as Korea, China, and Russia were neglected.

1920s would of course view Aristotle or Marx in his own culture-bound way, but so indeed would his European counterpart of the same age; both would have in common a conviction that such thinkers were an integral part of his personal intellectual heritage.

To minimize the "foreignness" of Western ideas to a modern Japanese intellectual, however, is not to underestimate the formidable language barriers. Thus the Shinjinkai members in this period, knowing that introduction must come before analysis and exposure before assimilation, devoted much of their considerable scholarly talent to translations of Western books. Because of these priorities, few of the early Shinjinkai translators made any mention of the specific applicability of their translations to the Japanese situation. The Shinjinkai magazine never became involved in any of the theoretical disputations over the Japanese situation which were being waged at the time among such luminaries as Minobe and Uesugi over the location of constitutional sovereignty, or Kawakami and Sakai over the interpretation of historical change, or Sakai and Takabatake over the nature of socialism. Individual members certainly had opinions on these hotly debated issues, but few records remain to trace them. For the group as a whole, introduction took decided preference over interpretation.

In the choice of Western works translated by the Shinjinkai was a haphazard quality which doubtless stemmed from the difficulty of locating specific Western writings. Foreign books were easily obtainable in Japan, to be sure, and such bookstores as Maruzen carried complete lines of the latest imports from Europe. These books were expensive, however, and there were no single comprehensive and accessible collections of such literature where interested scholars could choose at will. The Shinjinkai members thus tended to translate whatever they happened to run across: a work recommended by a professor, a title that caught their eye at Maruzen, or perhaps one of the books in Asō's or Sano's personal collection at the mansion. For such reasons, some of the works translated were little known or only mildly influential in the country of origin but achieved considerable popularity in Japan from the good fortune of a readable and well-marketed translation.

The variety of the literature translated by the Shinjinkai makes generalizations about the character of these influences difficult; each individual devoted himself to his own projects, with no overall coordination of translation and research efforts. A tentative classification of ideological influences at work in the translation efforts may nevertheless be made. Looking at the Shinjinkai magazine as a whole over the three years 1919–1922 (with the exception of *Dōhō,* which was unique in having a minimum of translation and research), perhaps the most consistent, if not always the most prominent, influence was the German Marxist tradition of political thought. Reflecting the monopoly of the early Shinjinkai by law students, the interest of the members was more political than economic and serious consideration of Marxism as a method of economic analysis was rare. Of much greater interest to the Shinjinkai was the ideology and history of the German socialist movement. The Shinjinkai magazine thus featured translations and introductions of Karl Liebknecht, Rosa Luxemburg, Karl Kautsky, August Bebel, and the Austrian socialist Friedrich Adler. This consistent interest in German Marxist political thought corresponded to the predominant influence of German thinking in many other areas of Japanese thought.

Three other major areas of Western ideological interest may be detected. These occurred in phases reflecting the Shinjinkai response to the historical development of the Japanese left-wing movement in this three-year period. While these phases merged and overlapped to a considerable extent and should not be considered in terms of any rigid "development" of Shinjinkai thought, they nevertheless suggest both the variety of influences within the group and its sensitivity to the organizational developments within the left-wing movement as a whole. These phases were, in chronological order, English social democracy, anarcho-syndicalism, and Soviet communism.

English social democracy was scarcely surprising as an influence in the Shinjinkai in 1919 in view of the group's commitment to pacifism and parliamentary democracy, tendencies characteristic of twentieth-century English socialism. The general sort of reading which influenced the Shinjinkai members may be seen in a "reading list" provided in the June issue of *Democracy:*

Correa Moylan Walsh, *Socialism* (1917).
J. A. Hobson, *Capitalism in War and Peace* (?).
G. D. H. Cole, *Self-Government in Industry* (1917).

Bertrand Russell, *Principles of Social Reconstruction* (1917).
John Stuart Mackenzie, *An Introduction to Social Philosophy* (1890).
Norman Angell, *The Great Illusion* (1910).[48]

This English socialist influence was prominent only in *Democracy*, and its virtual disappearance in later versions of the magazine reflects the general setback of the Taishō Democracy movement in early 1920 with the shelving of the universal suffrage bill and the blow to the labor movement dealt by the economic recession. Some individual Shinjinkai members—Rōyama Masamichi is the most conspicuous—remained firmly dedicated to the English style of social democracy and made it their creed in adult life, but such were in a small minority.

Anarcho-syndicalism received prominent treatment in the pages of *Senku* in the first half of 1920, reflecting both the increasing strength of the belligerent syndicalist faction within the labor movement in this period and the great interest in Kropotkin generated by the Morito Incident. The following items in *Senku* give a good indication of this strain within the Shinjinkai:

Hatano Kanae, "Research on Syndicalism—from Hecker's 'Social Considerations of Russian Social Thought'."
Sano Manabu, "Towards a Philosophy of Action."
Akamatsu Katsumaro, "Sorel's Pessimism and the Liberation Movement."
Kaji Ryūichi, "The Syndicalist Movement in Various Countries."
Sano Manabu, "Anarchists in Germany."
Hatano Kanae, "One Aspect of Max Stirner."
Kadota Takeo, trans., Kropotkin, "Political Rights and their Significance for the Working Class."
Akizeki Naoji [Shimmei Masamichi], trans., "Workers, Unite (The IWW Song)."

The shift from *Senku* to *Dōhō* in October 1920 was in a sense an extension of the heightened Shinjinkai interest in the radical labor

48. I have corrected numerous errors in spelling and citation and provided publication dates.

movement, for it represented an attempt for the Shinjinkai to establish communication with the workers and urge them in more activist directions. *Dōhō,* which lasted until the following May, corresponded almost precisely to the period of the short-lived Japan Socialist League (Nihon Shakai Shugi Dōmei), which attempted to bring together socialists of all persuasions into a united front but collapsed from a combination of suppression and internal squabbling between the "anarchist" and "bolshevik" factions for control of the labor movement. The Shinjinkai itself joined the League with Akamatsu as its representative.

Soviet communism was the last of the three major phases through which Shinjinkai interest was to pass and as such pointed the way to the next phase of the Japanese student movement and its domination by Marxism–Leninism. Interest in the Russian communist experiment emerged as a topic of great interest in the pages of *Narod* and is reflected in the Russian title. As with the two earlier phases, the shift accompanied and mirrored the vagaries of the socialist and labor movement as a whole, which saw in 1921 the intensification of the anarchist-bolshevist struggle for control of the labor union movement, reaching a climax in the attempt in October to create a single united labor federation including the unions of both sides. This project aborted over the failure of the two factions to agree on the critical issue of strong centralization versus loose federation.[49]

This climax, which marked the end of syndicalist strength in the labor movement as a whole, came during the publication of the early issues of *Narod,* which in the predominance of articles on Russian communism shows a leaning to the "bolshevist" faction. Russian influence in the Shinjinkai magazine was, however, by no means new at this time: *Democracy* two years earlier had featured translations of Turgenev and Gorky, and introductions of the deeds of Lenin, Chernov, and Babushka. But it was only in *Narod* that the Soviet example was clearly singled out for elaboration, a task much facilitated by the influx in these years of new books, mostly in English, describing the establishment and early years of the Bolshevik regime, such as Albert Rhys Williams, *76 Questions and Answers on the Bolsheviks and the Soviets* (New York, 1919), and Raymond Postgate, *The Bolshevik*

49. The new federation was to be called the Sōrengō. For an account of the Sōrengō movement and the issues involved, see *Sōdōmei gojūnen shi,* I, 542–565

Theory (London, 1920). Some of the articles in the pages of *Narod* showing an interest in bolshevism were:

> Hososako Kanemitsu, "The Current State of the Russian Intelligentsia."
>
> Chiba Yūjirō, "The 'Women's Festival' at the Kremlin," "The Youth Movement in Soviet Russia," and "Russia Under Famine."
>
> Nakagawa Minoru [identity unclear], "The 'Plight of the Bolsheviks' and Countermeasures."
>
> Hatano Kanae, "Thoughts on the History of the Russian Labor Movement."
>
> Kuroda Hisao, "Russian Labor Unions after the October Revolution."
>
> Matsukawa Ryōichi [identity unclear], "The New Economic Policy of Soviet Russia." [50]

The Shinjinkai efforts at translation and introduction of Western socialist thought were not limited to the magazine; the group also sponsored an important series of book-length translations which were published as the "Shinjinkai Library" (Shinjinkai sōsho). The project was conceived of as a means of commemorating the first anniversary of the Shinjinkai, and was announced in the magazine in March 1920.[51] A number of the translations which were planned never materialized; those definitely published were the following:

> Franz Oppenheimer, *Der Staat* (Kokkaron), trans. Okanoe Morimichi (Daitōkaku; May 1920).
>
> Gerhart von Schulze-Gävernitz, *Marx oder Kant* (Kanto ka Marukusu ka), trans. Sano Manabu (Daitōkaku; 1920?).
>
> Julius Hecker, *Russian Sociology* (Roshiya shakaigaku), trans. Hatano Kanae (Shūeikaku; October 1920).

50. Some of these articles, such as those by Hososako and Nakagawa, were translations, while others, although not direct translations, were based on specific Western secondary studies.

51. It had originally been planned that the series be published by Daitōkaku, but the Shinjinkai break with that publishing house shortly after resulted in two separate series, one put out independently by Daitōkaku and the other by Shūeikaku, the new Shinjinkai publisher. Only the latter series was officially called the "Shinjinkai Library."

Eduard Bernstein, *Der Revisionismus in der Sozialdemokratie* (Shūseiha shakai shugi ron), trans. Kaji Ryūichi (Shūeikaku; October 1920).

P. J. Proudhon, *Qu'est-ce que c'est que la propriété?* (Zaisan to wa nan zo ya), trans. Shimmei Masamichi (Shūeikaku; April 1921).

Paul Eltzbacher, *Der Anarchismus* (Museifu shugi ron), trans. "Wakayama Kenji" [Kuroda Hisao] (Shūeikaku; May 1921).

J. B. Arnaudo, *Le nihilisme et les nihilistes* (Nihirizumu kenkyū), trans. "Kazama Tetsuji" [Kazahaya Yasoji] (Daitōkaku; October 1922).

Karl Kautsky, *The Erfurt Constitution* (Erufuruto kōryō), trans. Miwa Jusō (Daitōkaku; February 1923).[52]

This substantial series, to which could be added several other independent book-length translations produced by Shinjinkai members in the period 1919–1923, plus the continuing series of partial translations and introductions in the pages of the magazine, gives some indication of the role of the Shinjinkai in importing Western ideology. This activity was the beginning of the left-wing translating and publishing empire which was to become a firmly established part of the modern Japanese socialist movement. These early efforts by the Shinjinkai members and others like them were to lead to more organized projects in the later student movement.

INTO THE PEOPLE

"I was searching for a lover. And then I found him. The worker is my lover. I can scarcely wait for his pale face to shine with cheer." So wrote Kadota Takeo in the second issue of *Democracy*, setting the tone of eagerness and condescension with which the Shinjinkai set out to involve itself in the labor movement.[53] It was this activity which carried on the "student-labor" concept of the Tokyo Rōgakkai and the impulse to enter "into the people" which dominated Asō and his group. The involvement of the Shinjinkai with the labor movement

52. I have attempted, where possible, to give the title of the original in the language from which the Japanese translation was made. Hence the Arnaudo book, for example, was made from a French translation of the Italian original.

53. *Shinjinkai kikanshi*, p. 37.

was a less notable activity than the intellectual efforts of publicity and translation but was nevertheless of importance in indicating some of the ways in which the members sought to turn their ideas into action.

The involvement of Asō and his group in the Yūaikai served to bring the Shinjinkai into close contact with the labor movement. By early 1919 Yamana, Tanahashi, and Sano were all living on Tsukishima, a tiny man-made island in Tokyo Bay, populated mostly by metal workers and skilled laborers who were relatively well off and easy to organize. Asō and his friends came to refer to Tsukishima as the "Kronstadt of Japan," an undisguised expression of their hopes that the workers under their tutelage would be no less revolutionary than the notoriously mutinous sailors and soldiers of that Russian island-port.[54] Although Tsukishima in the end failed to provide the fuse for revolution, the activities of the Shinjinkai members there did serve to draw into the Yūaikai a number of young workers who were later to become famous radical leaders. Most notable was Sano's Tsukishima roommate Yamamoto Kenzō, a central communist leader of the 1920s who is now enshrined in the Japanese Communist Party pantheon under the affectionate sobriquet of "Yamaken." The Tsukishima life of the Asō group in early 1919 served as a stimulating example for the student members of the Shinjinkai, who often visited Sano and the others, and at least one of them, Taira Teizō, went to live there himself.[55]

The Asō group not only literally entered "into the people" by living among workers but also led the movement to reform the Yūaikai and turn it in more radical directions. Asō and Tanahashi were the central figures in this reform, which was largely accomplished at the Seventh Annual Congress of the Yūaikai in the summer of 1919, shortly after Asō had quit his job as a reporter and entered the labor movement full-time. Although the more aggressive syndicalist elements were later to turn against Asō and Tanahashi and attack them under the slogan of "reject the intellectuals," the influence of these two men in determining the overall direction of the early Japanese labor movement is difficult to overestimate.

A number of the student members followed the example of Asō, Sano, and Tanahashi and became involved in the labor movement in

54. Asō, *Reimei*, p. 20.
55. Taira interview.

an individual capacity. These were the most "activist" members of the Shinjinkai, notably Miyazaki, Akamatsu, Yamazaki Kazuo, and Kadota Takeo. Akamatsu graduated in 1919 and, while serving as editor of *Kaihō,* had close ties with the labor movement. Miyazaki was the prime mover in the Shinjinkai celluloid union, while Yamazaki and Kadota were perhaps the most aggressive personalities in early Shinjinkai. These two men had both been converted to Christianity while in higher school, Yamazaki in Kanazawa and Kadota in Kagoshima, and both became boarders at the Hongō YMCA upon entering the university. Kadota was a unique combination of religious mystic and outgoing activist, a small, tough figure, fond of haranguing crowds, who made a name for himself in the labor movement in fiery speeches first at a rally in October 1919, protesting the choice of a Japanese labor representative to the first ILO convention in Geneva and then again at the May Day festivities in Ueno Park the following spring. Yamazaki also was involved in various labor activities and in the spring of 1921 went to live in the working-class district of Honjo.[56]

In addition to such individual involvement, the Shinjinkai as a group tried its hand at labor union organizing in 1919. The occasion came by chance at a massive universal suffrage demonstration in Tokyo's Hibiya Park on February 15, in which all of the Shinjinkai members participated. Immediately after the rally, Miyazaki Ryūsuke, while waiting for a trolley to return to the university, was suddenly approached by a young man in worker's clothes, who introduced himself as Watanabe Masanosuke, a laborer in a celluloid factory in Tokyo, and eagerly beseeched Miyasaki to take him into the Shinjinkai movement. Miyasaki proudly escorted this windfall back to the Shinjinkai offices in Hongō, and after some discussion within the group over the advisability of taking in laborers, it was agreed to let Watanabe and any of his worker friends join the Shinjinkai.[57] (It later became clear, however, that the "membership" offered to workers through the "branches" was distinctly second-class, consciously segregated from the *hombu,* or "main office" elite.)

So the Shinjinkai set up a "branch" at the Nagamine Celluloid

56. Yamazaki interview.
57. Miyazaki has repeated this story with slightly differing details in a number of magazine articles. For a representative one, see Miyazaki, "Shinjinkai to wakaki hi no Katsumaro-kun," pp. 44–45.

Company factory where Watanabe worked, in the Kameido area of Tokyo. The founding ceremonies of the Kameido Branch were held February 24, with eight Shinjinkai members attending. Miyazaki's description of the event gives an idea of the students' excitement at this development: "For a while after boarding the train [for Kameido] all was silent, but the boundless excitement could not be held back for long. Someone spoke out, 'Virgin soil! Unbroken ground! It is up to us to cultivate it. Japan is virgin soil, here, everywhere!' . . . [After the meeting,] the students bound back for Hongō parted reluctantly, promising to meet again. Outside, the dark clouds on the horizon opened in a downpour of rain, falling now and again in heavy torrents. They were without umbrellas and drenched by the rain, yet in the breast of each was an ineffable joy. 'Rain after breaking new ground, what a fine omen,' the youths whispered to one another as they made their way through the dark and rain." [58]

The Kameido Branch was an immediate success, and shortly afterwards a second branch was formed at another factory of the Nagamine Company, in the suburb of Nippori, under the leadership of Iwauchi Zensaku.[59] The two branches joined to expand and revitalize an existing union organization among the Nagamine workers, which was formally launched on May 6 as the National Celluloid Workers Union (Zenkoku Seruroido Shokkō Kumiai) and which became popularly known as the "Shinjin Celluloid Union" in testimony of the important role played by the Shinjinkai members in its founding. The union rapidly expanded, setting up chapters at factories other than those of the Nagamine Company, and demonstrated its strength in two strikes at the Nagamine plants in the summer of 1919.[60] These strikes were the first taste of battle for many of the Shinjinkai students, who mustered in strength to support the workers, turning the Takada-mura headquarters into a frenzy of activity.[61]

58. *Shinjinkai kikanshi*, p. 38.
59. Akamatsu, "Shinjinkai no rekishiteki ashiato," p. 71.
60. For details on the celluloid union and its strikes, see Ōhara shakai mondai kenkyūjo, ed., *Nihon rōdō nenkan*, 1 (1920), 21, 57, 391–392, 957, 961, 978. These entries present conflicting evidence on the dates and outcomes of the strikes. It would appear that a first strike was waged in early June but settled nothing, and a continuation of the same dispute flared up both in early and late July.
61. See Asō, *Reimei*, pp. 374–375, for a vivid description of the excitement. Asō's date of "early May" is erroneous.

The Shinjin Celluloid Union was a fleeting product of the great burgeoning of the labor movement in 1919 and did not survive long but did serve to provide the nucleus of one of the most radical factions in the Japanese labor movement in this period. Involvement of the students tapered off after the summer strike successes, and the union itself began to suffer from internal dissension, with the radical elements going on to form the Kameido and Nippori chapters of the Sōdōmei (the former Yūaikai) in 1920. Later withdrawing from the Sōdōmei under the leadership of Watanabe, this group formed the Nankatsu Labor Club (Nankatsu Rōdōkai) in 1922, which for its anarchist extremism became the target of police vengeance in the wake of the 1923 earthquake, when seven of its members were killed in the "Kameido Incident." [62] Watanabe was ironically spared by virtue of his arrest in the Communist Party suppression two months earlier and went on to become one of the greatest heroes of the Japanese communist movement, dying in a battle with the police in Taiwan in 1928.

After the successful but brief efforts of the Shinjinkai at organizing a labor movement, efforts which were more the product of a naive and flippant enthusiasm than of any genuine commitment to the labor movement as a whole, the only organized contacts of the group with the working class were through the provincial "branches" of the Shinjinkai. These "provincial branches" (*chihōbu*) were at first envisioned as a regular part of the group's activity, but during 1919 amounted to little more than the celluloid workers in Tokyo and pockets of sympathetic students in Kyoto (at Kyoto Imperial University) and Sendai (at Second Higher School and Tōhoku Gakuin).[63]

From late 1919, however, a new kind of Shinjinkai "branch" (now termed *shibu*) emerged, consisting for the most part of isolated groups of intellectually curious workers and farmers who were too few to create an independent organization, and managed to gain a sense of identity by tying in with the Tokyo student group and reading its magazine. In some cases these branches were launched by regular Shinjinkai members in their hometowns, such as that in Kanazawa by Shimmei Masamichi; in other cases local laborer-intellectuals took the

62. Kishi Yamaji, "Watamasa den," *Kaizō*, 13.4 (April 1931), 132–143.
63. Detailed information on the provincial branches may be found in the notes on Shinjinkai activity at the beginning or end of each issue of the magazine.

initiative of their own accord after chancing upon the Shinjinkai magazine and heeding its invitation to form a branch, the only requirement being subscription to the magazine.[64] By the spring of 1920, active provincial groups had been set up in Akita, Kanazawa, Hiroshima, Otaru, and Kumamoto.

This initial success was doubtless influential in leading the Shinjinkai to change its magazine from *Senku* to *Dōhō* in the summer of 1920. Unlike the other three versions of the Shinjinkai magazine, *Dōhō* was aimed primarily at the provincial branches, featuring numerous articles on the labor movement and labor problems. All the articles were anonymous, in keeping with the impersonal solidarity suggested by the word *dōhō* (brothers). Considerable space was devoted to correspondence and contributions from provincial members. By March 1921 the total number of branches reached ten, including, in addition to the above, Noto, Fukui, Kyoto, Osaka, and Sasebo. Most of these were, however, very small—the Fukui Branch consisted of five to six members in a tiny farm village south of Fukui City—and it was doubtless disappointment with the generally negligible effects of branch membership that led the Shinjinkai to abandon *Dōhō* and return in *Narod* to the earlier pattern of an intelligentsia-oriented magazine.[65] Few of the Shinjinkai branches produced any leaders of note, with the possible exception of that in Kumamoto, which included as one of its leaders Tokunaga Sunao, later a prominent proletarian writer.[66]

While many of the Shinjinkai members, in the manner of Asō Hisashi's group, entered the labor movement on a professional basis after graduation, the organized group efforts of the students themselves, first in the celluloid union and later in the provincial branches, amounted to little more than a boost to a few such individuals as Watanabe Masanosuke and Iwauchi Zensaku. Part of the fault for these paltry results lay with the relatively small number of members who had any positive interest in labor activities, for the majority belonged to the scholarship-oriented "research faction." Another serious obstacle

64. *Shinjinkai kikanshi,* p. 510.
65. A related consideration was doubtless the frequent suppression of *Dōhō,* which was probably due to the working-class audience, whom the police considered more dangerous than student-intellectuals.
66. Hisamatsu Sen'ichi *et al.,* eds., *Gendai Nihon bungaku daijiten* (Meiji shoin, 1965), p. 759.

was the education gap of student and worker. The laborers resented the condescending attitudes of the students and their insistence on using high-flown foreign jargon to explain the workers' own problems, while the students easily grew frustrated with the workers' failure to grasp theoretical issues.

INTERNAL TENSIONS AND THE NAROD DECLARATION

The first year of the Shinjinkai's existence was its most notable, a period of intense activity, bursting optimism, and a solidarity of spirit encouraged by the communal life in the Huang mansion. The first anniversary celebrations in December 1919 climaxed this eventful year, featuring a party at the Takada-mura headquarters attended by many of the leading lights of the liberal and socialist movements, such as Yoshino Sakuzō, Hasegawa Nyozekan, Morito Tatsuo, Yamakawa Hitoshi, and Sakai Toshihiko.[67] The academic lecture series and the Shinjinkai Library were both launched in commemoration of this eventful year, and both were conspicuous successes.

But in the course of 1920 and 1921, trends within the socialist and labor movements tended to erode the initial enthusiasm. The Morito Incident, the setback to the labor movement dealt by the depression of 1920, the growth of debilitating factionalism among competing socialist groups: all these events suggested that perhaps revolution was not just around the corner after all. The Shinjinkai members in these years came to have a good taste of the obstacles which were posed by police suppression; many of the issues of the group magazine were banned and the members themselves were closely watched by police spies (a detective of the Metropolitan Police Bureau is reported to have been on constant duty at the entrance to the Shinjinkai headquarters at the Huang mansion).[68] Such suppression was hardly crushing and may even in the end have proved more of a stimulus than an obstacle, but it suggested to the young students that the course of social reform was

67. Sakai Toshihiko, *Nihon shakai shugi undō shi* (Kawade shobō, 1954), p. 37.
68. Hatano Kanae interview. A number of the members were also classified as "persons requiring special surveillance" (*tokubetsu yō-shisatsunin*) or as "persons requiring thought surveillance" (*shisō yō-chūinin*). See for example an undated Home Ministry document, Naimushō, "Shisō yō-chūinin meibo" (c. 1921), now located in U.S. Library of Congress, where fourteen Shinjinkai members are listed.

by no means natural and that more than mere evangelism would be needed to accomplish specific goals. By 1921, the fervent idealism of 1919 had given way to much more realistic attitudes.

Disappointment over specific setbacks in the socialist movement did not necessarily breed frustration in the Shinjinkai. On the contrary, the three years following the founding of the group, if judged on any statistical scale, had witnessed a tremendous overall growth of the left-wing movement. One by-product of this growth had been a high degree of diversification in the movement. The unified, simplistic drive for "liberation and reform" of 1919 had given way to a large number of specialized movements, including a highly complex labor movement, a farm tenant movement in the Japan Farmers' Union, a proletarian literature movement in *Tanemaku hito* (The sower), a women's movement in the Sekirankai (Red Wave Society), a movement to free the outcasts in the Suiheisha (Leveling Society), and a number of others. In the face of such specialization, the Shinjinkai could no longer plausibly insist that their only necessary qualification was as "aroused youth": technical skills were now required.

These pressures in the direction of specialization joined with the natural tendency of political student groups to constant organizational and ideological changes in accord with the regular leadership turnover forced by graduation. This tendency was reflected in the Shinjinkai in the frequency of changes in the name and format of its magazine, which enabled each successive student class to assert its own identity. In the case of the Shinjinkai, however, this rapidity of turnover was slowed by the participation of alumni members in the activities of the group, a pattern which had been set from the very beginning when Asō Hisashi and his clique joined the Shinjinkai. The real problem lay less with alumni participation as such than in the lack of any guidelines to establish allotment of duties and privileges between student and alumni members. In its rejection of all formal organization, the early Shinjinkai exposed itself to the danger of factionalism in spite of the small size and cohesiveness of the group. This danger increased as more and more members graduated and scattered into professional life. The ratio of student members rapidly decreased from about three quarters in 1919, to one half the next year, to only about one quarter in late 1921.

In practice, of course, the student members tended to be in charge of most of the group's organized activities, such as editing the magazine, largely because the alumni members were too involved in their own professional lives to participate, or, as in the case of the large group in the Kansai area, geographically distant. One exception, and an important one, was Akamatsu Katsumaro, who even after his graduation in July 1919 remained the central leader of the Shinjinkai. Alone among the alumni members, Akamatsu insisted on retaining a controlling voice in running the group. The very lack of organization in the early Shinjinkai, in fact, was probably a reflection of the tacit acceptance of Akamatsu's leadership.

A number of fellow members, however, resented this domination by a single leader. The student members felt that alumni should play a passive role, while a number of alumni members were not pleased with Akamatsu's continued manipulation of the group. Related to this was the emergence of two fairly distinct groups among the Shinjinkai alumni members, known as the "activists" (*jissen-ha*) and the "scholars" (*kōgaku-ha* or *kenkyū-ha*). Akamatsu was the most important of the former group, which also included Kadota, Yamazaki, and others who were active in the labor movement. The "scholars" were in the majority and accounted for almost all of the seventeen members of the class of 1920, the largest delegation in the early Shinjinkai. These men for the most part became university teachers and lawyers and were disposed to moderate, scholarly activity, being distrustful and even contemptuous of attempts by intellectuals to enter "into the people." There is some indication that this majority group openly opposed the attempts of Akamatsu to lead the Shinjinkai in activist directions.[69]

Not only were personal disagreements a danger as the members of the Shinjinkai scattered, but the likelihood existed that factionalism within the socialist movement as a whole might split the group. This in fact occurred in the spring of 1921 as a result of the attack on Tanahashi Kotora by syndicalist elements within the Sōdōmei who demanded the "rejection of the intelligentsia." Fearing that this attack

69. Taira Teizō in Miwa Jusō denki kankōkai, ed., *Miwa Jusō no shōgai*, p. 196, mentions the reorganization of the Shinjinkai as a "plot" on the part of "certain members" (whom he identified in an interview as Akamatsu in particular). It is doubtful that Akamatsu's intentions were so insidious.

might be turned on the Shinjinkai as a whole, the March issue of *Dōhō* declared: "Certain people have approached us lately to ask, 'Are the views of Tanahashi those of the Shinjinkai?' The answer is simply that those are the opinions of Tanahashi as an individual, and are not the opinions of the group as a whole. Our group was born at a time when the cry of 'democracy' rang through society. Later, as social thought moved to the left, the individual members all proceeded in their own directions, and at present a number of intellectual tendencies have appeared within the group. To be sure, there are those who agree with Tanahashi, but this is not everyone. Within the Shinjinkai, the debate between labor unionism [the syndicalist faction] and socialism [the 'bolshevist' faction] is becoming more and more severe. Until a concrete and formal expression of this dispute appears, we will maintain the organization of a league of free individuals." [70]

These tensions were reflected in a decreasing membership within the Shinjinkai. From a high point in the seventeen-member class of 1920, the succeeding three classes had eight to ten members each, while the class of 1924 was completely vacant in late 1921 when a critical decision was made to reorganize the society as a purely student group. The statement which spelled out this decision and which came to be known as the Narod Declaration was made at a closed meeting of the Shinjinkai on November 30 and was announced on the first page of the December issue of *Narod* under the title "The Third Anniversary of the Shinjinkai":

Three quick years have passed since the birth of the Shinjinkai on the university campus in response to new trends in the intellectual world, summoning forth in the breast of each the tremors of a new age. Although short of duration, this period has seen a tremendous and unprecedented change in the intellectual world and in Japanese society in general. The new thought is gaining solid ground among the rising classes. We harbor a private joy at the thought that despite our meager strength we were perhaps able to contribute in some way to this situation today.

Over the past three years we have dauntlessly sought to make clear, both through written and spoken word, those things which

70. *Shinjinkai kikanshi*, p. 411.

we thought right. We have avoided all easy compromise and have faithfully defended these tenets. Our magazine for this reason has on several occasions met with the displeasure of the authorities and been banned from sale. Already several members of our group have fallen victims to suppression for the sake of the movement.

Our efforts have not of course been yet rewarded. We remain extremely weak. Our real mission lies in the future. Until the day that the people are finally victorious, there remain many things for us to do.

At the start when our tasks were clear, we felt our solidarity to be as firm as rock. Having joined together and taken our stand, we little doubted our determination to serve as martyrs for the cause in which we believed.

But now as we look back, we realize that men grow with the times. Today, when those who have graduated and entered into society account for over half the membership, we feel that there are a number of difficulties and inconveniences in maintaining the Shinjinkai as a social reform group in the present form.

The liberation movement in Japan has now reached a more concrete stage, and is entering a period of new activism. Our tasks are ever more numerous. We feel that in such a situation the best policy is to let those who have left the campus act each in his own free way, turning in those directions he thinks right. As we greet our third anniversary, we hereby declare that we will continue the Shinjinkai from this time on as a thought group within the university.[71]

With this the size of the Shinjinkai was cut from almost fifty down to the purely student membership of less than twenty. The magazine *Narod* was carried through until the end of the academic year in April, from which time its functions as the publicity and research organ of the Shinjinkai were inherited by the alumni members of the "scholar faction." This group organized itself as the Social Thought Society (Shakai Shisōsha) and published as a monthly organ *Shakai shisō* (Social thought), a magazine which in its stress on research, translation, and introduction followed closely in the model of the Shinjinkai maga-

71. *Ibid.*, p. 511.

zines and became an important and influential voice of noncommunist socialist intellectuals throughout the middle and late 1920s.[72]

The student members of the Shinjinkai, liberated from the dictates and pressures of its alumni, were now free to develop the group along the lines of specialization that were more appropriate to the recent developments in the left-wing movement. Over the next two years the Shinjinkai turned back to the university itself and sought to develop a strong campus base and large membership and to construct a nation-wide movement of and by students on a tightly organized base. The Narod Declaration marked a wholly new direction for the Japanese student movement.

72. The most detailed account of the Shakai Shisōsha and its activities is in Miwa Jusō denki kankōkai, ed., *Miwa Jusō no shōgai,* pp. 195–209.

4 | The Evolution of a National
Student Movement, 1922-1925

Abandoning their self-defined mission as "young intellectuals" and "new men," the Shinjinkai members after 1921 began to reinterpret themselves as students and turned to building a movement of students and by students—if not yet specifically *for* students. The natural direction in which to turn in this effort was to similar groups on other campuses, with whom they might forge an alliance and coordinate activities so as to enhance their impact on politics and society.

Although the Narod Declaration had eliminated a major conceptual barrier to the creation of an intermural radical student federation, there still remained two formidable obstacles: one was geography, the other was the duality of state and private higher education. Since the state educational system was designed at every level to achieve wide geographical distribution, the studentry in the elite higher school–imperial university channel was fragmented into geographically isolated congregations among which contact was difficult. Close ties were of course possible between the two levels in the case of the higher schools in Tokyo, Kyoto, and Sendai, all of which were adjacent to imperial universities, but this did not enable a true federation of equals. These higher schools did develop radical groups from an early date, which, however, were largely derivative of the university level movement and had little independent strength. The prime requirement for a radical federation was contact among schools at the same level, a task made almost impossible in the case of state schools by geographical dispersion. Only sporadic contacts, such as the memorable trip of the Tokyo Imperial Debating Club to Kyoto in October 1918, were possible.

Geography was favorable, by contrast, in the case of private universities, which were almost all located in the Tokyo or Kyoto–Osaka metropolitan areas. As explained in Chapter 1, however, the only private university with exceptional potential for student radicalism was Waseda, most of the others being too small, religious, technical, or conservative. The other law-school type universities such as Hōsei or Meiji had some radical potential but insufficient to take the lead in the creation of a nationwide student movement. The critical step, then, in creating a unitary radical student federation was to forge an alliance between Waseda and Tokyo Imperial, thereby serving to merge the segregated state and private channels of higher education. Only when the antagonism of state and private university students was broken down could the host of lesser schools—the provincial higher schools, other private universities, technical colleges, and so forth—be effectively organized. The Waseda–Tokyo Imperial coalition was finally effected in the years 1922–23; but to understand how this was done, it is necessary briefly to consider the nature of the early Waseda student movement and the ways in which it differed from the Shinjinkai.

THE WASEDA VARIANT

Waseda University might logically have been expected to precede Tokyo Imperial in launching a socialist student movement in the period 1918–19, both because of specific precedents in the Meiji socialist movement and because of the strong traditional interest of Waseda students in politics. And yet the first socialist group of note at Waseda at the time, the Minjin Dōmeikai, appears to have been founded at the encouragement of the Shinjinkai members, in February 1919.[1] Like the Shinjinkai and other radical student groups created in this period, the Minjin Dōmeikai was composed of the most progressive members of the university debating club, which at Waseda was called the Oratorical Society (Yūbenkai).

---

1. Takatsu Seidō, "Hata o mamorite," eight parts, *Gekkan Shakaitō*, nos. 55–62 (January–August 1962), pt. 1, p. 141, claims that the founding of the Minjin Dōmeikai was "stimulated" by the Shinjinkai.

The early association between the Shinjinkai and the Minjin Dōmei-kai, which was based more on common enthusiasm in the first flush of this "dawn period" than on any close personal ties, led to a shortlived attempt to bridge the traditional rivalry between the two schools and to form a league of radical students. In early July 1919 a meeting was held at the Shinjinkai headquarters in Takada-mura of leaders from four student groups: the Shinjinkai, the Minjin Dōmeikai, the Waseda Isshinkai (Renovation Society), and the Hōsei University Fushinkai (Society of Aid and Trust). The latter two groups were minor, and the informal "July League" which was created at this meeting was basically an alliance between the Shinjinkai and the Minjin Dōmeikai.[2]

Following summer vacation, plans were made for a formal organization to replace the provisional July League, and the resulting Youth Cultural League (Seinen Bunka Dōmei) was founded on October 10. Just before this, however, the Minjin Dōmeikai had undergone a factional dispute, with one segment of the membership seceding to create the Kensetsusha Dōmei (Builders' League), so that a total of five groups, three of them from Waseda, formed the league's membership. The statement of purpose of the league was vague enough to please all but a confirmed reactionary: "(1) This league is founded on the basis of truth. (2) This league aims for the liberation of all mankind. (3) This league will reform society in a just way." The autonomy of member groups was guaranteed, and headquarters were to be located at Takada-mura.[3]

The first recorded activity of the new federation was also its last. On October 25, a rally was held at the Hongō YMCA, at which representatives of each of the five member groups spoke.[4] The rally failed to fire any great enthusiasm for the league, which faded away before it had ever developed into a true federation. It may be postulated that the fatal weakness of this early attempt at intermural organization was the lack of any real accord between the Shinjinkai and the two groups

2. *Shinjinkai kikanshi*, p. 118, is the only documented evidence of the July League.
3. *Ibid.*, p. 171. No mention of the league is made in the Shinjinkai magazine after this.
4. *Ibid.* At this rally, three Shinjinkai members were among the speakers, but only one from each of the other four groups, suggesting that the entire project was the product of Shinjinkai enthusiasm.

into which the mainstream of the Waseda movement had splintered, since both the two Waseda factions proceeded in directions clearly and consciously distinct from the Shinjinkai.

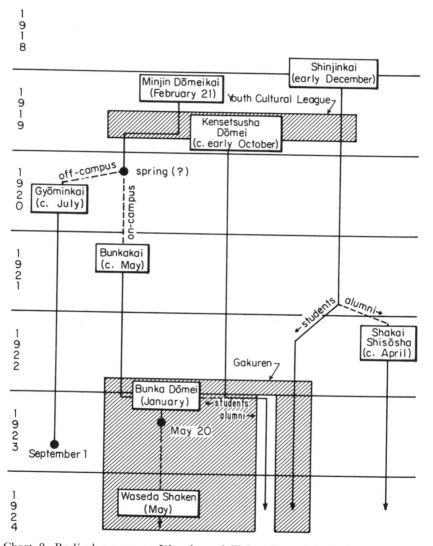

Chart 2. Radical groups at Waseda and Tokyo Imperial, 1918–1924

Symbols: Parentheses: founding date. Diagonal shading: federation. Black circle: dissolution. Broken lines: factions of existing groups or remnants of dissolved groups.

The faction which seceded from the Minjin Dōmeikai to create the Kensetsusha Dōmei was ideologically close to the Shinjinkai. The central leader in this group, Wada Iwao, was involved in the Yūaikai, and its major faculty adviser, Kitazawa Shinjirō, was cast in a mold not unlike Yoshino Sakuzō. An American-trained economist and member of the Reimeikai, Kitazawa was a key academic sponsor of the Yūaikai, serving as its acting president in 1919 while Suzuki Bunji was attending the ILO conference in Geneva. Like Yoshino, Kitazawa was a teacher of great personal appeal and attracted a group of loyal disciples, who formed the leadership core of the Kensetsusha Dōmei: Wada, Asanuma Inejirō, Inamura Ryūichi, and Miyake Shōichi. In the fall of 1919, this faction sponsored Kitazawa as official adviser to the Minjin Dōmeikai but was opposed by another group which looked in more radical directions for guidance to off-campus socialist leaders like Yamakawa Hitoshi and Sakai Toshihiko.[5] Under the leadership of Takatsu Seidō, a student whose early interest in social reform had led him to give up a post as Buddhist priest in his native Hiroshima and enter Waseda in 1918 at the age of 25, this radical group frequently participated in the study clubs of the Meiji socialists.[6]

The two Waseda lineages in the period 1919–1922 both exhibited interesting variants to the Shinjinkai pattern of development, helping explain the failure of any effective alliance between radical students at the two universities in those years. The Kensetsusha Dōmei, for example, although politically in much the same dimension as the Shinjinkai, embarked on a very different course of activity. After splitting away from the Minjin Dōmeikai in October 1919,[7] the group rented a

5. Some evidence indicates that the radical faction supported Takahashi Seigo, an uninspiring professor of political science, as adviser, but this was doubtless less from admiration for Takahashi than as a means of opposing the pro-Kitazawa group. This is the version of Miyake Shōichi, *Iku sanga o koete* (Kōbunsha, 1966), p. 18, which I consider to be the most reliable of a number of conflicting accounts of the Minjin Dōmeikai split.

6. For Takatsu's early development, see Takatsu, pt. 1, pp. 137–40.

7. The precise founding date of the Kensetsusha Dōmei, like so many other groups in this period, is obscure. Kikukawa, *Gakusei shakai undō shi*, p. 68, gives November, a possibility excluded by specific mention in the Shinjinkai magazine of the Kensetsusha Dōmei as among the Youth Cultural League founders on October 10. Shakai bunko, ed., *Taishōki shisō dantai shisatsunin hōkoku*, p. 39, gives a date of October 18; another government report, however, mentions an October 11 meeting of the Waseda Oratorical Society at which the Kensetsusha Dōmei declaration was distributed; Naimushō, *Tokubetsu yō-shisatsunin jōsei*

house in Ikebukuro adjacent to Kitazawa's as their headquarters and *gasshuku* and adopted a much less narrow policy on membership than the Shinjinkai, willingly taking in students from universities other than Waseda.[8] The most striking contrast with the Shinjinkai, however, was its emphasis on organization of farm tenant unions, an area of the left-wing movement which was barely beginning at that time and which presented far greater difficulties than the organization of the urban working class. The decision to embark upon this project was taken at the suggestion of Kitazawa that the Shinjinkai had already staked out a clear claim to leadership in the labor movement, so that it might be best to strike out in a new direction.[9] The traditional rivalry of Waseda and Tokyo Imperial was thus ironically responsible in part for the rapid growth of the organized peasant movement in Japan, since the members of the Kensetsusha Dōmei went on to form the mainstream of leadership in the national tenant union organization.

In contrast with the Kensetsusha Dōmei, the more radical wing of the early Waseda student movement moved within the tenebrous circles of the veteran socialists and anarchists, attending their small study groups and devoting more attention to underground agitation than to idealistic proselytism in the manner of the Shinjinkai. In the spring of 1920, this group—which had been continuing under the name of the Minjin Dōmeikai—was dissolved by the university authorities for inviting the anarchist Ōsugi Sakae to speak on campus. The group was reorganized off campus the following summer under Takatsu's leadership as the Gyōminkai (Dawn of the People Society). The ideological extremism of the Gyōminkai was matched by a far less ex-

---

ippan, 9 (November 1, 1919), 100–101. It would thus appear that the group was formed in early October, immediately before the Youth Cultural League.

8. The Kensetsusha Dōmei even included a number of Tokyo Imperial students, one of whom, Takatsu Wataru, found in the Waseda group an appealing alternative to the elitism of the Shinjinkai (Kinoshita Hanji interview); the report in Kaihō no ishizue kankō iinkai, ed., *Kaihō no ishizue* (Kaihō undō giseisha gassō tsuitōkai sewaninkai, 1956), p. 201, that Takatsu was a Shinjinkai member is erroneous. The Kensetsusha Dōmei also apparently had a few workers in its membership, although they were certainly a minority; see Tadokoro Terukai, "Zenki gakusei undō," *Shakai kagaku,* 4.1 (February 1928), 147.

9. See Kitazawa Shinjirō in Nōmin kumiai shi kankōkai, ed., *Nōmin kumiai undō shi* (Nihon minsei chōsakai, 1960), preface. A further influence leading the group into the farm movement was the strong interest of its leader, Wada Iwao, in agricultural problems.

clusive membership policy than either the Shinjinkai or Kensetsusha Dōmei. Although Waseda students remained the leaders of the group, workers were taken in as members on an equal basis and eventually came to form a majority. The Gyōminkai was represented in the Japan Socialist League in the fall of 1920 by Takatsu, for which he and two other student leaders of the group were expelled from Waseda on November 30.[10]

Both Waseda lineages were similar to the Shinjinkai in having a range of membership that included both students and nonstudents— whether recent graduates or laborers—and suffered the similar tensions engendered by such a mixed composition. Both Waseda groups were eventually forced, like the Shinjinkai, to reorganize into off-campus and on-campus wings which quickly parted ways. The Gyōminkai was the earliest to take this step, since the expulsion of the three student members from Waseda in late 1920 made it clear that overt connections with the university were hazardous. Thus in early 1921 the Bunkakai (Cultural Society) was organized by the surviving student members of the Gyōminkai as a campus group limited to Waseda students and began activity with the new term in the spring. Although of Gyōminkai lineage, the Bunkakai quickly began to go its own way, drawing guidance less from the off-campus veteran socialists than from Ōyama Ikuo, who had returned to Waseda as a professor in 1920, and from two young radical lecturers, Sano Manabu and Inomata Tsunao. By late 1921, when the leaders of the Gyōminkai were arrested for distributing propaganda leaflets, the Bunkakai was already an independent and self-sustaining organization.[11]

10. For this version of the demise of the Minjin Dōmeikai and founding of the Gyōminkai, I have followed Shakai bunko, ed., *Taishōki shisō dantai shisatsunin hōkoku*, p. 9. This version gives no date for Ōsugi's talk at Waseda, but presumably it was after his release from jail in March 1920. This account is far more plausible than the more commonly cited one of Kikukawa, *Gakusei shakai undō shi*, p. 112, which suggests that the Gyōminkai was formed after Takatsu's expulsion; that is impossible, since Takatsu was expelled (as Kikukawa himself relates) for serving as Gyōminkai representative in Japan Socialist League. Takatsu in his own memoirs follows Kikukawa, probably from lapse of memory after more than forty years; see Takatsu, pt. 1, p. 141.

11. The activities of the Bunkakai are described in detail in two accounts by its central leader, Takano Minoru, in Tōkyō daigaku shimbun sha henshūbu, ed., *Haiiro no seishun* (editor, 1948), pp. 13–32, and "Zengakuren [sic] no dekiru koro," *Daigaku ronsō*, 2.3 (May 1964), 85–88. These two accounts conflict on a number of points.

The Kensetsusha Dōmei managed to preserve its mixed membership considerably longer, balancing off-campus activity in the peasant movement with a continuing program of on-campus proselytism through manipulation of the Oratorical Society. The off-campus segment, however, began to bulk ever larger in the overall activities of the group, especially after October 1922, when the group began to publish a magazine, *Kensetsusha,* aimed largely at the tenant union movement.[12] Hence a decision was made in January 1923—two years after the Gyōminkai reorganization, one year after that of the Shinjinkai—to separate the student and nonstudent membership. The student wing was merged with the Bunkakai to form a united on-campus radical organization, the Bunka Dōmei (Cultural League).

The incompatibility of the three central student socialist groups in the period 1919–1922—the Shinjinkai and the two major Waseda lineages—stemmed largely from the different types of off-campus activity in which each was engaged. While the Shinjinkai indulged in the publication of an intellectual magazine and in labor union organization, the Kensetsusha Dōmei was active in the provincial farm tenant union movement, and the Gyōminkai stressed extremist underground agitation. It was only when off-campus activities and off-campus membership had been channeled into separate organizations that a true federation of students as students, coordinated on a national level, became conceivable.

THE FIRST COMMUNIST PARTY AND THE UNIVERSITIES

The Japanese Communist Party was a powerful if hidden element in the setting of Japan's first national federation of student radicals in the fall of 1922. The "first" Communist Party, the organization which was formally dissolved in March 1924, emerged in a curious process of flux, "from a gaseous state, to a liquid, and then to a solid" in the years 1920–1922.[13] The first of a series of confusing false starts and

12. For the contents of *Kensetsusha* and its successors, see Kanda Bunjin, comp., "Kensetsusha dōmei kikanshi *Kensetsusha, Seinen undō, Musan kaikyū, Musan nōmin* sōmokuji," *Rōdō undō shi kenkyū,* no. 36 (May 1963), pp. 28–34. The contents are analyzed in Kanda, "Gakusei no shakai shugi undō kikanshi." This series is scheduled for reprint by the Ōhara Shakai Mondai Kenkyūjo.

13. Takatsu, pt. 7, p. 148.

setbacks which made up the early history of the Japanese Communist Party was a trip to Shanghai in the summer of 1920 by anarchist leader Ōsugi to collect funds from Comintern representatives there. The sanguine expectation that Ōsugi would blithely swear off his anarchism upon receiving two thousand yen ($1,000) was rapidly disappointed as the anarchist-bolshevist antagonism grew ever more intense in the following two years.

Fiasco followed miscalculation when Kondō Eizō was selected as the next emissary to the Comintern outpost in Shanghai in the spring of 1921 and managed by sheer indiscretion to get arrested on the day of his return to Japan in possession of 6,500 yen ($3,250) in Comintern funds. Although the money was not confiscated, the two senior leaders of the embryonic party, Yamakawa and Sakai, realized that the police would be keeping close track of how the funds were spent and prudently advised Kondō to make use of it on his own. Kondō did so by enlisting the aid of the radical young Gyōminkai members for a campaign of pamphlet distribution in the fall of 1921. This effort ended abruptly when two rather crassly propagandistic handbills distributed to soldiers on maneuvers in Tokyo led the authorities to arrest Kondō and fifteen other Gyōminkai members in late November. Since the handbill in question was signed "Communist Party Headquarters," the arrests became known as the Gyōmin Communist Party Incident.[14]

The First Communist Party passed from a liquid to a solid state in the course of 1922, following the dispatch of a delegation to the Conference of the Toilers of the Far East in Moscow in January. The "party" that emerged was a tiny federation of the personal cliques of the major surviving Meiji socialists (with the critical exception of the anarchists, since the "anarchist-bolshevist dispute" was reaching a peak in the same months). The membership of the First Communist Party

14. There is good reason to doubt that an organization called the "Gyōmin Communist Party" ever existed; Kondō himself claims that it did, but this must be balanced against the conflicting testimony of the two central Gyōminkai leaders. Takatsu, pt. 2, p. 139, claims that the term was devised by the government authorities, while Takase Kiyoshi relates that the organization had no pretensions to being a communist party, but was rather called the "Gyōmin kyōsan shugi dan" (Gyōmin Communist Group). It is thus probably inaccurate to claim that this group was the earliest communist party in Japan. See Takase Kiyoshi, "Kakumei Sobieto senkōki," *Jiyū*, 5.2 (February 1963), 127–128. For Kondō's version, see Kondō Eizō, *Komuminterun no misshi* (Bunka hyōron sha, 1949), pp. 159–162.

was so motley as to defy any simple description, ranging from the classified advertising broker Yoshikawa Morikuni to the Okinawan schoolteacher Tokuda Kyūichi. Where the later Communist Party was to develop a heavy reliance on university-trained intellectuals drawn from the ranks of the student movement, the First Party was largely free of the atmosphere of university radicalism. To the limited extent that the First Communist Party was connected to the early student movement, it showed a clear preference for Waseda, the "outsider" university. Of particular influence in the party were three men, all of whom emerged from the early Waseda student movement:

Tadokoro Teruaki was a member of the Kensetsusha Dōmei who by 1922 had become one of Yamakawa's closest disciples and served as an editor of the Yamakawa-dominated magazine *Zen'ei* (Vanguard) in early 1922.

Takatsu Seidō, as the central figure in the Gyōminkai, was close to all the older socialist leaders and instrumental in the organization of the party after his release from jail in February 1922.

Takase Kiyoshi was a leader of the Gyōminkai with Takatsu and was selected for two critical missions to Moscow, first in January 1923 for the Conference of the Toilers of the Far East and again in November for the Fourth Congress of the Comintern. As Sakai's son-in-law, Takase enjoyed special preference within the First Communist Party.

Tokyo Imperial radicalism, by contrast, was of small importance in the First Communist Party. Both Sano Manabu and Nosaka Sanzō were members of the party, but both were exceptional as Shinjinkai members; Sano, although a Tokyo Imperial graduate, had close ties with Waseda, where he was employed as a lecturer after leaving the East Asian Economic Research Bureau in 1920, and Nosaka of course had been a Keiō graduate and only tangentially involved in the Shinjinkai. Of the regular Shinjinkai student membership, only three became members of the First Communist Party, and, with the possible exception of Koiwai Jō, who organized a party cell in Osaka, all were minor late-joiners.[15]

The distinct preference of Waseda over Tokyo Imperial within the

15. The other two were Akamatsu Katsumaro, who was minor enough to escape arrest in 1923, and Yamazaki Kazuo, who went to Moscow in late 1922 as a delegate of the party. Yamazaki's role in the First Communist Party is known to few people; Yamazaki interview.

circles of the early Japanese Communist Party is illustrated by the saga of the courtship of Sakai Magara, Toshihiko's only daughter, who by virtue of her parentage was considered a great prize among young bachelor radicals around 1920. Takatsu Seidō relates that four men were in the forefront of the heated competition for Magara's hand: the promising young novelist Shimada Seijirō (who had no university education), Shinjinkai members Akamatsu Katsumaro and Kadota Takeo, and Gyōminkai leader Takase Kiyoshi. In the end, Takase, the Waseda representative, won out and married Magara in 1922.[16] It is of further interest that the two Shinjinkai competitors went on to marry women who were very much within the Tokyo Imperial University sphere of influence: Akamatsu wed Yoshino Sakuzō's daughter, while Kadota took the younger sister of Yanaihara Tadao, a Christian liberal and professor of economics at Tokyo Imperial University who went on eventually to become president of the university in 1951.

Until the Communist Party finally took definite shape in mid-1922, no conscious attempt was made to influence the student movement, and even with the formal creation of the party it is difficult to detect any clear-cut "policy" towards university radicals. The one persuasive piece of evidence indicating early Communist Party concern for students is the testimony of Kikukawa Tadao, a founder of the Social Problems Study Group (Shakai Mondai Kenkyūkai) at First Higher School in the spring of 1922. Kikukawa asserts that Tadokoro Teruaki was "what might be called the party's man in charge of student agitation," and that in this capacity he masterminded the spread of the Russian famine relief movement among higher schools and universities in the summer and fall of 1922.[17]

"Party policy" in any event is a concept which probably had little relevance to the activities of the First Communist Party, a secret alliance of precarious cohesion among a small number of unique individuals. Of far greater importance in the development of the student movement in this period than any specific "manipulation" by the Party

16. Takatsu, Pt. 6, pp. 151–52.
17. Kikukawa, *Gakusei shakai undō shi*, pp. 122, 159. Kikukawa further claims that Tadokoro sought to advance the unification of the student movement under communist domination by propounding a strategy of "a single group in each school." Tadokoro's own version of the history of the early student movement makes no mention of this; see "Zenki gakusei undō."

was the voluntary commitment of several key student leaders to communism. While probably unaware of the movement towards an actual party organization, these students nevertheless defined themselves as "communists" and devoted themselves to living up to this definition. It may even be argued that in their youthful, doctrinaire commitment, these students were far purer communists than the actual leaders of the Communist Party, many of whom remained tainted by earlier bouts with anarchism, social democracy, and similar deviations.

Two young activists might be singled out as typical of this new mold of student radical. One was Takano Minoru, a preparatory-course student at Waseda in late 1920 when he was selected by Gyōminkai leaders to head the Bunkakai, its on-campus wing. As Bunkakai leader from the spring of 1921, Takano maintained frequent contacts with his Gyōminkai seniors and with the older socialists, and, he recalls, "prided myself as a bolshevik." [18] The other was Shiga Yoshio, who entered Tokyo Imperial University and the Shinjinkai simultaneously in April 1922 and quickly achieved a position of influence next to the senior leaders. But even from an earlier stage, as a student at First Higher School, Shiga had developed close ties with the older socialists, Sakai in particular, and hence was within much the same sphere of influence as Takano. Both Takano and Shiga were critical figures in leading the Japanese student movement to unification in the fall of 1922.

HORIZONTAL UNIFICATION: THE GAKUREN

The unification of the student movement was carried out during the final climax of the struggle for control of the labor movement between the anarchists and communists. The dispute had come into the open with the dissolution of the Japan Socialist League in May 1921 and by mid-1922 was at its peak. Since a major area of ideological disagreement between the two factions was over the validity of the Soviet experiment as a model for socialist revolution, the communist or "bolshevist" camp attempted to generate emotional sympathy for Russia as a tactic of opposition to the anarchists. One phase of this campaign was the movement launched in May 1922, demanding the withdrawal

18. Takano Minoru in Tōkyō daigaku shimbun sha henshūbu, ed., *Haiiro no seishun,* p. 19.

of the Japanese interventionist troops in Siberia. When the troops were actually withdrawn the same summer, the central demand was shifted to one for the diplomatic recognition of Soviet Russia.

Of far greater importance in generating student sympathy for the Soviet cause, however, was the relief campaign for the Russian famine of 1921–22. This drive was launched on May 22 with a special issue of *Zen'ei*, a semi-official organ of the embryonic Communist Party. The drive was taken up eagerly by many progressive groups and magazines throughout Japan and continued for about one year, lagging in the spring of 1923 and collapsing with the June arrests of the Communist Party. The humanistic appeal of the relief campaign made it an ideal vehicle for spreading the political influence of Soviet communism in Japan and certainly helped hasten the decline of anarchist strength.[19] (Whatever the political advantages of the movement, however, it was of only moderate financial success: as of April 16, 1923, the total amount collected was 7,627 yen, which ironically was even less than the ill-fated 8,500 yen the Comintern had sent into Japan in 1920–21 via Ōsugi and Kondō.)[20]

The famine relief campaign, a happy blend of political and humanitarian elements, was ideally suited for the spread of radical influence among students. Even before the campaign was officially launched by *Zen'ei*, in fact, the Shinjinkai magazine had carried several articles on famine relief, and the February 1922 issue of *Narod* had mentioned the students' desire to help out in some way.[21] Since the movement was begun rather late in the spring term, the first fruits of the campaign were borne in the provinces, where the students spent their vacation. Takano Minoru notes that the Waseda Bunkakai organized groups of vacationing students to collect money in their home provinces, while higher school students in Kyushu likewise generated interest in their newly formed radical study groups by summer relief campaign work.[22]

19. In November 1922 an official of the Workers' International Famine Relief Committee, Willy Munzenberg, "assured the Third International that the political importance of the relief campaign has been immense, particularly in the United States and Japan." H. H. Fisher, *The Famine in Soviet Russia, 1919–1923* (New York, 1927), p. 233n.

20. For the amount of relief money collected, see *Sekki*, no. 15 (May 1923), p. 80.

21. *Shinjinkai kikanshi*, p. 558.

22. Takano, "Zengakuren no dekiru koro," p. 87. For an example of the Kyushu activity, see Hayashi Fusao, *Bungakuteki kaisō* (Shinchōsha, 1955), p. 12.

When the new school term commenced in September, immediate steps were taken to coordinate the relief campaign among Tokyo students. The initiative was taken by the Waseda Bunkakai, which worked through the Oratorical Society to promote the formation of the Debating League for Russian Famine Relief (Yūben Remmei Roshiya Kikin Kyūsaikai) in mid-September. The league, which in October announced a membership of thirty-two chapters that included almost every university and professional school in the Tokyo area, embarked on an ambitious program of lectures, plays, and concerts to earn money for the relief fund. This campaign netted a modest total of 350 yen ($175) for famine relief; [23] its real importance lay rather in the contacts that it promoted among progressive students at a wide variety of schools. It was through this debating league, Takano recollects, that he first made the acquaintance of the leaders of the Shinjinkai and other groups.[24]

These intermural contacts soon led to a plan for a radical student federation, reviving the concept which had aborted three years earlier in the Youth Cultural League. This time, however, a far greater number of groups were involved, since rudimentary organizations had been set up for famine relief collection at many schools that had previously been unorganized. The majority of these groups were based on the debating clubs, the traditional birthplace of student radicals in Japan. Initial plans for the federation were drawn up in October, and the simple name of Student Federation (Gakusei Rengōkai), known commonly by the abbreviation "Gakuren," was chosen.[25] The founding meeting was held on November 7, 1922, the fifth anniversary of the October Revolution, on the Tokyo Imperial University campus. Over fifty representatives, even including some from a women's medical college, attended the semi-secret meeting.[26]

23. This figure is given in *Zen'ei*, no. 13 (March 1923), p. 203. Takano in Tōkyō daigaku shimbun sha henshūbu, ed., *Haiiro no seishun*, p. 22, claims that the student groups collected over 30,000 yen, which is a tremendous exaggeration, unless he is using postwar equivalents.

24. Takano, "Zengakuren no dekiru koro," p. 87, and Kikukawa, *Gakusei shakai undō shi*, pp. 119–126.

25. Shiga claims that the name Gakusei rengōkai was taken, at Shiga's own suggestion, from the Student Union (Hsüeh-sheng lien-ho-hui) in China, which was established in the wake of the May Fourth Movement in 1919. Shiga Yoshio interview. For the Chinese group, see Chow Tse-tsung, *The May Fourth Movement —Intellectual Revolution in Modern China* (Cambridge, Mass., 1960), pp. 122–123.

26. The only surviving accounts of the event by those present are Kikukawa, *Gakusei shakai undō shi*, pp. 138–139, and Takano in Tōkyō daigaku shimbun sha henshūbu, ed., *Haiiro no seishun*, pp. 24–26. These conflict on several points.

The Gakuren was larger than the Youth Cultural League had been, but the nature of the alliance consummated was similar. The central leaders were the Shinjinkai and the two Waseda groups, the Bunkakai and Kensetsusha Dōmei (which were soon to be merged into one). The other groups were mostly from private universities such as Meiji, Nihon, Keiō, and Hōsei: much like the Hōsei Fushinkai in 1919, these were clearly subordinate to the Waseda and Tokyo Imperial forces. One distinctly new element was the participation of various higher school groups. The founding of the Gakuren was informal, and no documents survive to provide the details. The declared purpose of the group was a camouflage of "mutual friendship among students." It appears that no statement of purpose was drafted, no real organization set up.[27] It was to be over a year before the Gakuren developed into a strong, tightly organized federation, but at least the first critical step of close cooperation between Tokyo Imperial and Waseda had been taken and the Japanese student movement was launched into a new era.

VERTICAL UNIFICATION: THE HIGHER SCHOOL LEAGUE

Of equal importance to the "horizontal" federation of Tokyo Imperial and various private universities in the Gakuren was the "vertical" contact established between the Shinjinkai and the provincial higher schools. The early Shinjinkai had made no systematic efforts to cultivate the higher schools as a source of future activists, reflecting a lack of interest in assuring its continuity as a student group. With the redefinition of the Shinjinkai as a pure student group in the Narod Declaration, however, and the reduction of the membership to less than ten following graduation in March 1922, recruitment from the higher schools became a matter of survival. The problem was made all the more pressing when the entire delegation of the class of 1924, a group of about four who were all graduates of First Higher, seceded from the Shinjinkai. This faction argued that the backbone of the socialist movement must be the working class and that any attempt to organize students, as students, in the manner of the Shinjinkai mainstream, was a mistake.[28]

27. Takano, *ibid.*, does mention officers and lists some "secretaries" (*kanji*) from memory, but his reliability is suspect.
28. The leaders of this faction were Murayama Tōshirō, Mizuno Shigeo, and Kinoshita Hanji. See below, Chapter 6, note 16.

Before 1922 few higher schools had radical groups, with the exception of First Higher and Third Higher, which were under the strong influence of the neighboring imperial universities. What left-wing political activity existed remained largely within the confines of the debating clubs until suddenly in the spring of 1922 a number of new groups appeared. Some of these were organized under the direct instigation of radical alumni, but most were spontaneous, the result of students' reading the left-wing literature which was increasingly available in this period. Two of the earliest provincial groups were in Kyushu, the R. F. Kai (R. F. Society) at Fifth Higher in Kumamoto and the Kakumeikai (Society of the Crane's Cry) at Seventh Higher in Kagoshima.[29] Reflecting the proud and rebellious spirit for which Kyushu is known, the leaders of these groups went on to become central figures in the Higher School League, then in the Shinjinkai, and finally in the reconstructed Japanese Communist Party after 1926. Most prominent were three Seventh Higher classmates, Koreeda Kyōji, Murao Satsuo, and Kiire Toratarō, while Fifth Higher's major contribution was Gotō Toshio, better known by his later pen name of Hayashi Fusao.

These two Kyushu higher school groups were followed by others in the following months, until by 1924 almost every higher school in Japan could boast a radical study group. The number of higher schools was rapidly increasing in this period, following the recommendations of the Special Council on Education; from 1918 until 1922, nine new schools were created, and another ten had followed by 1926. Most were located in provincial capitals, out of direct contact with the urban centers of political ferment; nevertheless, the newness of such schools encouraged a spirit of innovation among the students, and most saw the organization of a left-wing study group within a year or two after founding. Indeed, the new higher schools were in the course of the 1920s to produce activists of consistently more radical caliber than the established "number schools."

Shinjinkai interest in fostering higher school radicalism was expressed at the time of the Narod Declaration, in December 1921, when

---

29. The "R. F. Society" stood for the German "röte Fahne" (red flag). The "Kakumeikai," ostensibly named after an historical site in Kagoshima, was an intended play on words: *kakumei* means "revolution" when written with different characters.

it was noted that "At higher schools throughout the country, signs of the new thought are beginning to sprout. We would like gradually to make contact among the various higher schools and turn this into a large movement. We anticipate in the future the acquisition of a succession of strong fighters from these schools." [30]

The first major effort in this direction did not come, however, until the following autumn, when the Shinjinkai leaders at the time—Kuroda Hisao, Tomooka Hisao, Shiga Yoshio, and Itō Kōdō—embarked on a lecture tour to universities and higher schools throughout western Japan.[31] Making contact with radical student organizations where they existed or with interested individuals at unorganized schools, the delegation stirred up much enthusiasm as it went, instructing the eager provincial students in study programs and organizational techniques. Solid contacts were made at higher schools in Kyoto, Okayama, Kumamoto, and Kagoshima, and the success of the two-week expedition encouraged the Shinjinkai to promote a national federation of such study groups. These plans materialized during the New Year vacation in January 1923 when about ten delegates from higher schools ranging from Niigata to Kagoshima met in Tokyo.

The First Higher School radical leaders served as hosts to the provincial visitors. "During the day," recalls Hayashi Fusao, "we were taken around to various meetings and to the headquarters of different groups, receiving training in communist methods of propaganda, while at night we slept in the beds of an unheated sickroom at First Higher." [32] At a meeting in the judo hall at First Higher, the Higher School League (Kōtō Gakkō Remmei) was formally organized under a cloak of secrecy. The Higher School League differed from the Gakuren in that membership was by individuals rather than groups, and was limited only to the most dedicated communists (by the subjective defi-

30. *Shinjinkai kikanshi*, p. 526.
31. Shiga Yoshio, *Nihon kakumei undō no gunzō*, 4th ed. (Shin Nihon shuppansha, 1963), p. 230, mentions six people in this excursion; the other two were probably Sugino Tadao and Narazaki Akira. For Sugino, see Kikukawa Tadao, "Wakaki gakuto wa tatakau—Gakusei shakai kagaku undō no yokogao," *Chūō kōron*, 44.10 (October 1930), 171. For Narazaki, see unpublished manuscript of Kikukawa Tadao recording Kiire Toratarō's recollections of the student movement at Seventh Higher (undated, Kikukawa papers, now in the possession of Mr. Uchida Sakurō).
32. Hayashi Fusao, *Bungakuteki kaisō*, p. 5.

nition of the students themselves, of course). Kikukawa, one of the First Higher representatives of the league, relates that each member memorized the secret regulations to avoid committing them to paper: "The HSL will engage in communist propaganda among higher school students. HSL members must possess a spirit of zeal and sacrifice towards communism, and must be able to maintain strict secrecy. HSL members will function as the nucleus of each study group."[33]

The Higher School League did not survive as such, in part because the key members graduated in March to enter Tokyo Imperial and in part because of difficulty of contact among the widely separated schools. But the spirit in which it was founded set the tone of the student movement for many years thereafter. The higher school study groups continued to grow and prosper, participating in the Gakuren until educational authorities began to apply systematic pressure from 1925. Many of the higher school groups survived underground well into the 1930s, however, and were of significance in the history of the student movement in two respects. In the first place, the higher school groups made up a highly effective "farm system" both for the Shinjinkai and for the Kyoto Imperial student movement. Every spring, left-wing organizations at these key imperial universities could depend upon a revitalization with a new crop of tempered radicals from the higher schools, eager to prove their dedication. This kind of regeneration was not possible at private universities and helped maintain the supremacy of the Shinjinkai within the Tokyo student movement.

At the same time, the higher school study groups frequently played leading roles in the provincial socialist movements, participating in local labor and tenant unions and engaging in communist propaganda among rural workers and intellectuals. Because such activity was isolated and sporadic, it is difficult to assess its overall impact, but such documented cases as Mito, Matsue, and Okayama suggest that higher school radicals were often a critical element in instigating and supporting the provincial left.[34]

33. Kikukawa, *Gakusei shakai undō shi*, p. 140.
34. See Sugiura Katsuo, ed., *Aru seishun no kiroku—Kaisō no Suikō gakusei undō to Ogawa Haruo, Chiba Shigeo gokuchū shokanshū* (Wagatsuma shoin, 1969); Shimane daigaku shimbun bu, ed., "Shimane no gakusei undō shi," *Kyōdo*, no. 11 (November 1960), pp. 25–33; Misuzu shobō, ed., *Shakai shugi undō*, Gendaishi shiryō, vols. XIV–XX, (editor, 1964–68), XVI, 547–57.

THE GAKUREN: INTO THE OPEN

For five months after its founding, the Gakuren remained in a limbo, a loose, semi-secret federation with its only real strength in the Tokyo area and little sense of direction. The only memorable activity undertaken under Gakuren auspices in this period was participation in the February 1923 movement to protest the government's proposed Extreme Socialist Control Law. This protest was organized on a national scale by the labor movement, and Gakuren students acted merely as an auxiliary force, donning laborer's clothes to march in street demonstrations, distributing thousands of leaflets, and holding occasional on-campus rallies to demonstrate their solidarity with the off-campus left.[35] This activity was of some use in extending Gakuren influence to previously unorganized campuses but failed to inform the student movement with any sense of mission. The Control Law bill was shelved, accomplishing the aim of the protest movement (although the bill was to be enacted in even more stringent form as the Peace Preservation Law two years later), but students themselves found it difficult to claim a personal victory.

In the late spring of 1923, however, a burst of activity among radical students in Tokyo brought to the Gakuren the sense of confidence and direction which it had been lacking. This development owed much to the regeneration of the Shinjinkai with the entrance into Tokyo Imperial University of the leadership of the Higher School League. March saw the graduation of the class of Kuroda and Tomooka, the last generation of the early Shinjinkai, making possible a clean break with the past. The new group was to dominate not only the Shinjinkai but the entire Japanese student movement for the next three years and included three of the most influential and charismatic leaders of the later Shinjinkai: Kikukawa Tadao, Koreeda Kyōji, and Hayashi Fusao. Meanwhile, the Gakuren organization at Waseda had also been invigorated; in January 1923 the Bunkakai and the student wing of the Kensetsusha Dōmei merged into the Bunka Dōmei to repair the mod-

35. Kikukawa, *Gakusei shakai undō shi*, pp. 151–152. Since two other proposed laws were also being protested, this was known as the "movement against the three evil laws" (*san'akuhō hantai undō*).

erate-radical schism that had lasted over three years. Although a key leader had been lost with the arrest and subsequent illness of Takano Minoru in the February demonstrations, a number of talented young leaders were available, including Tokano Takeshi, Matsuo Shigeki, and Itō Ushinosuke.

This new leadership in the spring of 1923 at the two major citadels of Gakuren strength worked to turn the student movement away from political protests in which students acted simply in a supporting capacity and in the direction of campus-related radicalism initiated and dominated by the students themselves. Two variants of this new emphasis on the university itself emerged in 1923. One was a drive to increase the authority of students within the confines of the campus; such was the Shinjinkai campaign in early May to turn the Gakuyūkai (the existing student union) into an organ of student government, which will be described in the following chapter. The other was the attempt to launch protests of broad political significance in which the university was directly involved, in contrast, for example, to support of universal suffrage or socialist control laws. This type of activity was developed in a series of two dramatic protests on the Waseda campus, protests which brought about close cooperation of the Tokyo Gakuren members and served for the first time to bring the national federation into prominence.

The first protest was launched when the Bunka Dōmei leaders discovered in early May that the student equestrian club at Waseda was planning to reorganize as a Military Study Group (Gunji Kenkyūkai), with considerable encouragement and assistance from army officials. Drawing inspiration from the traditional Waseda animosity towards the military, the radical leaders immediately set in action a plan to disrupt the founding ceremonies of the proposed group on May 10. At a meeting of the Gakuren leadership on May 5, Waseda leader Matsuo won the support of groups on other campuses, who agreed to dispatch shock troops on the appointed day.

The Gakuren disruption of the founding ceremonies was a signal success. Student radicals, carefully dispersed throughout the crowd, relentlessly jeered each speaker who rose to the podium, shouting "Shame, shame!" to the professor heading the Military Student Group, "Have you forgotten Ōkuma?" to Waseda president Takada Sanae, and, to the vice-minister of the army, "Your medals are dripping with the blood of our comrades!" [36] To follow up this triumph, the students organized an open-air rally on the Waseda campus two days later. In the meantime, however, the right-wing forces, smarting from the humiliation inflicted by the Gakuren jeerers, had been carefully assembling their troops, both from the judo team (a traditional stronghold of student conservatism) and from the Jūō Club, an off-campus right-wing group of Waseda alumni. This time the tables were turned, and the speeches of the students at the afternoon rally were met with physical assault by their right-wing opponents. Takano was clubbed with a wooden clog by a Jūō Club member, while one of the judo wrestlers threw a pail of night soil over the crowd.[37] Several students were bloodied in the brawl that ensued.

These two confrontations greatly intensified the antagonism between the left and right on campus and shortly afterwards forced the dissolution of both groups involved. The victory tended, however, to be on the side of the Gakuren forces, for despite the official dissolution of the Bunka Dōmei, its members continued to operate through the Oratorical Society precisely as they had done before. The Military Study Group, by contrast, appears to have been permanently defeated.[38] Of greater importance than the fate of the immediate issue, however, was the confidence which the protest had given to the student radicals, who were left anxious for a new issue to extend their influence and organization still more. They did not have long to wait. In the course of a mass arrest of the membership of the Japanese Communist Party on the morning of June 5, a contingent of Tokyo police entered the Waseda campus to search the offices of lecturers Sano Manabu and Inomata Tsunao, both of whom were party members.

The police search of the campus triggered a vigorous protest among the Waseda students, all the more because Inomata and Sano had been

36. Kikukawa, *Gakusei shakai undō shi,* pp. 164–166, gives a detailed account of the jeering.
37. This detail is provided in one of the few accounts of the event by a right-wing participant; see Sasaki Mitsugu, "Gunji kenkyūdan jiken no shinsō," in Asanuma tsuitō shuppan henshū iinkai, ed., *Bakushin—Ningen kikansha Numa-san no kiroku* (Nihon shakaitō kikanshikyoku, 1962), p. 110.
38. At the same time, however, the Jūō Club reportedly made great gains after the incident. See Kōan chōsachō, *Senzen ni okeru uyoku dantai no jōkyō,* 3 vols. (1964), II, 308–309.

two of the closest advisers to the former Bunka Dōmei. The protest was begun through the Oratorical Society and widened through the Gakuren. At a special meeting of the Gakuren on June 18, a critical decision was made: some ten member groups agreed to issue a statement of protest signed in the name of the Gakuren and of its participating affiliates. For the first time the radical student federation emerged from semi-secrecy and began a course of open, coordinated activity on the campus. The protest movement against the Waseda police search was carried out under the slogan "protect the university" and was climaxed with a rally on June 20 at the Kanda YMCA, where Ōyama Ikuo, Miyake Setsurei, and Fukuda Tokuzō were the featured speakers. Ōyama's speech in defense of academic freedom and university autonomy was particularly stirring and has been compared by Kikukawa to the Yoshino–Rōninkai debate of November 1918 in its effect on the students.[39]

Summer vacation forced the "protect the university" protest to an early end, but only after it had served to generate wide support among the Tokyo student population. The Gakuren was greatly strengthened by both the Military Study Group incident and by the police search protest, for they gave the student movement the opportunity to take a clear stand on two political issues of immediate concern to the university campus, those of military education and academic freedom. The Gakuren acted autonomously and confidently, winning wide public attention for the first time. All this activity was limited to Tokyo, but the central Gakuren leadership was now clearly prepared to embark on much wider protests. The month of excitement on the Waseda campus in the spring of 1923 gave the Gakuren the sense of direction it had been seeking.

THE GAKUREN: TIGHTENING THE ORGANIZATION

The new sense of mission imparted to the student movement was reflected in the reaction of Shinjinkai member Hayashi Fusao to the Great Kanto earthquake of September 1, 1923, which destroyed much of Tokyo. Hayashi at the time was in his native Kyushu, where he had spent the summer trying his hand at agitation among local laborers.

39. Kikukawa, *Gakusei shakai undō shi,* p. 176.

Disappointed with the meager fruits of his efforts, Hayashi was gloomier still when he read the wildly exaggerated newspaper reports of the confusion in the capital:

> What surprised me was not the "total destruction" of the capital, or the "crumbling of Mt. Fuji," but rather the "street fighting in Tokyo." The revolution had occurred! The comrades had taken up arms, raised the barricades, unfurled the red flag, and were fighting the troops of the imperialists! . . .
>
> But I was too late. I alone had been left behind. While I wasted my time agitating in a boring provincial village, the revolution had broken out. If only I had advanced my scheduled return to Tokyo by a little, I would have made it. But now, by a mere day or two, I was a straggler from the revolution, a class traitor.[40]

Events proved Hayashi wrong, however, for the Kanto earthquake, far from precipitating revolution, gave birth to a white terror which produced the murder of anarchist leader Ōsugi Sakae and the massacre of many Koreans in a desperate search for a scapegoat to the natural disaster. These events forced upon the entire left-wing movement, following an initial surge of anger, the sober realization that only a period of moderation could counteract the setbacks. The expenditure of time and labor necessary to reconstruct the devastated city further worked to turn the socialist movement away from political extremism into a period of retrenchment and quiescence, a period of what has been termed "liberalization" or *ribekka*. The student movement too found the enthusiasm of the previous spring somewhat deadened and turned now to a period of low-key activism with primary stress on building up the organization and membership of national federation.

Within the Shinjinkai, however, the membership was not unanimously agreed on a policy of "realism" and moderation; a minority group of the most radical elements, including Hayashi, Koreeda, and Shiga, argued that the only proper course in the face of reaction was conversion to an underground organization relying on clandestine agitation to counter the white terror. Dominant within the Shinjinkai before the earthquake, this small group was known simply as the "lead-

40. Hayashi Fusao, *Bungakuteki kaisō*, pp. 6–7.

ership faction" *(kambu-ha)*, but in a general meeting of the membership in late November, it found that its plan to dissolve the Shinjinkai and create a secret vanguard elite was challenged by the majority. Thus the "anti-leadership faction" *(hi-kambu-ha)* led by Kikukawa Tadao won out, and the Shinjinkai committed itself to a program of membership expansion and concentration on moderate campus-oriented agitation.[41]

The victory of the "anti-leadership faction" under Kikukawa produced the Shinjinkai's first formal set of organizational by-laws. Although a number of revisions were made over the next several years, the basic format remained that of a dual system of organization. On the one hand were the study groups, varying in number from five to ten and classified either by the place or time of meeting. Each Shinjinkai member was automatically assigned to one study group, and attendance at the weekly study sessions was required. The elected heads of each study group made up the "section committee" (variously *bu-iinkai, han-iinkai,* and "presidium"). Parallel to this were "functional" groups, defined by the special tasks assigned them, such as planning of reading lists, Gakuren contact, accounts, editing of a mimeographed *Bulletin,* book procurement, or fraction activity in extra-curricular campus organizations. These functional groups were initially of rank parallel with the study groups, with their elected heads sitting on the section committee. Later, however, these functions were transferred from small groups to single individuals known as "secretaries" *(kanji)*, who met together as an "executive committee" *(shikkō iinkai)* and were headed by a "secretary-general" *(kanjichō)*. These officers were elected by a general meeting of the full membership.[42]

Parallel to this development of a rational internal organization within the Shinjinkai, which was followed in less elaborate variations by groups at other schools, was the expansion and coordination of the Gakuren itself. Whereas the Gakuren before the earthquake had been little more than a loose association of Tokyo groups with infrequent

---

41. See Kikukawa, *Gakusei shakai undō shi,* pp. 197–198. The victory of the anti-leadership faction is sometimes referred to in government accounts as the "Shinjinkai's November Revolution"; see, for example, Kawamura Tadao, comp., *Shisō mondai nempyō* (Seinen kyōiku fukyūkai, 1936), p. 39.

42. For the initial organization plan, see *Shinjinkai kaihō,* no. 3 (July 1, 1924), p. 1, quoted in Kikukawa, *Gakusei shakai undō shi,* pp. 198–199.

and tenuous provincial contacts, it now moved rapidly in the direction of a truly unified nationwide federation. In the period from the earthquake until the summer of 1924, as many as thirty new member organizations were founded. The degree of national unity was suggested by the uniform use of the term "social science study group," commonly referred to by the abbreviation *shaken,* as the official title of the Gakuren affiliates. Existing groups as well, with the sole exception of the Shinjinkai (justified by its long tradition), all dutifully changed their names to *shaken,* signaling the end of all literary coloring in the nomenclature of the left-wing student movement.[43]

The natural organizational subdivision within the national federation was geographical, and early in 1924 the Gakuren adopted the concept of "regional councils" (*chihō rengōkai*). The Tokyo Council (soon renamed the Kanto Council to include a number of provincial schools in central Japan) was the earliest, taking shape that spring. The Kansai Council and Tohoku Council were formally established in September, reflecting the burst of organizational activity which had occurred in Kyoto and Sendai since the earthquake.[44] Last was the Kyushu Council in 1925. In every case, an imperial university dominated the regional council. The organizational drive which characterized Gakuren activity in the year after the earthquake was crowned by a meeting of some fifty representatives at Tokyo Imperial University on September 14, 1924, at the beginning of the fall term. This meeting, which came to be known as the "First Congress" of the Gakuren, marked the final consolidation of the Gakuren as a united, nationwide student federation. The official Gakuren title was changed to Student Federation of Social Science (Gakusei Shakai Kagaku Rengōkai), and a report issued claiming a membership of 1,600 on 49 campuses.[45]

By late 1924, *shaken* had been established on almost every higher school and university campus in the country, as well as a number in technical schools and even middle schools. During the five-year period until the final dissolution of the Gakuren in November 1929, periodi-

43. In some schools, where the term "social science" was thought dangerous by school authorities, milder alternatives were used, such as "social thought study group" (*shakai shisō kenkyūkai*), "social problems study group" (*shakai mondai kenkyūkai*), or "reading society" (*dokushokai*).
44. See Kikukawa, *Gakusei shakai undō shi,* pp. 209–211, for details.
45. *Ibid.,* p. 216.

cal estimates of its membership were issued both by the students themselves and by government control officials. While the membership for a specific group occasionally showed wide variations from one list to another, the total Gakuren membership remained remarkably constant, ranging between 1,500 and 2,000, with 45 to 70 participating groups.[46] While the individual groups varied widely in permanence and authority, it is possible to distinguish three broad levels of Gakuren affiliation.

At the top were the "big three" of the prewar student movement, the Shinjinkai and the *shaken* at Waseda and Kyoto Imperial. National leadership of the Gakuren was heavily dominated by these three groups, all of which had large memberships, ranging from perhaps fifty to over one hundred. In terms of elitism, tradition, organization, and tolerance by the university administrations, these three groups stood out far above the rest, and among the three themselves the Shinjinkai was preeminent. These three accounted for roughly one fourth of total Gakuren membership.[47]

The middle-level membership of the Gakuren consisted primarily of the *shaken* at three different types of schools: secular private universities, such as Keiō, Nihon, Meiji, Chūō, and Hōsei in Tokyo, and Ritsumeikan and Kansai in the Kansai Council; Christian private universities, such as Rikkyō, Aoyama Gakuin, and Meiji Gakuin in Tokyo and Dōshisha and Kansai Gakuin in the Kansai Council; and the provincial imperial universities and higher schools. Membership tended to vary between twenty and forty, and though the commitment of the members was generally high, these groups were subjected to much greater pressure from the school administrations than the top three and were largely driven underground by about 1926. Although these *shaken* accounted for as much as two thirds of the total Gakuren mem-

46. Among the various lists are: Kikukawa, *Gakusei shakai undō shi*, pp. 216, 450; Hasegawa Akira, "Gakusei no shisō undō ni tsuite," *Shihō kenkyū*, vol. 15, pt. 4 (March 1932), pp. 101, 108, 111; Naimushō Keihokyoku, *Shakai shugi undō no jōkyō* (1927), p. 75; "Gakusei shakai kagaku rengōkai no soshiki oyobi kaiinsū" (mimeo, July 1927); Shihōshō, Keijikyoku, *Gakusei shakai undō shinsō* (undated, c. 1926), charts 3, 5.
47. This figure assumes the inclusion of the *shaken* at First, Third, and Waseda Higher, all of which were within the direct spheres of influence of the central three.

bership, they were able to exercise influence on a national scale only in the case of exceptional individual leaders.[48]

At the bottom of the Gakuren was a highly fluid grouping of *shaken* at a wide variety of minor schools, including women's colleges, technical schools, private higher schools, small Buddhist colleges, middle schools, and even some schools in the overseas colonies.[49] These groups tended to surface and disappear with frequency and totaled as many as thirty at the peak of Gakuren expansion in late 1925. Organized in schools with a low initial potential for student radicalism, such groups seldom had a membership of over twenty and were on the whole confronted with highly hostile administrators. Lacking any permanence, they had virtually no voice in Gakuren policy.

THE GAKUREN: LESSONS IN PROTEST

The enthusiasm which had been generated among student radicals by the events at Waseda in the spring of 1923 was only temporarily set back by the Kanto earthquake and the period of "realism" which it fostered. A number of Gakuren students were active in the revival of the universal suffrage movement in the winter of 1923–24, but it was not until the following fall that the Gakuren took the initiative in generating a nationwide, militant movement by and for students. Shortly before this, however, a glimpse of the possibilities of such a movement was provided in the Gakuren-led protests against the use of technical school students as strikebreakers in a labor dispute in early July involving the employees of the Osaka metropolitan trolley system. Gakuren representatives in both Kansai and Tokyo issued protests to the student strikebreakers and to the administrations of the three schools which they attended. The issue was a weak one for the creation of a broad protest movement, however, since responsibility for the incident seemed to rest largely on fellow students, whom Gakuren leaders were

48. Good examples were Shimizu Heikurō from Meiji Gakuin, Noro Eitarō from Keiō, and Tamaki Hajime from Tohoku Imperial.

49. The activities of a group at the Port Arthur College of Technology in Kwantung, for example, are detailed in the [*Gakusei*] *shakai kagaku rengōkai kaihō*, no. 1 (November 25, 1924), p. 3. See also Kikukawa, *Gakusei shakai undō shi*, p. 230.

predictably reluctant to condemn. It chanced that the strike collapsed and the academic summer recess commenced on the same day, so that the Gakuren protest, only just beginning, was left stranded.[50]

The Gakuren was launched into its most energetic era of legal political protest in the fall of 1924 by timely issues that were not only of specific concern to students *as students* but were at the same time linked with the two crucial political themes of militarism and the suppression of political freedom. One issue was the suppression of the higher school *shaken,* a move informally agreed upon at the annual conference of higher school principals in Tokyo in early October and effected in the months following. The problem of suppression itself will be treated in Chapter 7; suffice it to note here that the protest launched by the Gakuren in the winter of 1924–25 through campus rallies, handbill campaigns, and street demonstrations was vigorous and nationwide, although in the end ineffective.

The other issue was compulsory military education in secondary and college-level schools. The Special Council on Education had declared in 1917, "We believe it a matter of great urgency, in view of the present state of national education, that military-style training in schools be promoted so as both to benefit moral training and to contribute to physical education." [51] The council, however, provided no specific plan for implementing the recommendation, which was not acted upon until the summer of 1924, when Minister of Education Okada Ryōhei and Minister of the Army Ugaki Kazushige found themselves in close agreement on a plan to assign active-service army officers to military instruction duties in all schools above the primary level.[52] Several factors were involved in the timing of this decision. The Imperial Army, under Ugaki's direction, was just embarking on a dual program of retrenchment and modernization which involved the retirement of four divisions. This promised to create a surplus of active-service officers who might conveniently be assigned to military instruction. In

50. Kikukawa, *Gakusei shakai undō shi,* pp. 230–245, describes this "student scab incident" in great detail, and probably exaggerates its importance.

51. Kyōikushi hensankai, ed., *Meiji ikō kyōiku seido hattatsu shi,* 12 vols. (Ryūginsha, 1938–39), VIII, 565.

52. Ebihara Haruyoshi, *Zoku gendai Nihon kyōiku seisaku shi* (San'ichi shobō, 1967), p. 97, notes that the plan to introduce military education had actually begun under Minister of Education Kamada Eikichi (1922–23), but no concrete steps appear to have been taken.

addition, the universal conscription requirement of up to two years' service had been the focus of heated protest in recent years, so that the military was well disposed to barter a shortening of the term of service for the institution of military training in secondary schools and in special centers for young men who did not continue beyond elementary school. And finally, the educational authorities, for their part, were at this time becoming concerned over the rapid expansion of the radical student movement, especially at the higher schools, and envisioned compulsory military training as one way of countering left-wing influence.

The details of the plan were worked out in the fall of 1924, and following approval by the Council on Educational Policy, military education was made effective on April 13, 1925.[53] The scheme provided for the inclusion of military training in the physical education program of those state schools where physical education was compulsory, notably middle schools, normal schools, higher schools, and the various types of *semmon gakkō*. Private schools were not legally bound by the ordinance, but participated voluntarily in most cases. Universities were enabled to set up programs of military instruction which would, however, be voluntary—compulsory military training at the university level was not enforced until 1939. When in full effect, the military training program typically included from one to three hours of weekly calisthenics and classroom instruction as well as annual field maneuvers lasting several days.

When the proposed military education plan was revealed in the press in October 1924, the Gakuren leaders acted swiftly, mobilizing the now well-coordinated network of nationwide communication.[54] The center of the movement from the very start was Waseda, which the Military Study Group incident had firmly established as a leader of student antimilitarism. The prediction made by Bunka Dōmei leaders in 1923 that the Military Study Group was merely the first step in the institutionalization of militarism in Japanese education seemed now to have proved correct. The protest movement was launched November 10 with a rally on the Waseda campus, followed two days later

53. For the text of the law, see Kyōiku hensankai, ed., VIII, 568–570.
54. For details of the anti-military education protest, I have followed Kikukawa, *Gakusei shakai undo shi*, pp. 273–281.

by a meeting at Tokyo Imperial of delegates from various Tokyo universities who forthwith organized the National Student Anti-Military Education League (Zenkoku Gakusei Gunji Kyōiku Hantai Dōmei). Although set up in the name of student newspapers and debating clubs, the league was effectively controlled by the Gakuren and coordinated through Gakuren channels. Major demonstrations were held from November through January, sometimes in coordination with the simultaneous protest against higher school *shaken* suppression. January 25, 1925, was declared "Anti-Military Education Day" and observed by major demonstrations on campuses throughout Japan.

The anti-military education movement was frustrated when the plan was officially enforced in April but was revived again, heatedly if only briefly, in the fall of 1925 over a curious incident at the Otaru Higher Commercial School in Hokkaido. There, the army major in charge of military instruction had, on October 15, presented his students with a hypothetical incident as the basis for a discussion of military tactics. Consciously echoing the Kanto earthquake of two years before, the hypothesis envisaged a major earthquake occurring in the Sapporo–Otaru area and causing an "anarchist group" to instigate "disloyal Koreans" to revolt. The students were asked to explain how they might go about "annihilating the enemy." [55] This undisguised vaunting of the massacres of September 1923 was quickly seized upon by the Gakuren affiliate at Otaru Higher Commercial and soon emerged as a national protest issue not only among students but within every area of the left-wing movement. Students saw in the hypothesis incident clear proof that military training was not a means of "spiritual elevation" and "moral training" as its proponents had argued, but was rather being consciously manipulated to breed hostility to the left wing. Less than a week after the incident, Gakuren members presented a statement of protest to the Ministry of Education, which admitted that the hypothesis had been intemperate but refused to consider changes in the overall policy of military education. Throughout the rest of the year, protest demonstrations were waged on a number of campuses, although, as a year earlier, suppression was frequent.

After 1925, military education disappeared as an item of open, formal protest within the Gakuren, which was forced to devote the bulk

55. *Ibid.*, p. 337.

of its energy to countering the wave of suppression that was launched against the student movement beginning with the arrests of the Gakuren leadership in Kyoto in early 1926. The student left by no means abandoned its opposition to military education, however, and the individual *shaken,* notably at the higher schools, persisted in systematic efforts to disrupt and discredit the program of military instruction. Even into the late 1930s it is possible to find evidence of continuing student opposition to military education through boycotting classes and ridiculing instructors.

The Gakuren-coordinated protest movements in the winter of 1924–25 against the military education plan and the suppression of higher school *shaken* provided a laboratory for the newly completed reorganization of the Gakuren, consolidating the chain of command and giving the student leaders useful experience in protest organization. Further, these movements standardized within the arsenal of the student left the various techniques of physical confrontation which have since come to play a central role in the effectiveness of student protest in Japan. On December 17, 1924, for example, a student delegation to the Ministry of Education forced Minister Okada to lock himself in his office for three hours, a tactic commonplace today but novel at the time.[56] Then, on the following January 25, a large street demonstration of students attempting to march to the Diet to block passage of the military education bill was broken up by Tokyo police and several leaders arrested. Again, a familiar story today.

ONE WING OF THE PROLETARIAN MOVEMENT

Campus-based agitation and protests were only the most conspicuous forms of Gakuren activity in the mid-1920s. Just as the early Shinjinkai members had undertaken labor union organization under the slogan "into the people," so radical students under the Gakuren found themselves yearning to participate directly in the "proletarian movement." By early 1924, however, the possibilities had been substantially altered. The redefinition of university radicals as students, while enabling the

56. According to *ibid.,* p. 277, this tactic was known as the "piss torture" (*shōben-zeme*) in the expectation that Okada could not last long without the use of a urinal.

development of new potential in campus-bound protests, at the same time imposed limitations on their role in the labor movement. If students were now to join in the "proletarian" movement, an explicit theoretical framework was needed to define the limits of participation. Furthermore, the great expansion of both the student and labor movements since 1919 demanded a more organized approach than the haphazard and emotional efforts of the earlier "into the people" movement.

Student participation in the labor movement after the earthquake developed in two stages. The one-year period from April 1924 was characterized by the beginning of Gakuren participation in and even control over the labor education movement. Ever since the burgeoning of labor unrest during World War I, both government and industry in Japan had taken steps to promote the further education of adult workers, through the Ministry of Education's Bureau of Social Education (created in 1922), through the Kyōchōkai (Harmonization Society, a joint government-industry-financed institute set up in 1919), and through individual companies. But as the labor movement grew in size and belligerence, a different type of adult education emerged, sponsored by the unions themselves and designed not to pacify the workers but to enlighten them. In 1921 the Japan Labor School was established in Tokyo under Sōdōmei auspices as the first union-sponsored labor education institute in Japan. In the two years following, similar schools were founded in Kobe and Osaka and a second one in Tokyo, but it was not until 1924, in line with the trend of "realism" which dominated the labor movement after the earthquake, that the number of labor schools rapidly increased. In a one-year period from early 1924, fully eight new schools were established in Tokyo and the Kansai area.[57]

In addition to these formal schools, regular educational programs were set up within the individual labor unions, many of which came to have an "education section" to coordinate such activities. The Political Study Society (Seiji Kenkyūkai), which began in June 1924 as an advance organization in anticipation of a working-class political party, also created education courses for its substantial labor membership. At the outset, almost all these efforts at labor education were inspired and directed by middle-class intellectuals and liberal university

57. Nakamura Hideo, ed., *Saikin no shakai undō* (Kyōchōkai, 1929), pp. 941–966.

professors (many of them Christians), who interpreted the project as a type of "university extension" activity. Class consciousness was a far less dominant note in the founding philosophy than a certain philanthropic benevolence, and gradualism was the guiding political ideal. The model was the Workers' Educational Association in England, as reflected not only in a similar commitment to the ideals of political democracy and spiritual fulfillment but also in the frequent use in Japan of English jargon for the techniques and organization of labor education, such as "Dalton plan," "tutorial system," and "case method." [58]

The growth of the labor education movement in 1924 offered an ideal vehicle for students to contribute to the labor movement, and an article by Hayashi Fusao in the June 25 issue of the Gakuren *Bulletin* provided a clear theoretical rationale. "What Kind of Social Group Are Students?" asked the title of the article, and Hayashi answered that students are basically petty bourgeois, although he made a certain allowance for a degree of student proletarization in recent years owing to the effects of the economic depression on the Japanese middle class. The first task of the student movement, then, was to provide systematic instruction in Marxism to its membership in order to rid them of bourgeois attitudes and to "awaken [them] to a proletarian sense of justice." [59]

Hayashi went on to elaborate a second purpose to the student movement of "contributing to the proletarian movement *in those areas which are possible for students,*" and specifically cited the then-emerging labor education movement as one concrete example.[60] Hayashi also extended this duality of *purpose* in the student movement to a duality of *membership.* The bulk of the membership would devote its full time to the assimilation of texts in the study groups in order to overcome bourgeois attitudes, while a "small group with a clear-cut class consciousness and plentiful knowledge" would be charged not only with directing those below them but also with the larger task of "con-

58. See "K" [Kadoya Hiroshi] in Mombushō, Gakuseibu, *Sakei gakusei seito no shuki,* 3 vols. (1934–35), I, 38, and Kikukawa, *Gakusei shakai undō shi,* p. 267.

59. Hayashi Fusao, "Gakusei to wa ikanaru shakaigun de aru ka," quoted in Kikukawa, *Gakusei shakai undō shi,* pp. 251–252.

60. *Ibid.;* italics are in Kikukawa, but not necessarily in the original, which cannot be located.

tributing to the proletarian movement." In other words, those selected for labor education duties would be the elite few who were thoroughly trained in Marxist literature. Hayashi's formulation was accepted as the official theory of the Gakuren at the First Congress in September, and the "promotion of labor education" was adopted as a formal goal of the federation.[61]

Student participation in the labor education movement began in full in the fall of 1924 and continued at a high pitch for over a year until the movement itself began to decline. Students selected for labor education duties within the Gakuren affiliates were systematically dispatched as tutors to the various metropolitan labor schools or sent out to labor unions which had applied for study group instructors. It is difficult to calculate precisely how many students were involved in this activity, which was conducted in such a wide variety of settings, formal and informal; but it may be supposed that about one fourth of the Gakuren membership had at least some experience in tutoring laborers in Marxist theory. Some students became known as experts in certain areas of theory and were in frequent demand as tutors; thus, for example, Shinjinkai member Inamura Junzō gained fame as the leading "expert" on the Marxist theory of state.[62]

Hayashi's theoretical formulation made it clear that the function of the student tutors was not to uplift the workers or make them into responsible voters but rather to foster class consciousness and foment open rebellion. Where the liberal intellectuals who had pioneered the labor education movement looked to the Workers' Educational Association as a model, the young students turned to its radical rival, the Plebs League. In July 1924 the Shinjinkai Book Section was offering subscriptions to the organ of the League, *Plebs,* at three yen ($1.50) a year. In the months following, Eden and Cedar Paul, *Proletcult (Proletarian Culture)* (New York, 1921), explaining the principles of radical "independent working class education," became the standard handbook for Gakuren tutors. Abbreviated as *purokaru,* "Proletcult" became a catchword in radical student jargon and was defined as "the unified revolutionary theory of Leninism, which involves the training of or-

61. *Ibid.,* p. 254.
62. Okada Sōji, "Inamura Junzō no ashiato," *Shakai shugi,* no. 45 (April 1955), p. 4.

ganizers, anti-imperialism, the rejection of opportunism, and a common front of peasants with the urban proletariat."[63] Spiritual uplifting was clearly no goal of this kind of education.

The decline of the labor education movement—especially in the labor schools, which began to fold so rapidly that by 1928 there remained only three in Tokyo of the eight in late 1924—was an ironic indication of the success of the students' efforts at radicalization. By working at odds with the liberal academicians and moderate labor leaders who first began the movement, the students tended to create divisive tensions within the labor schools and to invite reprisals from the government and industry, so that workers attending the classes often found themselves jailed or jobless. Not only did the student tutors tend to counter the thrust of the moderate labor movement and thus abet the growing radical minority, but they helped heighten the emphasis within that minority on intellectualism and theoretical purity.

A new era of Gakuren affiliation with the labor movement began in the spring of 1925. This turn to the left was largely the result of the long-brewing rift in the labor movement which came to a climax in May with the secession of the radical wing of the Sōdōmei to form the Japan Labor Union Council, or Hyōgikai. The students, for their part, had only recently been frustrated by the failure to win any concessions in their energetic protests against military education and the dissolution of higher school study groups. Within the Shinjinkai, a still further radicalizing influence was the graduation in April of a class which was distinguished by its moderation and commitment to campus-related activities. With the notable exception of Shiga Yoshio, the Shinjinkai class of 1925 attended a meeting shortly before graduation to create its own alumni organization, the Kōjinkai (Wayfarer Club), committed to a course to the left of the older Shakai Shisōsha but considerably to the right of the younger Shinjinkai radical mainstream who had entered in 1923.[64]

Freed of the moderate drag of the class of 1925 and eager for a new start, the Shinjinkai greeted the founding of the Hyōgikai with great

63. This is from a Kyoto Imperial Shaken document of October 1925. See Hasegawa, p. 135.

64. Information on the Kōjinkai has been provided me by Ishidō Kiyotomo in personal correspondence, March 8, 1969. See illustration, p. 128, which shows nineteen members.

enthusiasm. The editor of the Shinjinkai *Bulletin* of May noted that "New work is piled up before the Shinjinkai like a mountain. The new excitement in the labor movement means new excitement for us as well. A new line-up for new activity! Prepare for the attack, prepare for the counter-attack. Close ranks, comrades, close ranks!" [65] In the same issue, Koreeda Kyōji, the prize theorist of the Shinjinkai, wrote an article "Thus We Proceed," in which he in effect rebutted Hayashi's formulation of the year before which had seen the student movement as "contributing" to the proletarian movement. No, insisted Koreeda, the student movement is rather organically related to a unitary radical whole, and must now be redefined as "one component element (*ichi kōsei bunshi*) of the proletarian movement." [66] Slightly reworded, this became the basis for the Kanto Council draft of a set of theses to be presented at the Second Congress of the Gakuren on July 16. The Kanto Draft declared that "the student movement must hereafter act as one wing (*ichiyoku*) of the proletarian movement with Marxism–Leninism as its guiding principle." [67] Although a considerably more innocuous version was promulgated as the "official" Second Congress Theses to enable legal publication, the Kanto Draft was secretly accepted by the leadership as the true Gakuren interpretation.[68]

In terms of student participation in the labor movement, "one wing of the proletarian movement" came to mean nothing more nor less than total dedication to the aims and activities of the Hyōgikai and its successor, Zenkyō (1928–1934). Gakuren support for these communist-controlled labor federations was never to falter, although isolated individual members of the student left might occasionally participate in the activities of the Sōdōmei and other federations to the right of the Hyōgikai. Even those students not fully committed to the ideology and methods of Hyōgikai activism tended to be drawn to support it by overwhelming majority pressure. Nakano Shigeharu thus describes the hero of his novel *Muragimo,* Yasukichi—who is actually Nakano him-

65. *Shinjinkai kaihō,* no. 4 (May 1925), p. 24.
66. Nakano-han no otoko [Koreeda Kyōji], "Wareware wa kaku susumu," *Shinjinkai kaihō,* no. 4 (May 1925), pp. 2–6; this article is partially quoted in Kikukawa, *Gakusei shakai undō shi,* pp. 305–306.
67. Hasegawa, pp. 121–122.
68. The published version appeared in *Gakusei shakai kagaku rengōkai kaihō,* no. 3 (October 20, 1925), p. 1.

self—as being very confused upon entering the Shinjinkai, since "they loved the Hyōgikai and hated the Sōdōmei. But Yasukichi had not the slightest idea of how the two differed." And yet shortly after, Yasukichi was to find himself deeply involved in assisting in the first of the Hyōgikai's great strikes, at Amalgamated Printing in Tokyo.[69]

The half year following the Gakuren Second Congress in July 1925 was a period of intensive student activity in concert with the Hyōgikai. It was such activity, especially in Kyoto, that was to provide much of the evidence for the arrest and indictment of the Gakuren leadership under the Peace Preservation Law in December and the months following. In this period, there was a notable shift in the emphasis of student participation from "education" to organization and agitation. The phrase "labor education" was replaced completely by "Proletcult," and the regular study of theoretical texts in labor groups, while by no means eliminated, gave way to much more clear-cut efforts at organization and attempts to breed revolutionary labor leaders.[70] From 1926, Gakuren students were frequently and systematically dispatched to the sites of strikes waged under Hyōgikai auspices. Of the Shinjinkai members, for example, Nakano Shigeharu's participation in the Amalgamated Printing dispute in January 1926 was followed in April by the dispatch of two newly recruited freshmen—one of them, Tateyama Toshitada, was later to become a central leader of the Shinjinkai—to help out in the Japan Musical Instrument Company Strike in Hamamatsu.[71]

How great, one is tempted to ask, was the solidarity of student and laborer in the decade of the Hyōgikai and Zenkyō, from 1925 to 1934? Certainly it was greater than in the era of the early Shinjinkai, which in trying to organize its "personal" labor union betrayed an undue anxiety to assume control in the defense of proletarian interests. By 1925, however, the control of much of the union movement was in the hands of the workers themselves and students were willing to accept

69. Nakano Shigeharu, *Muragimo,* Nihon no bungaku, XLI (Chūō kōron sha, 1967), 188. In the novel, the strike occurs a year later than it did in reality.

70. One of the best examples of such activity was student participation in the founding of the Proletarian Youth League (Musan Seinen Dōmei) in late 1922; see Kikukawa, *Gakusei shakai undō shi,* pp. 327–329.

71. For details, see Tateyama Toshitada, "Nihon Gakki daisōgi to watakushi," *Kikan rōdō,* no. 2 (January 1967), pp. 18–23.

a more humble role in tutorial and clerical capacities. Student-laborer solidarity was preserved and even strengthened in the years following by the gradual intensification of government suppression, which struck both groups alike.

Yet beneath this surface solidarity of worker and student, sustained by the abnormal conditions of intense suppression, lurked a gulf of social class, of privilege, and of education, presenting a constant dilemma for many student activists. One central theme of *Muragimo*, for example, is Yasukichi's constant grappling with the conflicting life styles of student and worker, a dilemma which the conclusion of the novel leaves ambiguous. No matter how humble the attitude of the students who joined them, many workers had good reason to suspect that students, both in jail and out, were treated far more leniently than they themselves. While the late 1920s and early 1930s may have been the period of the closest integration of left-wing student and laborer in modern Japanese history, the fundamental chasm of class antagonism and cultural orientation was rarely bridged in a meaningful way. The claim of the elitist students that they represented "one wing of the proletarian movement" was little more than a fiction of their romantic populism.

Democracy, No. 1, March 1919.

Senku (The Pioneer), No. 1, February 1920.

Dōhō (Brothers), No. 1, October 1920.

Narod, No. 1, July 1921.

The Early Shinjinkai Magazines

The Early Shinjinkai. The student membership of the Shinjinkai posing by the Takada-mura villa at the time of the group's first anniversary in December 1919 with Kawai Masaharu, a worker member from the Shinjinkai's Kanazawa Branch. Left to right: standing, Kawanishi Taichirō, Yamazaki Kazuo, Itō Takeo, Kaji Ryūichi, Kawai Masaharu, Miyazaki Ryūsuke; seated in middle, Kadota Takeo, Shimmei Masamichi, Miwa Jusō; seated in front, Akamatsu Katsumaro, Hayashi Kaname, Taira Teizō. Photo courtesy Miyazaki Ryūsuke.

The Shinjinkai Class of 1925. Known for its moderation, this class organized as the Kōjinkai (Wayfarer Club) just before graduation in March 1925, when this picture was taken near the Yamanoue Goten on the Hongō campus. Left to right: standing, Ozawa Masamoto, Ōyama Hikoichi, Oda Tadao, Uchimura (Ishijima) Harushi, Okabe Ichirō, Asano Akira, Kiyose Saburō, Kitano Seiichi, Fukuma Toshio; seated in middle, Orimoto Toshi, Tsuji Tsunehiko, Ōya Sōichi, Fugono Shinzō, Itō Kōdō, Matsuoka Hatayo; seated in front, Komiya Yoshitaka, Sugino Tadao, Hashimoto (Kaiguchi) Morizō, Hattori Shisō. Photo courtesy Tsuji Tsunehiko.

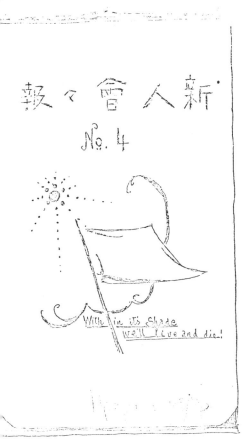

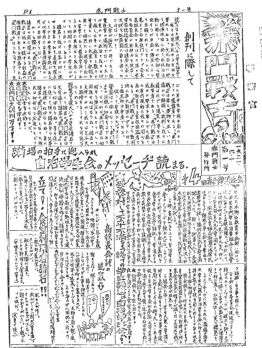

Akamon senshi (The Red Gate Fighter), No. 1, June 1, 1931. Mimeographed weekly organ of the Tokyo University cell of the Communist Youth League, the successor to the Shinjinkai.

Shinjinkai kaihō (The Shinjinkai bulletin), No. 4, c. May 1925, mimeograph.

Underground Student Publications

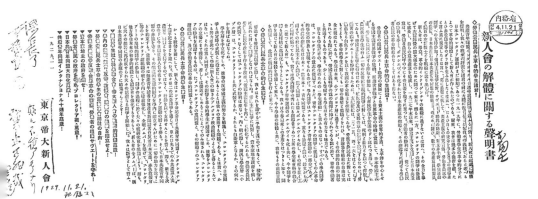

Printed handbill announcing the dissolution of the Shinjinkai in November 1929. The seal on the upper right and the handwritten notations are the work of censors in the Ministry of the Interior, where this copy was preserved.

The Shinjinkai Fiftieth Anniversary Reunion. Held on January 18, 1969, at the Gakushi Kaikan Annex on the Hongō campus of Tokyo University. The former Shinjinkai members appearing in this photograph are: (1) Aoyama Mitsuo, (2) Fugono Shinzō, (3) Hayashi Mutsuo, (4) Hikosaka (formerly Hirata) Takeo, (5) Hoashi Kei, (6) Hompu Ichirō, (7) Ishidō Kiyotomo, (8) Itō Takeo, (9) Iwauchi Zensaku (worker member of the Kameido Branch), (10) Kaiguchi (formerly Hashimoto) Morizō, (11) Kawai Yukichi, (12) Kim Chun-yŏn, (13) Kisamori Kichitarō, (14) Kitano Seiichi, (15) Kudō Eizō, (16) Kurazono Kiyoichi, (17) Masuo (formerly Tsunekawa) Nobuyuki (worker member of the Kameido Branch), (18) Matsuo Takeo, (19) Matsuzawa Kenjin, (20) Miyazaki Ryūsuke, (21) Miyazaki (formerly Kanazawa) Susumu, (22) Moriya Fumio, (23) Murata Fukutarō, (24) Nakanishi Fumio, (25) Nakano Shigeharu, (26) Nasu Tatsuzō, (27) Nishimoto Takashi, (28) Noma (formerly Matsumoto) Shinkichi, (29) Okada Sōji, (30) Ōmura Takeo, (31) Ōya Sōichi, (32) Ozawa Masamoto, (33) Sakamoto Yoshiaki, (34) Sakata Seiichi, (35) Sata Tadataka, (36) Shimmei Masamichi, (37) Soda Takemune, (38) Takayama Yōkichi, (39) Tanahashi Kotora, (40) Tanaka Seigen, (41) Tanaka Toshio, (42) Tanaka Toyonobu, (43) Tateyama Toshitada, (44) Toriumi Tokusuke, (45) Tsunoda Giheiji, (46) Uchida Sakurō, (47) Uchino Sōji, (48) Yamaguchi Tadayuki, (49) Yamauchi Tadayoshi, (50) Yamazaki Kazuo, and (51) Yoshikawa Sancharu. Also present were (52) Itō Yoshiko, the widow of Itō Kōdō, and (53) Nagasaka Seiko, the daughter of Nagasaka Keiichi. The radical student groups at Waseda and Kyoto Imperial were represented by (54) Inamura Ryuichi (Kensetsusha Dōmei), (55) Miyake Shōichi (Kensetsusha Dōmei), (56) Nishiyama (formerly Yamazaki) Yūji (Kyoto Imperial Shaken), (57) Takatsu Seidō (Gyōminkai), (58) Tokano Takeshi (Bunka Dōmei), and (59) Usui Yūzō (Kyoto Imperial Shaken). Other guests included Shinjinkai researchers, among them (60) the author. Photo courtesy Ishidō Kiyotomo.

5 | Shinjinkai Activity on the University Campus, 1923-1928

Street demonstrations and forays into the working class, though dramatic, accounted for far less of the whole of student radicalism in the 1920s than the less conspicuous, localized activity of left-wing students on their campus bases. While off-campus activities were subjected to constant surveillance and harassment, the campus itself was by comparison a sheltered haven—at least until educators began to assume the role of policemen after 1928. The campus was not only protected, it was convenient and manageable, offering the student radicals possibilities of effective organization which were denied them among the proletariat. It was in this arena rather than in the harsh world outside the university that the most lasting contributions of the prewar student movement were to be made. The details provided here refer only to the Shinjinkai, but the types of activities described occurred on campuses throughout Japan in this period, if generally on a less elaborate scale.

THE STUDY OF SOCIAL SCIENCE

The sole *stated* purpose of the Shinjinkai and similar groups in the Gakuren was the "study of social science," a phrase which was only partly a camouflage for political activism: group reading of radical literature was in fact the most systematically enforced and widespread activity of the prewar student left. While off-campus activism was generally limited only to the more daring core elements, study was required for all, and the "study group," or *kenkyūkai*, was the fundamental organizational unit of the student movement. The study groups

131

were the incubators in which radical leaders were hatched and nurtured; they were the "trenches" from which the students launched their offensive.[1] Because study groups were small and inconspicuous, surveillance was difficult, and the form survived long after other modes of activity had been suppressed.

The "study group," a small circle which gathered weekly for discussion of assigned texts, was a natural format. The habit of reading was valued highly by the intellectual elite of a nation which was already one of the most literate in the world, and the stress within the educational curriculum on language, both native and foreign, reinforced the habit. The tedium of impersonal lecture-style education further encouraged inquisitive students to devise their own programs of study to satisfy the strong "appetite for reading" (dokushoyoku) which has always been a common trait of the Japanese student left. Study groups for the digestion and discussion of new ideas had been common among reform-minded Japanese for long before the emergence of the "social science study group" after 1923. The initial membership of the Shinjinkai, for example, had been drawn largely from two small study groups, one which carried out research on universal suffrage under Yoshino Sakuzō, and one which met periodically at Asō's house to discuss socialism and the Russian Revolution. In the same period, the cliques which developed around the Meiji socialist veterans often devoted their meetings to the study of selected texts. Because of the lack of ideological consensus and a reliance on undirected enthusiasm in those years, however, study groups tended to be informal and irregular; the dominant approach to foreign texts was rather translation and research on an individual basis.

But by 1924, when "the study of social science"—a phrase popularized by Ōyama Ikuo [2]—became the catchword of the student movement, the pattern had greatly changed. Study came to be seen not as a tool for spreading the good word through translation and exhortation but rather as a technique of assimilation aimed at changing individual attitudes. Theoretical writings of the Shinjinkai leaders in the spring of 1924 argued along Marxist–Leninist lines that only through intense

1. The image of the study groups as trenches was used by the students themselves; see *Gakusei shakai kagaku rengōkai kaihō*, no. 3 (October 20, 1925), p. 4.
2. Kikukawa, *Gakusei shakai undō shi*, p. 254.

study and mastery of specific texts could each student overcome his petty bourgeois class character and attain a true "proletarian consciousness." The process, the students were warned, would require long hours and much sacrifice, for bourgeois attitudes are not to be shed overnight.[3] Although clad in Marxist terminology, this process seemed not unlike the attainment of enlightenment through Zen Buddhist meditation. By diligent effort, constant introspection, and ceaseless reading of the prescribed texts, the neophyte at the temple of Marxism would step by step cast off his bourgeois attitudes and at last attain the *satori* of proletarian consciousness.

The development of systematic study group programs was facilitated by the ever-increasing availability and range of radical literature. Foreign books, the raw material to be translated, absorbed, and applied, were imported with such regularity that Japanese readers might have them not long after their European or American publication. The inflation of the German mark in 1922–23 had enabled the import of quantities of low-cost left-wing literature in German which was quickly bought up by Gakuren students.[4] From America came the cheap and copious pamphlet literature of Charles H. Kerr, Inc., in Chicago, and from England the Marxist texts prescribed for reading courses by the Communist Party of Great Britain. Japanese government censors were apparently unconcerned with much of this literature, which was sold openly to eager students at all major bookstores specializing in Western books, such as Maruzen or Shirokiya, as well as many smaller ones. From about 1924 considerable quantities of Comintern literature began to enter Japan through Germany, and although much of it was officially banned by the censors, students had little trouble procuring it. Shinjinkai member Ishidō Kiyotomo relates that Kyōmeisha, a small bookstore adjacent to the university campus, which from the outside seemed one of dozens of innocuous textbook stores, had a back room full of Comintern literature for those interested.[5] In such stores, the

3. K. T. [Kiire Toratarō?], "Gakusei undō to kojin no nimmu," *Shinjinkai kaihō,* no. 3 (July 1, 1924), p. 35.

4. Takano Minoru in Tōkyō daigaku shimbunsha henshūbu, ed., *Haiiro no seishun,* p. 23. It was also the inflation of the mark that allowed such Japanese students in Germany as Fukumoto Kazuo to build up huge collections of Marxist literature.

5. Ishidō Kiyotomo, "Kōki no Shinjinkai," *Rōdō undō shi kenkyū,* no. 16 (July 1959), p. 36.

Comintern's English-language organ, *International Press Correspondence*, and a wide range of Marxist literature, largely in German, was made available to the students.

Translations likewise proliferated in the mid-1920s, gradually expanding the small base which had been laid by such pioneering translators as the Meiji socialists and the early Shinjinkai members. Although translations were treated by censors much more severely than the foreign originals (doubtless from fear of the proletarian audience which vernacular editions might reach), the literature of Marxism in Japanese grew steadily, and left-wing translations began to evolve as a distinctive and flourishing segment of the publishing world. Such well-established liberal publishers as Kaizōsha and Dōjinsha were now joined by a host of smaller and more radical firms like Hakuyōsha, Kibōkaku, Musansha, and Kyōseikaku, the proprietors of which were motivated in varying proportions by political commitment and the lure of profits. By about 1926 the literature of Marxism in translation had grown to the point that comprehensive, multi-volume collections of the Marxist classics were feasible. Earliest was the ten-volume *Writings of Lenin* (*Rēnin chosakushū*, Hakuyōsha, 1925–27), in the translation of which a number of young Shinjinkai members participated. This was followed by the sixteen volumes of the *Collected Works of Stalin and Bukharin* (*Sutārin-Buhārin chosakushū*, Hakuyōsha, 1928–30), but the greatest achievement of all was Kaizōsha's *Collected Works of Marx and Engels* (*Marukusu–Engerusu zenshū*), published over a period of six years from 1928 to reach a final total of twenty-seven volumes. Most of the work of translation for this project was undertaken by the members of the Shakai Shisōsha, the early Shinjinkai alumni group.[6]

A third major segment of the expanding array of left-wing publications was a continuous stream of periodical and pamphlet literature in Japanese. Unlike the foreign-language imports and the translations of Marxist classics, which were aimed primarily at intellectuals and usually sold for profit, this type of literature was propaganda directed at specific interest groups. Every left-wing political organization, no mat-

6. For various translations of Western communist literature, see Watanabe Yoshimichi and Shiota Shōbei, eds., *Nihon shakai shugi bunken kaisetsu* (Ōtsuki shoten, 1958), and Moriya Fumio, *Nihon marukusu shugi riron no keisei to hatten* (Aoki shoten, 1967), pp. 42–43.

ter how minute its following, attempted to publish a periodical organ, whether magazine or newspaper, so that the total number of such publications was enormous, although few lasted for more than a year, succumbing with confusing frequency to government suppression, financial difficulties, and factional squabbling. The bulk was undisguised propaganda and of little use for the study-group reading of students, who demanded more meaty, sophisticated fare. Around 1924 the demand was partly satisfied by such intellectual-oriented magazines as *Shakai shisō* or Kawakami Hajime's *Shakai mondai kenkyū,* but these were soon rejected as the hold of orthodox Marxism–Leninism tightened. By the late 1920s, the only periodicals approved for student study-group reading were the theoretical organs of the Japanese Communist Party and its front groups.

In the middle 1920s, most of the left-wing literature available to students was theoretical, dealing with the abstract principles of Marxism and confining pragmatic discussions to the description of Western models. Except for tactical disputations among left-wing leaders, the systematic application of Marxist theory to the Japanese situation began only in the late 1920s but then went on to become a flourishing (if often sterile) pastime in the 1930s. Complex theoretical battles were waged within the format of the "symposia" (*kōza*), multivolume projects by groups of Japanese scholars aimed at supporting fixed interpretations of the Japanese situation and its historical development. This body of literature provided the radical student study groups with still another source of provocative reading material; such texts, however, came into frequent use only after 1928, in the underground era of the prewar student movement. Before that time, most of the attention was devoted to the study of foreign classics rather than native interpretations.

So important were books to the life of the student left that the Shinjinkai in late 1923 established a Book Section (*shosekibu,* later *toshobu*) within its organization to facilitate and coordinate the acquisition of study materials. "If the Education Section [in charge of study group organization] is the heart of the Shinjinkai," claimed Book Section chief Orimoto Toshi in July 1924, "then the Book Section is the lungs, always sending forth new oxygen." He went on to report discounts not only on new books but on subscriptions to magazines both domestic (*Shakai shisō, Shakai shugi kenkyū,* and *Marxism,* for example) and foreign, including a number of British communist periodicals. Plans were also being made, Orimoto noted, to join the socialist literature cooperative of Charles H. Kerr, Inc.[7] The work of the Book Section was assumed in 1925 by Ishidō Kiyotomo, who tells of a booming business not only in supplying members with a wide assortment of reading (even obligingly filling orders for banned books) but in openly purveying Marxist literature to nonmembers as well. On one occasion, he recalls, the Book Section bought up three hundred pocket-sized copies of the *Communist Manifesto* (in English), and managed to sell the whole lot, at ten sen (5¢) a copy, in a single evening by canvassing the barrack dormitories on the university campus.[8]

THE SHINJINKAI READING PROGRAMS

The Shinjinkai inaugurated a systematic program of study group activity in early 1924, marking the beginning of the coordinated assimilation of Marxism in the Japanese student movement. The *Shinjinkai Bulletin* for July 1924 made note of six different study groups which had been in progress the preceding term. Typical was one led by Shinjinkai alumnus Tanaka Kyūichi, who was then a researcher at the East Asian Economic Research Bureau in Tokyo, on Borchardt's *The People's Marx,* a popular introduction to Marxism. The group met every Friday night and discussed two chapters a session, with attendance varying between twelve and twenty-two.[9] From the fall term, the study groups were rationalized along geographical lines and each member was required to attend the one within his area. The *Bulletin* for the spring of 1925 reported seven different study groups, six of which were held in the evening in different areas of Tokyo and a seventh in midday on the campus for those unable to make the evening classes.[10]

In 1924, when study group activity was just beginning both in the Shinjinkai and in *shaken* on other campuses, the reading was not yet

7. *Shinjinkai kaihō,* no. 3 (July 1, 1924), pp. 16–17.
8. Ishidō, "Kōki no Shinjinkai," p. 36.
9. *Shinjinkai kaihō,* no. 3 (July 1, 1924), pp. 6–7.
10. *Shinjinkai kaihō,* no. 4 (May 1925), pp. 22–23. The Honjo group was for students at the Teidai Settlement there.

uniformly Marxist–Leninist by Comintern definitions, and deviations such as the Borchardt introduction or works of the nineteenth-century German socialist philosopher Joseph Dietzgen were frequently encountered.[11] By the time of the Second Congress of the Gakuren in July 1925, however, reading was strictly limited to Comintern-approved texts, focusing on the classics of Marx, Engels, and Lenin and a number of introductions and elaborations by Soviet Marxists. The catholicity of the early Shinjinkai was a distant memory, and Russian communism, which had once been a single interest among many, now became orthodoxy. A few within the Shinjinkai continued to nurture personal interests in social democracy, anarchism, or revisionism but only outside the formal study groups and at the risk of harsh censure from the mainstream.

The most widely used introduction to communism in the study groups of the Shinjinkai and other Gakuren affiliates was Bukharin and Preobrazhensky, *The ABC of Communism*, which provided a thorough summary of the theoretical principles of Marxism–Leninism. This book was viewed with apprehension by the government authorities, and could only be read in secretly imported German or English editions. (A translation was finally produced in 1929 but was immediately banned.)[12] After this primer normally came the standard assortment of basic introductory Marxist classics: *The Communist Manifesto*, Engels' *Socialism: Utopian and Scientific*, Marx's *Wage, Price, and Profit*, and Lenin's *Imperialism* and *State and Revolution*. By 1924 all these works were available in Japanese translation and appeared without exception on any reading list of the study groups. From about 1925 Stalin's *The Fundamentals of Leninism* came to be added to this standard assortment.

Together with the introductory classics were prescribed a number of works by Soviet writers, such as Bukharin, *Historical Materialism*, or Bogdanoff, *A Short Course in Economic Science* (the latter was first used in an English edition but was soon translated into Japanese by Shinjinkai member Hayashi Fusao). With the emergence of communist

11. *Shinjinkai kaihō*, no. 5 (December 1925), p. 11.
12. This translation was by the Marukishizumu kenkyūjo (Marxist Research Institute), published by Isukurakaku. See Odagiri Hideo and Fukuoka Iyoshi, eds., *Shōwa shoseki, shimbun, zasshi hakkin nempyō*, 4 vols. (Meiji bunken, 1965–67), I, 77.

theorist Fukumoto Kazuo as a dominant influence in the student movement in 1926 (described in the following chapter), the emphasis in student reading programs shifted slightly. Fukumoto's own writings, both his articles in *Marxism* and his full-length books, were assigned as regular study group readings. Also, largely as a result of Fukumoto's own theories, certain classic works emerged in a place of new importance, most notably Lenin's *What Is to Be Done?*, which was virtually unknown in Japan before 1925. Fukumoto's exhortation to turn to intensive textual study of the Marxist classics also encouraged many students to proceed from introductory pamphlet literature to more substantial fare. The ultimate in this direction was *Capital*, which despite its immense difficulty was occasionally tackled in study groups with the aid of the Japanese translation by Takabatake Motoyuki and a handbook by Kawakami Hajime. Few made real progress save a handful aspiring to economic research as a profession, but *Capital* nevertheless has since remained the most revered, if least read, of the Marxist classics in Japan.

While the Marxist classics were the heart of the reading programs, later Marxist theorists were by no means prohibited and evoked serious interest among a minority of the student left. Prominent were Lukács, Varga, Deborin, and Rosa Luxemburg, the writings of whom were translated and widely read. These were specialized interests, however, limited to individual students or to small groups and were never accepted as standard material. In the study group reading programs, Marxism–Leninism in its classical theoretical form was considered the only conceivable starting point, and foreign texts the only acceptable channel through which it might be absorbed.

Since the assimilation of the standard texts was seen as a technique for instilling class consciousness, the method of conducting study groups was fully as important as the correct texts. Study group leadership was generally undertaken by senior members, who, it was prescribed, "must realize that left-wing education in its essence is revolutionary education." [13] But in fact, these "central elements" in charge of the study groups were often more preoccupied with their own pedantry than with the bourgeois attitudes of their charges. The heavily theoretical thrust of the prescribed texts made for tedious discus-

13. Hasegawa, pp. 125–26.

sions, and the difficulty of foreign-language editions worked to promote more confusion than enlightenment. Nakano Shigeharu tells of being utterly lost in study groups where unfamiliar words like *Kadett* or *Hegemonie* were bandied about.[14] The combination of tedium and difficulty worked to make lax attendance a constant problem of the study group leaders. Although the Shinjinkai by-laws provided that "members who fail without good reason to participate in the functions of the group for two continuous months will be expelled," study group attendance was erratic.[15] Yet in the long run, the study groups, whatever the discrepancies between the theory and practice of their operation, performed the critical function of establishing the communal reading of prescribed Marxist texts as the core of radical student activity, a pattern that has remained largely unchanged since.

LURING THE SYMPATHETIC

The "educational" efforts of the Shinjinkai extended beyond the closed study groups to systematic attempts at luring sympathetic nonmembers into the radical sphere of influence. These sympathizers were interpreted as petty bourgeois "liberals" with a nascent social consciousness which made them highly sensitive to political agitation. Whereas the Shinjinkai itself never grew beyond 3 percent of the total student body, these "liberals" were estimated at about one third of all students and were indispensable to the Shinjinkai itself, both as a reservoir for future membership and as partners for the creation of a common front on specific issues. The liberals were seen less as rivals than as radicals-to-be, needing only to be shown the way. They were at a stage of intellectual development through which most of the Shinjinkai members themselves had once passed, a stage characterized by an interest in religion, philosophy, and literature. The task of the Shinjinkai was to deflect their concerns from the ultimate to the immediate, from melancholy contemplation to belligerent activism, from literature to politics, from self to society.

One obvious means of gaining influence over the liberal segment of

14. Nakano Shigeharu, *Muragimo*, p. 188.

15. *Shinjinkai kaihō*, no. 4 (May 1925), p. 20, notes that a Section Committee meeting of February 9 decided to send warnings to those members who had been lax in study group attendance, suggesting that this was a major problem.

the student body was to work through the extracurricular organizations where they tended to congregate. Such conscious "fraction" activity [16] was begun in late 1923, when the "anti-leadership faction" won control of the Shinjinkai and launched a program of campus-oriented activism. Special cells were assigned to specific organizations and charged with developing them both as source of Shinjinkai membership and as independent political forces on campus.[17] Three organizations were of special interest to the Shinjinkai in its efforts to lure the sympathetic: the Debating Club, the *Imperial University News,* and the Teidai Settlement.

The Debating Club was a natural area of concern, since many of the Shinjinkai members themselves, beginning with the three founders, had received their political baptism as student orators. As many as one half of all Shinjinkai members had been active in higher school debating societies, although upon reaching the university they soon moved on to more radical pursuits.[18] The university Debating Club (which in 1920 had been broadened from the Faculty of Law to interested students of all faculties) posed the same problem which the Shinjinkai founders had faced in the fall of 1918, in its tendency to attract conservative as well as liberal elements (in addition to a fair number of romantic literary types given to declaiming on such topics as "The Cry of the Soul" or "The Red Sun Rises over the Endless Green Plains").[19] Since the literary-minded were hard to politicize and the conservatives were hostile to any overt political moves by Shinjinkai infiltrators, it

16. The term "fraction" is used in two very different senses in communist jargon. It sometimes refers (usually in the form "fractional" or "fractionalism") to the organization of a group within the communist party in opposition to the party line; this is of course a proscribed activity. The term is also used, however, to indicate a party member charged with infiltrating and radicalizing a noncommunist group, such as a trade union; this is an approved activity. In Japan, the word "fraction" appears to have been used only in this latter sense.

17. Of the original nine sections of the Shinjinkai in late 1923, six were in charge of such infiltration, covering the barrack dormitories, the Teidai Settlement, the consumer union movement, the *Imperial University News,* the Debating Club, and the Tōdai Shaken. See *Shinjinkai kaihō,* no. 1 (December 1923), p. 7.

18. The only available documentation for higher school debating experience of Shinjinkai members is for Third Higher alumni; out of thirty-four members from that school, twenty had been in the debating club, based on the list in Andō, ed., *Daisan kōtō gakkō benrombu bushi.* The proportion was considerably greater in the case of the early Shinjinkai (82 percent) than later (48 percent), suggesting the declining popularity of debating among student radicals.

19. *Teikoku daigaku shimbun,* no. 149 (January 11, 1926), p. 2.

was difficult to sustain constant control over the club.[20] The Shinjinkai nevertheless maintained a number of members in the Debating Club, taking advantage of the platform which it offered in on-campus debates and provincial lecture tours. The club also proved useful as a legitimate front through which liberal causes might be developed: in the anti-military education movement of 1924–25, for example, major on-campus rallies were held under the auspices of the Debating Club rather than the Shinjinkai.

The *Imperial University News* (*Teikoku daigaku shimbun*) was also a logical area of activity, since it offered an effective and legitimate mouthpiece for reaching the majority of students. The *News* had been created in December 1920 as a private, off-campus venture of three young alumni who envisioned a need to improve communication both among the students of separate faculties and between students and alumni.[21] A major stimulus for this project had been the inability of students in the Morito Incident earlier the same year to coordinate an effective inter-faculty protest. While the founders tended to be liberal, they were far from radical: all had been dedicated athletes and defined their mission as one of sustaining school spirit rather than of pressing reform.

For over two years, the *Imperial University News* remained a monthly tabloid filled with old-style sentimental essays. Gradually, however, as students with more journalistic than literary instincts came to edit the paper, it took on a progressive, news-oriented coloring, increasing in frequency to a weekly and in size to standard newspaper format. From the spring of 1923, Shinjinkai members began to join the *News* with the conscious mission of forging it into an organ of campus liberalism.

20. Conflicts between right and left seem to have been common in the Debating Club; see, for example, Kawamura, *Shisō mondai nempyō*, p. 68.

21. The three founders were Azuma Ryōtarō (from 1959 until 1967 governor of Tokyo), Kubo Kanzaburō, and Nagai Ryōkichi. For the history of the *Imperial University News*, see: "Honshi no jūgonen," *Teikoku daigaku shimbun*, no. 602 (December 4, 1935), pp. 57–58; "Honshi no ayumi—Sōkan kara konnichi made," *Teikoku daigaku shimbun*, no. 250 (April 30, 1928), pp. 3–5 (this valuable source includes the recollections of some thirty former editors, including many Shinjinkai members); Tokyo daigaku shimbunsha henshūbu, ed., *Haiiro no seishun* (this is a collection of reminiscences, mostly by former editors of the *News;* those by Matsuura Kenzō and Ozawa Masamoto contain details on Shinjinkai ties with the newspaper); Suzuki Tōmin, "Demokurashii no reimei," in Gakusei shobō henshūbu, ed., *Watakushi no gakusei no koro*, 3 vols. (Gakusei shobō, 1948), III, 62–77.

The *News* was a tempting target for manipulation, for it enjoyed both financial stability—thanks to its advertising appeal, especially among textbook publishers—and a degree of freedom from censorship not enjoyed by the regular commercial press.

By January 1924 Shinjinkai members occupied fully eight of the fifteen positions on the editorial staff of the *Imperial University News*.[22] Although this ratio dropped slightly over the next several years, the Shinjinkai continued to maintain substantial influence within the newspaper, which was consistently favorable towards the student left. Shinjinkai influence worked to establish in the *Imperial University News* a liberal tradition which was to continue well into the war years, long after all radical publications had been suppressed and most liberal ones cowed into restraint from criticism of government policy. The majority of Shinjinkai members active on the *News* were motivated less by an urge to foment rebellion than by a genuine interest in journalism. The down-to-earth skepticism required of professional journalists set them apart from the wild-eyed radicals at the core of the Shinjinkai, and it is no coincidence that not one of some twenty Shinjinkai members who served as editors of the *News* ever entered the Japanese Communist Party.[23]

The Tokyo Imperial University Settlement (Tōkyō Teikoku Daigaku Setsurumento, commonly abbreviated "Teidai Settlement") was the third major area of Shinjinkai activity in extracurricular groups. The settlement project was conceived in the wake of the Kanto earthquake by Professor Suehiro Izutarō, who had been impressed by English university settlements when studying in Europe. Curiously enough, it was Suehiro who had been responsible for leading Asō's clique into the working-class district of Tsukishima in 1918 when he chose Yamana to assist him on a government survey of laborer health conditions.[24] Now, five years later, he provided the opportunity for a new generation of students to enter "into the people." Almost all the legwork in the

22. A list of the newspaper staff appears in *Teikoku daigaku shimbun*, no. 62 (January 2, 1924), p. 3.
23. This number is based on a membership list of the alumni club of editorial board members, Ichō Kurabu, ed., *Ichō Kurabu kaiin meibo* (editor, 1967).
24. Tanahashi relates that Suehiro had originally wished to locate the 1918 health survey project in Honjo, which appealed to him as the most oppressed working class district in Tokyo, but was persuaded by Tanahashi to choose Tsukishima. Thus Suehiro's affinity for Honjo was satisfied in the Teidai Settlement. Tanahashi interview.

actual organization of the settlement was done by Shinjinkai members as a continuation of earthquake relief work which they had directed. The initial funding of the settlement was provided by money donated by the Tokyo city government in appreciation of the student relief efforts. Still further funds were produced by a delegation of Shinjinkai students who toured Kyushu with Suehiro under the grandiose banner of "Student League for the Restoration of Education in the Capital," showing the movie *Robin Hood* (an American version starring Douglas Fairbanks) to raise money for rebuilding Tokyo.[25]

In the months following the earthquake, Shinjinkai member Uchimura Harushi directed the efforts to win support for the settlement project and to choose an appropriate location. The site finally selected was located in the Yanagishima district of Honjo ward, close to the celluloid factories where early Shinjinkai members had tried their hand at labor organization. (Uchimura, incidentally, enjoyed a twofold success in his search for a settlement site, since he managed to marry the landlord's daughter, becoming an adopted son and taking his present name of Ishijima.) [26] The construction of the main settlement house was completed on June 6, 1924, and operations began immediately. Like the English and American social settlements after which it was modeled, the Teidai Settlement served a wide range of community needs, including adult education programs, a medical clinic, a small library, and an orphanage.[27]

The settlement was of importance to the Shinjinkai not only as a channel through which to recruit new membership but especially as a setting in which the members could work directly with the poor and oppressed whose cause they had undertaken. The Teidai Settlement Labor School, which was opened in the fall of 1924 and soon became the largest and most successful of all the left-wing labor schools in Tokyo, served as the center of the Shinjinkai efforts to turn laborers into class-conscious political activists through the techniques of "Proletcult." The free medical clinic operated by the Teidai Settlement was

25. The classic account of this episode is Hayashi Fusao, "Robin fuddo jiken," *Shinchō*, 26.9 (September 1929), 2–16, which also provides interesting information on the founding of the settlement. See also Kikukawa, *Gakusei shakai undō shi*, p. 192.

26. Asano Akira interview.

27. For the history and activities of the Teidai Settlement, see Ōmori Toshio, ed., *Tōkyō teikoku daigaku setsurumento jūninenshi* (Tōkyō teikoku daigaku setsurumento, 1937).

the chief area of activity for the ten-odd medical students who were Shinjinkai members. The settlement buildings were also convenient in providing a physical setting for Shinjinkai meetings and study group sessions.

Of the first hundred "settlers" in the Teidai Settlement, over thirty were members of the Shinjinkai, and many more Shinjinkai members are known to have paid occasional visits to the Yanagishima project.[28] The settlement served as an important outlet for the continuing urge of young intellectuals to associate with working people. Since the Teidai Settlement was created with substantial government backing as well as the support of many prominent Tokyo citizens and university alumni, it enjoyed a degree of prestige and financial stability that enabled it to survive and expand in years when similar projects were forced into bankruptcy. After the collapse of all radical student organizations in the middle 1930s, however, the Teidai Settlement increasingly became a haven for the student left and consequently the target of police suppression. In the wake of a series of arrests of students active in the settlement, it was ordered disbanded by the Ministry of Education in February 1939, after almost fifteen years of activity.

Beyond such undercover activities within extracurricular organizations, the Shinjinkai conducted considerable overt propaganda on the university campus in its own name. Most notable were open lectures, in effect a continuation of the early Shinjinkai institution of an "academic lecture series." The group sponsored over twenty major lectures in the period from its revival in 1923 until its dissolution as a recognized campus group in 1928, almost all of which were well attended (if the reports in the pro-Shinjinkai *Imperial University News* can be trusted). The lectures typically featured three speakers, of whom one would be a Shinjinkai member, another a senior academic figure, and a third perhaps a labor leader or progressive literary figure. Former Shinjinkai members, who remained in contact as "Friends of the Shinjinkai" (*kaiyū*, a type of honorary membership),[29] frequently appeared to speak on campus.

28. This is based on the list in *ibid.*, p. 233.
29. The *kaiyū* system was set up in December 1923 and is mentioned throughout the first issue of the *Shinjinkai kaihō*, the major purpose of which was contact with the *kaiyū*.

The academics who spoke at Shinjinkai lectures ranged from mild liberals to dedicated Marxists. Among the most radical was a trio of brilliant young Tokyo Imperial assistant professors known as the "Three Tarō" (Hirano Yoshitarō in law, and Ōmori Yoshitarō and Yamada Moritarō in economics),[30] all of whom were later to be purged from the university as communist sympathizers, Ōmori in 1928 and the other two in 1930. While popular, however, these men had less influence than more moderate figures such as Ōyama Ikuo and Morito Tatsuo. Ōyama spoke under Shinjinkai auspices on the Tokyo Imperial campus several times in the mid-1920s and was always greeted with tremendous enthusiasm. Morito, after serving a brief prison term for his article on Kropotkin, traveled abroad for over two years and returned in 1923 to settle down to a quiet life of scholarship at the Ōhara Social Problems Research Institute (Ōhara Shakai Mondai Kenkyūjo) in Osaka.[31] He lectured at the Shinjinkai's fifth and sixth anniversary celebrations in 1924 and 1925, stirring such a response that the speeches were later published in article, then in book form.[32]

A single example, but a striking one, of the Shinjinkai success at luring the uncommitted through such public lectures is offered by the case of a third-year law student named Ozaki Hotsumi, who in December 1924 was among the many non-Shinjinkai "liberals" attending Morito's lecture entitled "Thought and Struggle."[33] Ozaki was deeply impressed by Morito's eloquent insistence that man, in his search for truth, is forced to *struggle* with authority. Although Morito did qualify his "struggle" as one which would be "mainly in the realm of concepts,"[34] the tone of his talk was mildly anarchistic, as suggested by the later retitling upon publication as *An Appeal to Young Students*—a conscious echo of Kropotkin's famed *An Appeal to the Young*. Almost twenty years later, while awaiting execution following

30. Ishidō, "Kōki no Shinjinkai," p. 38.

31. For Morito's ties with the Ōhara Institute, see [Hōsei daigaku] Ōhara shakai mondai kenkyūjo, ed., *Ōhara shakai mondai kenkyūjo sanjūnen shi* (editor, 1954), *passim*.

32. The article forms appeared in *Kaizō* in January 1925 and February 1926. The pamphlet publications were as *Seinen gakuto ni uttou* (Kaizōsha, 1925) and *Gakusei to seiji* (Kaizōsha, 1926).

33. For a report on the lecture itself, see *Teikoku daigaku shimbun*, no. 100 (December 15, 1924), p. 2.

34. Morito, *Seinen gakuto ni uttou*, p. 58.

his conviction as a Soviet spy, Ozaki was to recall the impact of Morito's advocacy of "struggle" upon his decision to embark on the course which led eventually to communism and espionage.[35]

In addition to such formal endeavors at propaganda, Shinjinkai members were constantly striving to win converts on an individual basis by persuasion and argument, since the personal influence of a higher school classmate or old hometown friend was the most common factor in leading students to join the Shinjinkai (except for those who had been active at higher school and automatically entered the group upon reaching Tokyo). One highly productive setting for such agitation on a personal level was the barrack dormitory complex which had been constructed after the 1923 earthquake destroyed many of the private boarding houses in the university area. One room in the dormitories served in late 1923 as the temporary Shinjinkai headquarters, and there Kikukawa Tadao, an acknowledged master of persuasion, would gather unsuspecting students around the hibachi on a chill evening, catch their interest with a bawdy tale or two, and then shift deftly to the political education of the innocents. Not a few "liberals" were lured into the Shinjinkai in this way.[36]

Shaken: The Scholarly Front of the Shinjinkai

The Social Science Study Club at Tokyo Imperial, known as the Tōdai Shaken, was unique in that, unlike the *shaken* at most other schools, it served not as the vehicle for the radical vanguard of the campus left but merely as a front for that vanguard.[37] The Tōdai Shaken

35. See Misuzu shobō, ed., *Zoruge jiken*, 3 vols., Gendaishi shiryō, vols. I–III (editor, 1962), II, 6–7. I am indebted for this reference to Chalmers Johnson, *An Instance of Treason—Ozaki Hotsumi and The Sorge Spy Ring* (Stanford, 1964), p. 32, which however exaggerates in saying that Ozaki could repeat Morito's words "almost verbatim eighteen years later." Johnson's statement on p. 29 that Ozaki was a Shinjinkai member is also erroneous; this has been confirmed in interviews by numerous Shinjinkai members who knew Ozaki personally, including Shiga Yoshio, Taira Teizō, and Asano Akira. Ozaki did, however, attend various of the open Shinjinkai meetings, of which Morito's lecture was one.
36. See Asano Akira, "Tōdai jidai no Kikukawa-kun," in Kikukawa Tadao tsuitō shuppan iinkai, ed., *Kikukawa Tadao—Sono shisō to jissen* (editor, 1956), p. 4. Asano mentions Katsuki Shinji as one of those "educated" by Kikukawa.
37. Such a system existed briefly at other schools but was certainly exceptional.

was first proposed in May 1923 as part of the Gakuyūkai reform plan sponsored by the Shinjinkai and was formally established in November of that year.[38] The Shinjinkai had largely conceived and was totally to dominate Shaken, but no direct organizational links existed between the two groups. Although many (if not most) of the Shinjinkai members participated at some time in Shaken, only a minority of the total Shaken membership was simultaneously in the Shinjinkai. Entrance to the Shinjinkai was limited to those with the proper attitude and adequate introductions, but any interested students could participate in Shaken without obligation. For this reason, Shaken was considerably larger than the Shinjinkai and probably exceeded three hundred at its peak.[39]

Because Shaken was conceived by the Shinjinkai as a front group to bring uncommitted students into the sphere of political radicalism through the device of scholarship, the term "social science" in this case had a wider meaning than "Marxism–Leninism" as in the Gakuren-affiliated *shaken* on other campuses.[40] The Tōdai Shaken was organized into a fluctuating number of independent study groups corresponding to the various academic specialties of the students throughout the university, such as law, economics, political science, sociology, literature, agriculture, medicine, and engineering. This system gave the Shinjinkai, through its domination of Shaken, an opportunity for the systematic spread of radical influence far beyond its central base in the faculties of law and economics.

The Shaken study groups were not necessarily Marxist, especially in the first year, 1924–25, when one finds Yoshino Sakuzō (who resigned as a professor in early 1924 but remained affiliated with the university as a lecturer) leading one discussion group on Meiji political history and medical professor Nishi Seiho another on the theory of evolu-

For one documented example, that of the Mito Higher Shaken, see Sugiura, ed., *Aru seishun no kiroku*, pp. 31–32.

38. *Teikoku daigaku shimbun*, no. 59 (November 29, 1923), p. 2.

39. Estimates of Shaken size are difficult, since students did not formally join the group, but merely participated in one of its study sessions. The figure of three hundred is my own estimate based on the testimony of many former Shinjinkai members.

40. Kikukawa, *Gakusei shakai undō shi*, p. 268, flatly asserts that " 'social science' was merely another name for the scientific system of Marxism."

tion.[41] From the spring of 1925, however, younger and more radical teachers become conspicuous as leaders of the Shaken groups, men such as the popular "Three Tarō" or Rikkyō professor Kawanishi Taichirō, a former Shinjinkai member who often led a Shaken study group on agricultural problems. But while the emphasis in Shaken came eventually to be predominantly Marxist, it was less on Marxist–Leninist political education as in the Shinjinkai study groups than on the use of Marxist techniques for the scholarly analysis of specialized interests. Hence the literature group might read Plekhanov and Lunacharsky on Marxist esthetics and the farm problems group might study Kautsky's *Socialization of Agriculture*, but such openly political tracts as the *ABC of Communism* were rarely found in Shaken reading lists.[42]

The Tōdai Shaken served as a device for the spread of Marxist influence among the scholarly oriented liberals and was useful to the Shinjinkai in winning a number of new members, although the great majority of Shaken study group participants never made the decisive shift from theory to action. Of greater importance was Shaken's role in spreading the academic influence of Marxism beyond its stronghold in law and economics to other disciplines. The Social Literature Study Group and the Social Medicine Study Group within Shaken, both conceived at the start of the new academic year in April 1925,[43] were of particular interest in this respect. The literature group began full-scale activity in the fall of 1925 under the leadership of Hayashi Fusao and was consciously devised among the Shinjinkai leadership as a technique for the politicization of literature-minded students. Of the membership of some fifteen to twenty, a large number were drawn into the Shinjinkai, most notably a small clique of Urawa Higher graduates who had set up their own drama group and joined the Social Literature Study Group at Hayashi's urging.[44] In February 1926 the organization joined with a number of other young writers to form the off-

41. *Teikoku daigaku shimbun*, no. 65 (February 1, 1924), p. 2, and no. 73 (May 2, 1924), p. 3.
42. For a list of prescribed Shinjinkai reading according to discipline, see Mombushō, Gakuseibu, *Gakusei shisō undō no enkaku* (March 1931), pp. 192–197.
43. *Teikoku daigaku shimbun*, no. 114 (April 20, 1925), p. 7.
44. For the activities of this group and its relation to the Shinjinkai, see Hayashi Fusao, *Bungakuteki kaisō*, pp. 20–22, and the accounts of Ōta Keitarō,

campus Marxist Arts Study Group (Marukusu Shugi Geijutsu Ken-kyūkai), which played a critical role in leading the Japanese proletarian literature movement in new directions. Those of this talented group of young left-wing poets and novelists who entered the Shinjinkai came to be known as the *bungei-ha*, or "literary faction" (a term of abuse when used by more political types), which produced such writers as Nakano Shigeharu and Kamei Katsuichirō.

The Social Medicine Study Group, while less conspicuous than its counterpart in literature, strongly influenced a number of medical students seriously concerned with the role which their chosen profession might play in social reform.[45] They were specifically interested in such areas as health insurance, industrial sickness, public hygiene, and socialized medicine, and in their study sessions read the ponderous German work, Chages' *Kompendium der Sozialen Hygiene,* as well as studies by various Japanese scholars. Their keen interest in socialized medicine was reflected in a small book written by the members en-titled *The Socialization of Medical Care (Iryō no shakaika,* Dōjinsha, date unclear). Many were also involved in the operation of the free medical clinic at the Teidai Settlement. On the whole, their professional dedication tended to moderate any political extremism, al-though several became members of the Shinjinkai and, in one or two cases, communist activists. Katsuki Shinji, who was one of the group, became the secretary-general of the Shinjinkai in the fall of 1926, al-though less for his revolutionary ardor than for the image of quiet respectability which he provided in an era of increasing government pressure.

ALL POWER TO THE STUDENT MASSES!

The "awakening of proletarian consciousness" which the Shinjinkai sought to stimulate was, in theoretical terms, calculated to eliminate

---

Kawaguchi Hiroshi, and Kaji Wataru (all Shinjinkai members) in Kurahara Korehito and Tezuka Hidetaka, eds., *Monogatari puroretaria bungaku undō,* 2 vols. (Shin Nihon shuppansha, 1967), I, 85–109.

45. Information on the Social Medicine Study Group was provided by Katsuki Shinji in an interview.

the petty bourgeois class attitudes which were assumed to characterize university students as a whole. It was admitted, of course, that such endeavors would have no effect on the "student masses," the majority of whom were conceded to be politically apathetic. At the same time, however, the Shinjinkai engaged in a second line of activity which did in fact focus on the student masses but interpreted them not as petty bourgeois but rather as a special kind of "proletariat," spiritually and economically oppressed by their "employers," the educational authorities. On the basis of such an interpretation, the Shinjinkai undertook the initiation and support of a number of campus movements on behalf of student interests. Such activity profited the radicals in part because the student masses, grateful for the defense of their interests, might respond with support (if not commitment) on specific political issues and in part because the fomentation of student antagonism against the university administration might help hasten the collapse of authority within bourgeois society.

Whatever the precise calculations of the Shinjinkai leaders in promoting campaigns on behalf of the "student masses," the 1920s presented them with a golden opportunity. The economic depression which began in 1920 and was to last with varying intensity for over twelve years took a heavy toll among the middle-class families from which most university students came. Students were not only poorer while in school but found that their future as well was threatened by a rapid degeneration in employment prospects. The 1923 earthquake in Tokyo had an even more direct effect on student welfare, depriving many of adequate housing and exacerbating an already mounting sense of insecurity. These economic pressures, combined with the rapidly growing size of the total student population, led students in the early 1920s to sense that they were a special socio-economic grouping with its own interests and its own needs.

One result of this growing student self-consciousness was the institution of student "self-government," or *jichi*. This tradition had prevailed in the higher school dormitory committees since mid-Meiji, but had remained undeveloped in the more impersonal world of university students, where living quarters were scattered and where few students had any particular interest in campus affairs. But in 1920, in the case of Tokyo Imperial University, a movement began to create a unified student association both to coordinate extracurricular activities and to serve as an organ of student opinion.

Before 1920, extracurricular activities at Tokyo Imperial fell into two categories. One was athletics, which had been unified in July 1887 in the Athletic Association (Undōkai), a federation of the seven major sports clubs. Meiji Japan was the golden age of college sports, and the Athletic Association was the only powerful organized student force in that era.[46] A second type of organization emerged in the late nineteenth century, however, apparently originating in cheerleading groups which supported the crew teams (crew being the most popular of Meiji sports) within each faculty.[47] But whatever their origins, three such groups were given campus recognition in 1899 as the official clubs of each faculty involved: these were the Faculty of Medicine Tetsumon Club, the Faculty of Engineering Teiyūkai, and the Faculty of Law Midorikai.[48] These clubs, known generically as *gakuyūkai*, were seen as coordinating bodies for all nonathletic extracurricular activities and in the following decades were set up in schools throughout Japan, performing an important role in unifying student and alumni opinion. In the case of these early clubs at Tokyo Imperial, however, organization was exclusively along faculty lines, so that the interfaculty contact necessary for all-campus unity was discouraged. The early faculty clubs performed few functions on behalf of students beyond sponsoring occasional lectures and serving as a framework for such activities as debating and drama clubs.

The lack of any overall coordinating organ for student interests and opinion became an issue during the Morito Incident of early 1920,

46. For the organization of the Athletic Association, see Tōkyō teikoku daigaku, ed., *Tōkyō teikoku daigaku gojūnen shi*, II, 667–675.

47. The origins of the faculty clubs remain a mystery. For the cheerleading group theory, see Tōdai Arubamu, Keiyūkai, Midorikai iin yūshi konshinkai, ed., *Tōdai Arubamu, Midorikai, Keiyūkai iin meibo* (Yamagata Sahei shōten, 1967), pp. 4–6.

48. These names are difficult to translate. "Tetsumon" refers to the Iron Gate, an old entrance to the university campus near the Faculty of Medicine. "Teiyūkai" is most likely derived from the resemblance of the character *tei* to the letter "T", which appears on the emblem of the Faculty of Engineering (standing for the English "technology"); hence "the club of 'T' friends". Midorikai, or "Green Club", was doubtless taken from the color used by the cheerleading team.

when the students leading the protests were distressed by the necessity for each faculty to organize a separate demonstration. They put forth a proposal for the creation of an omni-faculty "student union" (Gakuseikai),[49] but the plan was defeated and in its place a considerably less radical reform was made in September 1920, when the Athletic Association was reorganized as the Tokyo Imperial University Gakuyūkai and provisions were made for the inclusion of "music, lectures, and literary activities to enable the cultivation of personality and the fostering of refined tastes." [50] As the language suggests, the reform was a conservative one, and progress in the area of student government was made difficult by the continued dominance of the athletic teams, which far outnumbered the two or three "cultural" clubs.

The publication of the *Imperial University News,* beginning in December of the same year, aided in building up student feeling of unity and of a need for a truly representative student association. The result was a movement beginning in early 1923 to reform the Gakuyūkai and to wrest it from the domination of conservative athletic interests. The Shinjinkai assumed leadership of the reform movement, and through the skillful use of jeering and parliamentary expertise managed to dominate a mass student meeting on May 5 to vote on Gakuyūkai reform. Under the slogan of "All power to the student masses!" the Shinjinkai radicals, led by Kikukawa Tadao and Sugino Tadao, forced the adoption of a set of resolutions which paved the way for a complete reform.[51] A drafting committee was created to consider various proposals and finally, after a considerable delay because of the earthquake, the reorganization plan was approved on March 25, 1924.[52] The major features of the new Gakuyūkai were as follows (refer to Chart 3):

Membership in both the Gakuyūkai and the appropriate faculty club was automatically granted to each student, with a compulsory assessment of five yen ($2.50) in annual dues. This rejection of volun-

49. Kikukawa, *Gakusei shakai undō shi,* pp. 127–129.
50. *Tōkyō teikoku daigaku gojūnen shi,* II, 676.
51. Kikukawa, *Gakusei shakai undō shi,* pp. 154–159, 183–185 provides a detailed account of the events leading to Gakuyūkai reform in the spring of 1924; this in fact is the only account now available, since those issues of the *Teikoku daigaku shimbun* published before the earthquake have not yet been located.
52. *Teikoku daigaku shimbun,* no. 70 (April 4, 1924), p. 2.

tary participation assured financial stability, encouraged student interest, and was to set a critical precedent for the later development of student government. Faculty members were made *ex officio* "special members" of the Gakuyūkai but paid no dues.

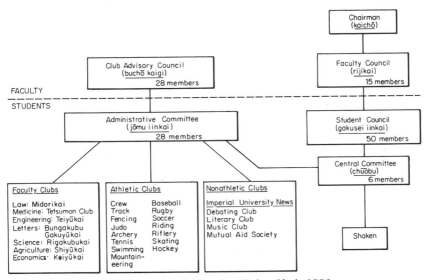

Chart 3. The Tokyo Imperial University Gakuyūkai, 1926

Source: Based on descriptions in *Tōkyō teikoku daigaku gojūnen shi*, II, 675–680, and *Teikoku daigaku shimbun*, no. 165 (May 10, 1926), p. 2.

Faculty Supervision was the key respect in which the Gakuyūkai pattern, which was followed in most other schools, differed from post-World War II Japanese student government. Supervision was exercised at the club level through faculty advisers who acted as titular heads of each individual club and who met as a group in the Club Advisory Council, having the power to review all decisions of the student-run Administrative Committee. On matters of overall Gakuyūkai policy, a Faculty Council of fifteen members had the power to review all decisions of the Student Council. The president of the university served *ex officio* as a member of the Faculty Council and as chairman of the Gakuyūkai. In practice, the faculty members tended to act in a purely advisory capacity and rarely initiated changes within the Gakuyūkai (although an important exception was to be the final

dissolution of the Gakuyūkai in March 1928, which was effected unilaterally by vote of the Faculty Council).

The Administrative Committee consisted of one student delegate
from each club, elected by the club memberships, which numbered
twenty-eight (including the Central Committee) in 1926. It was in
charge of contact among the separate clubs and of matters related to
club affairs in general. The athletic interests always had an absolute
majority on this body, which, however, was virtually powerless vis-à-vis
the Student Council.

The Student Council was the major innovation in the 1923 reform
plan and represented the first true organ of student government at
Tokyo Imperial University. It was composed of approximately fifty
members, elected proportionately from the separate faculties by popular student vote. The council met monthly and had power over the
creation and abolition of clubs, revisions of the Gakuyūkai charter, the
Gakuyūkai budget and all other affairs not specifically delegated to the
clubs. Even more important, the council was intended to serve as "an
organ of the expression of student opinion" and had the power to set
up special investigative committees on campus problems.

The Central Committee was the executive organ of the Gakuyūkai,
and consisted of six members appointed by a faculty adviser from
nominees chosen by the Student Council from its own membership. It
was charged with business matters, accounts, and the responsibility of
"advising" the chairman. It also had a number of special assignments,
the most important of which was control over the Tōdai Shaken, an
anomaly which was to bring about the destruction of the Gakuyūkai
itself. The Central Committee had the status of an independent club,
and hence had its own budget, adviser, and representative on the Administrative Committee.

By delegating the bulk of power within the Gakuyūkai to the popularly elected Student Council, the hold of the athletic interests on
extracurricular activities was broken, marking the end of an era in
university student life in Japan. Although initial student interest in
the council following its creation in 1924 was extremely low, the
machinery of student government was nevertheless available should
the need arise, as it soon would in the conflict between the Shinjinkai
and the student right wing.

DEFENSE OF STUDENT INTERESTS

The Shinjinkai leaders who led the Gakuyūkai reform movement realized that merely establishing the machinery of "student power" was hardly sufficient to win the support of the "student masses": specific activities in behalf of student interests had to be undertaken to show that the machinery worked. The most significant such endeavor was the student-run dining hall established under Gakuyūkai auspices in November 1923. The Gakuyūkai reform plan of the previous spring had included a demand for the "elimination of dishonest merchants" (kanshō taiji), referring to the commercial purveyors with whom the university contracted to provide on-campus dining and shopping facilities.[53] Students had long been disgruntled by these merchants, who often charged higher prices than off-campus shops, and the issue was made all the more urgent by the September earthquake, which created a serious food shortage in Tokyo.

The student dining hall, with a capacity of five hundred, was opened on November 13, offering such classic student fare as curried rice at prices far lower than before.[54] Shinjinkai members Kikukawa Tadao and Hayashi Fusao were instrumental both in the creation and the administration of the dining hall, which was under the supervision of the Central Committee of the Gakuyūkai. While the dining hall was a great success among the "student masses" for whom it was created, it appeared after a year that direct student management might not be the answer, for the Gakuyūkai was faced with a substantial debt from dining hall operations. Hayashi recalls that the Shinjinkai activists had been wholly unaware of the complexities of wholesale food purchasing and accounting which the project involved and were quickly disillusioned.[55] The persistent Kikukawa managed to keep the dining hall in operation despite Student Council complaints about the debt[56] but finally gave in, and after about two years of operation the manage-

53. Ibid., no. 86 (September 19, 1924), p. 2.
54. Ibid., no. 58 (November 16, 1923), p. 3; for a description of the dining hall, see Nakano, Muragimo, pp. 247–248.
55. Hayashi Fusao interview.
56. Teikoku daigaku shimbun, no. 90 (October 10, 1924), p. 2, and no. 98 (December 1, 1924), p. 2.

ment was returned to professional merchants. Even so, the franchises were thereafter controlled by the students through the Gakuyūkai rather than by the university, so that student welfare remained the paramount principle of dining hall operation.

The dining hall project was only one of many Shinjinkai activities in the period immediately after the earthquake but set the important precedent for radical students' assumption of the defense of "student interests." This type of activity receded in prominence in the mid-1920s as the student radicals came to view their role as "one wing of the proletarian movement" as overriding any concern for the welfare of bourgeois students. In the "age of chronic school disturbances" of the late 1920s and early 1930s, however, such manipulation of the nonpolitical interests of the student masses was to become of critical importance in sustaining the political student left and set an even more important precedent for the postwar student movement.

THE CLASH WITH THE STUDENT RIGHT

The reformed Gakuyūkai had originally been conceived by the student radicals as an organization through which students might unify in defense of their own interests. This was seen not only as desirable in itself but as contributing to the broader movement for social reform by posing a threat to the bourgeois educational order. These sanguine prospects were to be disappointed, however, and the Gakuyūkai was ironically turned from an offensive weapon of the student left to a defensive shield in the face of an attack by right-wing students. This threat emerged in late 1925 and forced a reinterpretation of the politically apathetic student masses, who were now seen not as potential allies but as potential reactionaries, to be "neutralized" rather than defended. Whereas the Shinjinkai in the spring of 1923 had exuberantly cried for "All power to the student masses," by late 1925 a set of Gakuren "Theses on General Policy for the Campus Movement" declared pessimistically that "to look with contempt upon the student masses in an age such as this, when reactionary suppression is becoming systematic, is to entrust the student masses to the hands of reaction and thus to abet the organization of reactionary forces." [57]

57. Hasegawa, p. 130.

An organized right-wing student movement had begun at Tokyo Imperial University from about the same time as the student left. Much as Yoshino Sakuzō served as a pivotal figure in the founding of the Shinjinkai, so the right-wing students tended to gather around the conservative professor of law Uèsugi Shinkichi, and as early as 1916 had organized an inconspicuous study group called the Thursday Club (Mokuyōkai). The aggressive activities of the Shinjinkai were conceived by Uesugi's followers as a threat demanding a clear response, which came with the formation of the Kōkoku Dōshikai (Brotherhood for National Support) in late 1919. This group won fame for its alleged role in instigating the Morito Incident the following spring but appears to have receded into inactivity not long after, weakened by a split between activist and scholarly factions in much the same way as its left-wing rival.[58]

Uesugi's followers banded together a second time in response to a perceived threat from the student left in November 1924 with the founding of the Shichiseisha (Seven Lives Society).[59] Taking its name from the pledge of the fourteenth-century imperial loyalist Kusunoki Masashige that he would give "seven lives" in the service of his country, thc Shichiscisha took the destruction of the Shinjinkai as its major goal and drew membership both from the serious intellectual conservatives who followed Uesugi and from an assortment of strong-arm toughs from the athletic teams, especially those in the traditional martial arts of judo and kendo. Particularly irritating to the Shichiseisha was the Shinjinkai leadership of the anti-military education movement on the university campus, and it was over this issue that the

58. The early history of the right-wing student movement at Tokyo Imperial remains unresearched. For two secondary accounts of modest reliability, see Kinoshita Hanji, *Nihon fashizumu shi*, 2 vols. (Iwasaki shoten, 1949), I, 160–162, and Kōan chōsachō, *Senzen ni okeru uyoku dantai no jōkyō*, pp. 262–265.

59. The characters for "seven lives" should properly be read, in Buddhist manner, as *shichishō;* the reading "Shichiseisha," however, was the one most commonly used by students at the time. The founding date of the group is unclear; both Kinoshita, *Nihon fashizumu shi*, and Kōan chōsachō, *Senzen ni okeru uyoku dantai no jōkyō*, give February 11, 1925, but this day was a patriotic holiday (Kigensetsu) and a most desirable one to put forth as a "founding day" for a right-wing group, hence probably artificial. I have followed Kawamura, *Shisō mondai nempyō*, p. 46, which gives November 15, 1924. Other versions are Kikukawa, *Gakusei shakai undō shi*, p. 309, which gives March 10, 1925, and Mombushō, Gakuseibu, *Kokka shugi teki tachiba o hyōbō suru gakusei dantai* (February 1934), p. 7, which gives November 11, 1925.

first outright clash between the two sides occurred in the fall of 1925. On November 21, the Debating Club sponsored an open "Forum on Military Education" in which representatives from both sides were permitted to speak. The final line-up was five Shichiseisha versus four Shinjinkai, and the "debate" rapidly degenerated into an animated jeering match between the two sides. Violence was averted but tension remained high.[60]

The confrontation then shifted to the Student Council, which until this time had been languishing from apathy on the part not only of the student masses but also of the Shinjinkai, now obsessed with being "one wing of the proletarian movement." The first two Student Council elections, in early 1924 and 1925, were wholly uncontested for lack of interest, and delegates had to be appointed by the separate faculty clubs.[61] Only one Shinjinkai member, Sugino Tadao, is known to have been on the council in this period. The right-wing threat abruptly revitalized the Student Council, however, and the elections of early 1926 showed heated competition in the faculties of law, economics, and letters, where political interest was high. The Shinjinkai delegation leapt suddenly from one to thirteen, over one fourth of the total Student Council membership. Several Shichiseisha members were also elected, and a minor feud broke out at the council's first meeting.

It was not until the fall of 1926, however, that a full-scale battle was touched off when the left-wing forces on the Student Council launched a drive to transfer Shaken from its anomalous position under Central Committee control to independent status similar to the other clubs, with its own budget and faculty adviser.[62] While the issue of Shaken independence was not in itself of great importance, it served as a convenient focus for all of the previously latent antagonism between the two sides. A meeting of the Student Council on November 10, at

60. *Teikoku daigaku shimbun,* no. 143 (November 24, 1925), p. 5.
61. The Shinjinkai proportions on the Student Council have been calculated from the scattered election reports in the *Teikoku daigaku shimbun* for each year. No single list of all the council members could be located.
62. The details of the Shaken organizational situation are complex and not entirely clear from the *Teikoku daigaku shimbun* accounts. It would appear, for example, that budgetary control was one point of dispute, but this was never mentioned in the open debate over Shaken independence, which became reduced exclusively to political issues. See, for example, *Teikoku daigaku shimbun,* no. 186 (November 15, 1926), p. 3.

which Shinjinkai leader Tanaka Toshio formally submitted a resolution for Shaken independence, produced a heated seven-hour debate, but the minority right-wing forces managed to win postponement of a vote until a special meeting later in the month. Held on November 25, this notable session produced the first open violence between left and right on the Tokyo Imperial University campus. The debate opened at three in the afternoon and went on into the evening as tension heightened with the approach of a vote. But when at last, around ten o'clock, Shinjinkai member Matsunobu Shichirō made a motion to close debate, Shichiseisha leader Suenobu Hifumi suddenly leapt onto a table and declared his opposition. One Shinjinkai member who tried to calm Suenobu was firmly stomped on the hand, whereupon the meeting broke into wild confusion and open brawling, forcing the chairman, Shinjinkai member Hōshaku Hajime, to declare adjournment.[63]

The Shichiseisha violence was widely condemned by moderates and radicals alike, and it soon became apparent that the left-wing forces would win on the substantial issue of Shaken independence. The left increased its Student Council majority by a vigorous campaign in the elections in December and January, and after a series of delays the Shaken independence resolution was passed by a vote of 34–13 at a council meeting on May 25, 1927. As a concession to the right wing, the name was changed to Cultural Science Club (Bunka Kagaku Bu) to obviate the political implications of the phrase "social science." Professor Hozumi Shigetō, who was by no definition a radical, was accepted as faculty adviser, and the Cultural Science Club was officially launched on November 1 following approval by the Faculty Council. Despite the concession on the name and the adviser, the new club meant a clear victory for the Shinjinkai, which the Shichiseisha could not long tolerate.

The climax came at a left-wing rally on January 24, 1928, sponsored by the Debating Club in opposition to the refusal of the educational authorities to permit the annual higher school debating meet at Tokyo Imperial. The rally was opened in a Law Faculty classroom with mes-

63. *Teikoku daigaku shimbun*, no. 188 (November 29, 1926), p. 2, and Nakano, *Muragimo*, pp. 249–251. The *Muragimo* account, written almost thirty years after the event and in fictionalized form, must be used with care.

sages of support from various liberal campus groups. All was calm until the Teidai Settlement representative rose to speak, whereupon Shichiseisha strong-arm man Soejima Tane leapt from the audience, ripped the message from the speaker's hand and pushed him from the podium. Soejima threw a chair at a Shinjinkai member who attempted to restore order, leading to an all-out melee of chair throwing and insult shouting between the two sides. Three Shinjinkai members were injured in the brawl, and the violence continued the following day as vigilante bands of Shichiseisha members roamed the campus in search of leftists. In one such attack, Soejima threw a brick at Shinjinkai member Maejima Masamichi, inflicting a serious head wound. A later investigation by the Student Council listed twelve students who had been assaulted or threatened by the Shichiseisha, of whom seven were Shinjinkai members.[64]

This wave of assaults set off strenuous protests among all the liberal groups on campus, and a "Group Council for Countermeasures to the Shichiseisha Assault Incident" (Shichiseisha-in Bōkō Jiken Taisaku Kaku-dantai Kyōgikai) was formed as a coordinating organization. But as the left-wing protest mounted, the right-wing forces worked quietly to destroy the Gakuyūkai from below. On February 3, the athletic clubs withdrew from the Gakuyūkai and shortly after reorganized as a new Tokyo Imperial University Athletic Association. On February 16, four of the faculty clubs, which had long harbored dissatisfaction with the Gakuyūkai system for a number of nonpolitical reasons, took the opportunity to announce their withdrawal.[65] As a last resort, senior Gakuyūkai adviser Hozumi Shigetō devised a reform plan which would bring the athletic teams back into the Gakuyūkai at the price of abolishing popular elections to the Student Council. When the Shinjinkai-dominated council refused to accept this plan, the Faculty Council met on March 29 and unilaterally decided to dissolve the Gakuyūkai.[66]

The concept of a coordinated student association at Tokyo Imperial

64. *Teikoku daigaku shimbun,* no. 238 (January 30, 1928), p. 2, and no. 239 (February 6, 1928), p. 2.

65. The main bone of contention of the faculty clubs was the allocation of the Gakuyūkai budget.

66. This series of events is described in detail in *Teikoku daigaku shimbun,* nos. 238–247 (January 30–April 2, 1928). The legal dissolution of the Gakuyūkai was April 5.

University thus collapsed, not to be revived until April 1941 and then not as a progressive organ of student opinion but as a wartime measure of patriotic unity. Efforts by the Shinjinkai in 1928 to reconstruct the Gakuyūkai proved futile, since the mass communist arrests on March 15 provoked a strong reaction against the campus left and forced the dissolution of the Shinjinkai itself as a recognized campus group. The forces of reaction were successful in destroying the Gakuyūkai, but in the process had firmly established it as a critical part of the machinery of the radical student movement.

Although the case of Tokyo Imperial was the most dramatic, the same sort of radical manipulation of gakuyūkai-type student associations, often in competition with the student right, was repeated on many other campuses. In this way the stage was set for the important role which the student "self-governing associations" (jichikai), the successors of the prewar gakuyūkai, were destined to play in the revival of student radicalism following the Pacific War.

6 | Under the Spell of Fukumoto, 1926-1928

The Japanese Communist Party was reorganized in December 1926, almost three years after it had been dissolved in the wake of a series of setbacks in 1923. These three years represent a near total break in the continuity of the communist movement in Japan and a thorough revision in the conception of the vanguard party. The distinction between the First Party and the reorganized party of 1926 may be expressed in a variety of ways: where the First Party was Marxist, the new one was Leninist; [1] where the membership of the First Party was socially diverse, the second party was dominated by university graduates; where the spokesman of the First Party was Yamakawa Hitoshi, that of the reorganized party was Fukumoto Kazuo; where the First Party was concerned with strategy and analysis, the later one was preoccupied with organization and tactics. The concern here is to trace the ways in which the student movement, in the period leading up to the mass communist arrests of March 1928, came to have a dominant influence within the Japanese Communist Party itself.

The First Communist Party had been formally dissolved in February 1924, in line with the insistence of Yamakawa Hitoshi and others that the situation did not warrant an illegal vanguard party. Yamakawa's view, which under later attack by his Leninist opponents became known as "Yamakawaism," stressed the primary need for the development of mass organizations, playing down the role of an elite party organization. While admitting the necessity of a highly trained,

1. For this distinction, see Gabriel Almond, *The Appeals of Communism* (Princeton, 1954), pp. 8–10.

"conscious" leadership, Yamakawa did not see the organization of the party itself and the maintenance of rigid party discipline as matters of great importance. This conception of the party was in part reflected in and perhaps molded by the membership of the First Party, which was so diffuse as to make inconceivable the kind of tightly knit, homogeneous group which Lenin had envisaged.

At the time of the dissolution of the First Party, a small committee called "The Bureau" had been formed to maintain contact with the Comintern, and in September 1925 this was expanded to a "Communist Group," charged with actively paving the way for actual party reorganization.[2] Since a number of the old leaders had fled the country, been jailed, or moderated their views on illegal activity, the recruitment of new leadership was urgent. It was from this need that a linkage with the student movement naturally developed. The Gakuren leaders who gathered for the Second Congress in Kyoto at the start of summer recess in 1925 had proclaimed Marxism–Leninism as their "guiding principle," and they faithfully based their study-group reading on Comintern-approved texts—including the writings of Lenin. The students clearly afforded a substantial reservoir of fully "conscious" elements for the new party. The "unreliable" class character of such young bourgeois intellectuals naturally posed a serious obstacle, but this was to be quickly overcome by the persuasive arguments of a brilliant new theorist who appeared just at this juncture.

FUKUMOTO KAZUO AND THE STUDENT MOVEMENT

Fukumoto Kazuo's emergence as the theoretical leader of the reorganized Japanese Communist Party in 1926 was the key to establishing a lasting organic relationship between the student movement and the party. Although Fukumoto himself was to be denounced by the Comintern in the 1927 Theses as a "left-wing adventurist," his profound influence on the Japanese communist movement could not be easily obliterated and remains felt to the present day. It was largely through his immense popularity among young student intellectuals

2. For details on the history of the Japanese Communist Party, see George M. Beckmann and Okubo Genji, *The Japanese Communist Party, 1922–1945* (Stanford, 1969).

that Fukumoto became for a time the high priest of the Japanese Communist Party and perhaps its last truly influential theorist. Conversely, it was through the grasp and espousal of Fukumoto's theories, known later by his opponents as "Fukumotoism," that a group of young intellectuals fresh from the ranks of the student movement were able to attain positions of high leadership within the Communist Party.

Fukumoto's debut on the stage of Japanese communism had the touch of a *deus ex machina*. Shinjinkai member Hayashi Fusao, who in late 1924 was working as an editor of *Marxism*, the legal magazine of the underground Communist Bureau, recalls the unprecedented manner of Fukumoto's appearance: "One day a bulky manuscript arrived at the editors' desk of *Marxism*. It was signed 'Fukumoto Kazuo,' but as I recall, he had not brought it in person but rather sent it by mail. Attached was a self-introduction saying that he was a professor at a certain higher commercial school who had just returned from Germany. Nishi Masao [the editor-in-chief of *Marxism*] read it first and concluded, 'It's a rather strange style, but there seems to be something here.' "[3]

Before his abrupt appearance in the pages of *Marxism*, Fukumoto had no ties whatsoever with the Japanese left.[4] Until 1922, when he left for two and a half years of study in Europe, he had followed a maddeningly routine course on the road to comfortable bureaucratic normalcy: First Higher '17, Tokyo Imperial Faculty of Law '20, Ministry of Interior post in Shimane prefecture, transfer to professorship at Matsue Higher, state-financed study abroad. He had been a classmate of at least eight Shinjinkai members at higher school and university and yet showed no ideological sympathy at the time. A strikingly different personality from most communist intellectuals in Japan, Fukumoto was driven less by soul-searching humanism and agonizing self-criticism than by a passion which was wholly cerebral and a self-confidence that bordered on arrogance. While in Germany, he had undertaken to master the totality of Marxist thought with methodical brilliance, and few Japanese communists were equipped at the time

3. Hayashi Fusao, *Bungakuteki kaisō*, p. 16.
4. For information on Fukumoto's career, I have relied largely on Fukumoto Kazuo, *Kakumei undō razō* (San'ichi shobō, 1962).

to challenge his boasts of success. This doubtless reflected more on the superficiality of Japanese Marxism in the mid-twenties than on Fukumoto's accomplishments, for it was merely the *impression* of his mastery that was telling. Hayashi Fusao recalls his feelings on reading Fukumoto's first essay: "The one thing which could not be doubted was his extreme erudition. The passages he quoted were all critical lines which I had never once read. Neither Yamakawa nor Sakai nor Inomata nor Sano Manabu nor Sano Fumio nor Aono Suekichi had once quoted these for us. These fresh contents forced me to realize the ignorance of Japanese Marxists—or at least so I, as a student theorist, thought." [5]

Fukumoto's very language and sentence structure were a source of delight for the students. His style was a well-crafted confusion of lengthy Sino-Japanese coinages and superfluous translationese, truncated by batteries of commas, dashes, equal signs, and quotation marks, and filled with quotable formulas which became the basis of a new student jargon. Nakano Shigeharu's hero in *Muragimo* was one of many captured by Fukumoto's style (for "Iwasaki" and "Yamada" read Fukumoto and Yamakawa, and for *"Marxist Studies," Marxism*): "Yasukichi had been reading Iwasaki's writings in the greenish-covered *Marxist Studies* for some time before. It was quite intriguing (*omoshiroi*). In the first place, titles like 'We Must Start with a Change of Direction in Yamada's "Change of Direction," ' or 'Union Afterwards Cannot Exist without Division Beforehand' were intriguing. His style of thinking, as in 'The question of what must later become of a particular thing is already answered in the realization of where it is at the present' was also intriguing. Yasukichi could not quite understand how those much more deeply involved in the movement than himself could treat Iwasaki's essays like a bible, but for himself, he found a vivid appeal not in the content of what was written but rather in the way it was written." [6]

For the majority of the student activists, more adept at theory than the literary Yasukichi, however, the content of Fukumoto's writings was indeed of great importance. The breadth of his theoretical endeavors offered something for every kind of specialized interest among student radicals. In his last six months in Europe, Fukumoto had

5. Hayashi Fusao, *Bungakuteki kaisō*, p. 16.
6. Nakano, *Muragimo*, p. 267.

secluded himself in a Parisian apartment and, drawing on the thousands of German books which he had purchased, prepared three weighty manuscripts which were to provide the raw material for his steady outpouring upon returning to Japan.[7] One of these treated "the methodology of economic criticism" and was the basis of his earliest articles in *Marxism* (which began in December 1924 and were to continue in almost every issue for over two years). In these writings on Marxist economics, Fukumoto persistently and scathingly attacked the interpretations of Kawakami Hajime, whom he managed to discredit in the eyes of many student radicals, including even some of Kawakami's own students. Fukumoto's views in this area did not achieve wide currency, however, and were largely limited to those students with a professional or scholarly interest in economics.

Another of Fukumoto's three manuscripts dealt with the dialectical materialist view of history. Previewed in a single article in the February 1925 issue of *Marxism,* this theme was developed in full at a two-day lecture series in early November at Kyoto Imperial University. This occasion was of special importance in marking Fukumoto's first personal contact with the student radicals, who had been reading his essays in *Marxism* (a standard item on the *shaken* study lists) but had never met the man. The lectures were published by Hakuyōsha the following February as Fukumoto's first book, *The Structure of Society and the Process of Social Change,* which was avidly read among left-wing students and commonly referred to as the "bible" of Fukumoto's worshipers.[8] As one of the first systematic attempts to explain dialectical materialism to the Japanese left, this work was warmly greeted by students, whose philosophical predilections were titillated by the concept of dialectical change.[9]

7. Fukumoto, *Kakumei undō razō,* pp. 16–17. Fukumoto's claim that his library of European books numbered "several tens of thousands" seems rather exaggerated.
8. Fukumoto Kazuo, *Shakai no kōsei narabi ni henkaku no katei* (Hakuyōsha, 1926). Yamazaki (now Nishiyama) Yūji, one of the Kyoto Imperial students who heard Fukumoto's lecture and was shortly thereafter arrested in the Gakuren incident, placed great emphasis on the importance of this work among Kyoto radicals. Nishiyama interview.
9. The dialectic was not, however, a complete novelty to student radicals, for the brilliant Shinjinkai theorist Koreeda Kyōji had written an article under the pen name of Akiyama Jirō in the May 1924 issue of the Gakuren *Bulletin* in which he clearly outlined the dialectical concept of the unity of theory and practice with reference to the perennial debate in the student movement over "study

While Fukumoto's writings on Marxist economics and on dialectical materialism offered provocative fare for student economists and philosophers, it was rather the third manuscript, on the theme of political party organization, that was to leave the most profound mark on the history of Japanese communism. It is only to Fukumoto's views on this problem, thus, that the term "Fukumotoism" is properly applied. Later critics of Fukumoto have claimed that his theory of party organization was nothing more than warmed-over *What Is to Be Done?* with a sprinkling of Lukács. This was perhaps true, but in modern Japan, where the introduction of a new Western idea wins quicker and surer acclaim than an original indigenous theory, Fukumoto's success was guaranteed. It is surprising that the concept of a Leninist party should have been so novel in Japan in 1925, for it was first outlined in *What Is to Be Done?* over two decades earlier; yet whether from oversight or unpreparedness, that classic was almost wholly unknown until Fukumoto. Ishidō Kiyotomo recalls that Fukumoto's message came just as the students were discovering Lenin's theories of organization on their own. In the fall of 1925, a one-volume collection of Lenin's writings (in German) had been imported to Japan and was widely read among Shinjinkai members.[10] The following year, Hakuyōsha began publication of *The Writings of Lenin*, which included *What Is to Be Done?* in the fourth volume. Fukumoto thus both profited by and himself heightened a Leninist trend on the extreme left.

Indeed, the Leninist concept of an elite vanguard party seemed made to order for student intellectuals. In preaching the need for a secret, highly disciplined, centralized party of "professional revolutionaries," Lenin had specifically provided for young intellectuals. He had further stressed the importance of the proper consciousness and the need for "theoretical struggle," a phrase which Fukumoto popularized (it became the title of one of his books, *Riron tōsō*) and which became a key slogan of student radicals. This concept gave specific validation to the study circles, the heart of the student movement, where total attention was focused on the mastery of theory and the attainment of the "proper consciousness."

---

or action." See Kikukawa, *Gakusei shakai undō shi,* pp. 250–252; the original article cannot be located.

10. Ishidō Kiyotomo, "Sono koro no Fukumoto shugi," *Gendaishi shiryō geppō,* supp. to Misuzu shobō, ed., Gendaishi shiryō, XX (editor, 1968), 2.

Fukumoto first broached his ideas on party organization in *Marxism* under the pen name of Hōjō Kazuo in a series of three articles in the spring of 1925 on the development of party organization theory in Europe, but it was not until the October issue that he first applied these ideas to the Japanese situation. Bearing the uniquely Fukumoto-like title of "Through What Stages Will the 'Change of Direction' Pass, and Which Stage Are We Staging Now?", this article—similar to *What Is to Be Done?* itself—was a systematic cataloguing of all the theoretical errors of rival left-wing leaders, whom Fukumoto dismissed as opportunistic and economistic. Citing Lenin, Fukumoto declared that a "separation" out of these revisionist elements was necessary before a "unification" of the left-wing movement into a truly Marxist party could be effected.[11] He made it clear that Yamakawa, for his gross underestimate of the necessity of a vanguard party, was the chief among the opportunistic elements to be separated out.

The dispute between Fukumoto and Yamakawa thus centered in the first instance on a major strategical alternative, that of a secret vanguard party versus a mass legal common-front organization, although such a fundamental disagreement of course came to involve differences on a wider variety of issues. The details of the confrontation were complex to start with and were considerably complicated by rapidly changing developments at the time within the labor and proletarian party movements, as well as by shifting dictates from the Comintern.[12] In the broadest sense, however, the Yamakawa–Fukumoto rift was one of fundamental political style, for which reason the confrontation was raised to the level of "isms" and became a permanent division within the left-wing movement in Japan. In a rather simplified way, Yamakawa might be seen as the pragmatic humanist, sensitive to the importance of theoretical rigor and as a matter of principle loyal to the Comintern, but in the last analysis highly preoccupied with the special

11. Fukumoto Kazuo, "Hōkō tenkan wa ikanaru sho-katei o toru ka, wareware wa ima sore no ikanaru katei o katei shitsutsu aru ka," *Marukishizumu,* 3.4 (October 1925), reprinted in Takeuchi Yoshitomo, ed., *Marukishizumu II,* Gendai Nihon shisō taikei (Chikuma shobō, 1965), XXI, 61–87. For a list of Fukumoto's articles in *Marxism* in 1925, see Fukumoto, *Kakumei undō razō,* pp. 227–28.

12. For accounts in English of these developments, see George O. Totten, III, *The Social Democratic Movement in Prewar Japan* (New Haven, 1966), pp. 39–66, and Beckmann and Okubo, *The Japanese Communist Party,* pp. 79–137.

realities of the Japanese situation. It was a style that was at once more "popular" in its human concern for the Japanese masses and more "personal" in its preference for affective bonds over organizational discipline as the basis for leadership in the movement. Fukumoto represented the other extreme of the theoretical purist and the intellectual elitist. So extreme was Fukumoto, in fact, that his political position with the movement was quickly undermined, but the general style which he introduced became the mainstream of the Japanese communist movement thereafter. The Yamakawa alternative survived as a proud and important minority faction, organized academically in the Rōnō School and emerging politically in the postwar period as the left wing of the Japanese Socialist Party.[13]

The year 1926 saw Fukumoto's popularity rise to a frenzied peak in the student movement. Besides his articles in *Marxism,* Fukumoto began a personal magazine and in the course of one year published five books, most of them collections of earlier magazine articles; all were intensively studied by Gakuren members. In late March, Fukumoto was dismissed from Yamaguchi Higher Commercial School, where he had been teaching since shortly after his return from Europe, and moved to Tokyo.[14] Not long after his arrival, he took up residence in the Kikufuji Hotel, close to the Tokyo Imperial campus, and soon was invited to join the Communist Group. Despite his proximity to the students, however, Fukumoto's personal ties with them were formal and distant and he made only two or three appearances on university campuses.[15] His unapproachable personality (which was known, however, to make exception for the opposite sex) ironically heightened his influence all the more, for he was worshiped as an oracle rather than

13. For a general history of the Yamakawaist alternative, see Koyama Hirotake *et al., Nihon no hi-kyōsantō marukusu shugisha—Yamakawa Hitoshi no shōgai to shisō* (San'ichi shobō, 1962). A good analysis of the differences between Yamakawa and Fukumoto may be found on pp. 117–128.

14. Fukumoto, *Kakumei undō razō,* p. 52, merely notes that he "resigned"; Noguchi, p. 232, claims that he was dismissed for his left-wing tendencies. The real reason was apparently a combination of his political views and a wage dispute which he had been having with the school administration; see Fukumoto's own detailed explanation in his interrogation record, Misuzu shobō, ed., *Shakai shugi undō,* Gendaishi shiryō, XX, 299–300.

15. *Ibid.,* XX, 303, mentions only two appearances, one at Waseda and one at the Tokyo Imperial Faculty of Agriculture.

admired as a teacher. This relationship was by the same token to hasten his fall, since he left no personally committed disciples to follow him once his theories had been repudiated.

STUDENTS AND THE PARTY

Fukumotoism was the vehicle on which the young intellectuals produced by the student movement rode to power within the Japanese Communist Party. The earliest of these were Shinjinkai members such as Shiga Yoshio, the only known student member of the First Communist Party (which he claims to have joined in November 1923, not long before its dissolution).[16] Shiga was brought into the Communist Group in the fall of 1925 as one of its first recruits but was drafted into the army for one year in December and exercised little influence until after the formal reorganization of the party in December 1926. Of greater importance in this period were Koreeda Kyōji and Murao Satsuo, both of whom had followed identical careers through the Kakumeikai and Higher School League while at Seventh Higher, and on to Shinjinkai leadership as students in the Tokyo Imperial Department of Sociology. When admitted to the Communist Group in the fall of 1925 at the invitation of Tokuda Kyūichi (who himself had briefly attended Seventh Higher and shared the fiery southern personality), both Koreeda and Murao were third-year university students and thus became not only very early members of the Group but the only ones to join while still students.[17] Exceptional in their talents at theory and organization alike, this pair of Kyushu radicals paved the way to extensive Shinjinkai membership in the reconstructed Communist Party.

The stock of student intellectuals in the communist movement rose dramatically with the winter arrests in 1925–26 of over forty Gakuren leaders, mostly in the Kyoto area, for violation of the Peace Preservation Law. Students thus became the first victims of a law designed

16. *Ibid.*, XIV, 124, confirmed in interview. In Tokuda Kyūichi and Shiga Yoshio, *Gokuchū jūhachinen* (Jiji tsūshinsha, 1947), p. 114, Shiga notes that he "fortunately escaped arrest" in June 1923, implying that he was a party member at the time; this would appear, however, to be incorrect.

17. Misuzu shobō, *Shakai shugi undō*, Gendaishi shiryō, XVI, 135, 169.

specifically to control communism, impressing upon many, both in government and on the left itself, that students were in the vanguard of the Japanese communist movement. A sizable increase in the young intellectual delegation within the Communist Group in late 1926 reflected this new-found prestige.[18]

When the Japanese Communist Party was officially reorganized at Goshiki Spa in the mountains of northern Japan in early December, Tokyo Imperial graduates already comprised a powerful group, including not only Fukumoto and Sano Fumio (his key supporter among the senior intellectual leadership), but also nine younger Shinjinkai products, all of whom were dedicated advocates of Fukumoto's theories. Out of seventeen attending the Goshiki conference, seven were Tokyo Imperial University intellectuals and the rest laborers.[19] The laborer element was uneasy about this heavy dose of elitist intellectuals, and their support for Fukumoto and his followers stemmed at best from a feeling of *faute de mieux,* the only alternative to Fukumoto being the moderate and already discredited Yamakawa. This

18. The sudden influx of young intellectuals into the Communist Group was eased by Fukumoto's appearance in Tokyo in the spring of 1926 and by the simultaneous imprisonment, as a result of convictions following the 1923 communist arrests, of several leading First Party members (notably Sakai Toshihiko and Arahata Kanson) who might have challenged Fukumoto's ascendancy. In the six months leading up to the reorganization of the Party in December 1926 eight young student movement alumni joined the Communist Group: Kadoya Hiroshi, Kawai Etsuzō, Kiire Toratarō, Mizuno Shigeo, Murayama Tōshirō, Nakano Hisao, Ōshima Hideo, and Toyoda (later Hirai) Sunao. For details on their recruitment, see Misuzu shobō, ed., *Shakai shugi undō*, Gendaishi shiryō, XVI, 129, 148, 157, 159, 165, 166, 405, 486. Of these eight all but Kawai, a Kyoto Imperial student, were Shinjinkai members, although the so-called "Mizuno faction" (Mizuno, Murayama, and Toyoda), the members of which had been together in the judo club at First Higher, had participated in the Shinjinkai only briefly, soon bolting to enter "into the people", participating in the labor movement in the Kansai area (where Kawai joined the faction). For details on the Mizuno faction, see Asano Akira, *Izumu ni ugoku mono* (Nihon kyōbunsha, 1955), pp. 40–42. This account, however, is second-hand (Asano knew Mizuno well, but only *after* the faction had left the Shinjinkai); the only information on the group by a member is in Mizuno Shigeo, "Kukyō no aji," *Chūō kōron*, 47.3 (March 1952), 148–152. The precise timing of the group's entrance to and secession from the Shinjinkai remains unclear. Kinoshita Hanji in an interview was unclear or possibly evasive on this point.

19. This is based on the government's reconstruction of those present; Kōan chōsachō, *Nihon kyōsantō shi (senzen)* (reprint by Gendaishi kenkyūkai, 1962), p. 115.

worker-intellectual rift was to become critical in the confrontation with the Comintern in Moscow the following summer, when Fukumoto was deposed as chief party theorist.

In the fifteen months from Goshiki until the "3.15" (March 15, 1928) arrests, the reorganized Communist Party embarked on a course of gradual expansion climaxed by an intensive membership drive just before the general elections—the first under universal suffrage—in late February 1928. In this period, the influence of young intellectuals fresh from the student movement became still more pronounced. In a snowball effect, the existing young intellectual group encouraged the admission of its own kind, a tendency clearly revaled in recruiting patterns. A graphic example is that of Nakano Hisao, who in the brief period from March to May 1927 brought eight more young intellectuals—of whom three were former Shinjinkai acquaintances—into the party in responsible positions.[20]

The importance of the Shinjinkai in the Communist Party in the period leading up to the 3.15 arrests is suggested by the composition of the central leadership group, as reconstructed by the government prosecutors.[21] Out of a total of thirty-seven leaders, fourteen had been Shinjinkai members. Two others, Sano Fumio and Fukumoto, had attended Tokyo Imperial University, while only one, Mizuno Hideo, was a product of Waseda. Thus the predominance in the First Communist Party of Waseda student radicals over those from Tokyo Imperial was now reversed. Of the other twenty members of the central group, most were of proletarian origin, although a few survivors of the First Communist Party, such as Tokuda Kyūichi or Nakamura Yoshiaki, were of the renegade pattern, neither pure laborer nor pure intellectual, which characterized the older Meiji style of radicalism. In percentages, university-educated intellectuals accounted for 48 per cent of the entire group, and Shinjinkai members alone for 38 per cent.

Until the March 1928 arrests, intellectuals were generally taken

20. The three Shinjinkai members were Asano Akira, Irie Shōji, and Uchigaki Yasuzō; of the rest, two were leaders of the *shaken* at Tokyo Women's College (Watanabe Taeko and Hatano Misao), and the others had attended various private universities (Inokuchi Masao from Keiō, Shindō Kyūzō from Meiji, and Mizuno Hideo from Waseda). For Nakano's recruiting activities, see Misuzu Shobō, ed., *Shakai shugi undō*, Gendaishi shiryō, XVI, 160.

21. *Ibid.*, pp. 95–182.

into the party only after they had left the student movement and become professional underground activists. The student movement itself was thus a kind of training ground for party recruits, and a point was eventually reached in the early 1930s when mass arrests became so frequent that students still engaged primarily in campus activities were taken directly into positions of high party leadership. It must be remembered, however, that the actual membership of the party was at most times very small and always clandestine, so that the majority of Gakuren members rarely knew at a given time whether a communist party even existed and few were ever given the opportunity to join. Yet the party had an existence within the student movement independent of its ephemeral reality, as an ideal deeply inculcated in the thought patterns of student radicals. The gap between the professed ideal of a communist party and its uncertain reality created a constant tension among students who considered themselves "communists." Nakano Shigeharu has captured this tension in *Muragimo*, where Yasukichi recalls a conversation with a fellow Shinjinkai member:

One day when there was no one in the house (although that probably had nothing to do with it), Murayama took out the latest issue of *Marxist Studies*, with Nagano's article, and, indicating a particular passage, asked me how to interpret it . . .

"In other words, isn't it like this? Doesn't it mean that there must be a revolutionary organization of the fully conscious elements?" I replied.

"Well, of course, there must. But *is* there one? Has it actually been formed?"

"Well . . ." Feeling a bit foolhardy, I answered, "Probably not."

"Probably not? If there isn't, shouldn't there be? Logically, the problem of leadership comes up. If there's no organization, how can you pose the problem of organized leadership?"

Since it seemed like a problem of mathematical logic, I was at a loss for a reply. But I could not bring myself to ask Murayama, "Well, then, *is* there one?"

Why did that cynic Murayama ask me about that? Was it a hint, given out of his peculiar indirect kindness? In short, he's talking about a communist party, isn't he? Is there a communist party? It seems there might be, but then it seems there might not be.[22]

Thanks to their theoretical grasp of the necessity and importance of a communist party, student radicals after 1925 afforded a substantial reservoir of "fully conscious elements" who were prepared to join if called. An invitation to a young university intellectual to join the clandestine Japanese Communist Party was not, as the wording of Peace Preservation Law indictments was to claim, an "inducement" (*kan'yū*) but rather an honor which allowed only immediate and un-conditional assent.[23] The relationship between the Communist Party and the students was less one of an organization in search of recruits than of recruits in search of an organization.

The student movement thus came *in fact* to serve as a natural train-ing ground and reservoir for party membership, especially as suppres-sion intensified after 1928; *in theory,* however, such a role was never admitted, creating a highly ambiguous relationship between the stu-dent movement and the party. This confusion was clearly revealed in Tokuda Kyūichi's testimony on the communist youth movement at the mass public trial of the communists in September 1931. Tokuda claimed that "petty bourgeois elements have greatly overestimated the role of students, and many appear to view students as the vanguard of revolutionary activity. But this is fundamentally mistaken." When the bemused Judge Miyagi inquired why, then, did so many student intel-lectuals enter the party, Tokuda (after contemptuously warning Miyagi that a bourgeois judge could not comprehend his argument, which was doubtless true) resorted to the same arguments developed by stu-dent theorists years before, admitting that intellectuals could in fact be turned into revolutionary militants through proper training and theoretical mastery.[24]

The official party view of the student movement followed naturally from this theoretical deprecation of bourgeois intellectuals as party

22. Nakano, *Muragimo,* pp. 274–275.
23. Matsuzawa Kōyō, "Marukusu shugi ni okeru shisō to shūdan," in Chikuma shobō, ed., *Kindai Nihon shisō shi kōza,* 8 vols. (editor, 1959–61), V, 236–240.
24. Misuzu shobō, ed., *Shakai shugi undō,* Gendaishi shiryō, XVII, 655 656. The contempt for intellectuals at this time was related to the activities of the "Worker Faction" (Rōdōsha-ha, led by Mizuno Shigeo and other intellectuals) in advocating the dissolution of the Communist Party.

members. The student movement was seen as comparable to any movement in defense of the interests of a specific social grouping, such as the trade union movement, the consumer movement, or the women's movement. Student activists would not be concerned with providing leadership for the elite ranks of the party itself but would merely direct activities which advanced the interests of students as a social class. If they did participate in the labor movement, it would merely be in a technical role as tutors and clerks. In short, the student movement was, as Hayashi and Koreeda had theorized first in 1924–25, merely "one wing of the proletarian movement" with no special claims to overall leadership. This general line was maintained consistently thereafter, although occasionally rephrased, as for example in an article by Shinjinkai member Nakano Hisao in the February 1927 issue of the Fukumotoist monthly *Seiji hihan* (Political criticism). Here Nakano simply reclothed the "one wing" theory in Fukumotoist cant, calling for a "merging with the total front of the proletarian movement" and a "progressive shift to an all-proletarian political struggle."[25]

It followed from the official interpretation of the student movement as a mass interest group that it could be infiltrated and influenced in much the same way as similar groups, through the use of party fractions. The creation of a fraction for the student movement was in fact specifically authorized by the Moscow Theses of March 1926, but action on the matter was apparently not taken until one year later.[26] The resulting "Student Fraction" (Gakusei Furakushon), supplemented by an enigmatic "Student Semi-Illegal Committee" (Gakusei Han-higōhō Iinkai)[27] which was alleged to have served as its auxiliary organization, had a shifting membership in which a total of ten persons were at some time involved. All were either students or recent

25. Sugi Michio [Nakano Hisao], "Gakusei shakai kagaku undō no hōkō tenkan," *Seiji hihan*, no. 1 (February 1927), pp. 51–67. This magazine was edited by a strongly pro-Fukumoto group of young intellectuals associated with the Industrial Labor Research Institute (Sangyō Rōdō Chōsajo), most of whom had been active in the student movement. Nakano had already left the university and the student movement when he wrote this article.

26. Misuzu shobō, ed., *Shakai shugi undō*, Gendaishi shiryō, XIV, 48. Tokuda in his 1931 trial testimony asserted that a student movement fraction was created by the party in 1925, but no other evidence corroborates this. See *ibid.*, XVII, 660.

27. The term appears to be a translation of the German (?) *halbirregale kommision* (*sic*). See Hasegawa, p. 169.

graduates, of whom seven were from Tokyo Imperial, and one each from Kyoto Imperial, Waseda, and Tokyo Women's College (the latter in charge of the recently founded Women's Gakuren). Most appear to have been Communist Party members at the time of their participation in the group.[28]

It should be clear that the Student Fraction was little more than an organizational redundancy, existing only to fit the dictates of official theory.[29] A fraction was normally expected to work within a mass interest group to subvert it and force upon it policies advantageous to the Communist Party. But in fact the student movement was very different from other mass interest groups, being already dominated and controlled by young intellectuals who pride themselves on their Marxist–Leninist purity. Clearly, there was little "subversion" to be carried out, since the student movement represented the most radical segment of the entire left wing. All that the Student Fraction accomplished, it would seem, was to accord official party recognition (and membership) to certain de facto leaders of the Gakuren. The case of the Student Fraction thus serves as ironic testimony to the confusion created by the gap between the theory (a mass interest group) and the reality (a reservoir for party leadership) of the student movement after 1926.

DAILY LIFE AMONG STUDENT COMMUNISTS

Ideology and organization, while essential to understanding the overall function of a student movement, fall short of giving any sense of the day-to-day functioning of student activism. What was it like, quite simply, to be a student communist in Japan in the late 1920s? The Shinjinkai around the winter of 1926–27, when radical purity was at a confident crest, offers a well-documented example of the life style of student communists. The Shinjinkai then had a membership upwards of 120; in contrast with the early Shinjinkai, however, it was not

28. For information on the Student Fraction, see Misuzu shobō, ed., *Shakai shugi undō*, Gendaishi shiryō, XVI, 236–240, under the indictment information on Soda Hidemune and Tanaka Toshio. Secondary summaries may be found in Hasegawa, pp. 166–177, and Mombushō, *Gakusei shisō undō no enkaku*, pp. 198–201.

29. In interviews, two former members of the Student Fraction (Tanaka Toshio and Tateyama Toshitada) were unable to recall any overall function or policy for the group.

a manageable, coordinated unit. With wide-ranging activities both on and off campus, much of the membership was scattered into isolated pockets, intensely involved in specialized projects which allowed little concern for the group as a whole. Degree of commitment also varied widely. Although proven dedication was in principle required for membership, with prospective joiners being closely scrutinized, many participated irregularly or only in specific, limited activities. It would be unusual for more than twenty or thirty to attend the regular monthly meetings of the Shinjinkai, and the "core" of the most dedicated and active members totaled no more than forty.

A variety of specialized interests and personality types were to be found within the group. As the Shinjinkai grew, it rapidly branched out from its exclusive base in the Faculty of Law to the Faculties of Economics, Letters, and Medicine. Temperamentally, the Shinjinkai students in 1926 diverged along factional lines not unlike those of the earlier period. The "activists" (*kōdō-ha* or *jissai-ha,* both informal terms) were those in control of overall policy and tended to prefer activities, such as union organizing, which enabled direct contact with the proletariat. On the other extreme were the scholarly types, who in early 1927 were condemned by the activist mainstream as the *shosai-ha,* or "study faction." These were most commonly found in the Faculty of Economics, and their major preoccupation was the academic one of Marxist economic theory. Fewer in number than either the activist or scholastic personalities were the two cliques of students, in literature and in medicine, which had been developed through the specialized study groups within the Tōdai Shaken. None of these various groupings, however, were clearcut factions competing for power within the Shinjinkai. They were rather tendencies, broad conflicts of temperament and vocational aim which created a constant tension among the membership but seldom sharp division. No matter which "tendency" a given member had, he participated with the rest in communal living, in study groups and in off-campus agitation.

As with the early Shinjinkai, communal life in a *gasshuku* sustained the enthusiasm and cohesiveness of the group. Following the earthquake, the severe student housing shortage made a *gasshuku* impractical, and temporary Shinjinkai headquarters were set up within the barrack dormitories in which a large number of members lived. In the course of 1924, however, with the increase in membership and the need for a more convenient and private headquarters, a *gasshuku* was set up north of the university in Komagome.[30] It chanced that the father of member Hayashi Fusao died that year, and his widowed mother, Gotō Hideko, was asked to come to Tokyo to act as caretaker of the Shinjinkai lodging. Mrs. Gotō served as house mother of the central *gasshuku* for the next two years, as it moved from Komagome to Sakuragi-chō on the heights behind Ueno Park in the spring of 1925 and thence to nearby Shimizu-chō in 1926. Wholly ignorant of the political activities of the Shinjinkai members when she came to Tokyo, the kindly old lady solicitously watched after their needs, providing cooking, cleaning, and motherly advice, for which she was held in great affection by the young radicals.[31]

From the spring of 1926 *gasshuku* life flourished, and by 1927 the Shinjinkai operated three separate establishments. The Shimizu-chō *gasshuku* was the central headquarters, located in a house rented from Ōkōchi Masatoshi, a member of the House of Peers whose son Nobutake was a member of the Urawa Higher literary clique within the Shinjinkai. The two others were located at Morikawa-chō and Oiwake-chō, both near the Hongō campus.[32] Each *gasshuku* housed from ten to fifteen members, and those living in them, while never more than one third of the total Shinjinkai membership, accounted for most of the "core." These off-campus houses were the heart of the Shinjinkai. It was here that the study groups and endless arguments took place, here that the theory and tactics of the entire Japanese student movement were worked out, and here that contact with the whole spectrum of the Japanese left was maintained by frequent visits from labor leaders, radical politicians, progressive academicians, and left-wing artists.

The tone of radical student life was not such as to lure recruits for

30. Hayashi Fusao interview.

31. For a portrait of Mrs. Gotō, which a number of former Shinjinkai members have praised for its effectiveness, see Nakano, *Muragimo*, p. 186. Hayashi appears in the novel as "Saeki Tetsuo."

32. For information on the various *gasshuku* and other aspects of Shinjinkai life in this period, see Nakahira Satoru *et al.*, "Shōsetsu *Muragimo* to Shinjinkai jidai," *Chūō hyōron*, no. 36 (December 1954), pp. 76–86; this is a discussion including former Shinjinkai members Nakahira Satoru, Ōmachi Tokuzō, and Yamauchi Tadayoshi.

its comforts, for it was puritanical, physically demanding, and intensely serious. The *gasshuku* itself was plain and almost wholly undecorated. The boarders rarely drank, in a country where heavy student drinking was not only a tradition but at times a major social problem: Nakano Shigeharu recalls his disbelief upon entering the Shimizu-chō *gasshuku* in 1926 to discover that all the other students were teetotalers, ignorant of the very taste of *sake*.[33] Behind the puritanism of the Shinjinkai lay a sense of discipline and moral rigidity that bordered on the masochistic. In *Muragimo*, Nakano describes "personal life criticism meetings" (*shi-seikatsu hihankai*) at which each student was subjected in turn to the open criticism by fellow members of any aspect of his private life which they found improper.[34] In such ways the tone of severity in *gasshuku* life was sustained. Flippancy, extravagance, lewdness, and even humor were all out of place.

A visitor to the Shinjinkai *gasshuku* in 1927 would also have been struck by the air of secrecy which dominated it. Many of the students, especially those participating in off-campus agitation, went by aliases, some having perhaps two or three different names for underground work, as well as a pen name or two for articles in left-wing magazines. Few of the radical students in this era wore the traditional uniforms, preferring working class clothing both as a camouflage and as a mark of solidarity with the proletariat. Much of the secrecy was forced by necessity. Plainclothes detectives were on constant watch outside the Shinjinkai *gasshuku*, and the individual members themselves were often followed. Vigilance had to be paid against the possibility of spies within the membership (one or two such cases were actually discovered) or of police attempts to bribe the less committed.

One doubts, however, that police pressure, at least before 1928, warranted such secrecy as the students maintained; a stronger motivation may have been the sheer excitement of underground work. Imagine, for instance, the tingling satisfaction of giving the slip to a plainclothesman tailing you, of sauntering out of a radical bookstore with a brand new copy of the *Communist Manifesto* in a plain brown wrapper, or of writing hidden notes to a jailed comrade in secret code. But what in the early stages may have been the "shivering thrill

33. Nakano, *Muragimo*, p. 190.
34. *Ibid.*, pp. 196–197.

of intrigue" had by the early 1930s, under intensified suppression, become a near obsession.[35] The novelist Dazai Osamu, who was involved in the underground student movement in 1931, later had the hero of *No Longer Human* reflect on the "ludicrous degree of secrecy" of the student movement, "perpetually prey to life-and-death tensions" and fraught with "frantic excitement over missions . . . of stupefying inconsequentiality."[36]

Out of the milieu of radical student life emerged a new jargon. In striking contrast to the thoroughly Japanese and intricately constructed cant of a similarly suppressed minority, the underworld, the jargon of the extreme left was wholly Western in origin, although sometimes contorted beyond recognition. Such terms as *furaku* (fraction), *repo* ("reporter" or contact man), *shimpa* (sympathizer), *orugu* (cell organizer), and *kyappu* (captain, or cell leader) were everyday language among radical students and many remain common today. It was as much a mark of shame to be labelled *buru* (bourgeois) as it was an honor to be called *puro* (proletarian). The more pedantic would insist on using the original German or English phrases picked up from study group texts. *Muragimo* depicts a scene in which "Ijūin" (Koreeda Kyōji) appeared one day at a discussion on the role of mass demonstrations. "When the talk reached a certain point, he thrust the upper part of his body across the table and as he leaned forward, Yasukichi from the corner heard him say in hushed tones, '. . . . No, the problem lies in *Aufstand*. There must be a future *Aufstand.*' " By using the German instead of an easily available Japanese word for "uprising," Ijūin gave his pronouncement an air of esoteric authority.[37]

In the late 1920s, one even finds the original Japanese titles of student organizations being translated into English; still more circuitously the abbreviation of the translation was then used to designate the group. Hence the Shinjinkai was frequently called the N.S. (New Men's Society), the Gakuren the F.S. (Federation of Students' Social Science), and a *shaken* an S.S. (Society of Students' Social Science).[38] In the early

35. The phrase is from Asano, *Izumu ni ugoku mono,* p. 18.
36. Dazai Osamu, *No Longer Human,* trans. Donald Keene (Norfolk, Conn., 1958), pp. 69–70.
37. Nakano, *Muragimo,* p. 193. The attribution to Koreeda is by Ishidō Kiyotomo in an interview.
38. The translations are given as in Hasegawa, p. 1.

1930s, as organizational forms proliferated, so accordingly did the array of contractions and abbreviations used to refer to them. Student manifestoes were filled with talk of "PN groups," "Anti-Imp," and "SL-like protests" [39] : small wonder that government officials found it necessary to compile and distribute glossaries of communist jargon to educational personnel throughout the country. In 1932, for example, the Ministry of Education issued a confidential pamphlet, "An Illustrated Explanation of the Student Thought Movement," which included a list of almost two hundred left-wing terms.[40]

The pace of life of a student radical in prewar Japan was hectic. During the day the Shinjinkai *gasshuku* were deserted as the members scattered to their wide-ranging activities on the campus, in labor unions, in the settlement, or traveling to make contact with rural peasant groups. Upon returning in the evening, the students would gather for study circles or informal theoretical discussions. Time also had to be allotted for the study of texts, a time-consuming task if the books were in a foreign language. With the many preoccupations of the movement itself, two areas which were conspicuous by their absence in the daily agenda were relaxation and academic life. Shinjinkai members, at least the more committed, rarely had time for frequenting cafés, strolling the Ginza, picnicking, athletics, or other conventional student pastimes. What entertainment they did enjoy would normally have a political dimension; if they attended the theater, it would be proletarian drama at the Tsukiji Little Theater, and when they engaged in rugby practice, it was to temper their reflexes for encounters with the police.[41]

In their academic life, the later Shinjinkai members continued the earlier patterns of near-total neglect of classes, except for such special cases as medical students or the lectures of young radical professors. Shinjinkai members were on the whole academically uninvolved, devoting themselves to the prescribed curriculum only for a week or two before the annual examinations in March—hence a consistent lull

39. For example, see the Gakuren document quoted in Naimushō, *Shakai undō no jōkyō* (1930), p. 369.

40. Mombushō, Gakuseibu, *Gakusei shisō undō zukai* (September 1932), pp. 85–98.

41. For the activity of the Shinjinkai rugby team, see *Teikoku daigaku shimbun,* no. 105 (January 31, 1925), p. 3. The explanation (perhaps apocryphal) of the Shinjinkai motive was provided me by Professor Matsumoto Kaoru of Waseda, who was at the time a Tokyo Imperial student and a dedicated rugby player.

in campus radicalism in that month. Like their predecessors, Shinjinkai members in the late 1920s seemed anxious to graduate, if only to satisfy the parents who in many cases had undergone privation and anxiety to send them to the university. After the initiation of systematic suppression following the 1928 arrests, many Shinjinkai members failed to graduate, but it was more often because of disciplinary action taken by the university than from any voluntary renunciation of university education and its privileges. Only two Shinjinkai members in the class of 1927 failed to graduate; approximately one third of those in 1930 did not. A few who were expelled for left-wing activity, however, were readmitted after several years and eventually graduated.[42]

School vacations, especially the two-month summer recess, were seen by radical students not as a time for rest and recreation but rather as an opportunity to extend their influence in new directions. Like all students in Tokyo, the Shinjinkai members returned to their native provinces but less to pay the ritual family respects than to try their hand at agitation on the local level. Systematically organized as early as 1923 under the euphemism "summer work" (*sāmā wāku*), this kind of activity continued thereafter as a regular Shinjinkai project.[43] The most common targets were the provincial higher schools; Shinjinkai members would regularly visit their respective alma maters to encourage and coordinate the activities of the *shaken* there.[44] In the late 1920s, some students even attempted to set up study circles in their former middle schools, although in most cases these groups collapsed, either under school pressure or for lack of interest, soon after the Tokyo organizer departed. Still another area of provincial agitation during academic recess was in local labor and tenant unions, although here again the vigilance of the local authorities, who were constantly on the lookout for these students from Tokyo ("outside agitators" in contemporary American parlance), inhibited any lasting success.

Women comprised another area in the life of the student radical where political considerations, if not overwhelming, were important.

---

42. This pattern became much more frequent in the early and middle 1930s, when the forcing of recantation became standard government policy.

43. Kikukawa, *Gakusei shakai undō shi,* pp. 185–186.

44. Nakano, *Muragimo,* chap. 4, describes a trip by Yasukichi during the summer to make contact with *shaken* at Fourth Higher (Nakano's alma mater) and Toyama Higher.

The liberal convictions of the Shinjinkai members generally extended to their attitudes towards the opposite sex, leaving a minor stain of feminism throughout the history of the group. In April 1920 Kadota Takeo wrote an article on "The Creation of a Feminine Culture," arguing that women were subjected to a twofold oppression of "wage slavery and sexual slavery" and urging them to "break free of these shackles." [45] Student radicals were at the same time strongly opposed to legalized prostitution, condemning it as an institution of bourgeois decadence, and resolutely refrained from frequenting the brothels popular among many other students. Thus in 1923, for example, the Tōdai Shaken sponsored a discussion group with the aging crusader against prostitution, Miss Hayashi Utako.[46] Again, in late 1926, a student magazine attacked the oppression of women in female colleges, which they claimed was rationalized "in the name of a lifeless, traditionalistic, nunnery-like 'school spirit.' " [47]

Ideological convictions strongly colored the personal ties of Shinjinkai members with women, who were seen less as lovers than as partners in the movement for social and political reform. It was largely under the tutelage of Shinjinkai members that a minute but vigorous female student movement emerged in the late 1920s. Even in the period of the early Shinjinkai a study group had been organized at Tokyo Women's College, under the guidance first of Morito Tatsuo and then of Sano Manabu.[48] Although short-lived, these groups were succeeded in about 1925 by *shaken* both at Tokyo Women's College and Japan Women's College. Shinjinkai members Koreeda, Shiga, Asano, and others offered their services as tutors and were joined in 1926 by Fukumoto Kazuo (whose interest in the female study circles appears to have extended beyond the intellectual; rumor has imputed to him amorous associations with as many as six of his pupils).[49] Romance blossomed in a number of cases, and several Shinjinkai members found wives (as often as not on a common-law basis) in the *shaken* at these

45. *Shinjinkai kikanshi*, p. 238.
46. *Teikoku daigaku shimbun*, no. 62 (January 2, 1924), p. 3.
47. Kobayashi Kōzō, "Gakusei no jiyū kakutoku undō," *Gakusei undō*, no. 2 (November 1926), p. 7.
48. Amakusa Rintarō, *Nihon kyōsantō daikenkyo shi* (Bukyōsha, 1929), p. 404.
49. *Ibid.*, pp. 408–410, 412, 415, and Tateyama Takaaki, *Nihon kyōsantō kenkyo hishi* (Bukyōsha, 1929), p. 340.

two colleges. Among the most noted of their prizes were Watanabe Taeko, the central leader at Tokyo Women's who married Shiga shortly after her graduation in 1927, and Hatano Misao, also from Tokyo Women's, who became Koreeda's mistress. These two were among the leaders of the Women's Gakuren (organized in early 1927) who were arrested in the 1928–29 communist roundups, creating a public sensation at the time.

While ideological sympathy was certainly desirable in the female companions sought after by Shinjinkai members, women also served more realistic functions, especially for students intent on careers as professional revolutionaries. Many of the students at women's colleges were of wealthy family background and could be counted on for financial support in a movement constantly hampered by lack of funds. Women were of further use as a camouflage for underground activity, since they enabled a minimum of exposure by undertaking the purchase of daily necessities and maintaining contact with other comrades. With a "housekeeper" (hausukīpā), as they were known in the jargon of the left, a communist activist could minimize suspicion and protect his cover.

A very few Shinjinkai members related their political convictions to romance not by seeking out like-minded female intellectuals but rather by entering "into the people." The most famous of these was Mizuno Shigeo, who, after withdrawing from the Shinjinkai in 1923 to enter into the Kansai labor movement, discovered a nearly illiterate eighteen-year-old named Nakagawa Hanako, then employed as a waitress in a Kyoto restaurant. Enticed by her thoroughly proletarian qualities, Mizuno wooed, radicalized, and eventually married her; he has since become one of postwar Japan's most powerful businessmen, and Hanako remains his wife.[50] On the whole, however, those Shinjinkai members who sought women either for their political radicalism or their proletarian purity were in the minority; ultimately, most chose the much less revolutionary course of a traditional arranged marriage.

The economic life of the Shinjinkai members also deserves mention. Most, while not in desperate poverty, were far from well-to-do, sharing in the economic plight of the majority of students in the late 1920s. The typical Shinjinkai member received a monthly allowance, either

50. Okamoto Kōji, *Nagatomi Ryūken to iu otoko—Kyosetsu Mizuno Shigeo den* (Dōmei tsūshinsha, 1965), pp. 90–91.

from his parents, from a hometown benefactor, or from one of the provincial scholarship associations (*ikueikai*) of forty to fifty yen ($20–$25) a month. Over half of this had to be spent on tuition (almost ten yen a month) and room and board—the latter of very low quality. When the expenses of clothing, school supplies, and, above all, books—a major expense for radical students—were added, little was left for any extravagances.

Student activists supported their political activities almost entirely with their own money, supplemented perhaps by occasional contributions from sympathetic senior intellectuals. No evidence may be found to suggest provision of student movement funds by the Japanese Communist Party or by foreign agents; on the contrary, students gave what little they could afford to the movement itself. Many young radicals were so consistently in debt that they were forced to seek side jobs to support themselves. While some engaged in the traditional job of tutoring middle school students for entrance exam preparation, it was more usual for Shinjinkai members to earn money by translating left-wing literature or by working in a clerical capacity in labor unions in return for small wages.[51] Certain Shinjinkai extracurricular activities, such as editing the *Imperial University News* or administering the dining hall project, also provided the members with extra income.

The radical life style was, above all, a *total* life style, at least for the dedicated "core." Commitment to communism was seen not simply as the advocacy of certain political reforms or adherence to a certain method of economic analysis; it was considered rather a new way of life. In fact, however, the radical life style offered little that was really new, except perhaps its language. Far from iconoclastic, the student radicals were cast in a familiar Confucian mold, stressing the importance of such conservative values as discipline, moral propriety, and secrecy. These tendencies were progressively intensified by the solemn and uninspiring tone of Japanese life in general in the 1920s and by the increasing government suppression of the left. The exuberance of the early Shinjinkai would have seemed inexcusably flippant in the context of the mood of grim and total determination which had enveloped the student movement by the end of the decade.

51. Kadoya Hiroshi in Mombushō, *Sakei gakusei seito no shuki*, I, 21, mentions that students could make twenty to thirty yen ($10–15) a month at such work.

7 | Suppression

Government control was the single most critical factor in molding the forms of student radicalism in prewar Japan. The constant threat of suppression gave to left-wing student life a tone of tension and excitement which did much to sustain the movement at the same time that it drove it to ever greater extremes of belligerency and ideological dogmatism. The prevalence and variety of government control gave to the students a wide array of issues and incidents on which to further build their movement in the name of academic freedom and student autonomy; yet such gains were offset by a concomitant tendency to relegate the original issues of social injustice to secondary importance. The effects of suppression were thus great but paradoxical: it served as a stimulant to student activism when mild but as a depressant when thorough; it encouraged the quantitative growth of the movement but degraded its quality; it forced the evolution of elaborately devised organizational schemes but worked to detract attention from theoretical fundamentals.

Two different segments of the state bureaucracy had a direct interest in control of the student movement. The police officials in the Ministry of the Interior were concerned with student radicals as one part of the overall left-wing movement and interpreted the problem within the relatively narrow, negative context of criminal behavior and threats to security, whether internal or national. The police approach to control was rational and authoritarian, relying on the usual techniques of banning books, dissolving meetings, surveillance, arrest, torture, and imprisonment. The educational officials in the Ministry of Education, however, tended to take a broader view of the problem, focusing on deficiencies in the educational system as the root causes of student dissent. To educators, student radicals were not criminally misfit but spiritually misguided, either because of liaisons with the off-campus left ("outside agitators") or because of a lack of adequate patriotic education.

Within both the police and the educational bureaucracies there occurred a gradual intensification and elaboration of suppression in the decade following the emergence of an organized national student movement in 1923. The mass arrests of March 15, 1928, emerge as a clear turning point in this evolution. Before that point, control efforts were on the whole haphazard, uncoordinated, and notably ineffective in stemming the growth of the student movement. After the 3.15 arrests, however, rapid steps were taken in the direction of a broadly coordinated apparatus of suppression, although the formal machinery was not completed for another five years. This period saw the police officials greatly intensify their own approach of control through arrest and prosecution, while the Ministry of Education turned to its own distinctively "soft" approach stressing persuasion and reeducation as key deterrents. Where the police approach was rational and "paternal," the educators' approach was affective and "maternal," striving to encourage a reintegration of radical students with the womb of Japanese tradition and the family. This "soft" approach was greatly extended through the Ministry of Justice in its efforts after 1931 to force the recantation of convicted communists.

HIGHER SCHOOL SUPPRESSION, 1924–1925

Systematic control of the student movement appeared first not at the university level, but in the higher schools. This was in large part because strict discipline and close surveillance were far more in keeping with the higher school stress on character formation than with the spirit of professionalism and free inquiry which dominated the universities. While universities, both state and private, harbored an instinctive hostility towards any Ministry of Education efforts to interfere with student discipline, the higher schools—excepting to some extent the oldest and most prestigious schools such as First and Third Higher

—were on the whole servile to the dictates of the central bureaucracy in matters of student control.

From the moment that higher school *shaken* began to emerge in 1922, higher school principals (who, unlike their university counterparts, tended to be professional administrators rather than teachers serving in a temporary administrative capacity) demonstrated their concern and are rumored to have discussed control measures at their annual conference that year.[1] Official school recognition was granted the *shaken* grudgingly, if at all. Suspicion increased in the year following the Kanto earthquake when officials discovered that the higher school *shaken* were part of a national left-wing student federation. In May 1924 a group of Shinjinkai and Kyoto Imperial Shaken members under the leadership of Asō Hisashi embarked on a lecture tour to western Japan to stimulate the growth of study groups there. This trip much resembled that of earlier Shinjinkai leaders in the fall of 1922, which had resulted in the formation of the Higher School League. This time, however, provincial school officials were alert to the coming of the big-city radicals and took special measures to discourage them. The Gakuren visitors had the most trouble at Fifth Higher in Kumamoto, where principal Mizobuchi Shimma, an outspoken hardliner, firmly refused them permission to speak on campus and even attempted to counter their efforts by encouraging a rally of a local right-wing student group.[2]

Not long after, Okada Ryōhei became Minister of Education, a post he was to hold for almost three years, earning a reputation among student leftists as the leading architect of suppression policy. Ironically, Okada himself had been involved in the socialist movement when a student at Tokyo Imperial University some twenty years before and was a relative moderate on the question of control.[3] Nevertheless, it was under his direction that the first steps towards coordinated suppression were taken at the annual conference of higher school principals in early October 1924. After evidence of Shinjinkai efforts to link

1. *Teikoku daigaku shimbun,* no. 100 (December 15, 1924), p. 5, also quoted in Kikukawa, *Gakusei shakai undō shi,* pp. 288–289.
2. For a detailed report on this trip, see *Shinjinkai kaihō,* no. 3 (July 1, 1924), pp. 10–12. See also Kikukawa, *Gakusei shakai undō shi,* pp. 211–286.
3. Nijō Einosuke, "Gakusei jiyū yōgo dōmei no seiritsu oyobi sono nimmu," *Gakusei undō,* no. 1 (October 1926), p. 17.

the higher school *shaken* into a national left-wing student organization was presented, Fifth Higher's Mizobuchi put forth a resolution calling for the dissolution of these groups. The first public indication of the new policy came on December 5 when Mizobuchi ordered the dissolution of the Fifth Higher Shaken, citing the authority of the Minister of Education. In the ensuing two months, most of the remaining higher school study groups were dissolved in the face of an assault which relied on threats and cajolery rather than outright force, in an attempt to dull student response. The longest to survive were the *shaken* at First and Third Higher, which were finally dissolved in the fall of 1925.[4]

The effectiveness of higher school *shaken* dissolution was minimal. Deprived of formal school recognition, students simply carried their organization underground. Study activities, which were easy to camouflage, continued precisely as before, while open on-campus agitation was conducted by manipulating debating clubs or literary groups. Far from suppressing left-wing activity in the provincial higher schools, *shaken* dissolution did much to fan it. Not only was suppression itself a highly effective issue for mobilizing moderate student support in the name of "academic freedom," but it also enabled the radical leaders to savor the excitement of clandestine activism with little fear of serious consequences. By heightening the frustration and hostility of the educators, this first step at suppression paved the way for the institution of the far broader control apparatus which was to follow.

THE KYOTO GAKUREN INCIDENT, 1925–1926

Although educational authorities were the first to take systematic action to stem student radicalism, the police officials had displayed a strong interest in the student movement ever since the period of the early Shinjinkai. The police were beset, however, by the lack of an effective legal apparatus to deal with the students. They were hamstrung first by the strongly autonomous attitudes of Japanese university officials, who adamantly refused cooperation with early police control efforts. Although police spies were known to enter the campus to

4. For details on the suppression of each group, see Kikukawa, *Gakusei shakai undo shi*, pp. 289–292.

watch suspicious students and professors, they had no powers of arrest or of dissolution of assembly. The focus of police control was thus concentrated on student ties with the off-campus left in the labor, farm, and socialist intellectual movements. Yet even in this area, little effective control legislation existed. The Peace Police Law of 1900 gave law enforcement officials broad power over political assembly and specifically forbade the participation of students in political associations but carried only a twenty-yen ($10) fine for violation. Since the law was designed originally to regulate dissent rather than to eliminate it, the penalties were light, amounting at the most to one year's imprisonment (for clandestine association, the crime for which the leaders of the First Communist Party were convicted).

Thwarted by the weakness of the Peace Police Law, the law enforcement authorities could control student radicals only on tangential charges, such as disturbing the peace, lese majesty, or violation of the press laws, all of which required elaborate vigilance and could be pressed only against a single individual, leaving the organization intact. Frustration was even greater in the area of censorship, for the antiquated Book Section in the Ministry of the Interior found itself unable to keep up with the explosive growth of the publishing world in the 1920s. The very machinery of censorship was ludicrously ineffective; almost all radical periodicals and handbills, for example, were officially banned only after they had been completely distributed. Prosecution under the press laws for inflammatory statements was time-consuming and unrewarding for want of severe penalties.[5] Ministry of Interior officials, while well aware that students were absorbing huge doses of Western radical literature and were closely involved with the off-campus left, found themselves unable to pursue any but circuitous and stopgap methods of control.

The Peace Preservation Law of April 1925 dramatically improved the prospects for strict control. Reflecting a wholly different approach from the Peace Police Law, the new legislation defined unlawful association not in terms of secrecy or sedition but rather of ideology, forbidding various types of involvement in activities aimed at "altering

5. For an interesting account of the frustrations of the censors, see Mitamura Takeo, *Sensō to kyōsan shugi* (Minsei seido fukyūkai, 1950), pp. 85–97. The author served as a Ministry of Interior censor in 1928–29.

the national polity (*kokutai*) or denying the system of private owner-ship." Most important, penalties ranging up to ten years of imprison-ment with heavy labor were provided, enabling a serious threat to the continuity of left-wing leadership. While communism was not specif-ically mentioned in the law, the target was obvious enough to all in-volved and would be confirmed by the practice of the following years.

It was probably a coincidence—albeit a fortuitous one for the stu-dent left—that the Peace Preservation Law was first used against the Gakuren.[6] The central figure in the case was Kubota Shun, a police official who in 1923 had figured prominently in the arrests of the First Communist Party in Tokyo and who was appointed head of the Special Higher Section of the Kyoto Police Bureau in late 1924.[7] Eager to further his reputation for ferreting out left-wing conspiracies, Kubota became interested in the Gakuren when it held its Second Congress in his bailiwick in July 1925, not long after the passage of the Peace Preservation Law. Kubota and his men kept tight watch over the Kyoto Gakuren leaders during the several months following, watchful for any suggestions of a new communist party. Suspicion mounted in late September when Kyoto students managed to make contact with a visiting Soviet trade union representative in spite of tight police security.[8] The anti-military education movement generated by the Otaru hypothesis incident provided still more grist for Kubota's mill, and by the end of November he was confident that enough activity was underfoot to warrant mass arrests.

The student arrests were made in the early morning of December 1. Thirty-seven members of the Gakuren, almost all from Kyoto Imperial

6. A huge amount of government materials is available for study of the Kyoto Gakuren incident. Sets of the entire preliminary investigation interrogation records, Shihōshō, "Taishō jūgonen Kyōto o chūshin to suru gakusei jiken chōsho kiroku," 21 vols. (mimeo., 1926), may be found in Dōshisha University (Kirisutokyō Shakai Mondai Kenkyūjo), Kyoto University (Jimbun Kagaku Kenkyūjo), and Hōsei University (Ōhara Institute). For a convenient summary of the case and the background of the defendants, see Shihōshō, Keijikyoku, *Gakusei chian iji hō ihan jiken kōgai*, Shisō kenkyū shiryō, no. 7 (June 1928).

7. The role of Kubota in the 1923 arrests is mentioned only in Kikukawa, *Gakusei shakai undō shi*, p. 364. In a personal letter to the author dated Septem-ber 28, 1970, in response to queries on this point, Kubota neither confirmed nor denied his involvement in the 1923 arrests, merely indicating that prior to his Kyoto appointment he had served as a police official in Aichi Prefecture.

8. For accounts of this incident, see Hasegawa, p. 112, and Kikukawa, *Gakusei shakai undō shi*, pp. 331–333.

and Dōshisha, were detained in two police stations for interrogation while their rooms were seached for evidence.[9] The announced reason for the arrests was suspected violation of the Publication Law in an anti-military education handbill distributed at Dōshisha in mid-November. It seems clear, however, that the police had hoped from the beginning to prosecute for violation of the still untested Peace Preservation Law. But to their disappointment, the bulk of the evidence seized consisted of bushels of German and English left-wing texts that had legally passed censorship controls; the press mercilessly twitted the police for being unable to read the documents. More serious than the lack of evidence were the massive student protests triggered by the arrests. Huge rallies were held on a number of campuses, and angry manifestoes issued by students and faculty alike. Protests were based not only on the broad issue of intellectual freedom but also on the more technical grounds of the alleged illegality of the arrests and the violation of university autonomy in the search of a campus dormitory without university authorization.[10]

Apparently startled by the adverse publicity and wide protest, the Kyoto police released all the arrested students within a week, and by the middle of the month press reports began to hint that charges would not be pressed except for the minor press law violations. But while the incident on the surface seemed to have petered out, in reality the Kyoto police officials, smarting from their public disgrace, were preparing a second offensive. Confident that certain of the documents gathered in the December searches would enable conviction under the vague wording of the Peace Preservation Law, the police this time took the critical precaution of banning all press notices pending indictment.

The second roundup, which included about half of those arrested previously, began on January 15, 1926, and continued sporadically through April, reaching a final total of thirty-eight students (of whom a small number were dropouts or recent graduates). Twenty of these

9. Press reports at the time varied widely as to the number arrested; the *Tōkyō asahi shimbun* reported 20 on December 2, 26 on the 3rd, and 34 on the 4th, while the *Ōsaka asahi shimbun* of December 3 gave 32. The *Teikoku daigaku shimbun* on December 14 gave still another figure of 33, which has been followed by Kikukawa, *Gakusei shakai undō shi*, p. 353. I have preferred to accept the government figure of 37, which appears, for example, in Hasegawa, p. 115.

10. For details of the protests, see Kikukawa, *Gakusei shakai undō shi*, pp. 353–358.

were from Kyoto Imperial and nine from various other Kansai schools. Nine Tokyo leaders (including four Shinjinkai members) who had participated in Gakuren affairs in Kyoto in late 1925 were included as a token to establish the nationwide extent of the federation. The students were all released on bail or recognition following indictment in September; and in April 1927 all were convicted of violations of the Peace Preservation Law and given sentences ranging from eight to twelve months.[11]

The precise aims of the officials who masterminded the Kyoto Gakuren arrests have never been made clear; perhaps a precedent for the use of the Peace Preservation Law was desired, or perhaps Kubota's inordinate ambition was the deciding factor.[12] Whatever the hidden motives, however, the ulterior aim of crushing the radical student movement was seriously disappointed. The attitude of the Gakuren students throughout their several months' stay in the Kyoto penitentiary was defiant and unrepenting. Indeed, they were given little cause for regret; in contrast to the torture inflicted on many thought prisoners in the 1930s, the Gakuren students were treated with respect by police and justice officials and given all the comforts they might desire —including large shipments of the latest communist literature from their comrades outside.[13] Little wonder that when questioned by justice officials as to their future plans, the students almost without exception announced their intentions to dedicate their lives to the proletarian movement.[14] They kept their word. All the defendants were suspended from their respective universities following indictment and immedi-

11. The initial decision in the Kyoto Gakuren incident was appealed and became a highly complex and protracted case, largely because of the complications introduced by the re-arrest of many of the defendants in 1928–29. The first appeal, which was heard in the Osaka Court of Appeals, lasted for over two and a half years, with a new verdict (but only for those who had not been re-arrested in the meantime) on December 12, 1929, which increased the sentences for a number of the defendants. A final appeal was made by a group of nine, but was dismissed on May 27, 1930. The case created some unusual legal problems with respect to the possibility of double jeopardy; see, for example, the *Tōkyō asahi shimbun* accounts of the cases of Ikeda Takashi (December 14, 1929, p. 7) and Kumagai Takao (June 10, 1930, evening ed., p. 2).

12. Kubota claims that the arrests were fully approved by the Ministry of Interior in Tokyo, but this may have been rather passive assent. Letter cited.

13. Hayashi Fusao, *Bungakuteki kaisō*, p. 24, tells of receiving the latest copies of *Imprecorr* while in jail.

14. Shihōshō, "Taishō jūgonen . . . gakusei jiken chōsho kiroku," *passim*.

ately embarked on careers of professional activism. The Ministry of the Interior noted with concern in its 1927 report on the left-wing movement that many of the Kyoto Gakuren defendants had become active in communist front organizations after release pending trial and appeals.[15] These qualms were substantiated in the 1928–29 mass communist arrests, when twenty-two of the thirty-eight were rearrested as members of the Japanese Communist Party.[16]

THE STALEMATE OF STUDENT CONTROL, 1926–1927

Following the Kyoto Gakuren arrests, initiative in student control policy shifted from the police back to the Ministry of Education. Educators quickly concluded from the Gakuren roundup that the central problem of the left-wing student movement lay in its ties with groups outside the campus, whether labor unions, socialist parties, or radical students on other campuses. Not a few educational officials appeared angered and embarrassed over what was seen as a police intrusion into campus concerns. The keynote in the period after the Gakuren arrests, then, was to *isolate* the student movement, to contain it within the confines of the campus. In this way, it was argued, students would be completely under the control of educators and free from the corrupting "outside" influences that were seen as the lifeline of student radicalism. This reasoning was based on two assumptions which were quickly to be disproved: first, that students *could* be isolated from the outside world short of total incarceration; and second, that the sources of student radicalism were independent of the educational institutions themselves.

The Kyoto Gakuren arrests were not long in producing an escalation of control within the educational bureaucracy. The higher school principals' conference in Tokyo in early May 1926 discussed the ambiguous results of *shaken* dissolution and concluded that stiffer measures were necessary. In the wake of the conference, minister Okada issued a directive to the heads of all college-level schools, spelling out a new policy.[17] The previous prohibition of the group study of left-wing

15. Naimushō, *Shakai shugi undō no jōkyō* (1927), p. 87.
16. Of the sixteen *not* rearrested, most were active in the left-wing movement, including such notable activists as Hayashi Fusao, Noro Eitarō, and Suzuki Yasuzō.
17. The precise form taken by this directive is unclear. Such government reports as Hasegawa, p. 145, claim that it was a resolution (*ketsugi*) passed at the con-

literature was now extended to individual study. Student participation in any sort of off-campus activity was forbidden and debating and literary clubs, which had in many cases become pawns of the student left, were placed under strict school supervision. But although this "Okada Directive" was the first explicit statement by the government on control of the radical student movement, it did little more than affirm existing policy in most higher schools and was weakened by the absence of any specification of concrete control procedures. The Okada Directive was probably less important in tightening campus control of the left than in providing a timely new issue in the protest repertoire of the student radicals.

The release of the news ban on the Kyoto Gakuren Incident in the fall of 1926 led to a new phase of control activity, with official concern now escalating to the previously inviolate university level. The first step was the dissolution of the Kyushu Imperial University Shaken on September 29, two weeks after the press ban release, on the specific grounds of Gakuren affiliation.[18] Politicians for the first time began to query the government in regard to its policy towards student radicals, and in early October the Ministry of Education announced that all ties with the Gakuren must be renounced by recognized groups on state university campuses.[19] Specific guidelines aimed at eliminating outside contacts by radical study groups were laid down at all the imperial universities. Private universities as well took steps paralleling those of the government. In almost all cases, however, the university authorities stopped short of outright dissolution, remaining hesitantly loyal to their professed ideals of academic freedom. Even the Kyushu Imperial Shaken, thus, was reestablished with university approval in January 1928.[20] In all, the new restrictions had little effect, especially on the most active campuses of Tokyo Imperial, Kyoto Imperial, and

---

ferences of higher school and college principals, while Kikukawa, *Gakusei shakai undō shi*, pp. 376–378, terms it a *tsūtatsu*, or "directive," issued by the minister; both agree that the term *naikun*, or "informal instruction," was one which was inaccurately used among the students to refer to the document. Still a third explanation is that it was in the form of a *kunji*, or "oral explanation," given by Okada at the higher school principals' conference; see Ebihara, *Zoku gendai Nihon kyōiku seisaku shi*, p. 101.

18. Ōhara, *Nihon rōdō nenkan*, VIII (1927), 449.
19. *Tōkyō asahi shimbun*, October 8, 1926, p. 2.
20. Kawamura, *Shisō mondai nempyō*, p. 75.

Waseda, where left-wing students remained in touch with the "outside" left and often dominant within it.

The Okada Directive and the prohibition of Gakuren affiliations gave the student leadership an opportunity to develop some new techniques of organization and agitation. In early June, for example, in protest against the Okada Directive, a number of liberal groups on the Tokyo Imperial campus banded together to organize the Tokyo Imperial University Student League for the Defense of Liberty. Parallel groups were set up in Kansai and elsewhere, all of which were united in a national organization on June 28 as the All-Japan Student League for the Defense of Liberty (Zen-Nihon Gakusei Jiyū Yōgo Dōmei). Much like the Anti-Military Education League in the fall of 1924, this organization was little more than a puppet of the left, duplicating the Gakuren in leadership and organization while enjoying the support of a number of moderate campus groups which rallied to the cry of the "defense of liberty." When the Gakuren itself came under fire in the fall of 1926, the leadership simply relegated the term "Gakuren" to underground status and proceeded to act precisely as before through the Defense of Liberty League. Such shifting of labels while maintaining identical policies appears to have been enough to satisfy the school authorities at this stage.

From the fall of 1926 the student left launched a counteroffensive against the educational establishment which came to be known as the "student self-government movement" (gakusei jichi undō). The Okada Directive and the announcement of the Kyoto Gakuren arrests released a great deal of sympathy for the persecuted student left. Senior intellectuals filled the pages of the liberal monthlies like Kaizō, Warera, and Chūō Kōron with turgid tracts in defense of academic freedom,[21] while the liberal and moderate segments of the student population showed a new willingness to join with the left. To capitalize on this widespread sympathy, the radical leadership adopted a policy of encouraging specific, campus-oriented reforms under the broad label of "student self-government." The model for this activity had been established several years earlier by the Shinjinkai in the Gakuyūkai

21. For a bibliography of such articles, see Kokuritsu kokkai toshokan, Rippō kōsakyoku, comp., Daigaku no jiyū ni kansuru bunken mokuroku (Compiler, 1952), pp. 89–99.

reform movement, but now for the first time it was sponsored on a coordinated national scale. To provide a voice for the movement, a magazine entitled *Student Movement* (*Gakusei undō*) was begun in October by Gakuren leaders from Waseda and Tokyo Imperial.[22] This was the first time since the termination of *Narod* in 1922 that the Japanese student left attempted to launch a wide, popular student movement through the medium of a legal magazine; [23] it was also to be the last.

The range of the student "self-government" movement was explained in an article entitled "The Student Movement to Win Freedom" in the second issue of *Student Movement*, by "Kobayashi Kōzō" (whose true identity is unclear). The author first stressed the need to defend the students' right to study social science but went on to explain that radicals must not stop there, they must proceed to the reform of the university itself, to create a truly student-oriented student movement. In suggesting some possible approaches, Kobayashi touched on many of the basic issues of Japanese student autonomy for years to come:

In higher schools, colleges, and universities throughout the country there exist no organs of student self-government. Wholly tyrannical schools are found in great number. Even where there are such organs, they exist in name only and do not serve truly to represent the will of the students and to transmit it to the authorities. Student councils and assemblies, just like the Imperial Diet, are wholly powerless. And above this is the Faculty Assembly, which admits no student participation whatsoever, and then the antiquated, bureaucratic Board of Directors and University Senate, not unlike the genro or Privy Council. Thus it is a system in which the student right of self-government is clearly and completely denied, and the school, the very institution which claims to

22. The chief editors of this magazine were Nagashima Matao (a Waseda Shaken leader), Yoshikawa Saneharu (a Shinjinkai member who then went under the alias of Futatsugi Takeshi), and Ōta Keitarō (Shinjinkai). Ōta Keitarō interview and Ishidō Kiyotomo correspondence.

23. The magazines of the Kensetsūsha Dōmei were not, in my opinion, student movement organs, while the various "bulletins" (*kaihō*) put out by the Shinjinkai and Gakuren in the mid-1920s were irregular newssheets for circulation among the membership alone.

be independent from society, ironically manifests a system of oppression which is a replica of the Japanese state itself.

Again, if we consider the instruction which we receive every day, we find that absolutely no student participation is permitted in deciding upon curriculum, professors, or schedules, and that through the system of attendance, grades, and examinations, a unilaterally decreed system of force-fed education is imposed on the students. Accordingly, military education has been set up in schools to make barracks of them, in spite of the student masses rising as one in protest, and has been forced on them by using a combination of threats and favors . . .

Further, if one considers the students' daily life, do the school authorities *really* strive sincerely for its betterment? We demand the construction and student management of free dormitories which are not mere prisons. We desire adequate campus hygienic facilities. We seek the establishment of a mutual aid system. We demand the free student use of campus facilities. Just look at the Yasuda Amphitheater which was recently constructed at vast expense at Tokyo Imperial University. To what extent is this for the benefit of students? Of course, students have the right to use it. They just have to pay two hundred yen ($100) each time! We demand the construction of assembly places which we can use freely.[24]

The self-government movement has traditionally been accorded its first success in a major student strike at Matsuyama Higher School in December 1926, although the incident was a classic oust-the-principal type with little or no political coloring. The importance of "self-government" activity, however, lay precisely in its nonradical orientation, which in theoretical terms served to heighten the consciousness of liberal moderates and make them more susceptible to radicalization. A graphic example is provided by the case of Miyamoto Kenji, a leader of the Matsuyama Higher strike with only a budding interest in social causes at the time; in 1968, as secretary-general of the Japanese Com-

24. Kobayashi, "Gakusei no jiyū kakutoku undō," p. 6. The irony of the mention of the Yasuda Amphitheater will impress anyone who was on the Tokyo University campus from June 1968 until January 1969 when that building was occupied and in the end heavily damaged by student radicals.

munist Party, Miyamoto looked back most kindly on his student strike experience.[25]

Despite the wide publicity generated by the Matsuyama Higher strike and several other similar incidents (mostly at higher schools) in 1927, the student self-government movement was not an immediate success. The magazine *Student Movement* collapsed after the second issue, and the concept of moderate, campus-limited agitation was lost in the vogue for theoretical purism which then dominated the student movement under the influence of Fukumoto.[26] But the idea of merging left-wing student politics with basic campus discontent was clearly established and lay waiting to be mobilized on a far more impressive scale when the "era of chronic student disturbances" began in earnest after 1928.

THE EDUCATIONAL CONTROL APPARATUS

The mass communist arrests of March 1928 were a decisive turning point in the direction of an integrated system of control over all forms of protest. The basic conceptual lines were clearly drawn in the several months following the 3.15 arrests, although the apparatus was to swell in size over the following years, culminating in formal interministerial coordination with the Deliberative Committee on Thought Control in 1933. Before 1928 control over the left had been basically punitive in concept, effected through negative, stopgap measures. After the mass arrests, however, the legal machinery of suppression was greatly strengthened to give police officials a new measure of authority and confidence, while at the same time the softer approach of the educator was for the first time developed in a highly organized way. Thus both the "carrot" and the "stick" (or, in the Japanese idiom, the "whip and the candy") were stressed in a new philosophy of integrated control. Willing legal and budgetary authorization by the Imperial Diet per-

25. Ōgiya, ed., *Ā gyokuhai ni hana ukete*, pp. 278–282. Upon entering Tokyo Imperial, Miyamoto joined one of the left-wing reading societies, but was never a Shinjinkai member.

26. The second issue of the Fukumotoist magazine *Seiji hihan*, in March 1927 announced in the editorial notes (p. 125) that *Gakusei undō* had merged with it; this accounts for the large number of articles on the student movement in the early issues of *Seiji hihan*. The approach to the problems of the student movement, however, was totally different in the two cases.

mitted the system to expand until radical protest was effectively channeled into all but the most isolated and sterile activities.

The immediate effect of the 3.15 arrests on the student movement
was to precipitate a host of measures of outright suppression. The news
of the arrests was officially released on April 11 and the role of students
given wide publicity. The *Tōkyō asahi shimbun* announced in one
front-page headline that

MAJORITY OF STUDENTS ARRESTED ARE IMPERIAL
UNIVERSITY STUDENTS
AUTHORITIES ARE ASTONISHED
STUDENT PARTICIPATION ON A NATIONAL SCALE

The public scare generated by the evidence of student communist involvement gave the educational authorities clear sanction to take immediate and extensive reprisals. The traditional freedom of student
activity at the two great imperial universities was finally overridden
with the forced dissolution of the Shinjinkai on April 17 and of the
Kyoto Imperial Shaken the following day. By these moves, which were
taken by the respective university senates at the prodding of the Minister of Education, the last centers of legal student radicalism were
eliminated and all dissent driven underground or into camouflaged
fronts. The Ministry of Education went still further and forced the
dismissal of a number of prominent left-wing scholars at various imperial universities, including such radical student heroes as Kawakami
Hajime and Ōmori Yoshitarō.

Simultaneously, the educational officials began the formulation of a
system which came to be known as "thought guidance" (*shisō zendō*).
The tone was set by a formal instruction issued on April 17 by Minister
of Education Mizuno Rentarō in which left-wing ideas were traced to
the social and political maladjustments of post-World War I Europe
and were seen as a purely outside threat to Japan's stability. The basic
strategy thus remained that of isolation; but where the 1926 Okada
Directive had simply provided administrative guidelines aimed at the
selective isolation of the most extreme elements, the Mizuno instruction now stressed the importance of *total* control. In highly Confucian
language, Mizuno declared, "It is first necessary for those who educate

and guide [the young] to ponder deeply, that they may have convictions about the principles of the *kokutai* and about the nation's founding spirit which are firm and unswerving, and to serve as models themselves, that they may instruct by example within every area of daily life. It is also urged that they fathom the intentions of students, establish appropriate means of guidance, and eliminate the slightest opportunity for the interference of outside temptations. Thus can we nurture healthy, responsible citizens and assure the effectiveness of education." [27]

During the summer of 1928 plans were made for machinery to implement this abstract formula; the resulting scheme was approved by the government in September and formally established on October 30. The thought guidance apparatus consisted first of a central organ within the Ministry of Education in charge of basic research and dissemination of information on student thought. Initially set up as a Student Section (Gakuseika) within the Bureau of Special Education, this organ was elevated to an independent Student Division (Gakuseibu) in July 1929 with a staff of seven. A still further upgrading was effected in June 1934 with a reorganization as the Thought Bureau (Shisōkyoku), the change in name suggesting the expanding focus of the office. [28]

Parallel with this central office was a network of control officials on the campus of every state school above the secondary level. With the creation of the Student Section, the existing "proctors" (*gakuseikan*), who until then had been minor administrative officials in charge of student disciplinary matters, were given a new and less threatening title of "student supervisors" (*gakusei shuji*) at a higher bureaucratic rank and were charged with all duties related to student thought control, guidance, and discipline. [29] The number of such officials was greatly increased, and in large universities such as Tokyo Imperial (where there were five student supervisors), an independent "student section" was set up. By 1934 there were 664 student supervisors through-

27. The title of the instruction was "Shisō zendō no shushi tettei kata," (Means of accomplishing the aims of thought guidance), Instruction (*kunrei*) no. 5 (April 17, 1928); for the text, see *Tōkyō asahi shimbun,* April 17, 1928, p. 7.
28. The Thought Bureau was later renamed the Education Bureau (Kyōgakukyoku), in 1937.
29. See Mombushō, Gakuseibu, *Shisō chōsa sankō shiryō,* no. 3 (April 1929), pp. 196–202, for a list of those attending the first conference of student directors in December 1928 and a speech by the Minister of Education explaining the purpose of the system.

out the country, including 224 at various private schools.[30] Because of its size, the student supervisor system accounted for the bulk of the Ministry of Education's budget for thought guidance, which rose from 422,038 yen ($211,019) in 1929 to 619,778 yen ($309,889) in 1934.[31]

Through this basic machinery, the Ministry of Education embarked on a wide variety of projects designed to undercut the perceived causes of student radicalism.[32] To begin with, steps were taken to alleviate the economic causes of student unrest, to which most of the government-sponsored research reports on campus radicalism assigned great importance. Through the student supervisor network, student welfare facilities were developed on a scale previously unknown in Japan, subsuming and often surpassing earlier student initiative in this area. Employment counseling, mediation for part-time jobs, increased scholarships, loans at favorable interest rates, exemption from tuition payments for impoverished students, health and hygienic facilities, discounts on school-related supplies and equipment, and construction of new dormitories and student amusement facilities were undertaken as a means of undercutting economic dissatisfaction that might lead to ideological extremism.[33] In addition, pastimes which might divert energies from left-wing activism were strongly encouraged. Sports were singled out for special attention through the planning of organized athletic meets and according of special privileges to sports clubs and cheerleading groups. For others, tours, picnics, and special entertainment were arranged, not infrequently involving some mild patriotic indoctrination.

Extensive counseling facilities were also instituted on the principle that continuous guidance on an individual level is the best way both to detect radicalism in its early stages and to change the thinking of those already involved. In the higher schools, a "faculty counselor" was assigned to each student in an effort to keep track of ideological tendencies, and those with suspected radical leanings were reported on a

30. Mombushō, Shisōkyoku, Shisōkyoku yōkō (1934), pp. 9–10.
31. See ibid., pp. 13–18, for more details on the thought control budget.
32. For a concise summary of the thought guidance policy, see Mombushō, Gakuseibu, Gakusei shisō undō no keika gaiyō (1930), pp. 27–42. Convenient yearly summaries of these policies may be found in Ōhara, Nihon rōdō nenkan, vols. X–XVII (1929–36).
33. For a detailed directory of such facilities, see Mombushō, Shisōkyoku, Gakusei seito no fukuri shisetsu (1935).

blacklist upon entering the university. These students would then be closely watched by the student supervisor's office and called in for informal chats at regular intervals. One government manual on the techniques of thought counseling recommended a combination of sympathy and wheedling with veiled threats of future reprisals as the best way of dissuading a potential student leftist.[34] Student supervisors attempted to maintain contact with the parents of student radicals to enhance the pressure. Such individual coaxing and consultation was a key element in forcing the *tenkō,* or recantation, of student communists, which became standard policy after about 1933.

Efforts were further made to discourage the academic study of Marxism while encouraging the appreciation of Japanese tradition. In 1930 a regular program of higher school lectures by anti-Marxist scholars was instituted, while a project for the translation of Western anti-Marxist tracts was sponsored at government expense. The curriculum in ethics, Japanese history and culture, and religion was expanded in many schools, and special scholarships offered to interested students. The Ministry of Education compiled regular lists of "good books" (*ryōsho*) to counter the influence of left-wing literature and even financed a project to publish new editions of such native classics as the *Kojiki, Nihon shoki,* and *Man'yōshū.*

To aid in the formulation of more effective control policy, the central Student Section (Division) produced a constant flow of research materials on student life, thought, and politics. In addition to a basic periodical series entitled *Thought Investigation Materials (Shisō chōsa shiryō),* which appeared two to five times yearly until the Pacific War, the Ministry of Education published a wide variety of reports and analyses on the student movement, aimed at various levels of the control officialdom.[35] Thanks to such materials, the causes, history, and

34. Tōkyō teikoku daigaku, Gakuseika, *Shōwa kunenjū ni okeru hongakunai no gakusei shisō undō no gaikyō* (February 1935), pp. 24–33.
35. The basic series was entitled *Shisō chōsa sankō shiryō* (Thought investigation reference materials) for the first four issues, and was renamed *Shisō kenkyū* (Thought research) with the founding of the Education Bureau in 1937. Many of these Ministry of Education materials are listed in Cecil H. Uyehara, *Leftwing Social Movements in Japan—An Annotated Bibliography* (Tokyo and Rutland, Vt., 1959). For a more complete analysis, see Okamoto Yōzō, "Mombushō kankei no kaikyū undō chōsa shiryō ni tsuite," *Rōdō undō shi kenkyū,* no. 33 (September 1962), pp. 38–45.

techniques of the Japanese left-wing (and even right-wing) student movement in the early 1930s are documented in copious detail. A further area of government-sponsored research began with the institution of the Student Thought Problem Investigative Commission (Gakusei Shisō Mondai Chōsakai) to study the causes and possible remedies of student unrest. This thirty-eight-man team of scholars, educators, and bureaucrats produced a lengthy report in March 1932, containing a number of specific policy recommendations.[36] The only real innovation to result from the investigation, however, was the establishment of the National Spirit and Culture Research Institute (Kokumin Seishin Bunka Kenkyūjo) the same fall to pursue the academic development of Japanese studies. Among the numerous projects of this institute was a thorough statistical study of the motivation and personality of left-wing students.[37]

The fruits of these efforts were mixed. While they may have brought some long-term strengthening of patriotic sentiment on the campus, the immediate effects were less desirable. The radical students themselves greeted many such projects with contempt and amusement, skillfully milking them for political advantage. Anti-Marxist scholars dispatched to lecture at higher schools, for example, found themselves mercilessly jeered when they were unable to answer tongue-in-cheek questions posed by student radicals on abstruse fine points of Marxist theory. Entertainment sponsored by the student supervisors also presented tempting opportunities for ridicule, as for example in an athletic meet at Kyushu Imperial University in April 1929 which featured a "thought guidance race" in which the participants attempted to run while holding down a hydrogen-filled red balloon with a white fan. The symbolism was apparently clear to all, including the student supervisor whose efforts were being mocked.[38]

These "soft" approaches were by no means the whole of Ministry of

36. For a list of the commission members, see Ōhara, *Nihon rōdō nenkan*, XIII (1932), 793–794. A summary of the report may be found in *ibid.*, XIV (1933), 736–738. A minority report was written by the two lone liberal members of the commission and published independently; see Kawai Eijirō and Rōyama Masamichi, *Gakusei shisō mondai* (Iwanami shoten, 1932).

37. The report was Okada Tsunesuke, *Shisō sakei no gen'in oyobi sono keiro* (Kokumin seishin bunka kenkyūjo, 1935).

38. Kyūshū daigaku sōritsu gojusshūnen kinenkai, ed., *Kyūshū daigaku gojūnen shi—Tsūshi* (editor, 1967), p. 308.

Education efforts to control the left-wing student movement. Of equal emphasis in the philosophy of control and of far greater importance to the radicals themselves was a tremendous extension of the use of disciplinary measures against the student left. Strict limitations were placed on left-wing activity of any sort on *all* campuses, including imperial universities. Those caught indulging in on-campus agitation were promptly subjected to measures ranging from simple reprimand to permanent expulsion in the most extreme cases (usually only for conviction under the Peace Preservation Law). Educators came to cooperate closely with the police to ensure a high degree of continuity in off- and on-campus surveillance. While regular police were rarely allowed within school gates, special police were attached to the student supervisor offices for the purpose of on-campus arrests. By 1933 campus control was tight enough so that any student who persisted in agitation could count on eventual arrest and discipline.

8 | The Student Movement Underground, 1928-1934

The March 1928 arrests ushered in a period of systematic suppression. Waves of mass arrests of the communist movement followed with remarkable regularity at intervals of six to twelve months, interspersed with numberless roundups of small, isolated cells of students, workers, or writers.[1] The effects of this atmosphere of permanent suppression on the student movement were contradictory. Quantitatively, it encouraged a dramatic increase in the number of students involved in clandestine activity until about 1932, when a general decrease began. In the five-year period 1930–1934, over six thousand students were arrested for "activities related to the social movement," ranging from two girls enrolled at a "Ladies Sewing Institute" to almost seven hundred at Tokyo Imperial.[2] Since the Gakuren before 1928 never claimed a membership of over two thousand, the leap in sheer numbers was impressive.

Yet suppression worked also towards a steady deterioration in the *quality* of student radicalism. Initially, government efforts to curb the student movement provoked an aggressive counterattack, fanning student anger and winning support for the extremists from the liberal middle. But the authorities were rewarded at the same time by the growing frustration and hollowness of student protest, which despite

1. A convenient listing of these arrests may be found in Shakai bunko, ed., *Shōwaki kanken shisō chōsa hōkoku* (Kashiwa shobō, 1965), p. 59.

2. Calculation from the annual reports in Naimushō, *Shakai undō no jōkyō*, gives a total of 6,142 student arrests in these five years. Mombushō figures, however, conflict in a number of ways and give a total for the same period of only 4,214; see Ōhara, *Nihon rōdō nenkan*, XVIII (1937), 322–323. The reasons for the discrepancy are not clear.

numbers was drained of all creative drive by the relentless suppression. Forced ever deeper into underground isolation, the student left resorted increasingly to heavy reliance on formulas and simplistic slogans to the detriment of working out any theoretical framework for rapidly changing circumstances. All policy lines came to be determined primarily by unthinking, formulistic adherence to Comintern directives, with scant allowance for problems unique to Japanese students. Few new approaches or areas of activity were pioneered in this period, which featured mostly complex and futile elaborations on patterns set in the mid-1920s.

The Dissolution of the Shinjinkai, 1928–1929

The two-year period following the 3.15 arrests saw a critical transition on the student left from the confidence of the mid-1920s to the frustration of the early 1930s. This was a period of greatly heightened suppression on the university campus and of the evolution of a new variety of organizational devices, both on campus and at the national level, aimed at coping with severely decreased freedom of activity. The case of the Shinjinkai on the Tokyo Imperial University campus provides the best-documented example of this general phase of the student movement. The campus activities of the Shinjinkai have already been followed up until the March 1928 arrests. It will be recalled that the climactic battle with the student right and the resulting dissolution of the Gakuyūkai had occurred just shortly before the 3.15 arrests. The campus was thus already in a state of ideological tension when the arrests occurred, and the result was a dramatic reduction in the freedom afforded to on-campus political activists.

The dissolution of the Shinjinkai had been ordered, as recounted in Chapter 7, by the university authorities in the wake of the 3.15 arrests, thus terminating the group's status of over ten years as a recognized campus organization with the right to hold open meetings in school facilities. This action, together with the dismissal of Professor Ōmori, led to an animated protest movement in the late spring. In the usual manner, a broad front organization (the "Anti-Suppression League") was set up, rallies held, and a series of petitions presented to the university administration. The students were quick to discover, however, that the latitude of political activity formerly allowed was being rapidly narrowed. The university proctors issued regulations imposing strict controls on (and, for a brief period, even total prohibition of) handbill distribution and the display of standing posters.[3] Students were now for the first time disciplined for on-campus propaganda, one of the earliest victims being Shinjinkai member Kawai Atsushi, who was suspended in June 1928 for the remainder of the school year on a charge of handbill distribution.[4] The number and severity of such measures mounted over the years following.

The Shinjinkai survived the official university dissolution by going underground but could not agitate on the campus in its own name, and indeed found it difficult to hold meetings even in secret off-campus locations. Accustomed to years of campus extra-territoriality, the students were apparently incautious of the dangers of off-campus suppression, as was dramatically demonstrated in late September 1929 when Tokyo police, on a tip from a suspicious housewife, broke up a clandestine gathering of students in a wooded area on the outskirts of Tokyo. Investigations proved that this "picnic," at which twenty-two were arrested, was in fact a Shinjinkai reorganization meeting in preparation for the fall term.[5] Although charges were not pressed by the police, the university authorities meted out disciplinary action to all involved, including the unprecedentedly heavy penalties of suspension for twelve and expulsion for the central leader, Niwa Fumio.[6]

The sudden increase in on-campus suppression forced a search for new forms of organization. Not only had the Shinjinkai itself been dissolved, but such groups as the Cultural Science Club (the former Shaken) and the Debating Club were now defunct, having collapsed with the Gakuyūkai and been denied permission by the university to reorganize independently. The radical core in the now-underground Shinjinkai hence sought a new format for political activity. The solution was found in the "reading societies" (dokushokai, often referred

3. *Teikoku daigaku shimbun*, no. 245 (March 19, 1928), p. 2, and no. 248 (April 16, 1928), p. 3.
4. *Ibid.*, no. 257 (June 18, 1928), p. 2.
5. These arrests became known after the location as the "Toshimaen Incident." The names of all those present are not known. For the government account, see Naimushō, *Shakai shugi undō no jōkyō* (1928), pp. 170–172. The incident was also covered in the press.
6. *Teikoku daigaku shimbun*, no. 270 (November 5, 1928), p. 1.

to as "R.S."), small groups which had originally been organized among acquaintances for the promotion of mutual friendship and intellectual exchange. From the spring of 1928 the Shinjinkai began to take over the reading societies, expanding and reorganizing them on the basis of higher school affiliation. In this way, a study group network fully as extensive as the old Shaken was built up. With the Shinjinkai itself now driven underground, new membership was taken into the reading societies rather than the Shinjinkai proper, which began to function as a leadership cell. University authorities were aware of the radical manipulation of the reading societies but granted them official recognition as a controlled outlet for political passions and issued warnings that any signs of activism would bring dissolution.

Thus a new pattern of organization gradually emerged in the student movement, the old format of a single legal (or semi-legal) radical group on each campus giving way to a dual structure of a dedicated underground core plus a network of legal front groups. This pattern emerged only partly in response to on-campus restrictions: an equally important influence was the demand by the off-campus communist movement for a ready supply of new recruits in the face of periodic mass arrests. In the period before 1928, as we have seen, the student movement began to emerge as a de facto reservoir for Communist Party membership, but this relationship had never been regularized by direct organizational links between campus and party (with the exception of the minor "Student Fraction"). In the course of 1928, however, it became clear that a smooth, formal tie-up was needed; the only obstacle remained the theoretical denigration of students as unreliable bourgeois intellectuals.

This theoretical dilemma was solved in 1929 by the mobilization of the Communist Youth League as a halfway house for campus activists headed for party membership. Prior to this, the concept of a "communist youth movement" had been ambiguous in Japan. A "Proletarian Youth League" had been formed in the summer and fall of 1925 but, as the name suggests, was intended exclusively for working-class youth—even though Gakuren members were instrumental as patrons in the preliminary stages of organization.[7] This league was a legal front and was controlled by an underground core originally

7. Kikukawa, *Gakusei shakai undō shi*, pp. 327–329.

termed simply "Youth" (*Yūsu*) but later renamed the "Communist Youth League." [8] Neither organization appears to have been extensive and both collapsed in 1928 with the arrest of the underground leaders and the forced dissolution of the front group. This cleared the way for a reinterpretation of the function of the "youth movement," which had always seemed rather superfluous anyway in a situation where very few communists were over thirty. The new conception in essence deemphasized the function of the youth movement in mobilizing young workers and stressed rather its role as a youthful reservoir for party membership regardless of class. In this way students—who, after all, *were* "youths"—could be taken into the "communist youth movement."

When the task of reconstructing the underground Communist Youth League was taken up in the summer of 1928, intellectuals were thus for the first time conspicuous among the leaders. While the central figure, Itō Masanosuke, was of worker origin, the other positions were filled by such student movement alumni as Abe Ken'ichi, Katayama Satoshi, and Ōyama Iwao (the latter two being ex-Shinjinkai members).[9] Most of this group was arrested in the fall, and a new start undertaken in December when Sano Hiroshi returned from a period of study at the Lenin Institute in Moscow. Sano bore with him the magic key for reorganizing the national student movement, a set of theses on the Japanese "youth movement" which had been approved at the Fifth Congress of the Young Communist International in Moscow the previous August. Announced to Japanese communists in February, 1929, these "Theses Regarding the Tasks of the Japanese Communist Youth League" touched specifically, if briefly, on the student movement, decreeing that "students should be made to participate actively in the League, with the central elements organized within the league itself, and sympathizers into support groups for *Proletarian News* and *Proletarian Youth* [the Party and League organs, respectively]." [10]

8. For the history of the Communist Youth League, see Tsukada Taigan, *Kyōsan seinen dōmei no rekishi* (Nihon seinen shuppansha, 1968) for the official communist version, and Kōan chōsachō, *Nihon kyōsantō shi (senzen)*, *passim*, for the government version.

9. *Ibid.*, pp. 227–228. Abe had been expelled from Fifth Higher for radical activity and hence did not enter the university.

10. For the text of the theses, see Naimushō, Keihokyoku, *Tokubetsu kōtō keisatsu shiryō* 2.4 (August 1929), 1–38. For an abbreviated summary in English see "Resolution of the Young Communist International on Japan (Extract),"

To effect this wholly new approach to student movement organization, Sano delegated Tateyama Toshitada, a former Shinjinkai leader and Communist Youth League organizer since mid-1928, who by coincidence had been one year below Sano in the left-wing Kakumeikai at Seventh Higher School. Tateyama elaborated on the basic Young Communist International directive in an article in the April 4 issue of *Proletarian Youth* entitled "Regarding the Tasks of Revolutionary Student Youth." In this article, which came to be known as the "Student Theses," Tateyama condemned the Gakuren for an inappropriate mixture of legal study activities with illegal political campaigns, resulting in a "distortion into an equivocal, semi-communist organization." To correct this, he decreed, the most revolutionary core elements should be organized as members of the Communist Youth League in underground groups on each campus. Moderate and legal front activities would be coordinated via these groups by the league itself and thus the Gakuren would not be needed. Provision was made for the survival of the Gakuren while the details of the new system were worked out.[11]

The first steps at implementation were taken even before the Student Theses were published. The "central elements" in each Gakuren affiliate (normally a *shaken*) were organized into a core group (known officially simply as a "student illegal group") directly under Communist Youth League control, while the organization of the Gakuren itself was greatly simplified in preparation for dissolution. These efforts were slowed but not disrupted by the second wave of mass communist arrests on April 16, 1929, and by the fall term the new system was operating smoothly enough to warrant the final elimination of the Gakuren. On November 7, 1929, the twelfth anniversary of the Bolshevik Revolution, the Gakuren formally announced its dissolution and the assumption of its functions by the Japanese Communist Youth League. The Shinjinkai followed on November 23 (as the tenth anniversary of the Young Communist International) with a separate declaration of "dissolution to a higher stage of development" (*hattenteki kaishō*), which

---

International Press Correspondence, 9.4 (January 18, 1929), 69, which makes no mention of students. It is possible that the expanded version was written by Sano alone, on the basis of the resolution of the Young Communist International: this is suggested in Kawamura, *Shisō mondai nempyō*, p. 93.

11. For the text of these theses, see Hasegawa, pp. 213–218.

was drafted by Kawai Yūkichi and distributed as a handbill on the Tokyo Imperial campus.[12]

Thus the eleven-year era of the Shinjinkai gave way to the era of the Tokyo Imperial Branch of the Japanese Communist Youth League, which was to survive for five years. The change did not alter the basic modes of radical student activity but merely facilitated the use of student groups as personnel reservoirs for the Communist Party. The scheme was that of a pyramid leading upwards from the low-level campus front groups, through an intermediate student cell, into the Communist Youth League, and thence up to the apex of the Communist Party itself. The two years following the dissolution of the Gakuren saw a number of shifts in the terminology and theoretical definition of the intermediate campus cell level which would be tedious to detail here. Suffice it to note that the student cell members were alternately defined as *actual* league members and as "candidates" for league membership. The final solution was the former, in accordance with the "New Student Theses" in the spring of 1931.[13]

It is difficult to say whether the great attention devoted to such organizational manipulations really affected the functioning of the student left, although it doubtless made considerable psychological difference to those involved. It can be definitely shown, however, that the period following the 3.15 arrests did see a substantial increase in the number of student-intellectuals entering the leadership ranks of the Japanese Communist Party. Of all persons indicted for communist activities under the Peace Preservation Law, the proportion of those with formal education beyond middle school increased from 29 per cent in 1928 to 31 per cent the following year, and then to 39 per cent

12. Details of Gakuren activity from the 3.15 arrests until dissolution are provided in elaborate detail in many government accounts; the best is the Naimushō annual, *Shakai (shugi) undō no jōkyō*, for 1928 and 1929; Hasegawa provides a competent summary. The text of the Shinjinkai dissolution statement appears considerably abridged in Kikukawa, *Gakusei shakai undō shi*, pp. 474–475. The full text is in Mombushō, *Gakusei shisō undō no enkaku*, pp. 248–251, and has recently been reprinted in "Shinjinkai shiryō" (Shinjinkai documents), supp. to vol. II of San'ichi shobō henshūbu, ed., *Shiryō sengo gakusei undō* (San'ichi shobō, 1969), pp. 6–8. A copy of the original handbill by which the dissolution statement was publicized is in Naimushō, Keihokyoku, "Banned newspapers, pamphlets, and handbills, 1928–1940," microfilm no. MJ-143, U.S. Library of Congress, item 3422. The attribution of. the Shinjinkai statement to Kawai is from Kawai himself, as told to Ishidō Kiyotomo; Ishidō correspondence.

13. Tsukada Taigan, pp. 93–96. For a summary of the New Student Theses, see Naimushō, *Shakai undō no jōkyō*, 1931, pp. 353–354.

in 1930.[14] The great majority of these, excepting only a few older intellectuals like Fukumoto Kazuo, had been nurtured in the campus groups. It should be further noted that the proportion of intellectuals was considerably higher in the central leadership groups than in overall percentages.[15]

Government statistics allow a few further observations on the composition of the communist leadership in this period. One finds, for example, that of the "intellectuals" involved, the great majority came from a very few universities: most dominant were Tokyo Imperial with 95 indictments (22 per cent of the intellectual group), Kyoto Imperial with 56 (13 per cent), Waseda—including the preparatory course—with 44 (10 per cent), Nihon with 26 (6 per cent), and Meiji with 16 (4 per cent). Also of interest is the increasing youthfulness of the communist movement: while the average age of those arrested in 1923 in the First Communist Party was over thirty, the arrestees in 1928 averaged twenty-six, and in 1929 only twenty-five.[16] Confirming a growing tendency in the period after 1928 to rely on the campus as a membership reservoir is a leap in the proportion of arrestees actually enrolled in an institution of higher education (as opposed to drop-outs and alumni), from 24 per cent in 1928 to 41 per cent in 1930. The communist movement, in other words, came increasingly to depend on the student groups themselves, rather than their alumni, to replenish the leadership ranks.

THE AGE OF CHRONIC STUDENT DISTURBANCES

In precisely the same years that the student left was being driven underground into ever closer integration with the off-campus communist movement, the entire system of higher education was undergoing a period of intense strain that did much to generate wide stu-

14. Statistics for these three years are tabulated in Hasegawa, pp. 179–187. Similar statistics for each year may be found in the annual Naimushō reports, *Shakai undō no jōkyō*, in the sections on the student movement.

15. Thus, for example, nearly half of the central leadership group in the 1928 arrests were intellectuals (that is, having an education beyond middle school), while almost all of those in the major 1930 roundup (centering around ex-Shinjinkai member Tanaka Seigen) were young student activists.

16. Ikeda Katsu, "Nihon kyōsantō jiken no tōkeiteki kōsatsu," *Keisatsu kenkyū,* 1.5 (1930), 61–62.

dent unrest, far beyond the confines of political radicalism. The roots of the unrest were economic. Depression, which had begun to affect the material comfort of student life from around the time of the Kanto earthquake, persisted throughout the 1920s, and was further exacerbated by the world depression after 1929. By 1931 food and housing were acute problems for many students, particularly those crowded in the capital city.

The most serious dislocation imposed on students by the economic situation, however, was the threat of unemployment after graduation, since the expansion of the higher educational system begun in 1918 had created far more talent than a lagging economy could absorb. The employment rate of 81 per cent among university and college graduates in 1923 had fallen to 65 per cent two years later, to 54 per cent in 1928, and finally to a dismal low of 37 per cent in 1931.[17] A student who had managed to enter higher school in 1923 with high hopes of ascending to the loftiest heights of elite preferment found upon graduating from the university six years later that his chances of mere employment were no better than fifty-fifty. As the *Imperial University News* observed in a June 1930 article on the student employment crisis, "Having spent some seventeen years of preparation all the way from grade school through the university and about to enter the 'real world,' the graduate finds a situation of reckless over-supply and stands on the brink of joblessness, his status of 'Bachelor of Arts' having little value." [18] Such disappointment was readily translated into feelings ranging from insecurity and brooding resentment to vocal bitterness.

This constriction at the terminal of the elite pipeline of education was made all the more serious by a corresponding tightening at the earlier bottlenecks of competitive entrance examinations. The "examination hell" undergone by students attempting to enter higher school, which became a familiar theme of countless magazine articles and government reports in the late 1920s,[19] placed students under psycho-

17. Hasegawa, p. 24.
18. *Teikoku daigaku shimbun*, no. 342 (June 2, 1930), p. 2.
19. The "examination hell" had become the focus of major concern by 1927, leading to a series of important reforms. The effects of these reforms are difficult to gauge, however, since old practices apparently survived in many cases. These reforms were reversed after the war. For a detailed study of this problem, see Ikeda Susumu, "Nihon no nyūgaku shiken seido no enkaku," *Kyōto daigaku kyōiku gakubu kiyō*, vol. 4 (1958), pp. 96–124.

logical strains that could easily surface in activist discontent on the higher school and university campuses. Suddenly released from the pressure and tension of years of cramming, students often found protests and demonstrations a welcome relief and a novel opportunity for self-expression. At the same time, the difficulty of entrance made the eventual disappointment upon graduation even keener. This vicious circle of psychological pressures was further complicated by the emergence of a significant degree of competition in the examinations to enter the imperial universities from higher school; the entrance rate for this transition at Tokyo Imperial, which had been 88 per cent in 1919, had dropped to under 60 per cent by 1930.[20]

These economic and psychological stresses reached a peak in the early 1930s precisely at the time when the left was ready and eager to turn them to political advantage. The result was a tremendous, unprecedented wave of student rebellion in the period from 1928 until about 1932, an era which has been tagged "the age of chronic student disturbances" (gakusei sōdō mansei jidai).[21] Radical students had, of course, attempted before 1928 to capitalize on generalized student discontent, as seen in the Shinjinkai efforts to reform the Gakuyūkai in 1923–24 or in the "student self-government movement" espoused by Student Movement in late 1926. These earlier efforts, however, had been temporary and peripheral tendencies within the broad thrust of the student movement in the direction of theoretical purity and contempt for pragmatic goals. But after March 1928, with the alternatives radically narrowed by the threat of massive suppression, this secondary tendency to agitation on the basis of specific, campus-based struggles was revived and elevated to a position of high priority within the mainstream of the student movement.

Two qualifications of the role of the radical left in this period of student unrest deserve emphasis. First, both the underlying and the precipitating causes in the majority of these disputes were nonpolitical, and the student left merely took advantage of situations which it had little part in creating. Even if student radicals had been quiescent in the early 1930s, a great many spontaneous disturbances would have

20. Mombushō, ed., Nihon teikoku Mombushō nempō, vols. XLVII–LIX (1919–31), sections on higher schools.
21. Kikukawa, Gakusei shakai undō shi, p. 399.

occurred all the same. Second, the left-wing leaders themselves never envisaged the fomentation and leadership of *gakkō sōdō* as the primary goal of the student movement, which continued to be defined strictly in relation to its contribution to the "proletarian movement." Nevertheless, the "chronic student disturbances" do occupy a significant place in the history of the student left. Not only were the most highly publicized incidents inevitably characterized by the leadership of the radical left, but the educational authorities themselves tended to view left-wing agitation and nonpolitical disturbances as part of a single phenomenon, the "student thought problem." The control apparatus was thus aimed at both tendencies at once, and the outburst of widespread student strikes had the automatic effect of increasing suppression of the left wing. Conversely, nonpolitical dissenters in the traditional mold were now subjected to far more heavy-handed disciplinary measures than in the past.

Perhaps the most dramatic example of left-wing influence in the *gakkō sōdō* of this period was the conscious use of the vocabulary and techniques of the labor movement. The device of the student strike, or *dōmei kyūkō,* which had been so common in school disturbances since Meiji, was now removed from its traditional ethos of festivity and reclothed in advanced techniques of organization and confrontation taken directly from the labor movement. The flowery speeches of traditional school strike leaders were replaced by bundles of handbills riddled with Marxist jargon. Strike leadership groups were organized in two or three independent groups on the cell principle, to provide against the mass arrest of the top level. Strike headquarters were made clandestine, and the location shifted with each meeting to discourage raids by the police, upon whom school administrators were increasingly forced to rely. By the conscious use of such techniques, confrontation was dramatized and many disturbances were prolonged far longer than had been possible in the past.

The number, variety, and scale of school disturbances in this period were unprecedented. In the mid-1920s, school disputes and strikes had occurred intermittently in the familiar Meiji pattern, but it was only with the major incidents at Matsuyama Higher and Second Higher in 1926–27 that signs of a wholly new trend appeared. From 1928 the number of school disturbances gradually increased, taking a sudden upward turn in the fall of 1929. In the winter of 1929–30, nine different higher schools, out of a total of thirty-two, underwent major disturbances, usually reaching the strike stage. By October 1930 the *Tōkyō asahi shimbun* could observe in a large headline that an "age of student disturbances" had emerged, with thirty-eight schools being hit in the space of a single year.[22] In the following few months through the winter of 1930–31 a tremendous peak was reached, not a day passing without some mention in the press of the progress in at least one of many concurrent disputes. From mid-1931, the tide began to slack, in part from the sobering influence of the Manchurian Incident in September, but for the next few years the number of school disturbances remained substantially higher than the level of the mid-1920s.[23]

Disturbances were by no means limited to the elite universities and higher schools, although not one major university or higher school in Japan remained unscathed; several of the more notorious—such as Waseda, the classic center for *gakkō sōdō* in the old style—suffered as many as three or four separate rebellions. But even the most obscure reaches of the educational system, where the possibility of purely political activity was minimal, were affected and in fact produced some of the most celebrated disputes. Such Buddhist colleges as Ryūkoku and Ōtani suffered multiple disturbances. Women's schools were also prominent, typified by a protracted dispute at Tokyo Women's College of Dentistry in late 1930. At least six strikes in 1930 alone are recorded in higher and technical schools in the colonies of Taiwan and Korea. Schools of the most specialized nature appear in the long lists of disputes, including dental schools, music schools, sericultural schools, and an electrician training institute. Epitomizing the breadth of student unrest in this period was a strike by the entire student body of the Technical School for the Blind in June 1930. (The issue was the resignation of a popular teacher in an intra-faculty squabble; the students in the end succeeded in restoring him to his position.) [24]

22. *Tōkyō asahi shimbun*, October 23, 1930, p. 11.
23. The most complete catalog of *gakkō sōdō* in this period is to be found in Ōhara, *Nihon rōdō nenkan*, in the annual sections on the student movement. Kikukawa, *Gakusei shakai undō shi*, pp. 457–468, provides a less complete list through 1930. Daily newspapers, such as the *Tōkyō asahi shimbun*, also had detailed coverage.
24. Nose Iwakichi, *Saikin gakusei sayoku undō hiroku* (Banrikaku, 1931), pp. 319–327.

The issues which occasioned school disturbances in the early 1930s were as varied as the types of schools involved. The only issue of immediate concern to the student left was the suppression of their own study groups, either though disciplinary actions against the leaders or through outright dissolution. This issue, however, generated only a small percentage of the total number of disputes, even at the most highly politicized university level. Since the issues were always limited to the particular situations on specific campuses, they are difficult to categorize meaningfully. How does one classify, for example, the demand of Yamagata Higher students in the spring of 1929 that term examinations be postponed to allow for time lost in a dysentery epidemic which struck the school dormitories? Or the intense strife at Waseda in the fall of 1930 over an allegedly unfair distribution of tickets for the annual Waseda–Keiō baseball game? In a number of instances, the overt "issues" of a disturbance appeared so trivial that one suspects contrivance in an effort to keep up with the times.

Nevertheless, students had many genuine causes for complaint, and some of the most frequently encountered areas of protest, other than the above-mentioned issue of left-wing suppression, were the following (although in any given disturbance, a number of different issues were likely to be combined in a lengthy composite list of demands): 1. demands for more democratic organization of the extracurricular associations (gakuyūkai), especially with respect to faculty control, election methods, and the role of the athletic clubs; 2. demands for the abolition or reduction of various student expenses, such as tuition, gakuyūkai fees, and dining hall prices; 3. demands relating to the improvement of the quality of education, such as the ousting of incompetent teachers, the censure of lectures which were never updated, and requests for additional instructors; 4. demands for more student control over dormitories, dining halls, and mutual aid facilities.

The "age of chronic student disturbances" not only firmly established the campus-based dispute within the standard repertoire of the student left but also brought into the dynamics of student radicalism the crucial element of publicity, which had hitherto been accorded only a few isolated incidents such as the Gakuren arrests of 1925–26. The extensive publicity stirred up by the many disputes, especially those at famous universities and higher schools, on the one hand made the reading public for the first time aware of the scope of student discontent and thus greatly heightened the general influence—both positive and negative—of student activism. On the other hand, publicity served as an effective vehicle of communication among students on separate campuses, ironically at precisely the time that educational authorities were doing their best to "isolate" the students. Students had only to pick up a newspaper or one of several books on student disturbances published in 1930–1932 to find a complete catalogue of the issues and techniques involved.[25] In this way, the element of faddism was introduced to the student movement, with those at tranquil schools turning to protest less from conviction than from a desire to be considered up-to-date.

THE STUDENT LEFT AND THE RISE OF FASCISM, 1931–1934

The relationship between the underground student left and the above-ground *gakkō sōdō* was symbiotic, so that each worked to expand and develop the other. By the same token, both reached a peak at about the same time, in 1931, and both began a period of gradual decline over the ensuing two or three years. By 1934 both phenomena had largely disappeared; student disturbances now rarely reached the headlines of the national press, while the underground student movement had lost all semblance of continuity and national organization. This decline of student activism, both political and nonpolitical, must be understood within the context of the resurgence of nationalist sentiment and the rise of Japanese "fascism" in the early 1930s.

Throughout the two and a half decades following the war with Russia, Japan's international position had been relatively secure in the popular mind. The only issue which stirred nationalist passions to any degree was the exclusion of Japanese immigrants by the United States, but this was a limited problem relating to racial pride rather than

25. The only major secondary works (largely journalistic in tone) on the prewar student movement appeared in this period: Fujimura Kazuo, *Gakusei shisō mondai zatsuwa* (Nihon hyōronsha, 1930) in February 1930; Sugiyama Kenji, *Nihon gakusei shisō undō shi* (Nihon kirisutokyō seinenkai dōmei gakusei undō shuppan bu, 1930) in October 1930; Nose, *Saikin gakusei sayoku undō hiroku*, in April 1931; Kikukawa, *Gakusei shakai undō shi*, in October 1931; and Takayama Shūgetsu, *Kōtō gakkō to sakei mondai* (Nihon hyōronsha, 1932) in April 1932.

national security. It was only with the controversy over the London Naval Conference in 1930 that widespread public concern over Japan's security was regenerated, serving as a prologue to the Manchurian Incident in the fall of 1931. These events injected into the public consciousness a sense of national crisis which mounted steadily over the following decade. The invasion of Manchuria was followed in 1932 by a series of right-wing assassination plots and by mounting Japanese concern over the situation on the continent. It was within this context, known rather imprecisely as Japanese "fascism," that the student movement met its demise.

The changed setting after 1930 was reflected among students in a number of ways; one of the most dramatic was the sudden resurgence of student nationalism. Given the interest of mid-Meiji youth in national identity, it was scarcely surprising that a new sense of national crisis would provoke a new movement among concerned young Japanese. Organizationally, this movement was lineally descended from the right-wing student movement of the 1920s, and yet its concerns were very different. Whereas such earlier groups as the Kōkoku Dōshi-kai or Shichiseisha at Tokyo Imperial had been created almost wholly in a defensive reaction to the success of the student left, the new young nationalists of the 1930s were only tangentially preoccupied with the communist threat. The driving force of this new nationalism was far more positive, rooted not in a fear of social revolution but in an affirming vision of Japan's newly perceived mission in Asia.

The invasion of Manchuria was clearly the catalyst for the new wave of student nationalism. Where only twenty-two right-wing campus groups existed prior to September 1931, four times that many were active by early 1933.[26] These groups were basically of two types. Roughly half were defined in rather mystical terms, focusing on the cult of the emperor and the "exaltation of Japanese tradition," often involving scholarly interests in Shintō and ancient Japanese rituals. The other type was much more pragmatic and specifically related to Japan's immediate national interests; some were created in the name of "national defense" and were interested in the military aspects of Asian expansion, while others were known as "Manchuria—Mongolia research groups" and aimed at a broad understanding of the areas

26. Mombushō, *Kokka shugi teki tachiba o hyōbō suru gakusei dantai*, p. 4.

into which Japan was expanding. The activities of the majority of right-wing student groups in the 1930s were on the whole quiet and committed, involving study group sessions, the publication of magazines, sponsorship of lectures, and so forth. Only a tiny minority were conceived to be groups for anti-communist political action in the sense that the Shichiseisha had originally been.[27]

The most dramatic indication of the new vigor of student nationalism came with the revelation of the Blood Pact Group (Ketsumeidan) assassination plots in early 1932. Of the fourteen arrested in connection with this scheme to assassinate prominent political and business leaders (of which the first two succeeded), six were radical agrarian nationalists from Ibaraki prefecture, who might with justice be considered as negligible minority malcontents. The other eight, however, were all students, seven of them from imperial universities: four were members of Shichiseisha at Tokyo Imperial, and three from a similar group at Kyoto Imperial. No obscure fanatics, these students bore remarkable similarities to many left-wing student radicals. Most were from Kyushu, and all were intelligent students of good character, driven by intense idealism and willing to commit themselves to extreme solutions. Their perceived enemies—big business and party politicians—were precisely the same as those of the radical left.[28]

The real differences between left- and right-wing students in the early 1930s appear to lie less in political antagonism than in temperament and emphasis. Student leftists tended to prefer clandestine plotting and aggressive action, while those on the right devoted themselves rather to more docile and studious pursuits of the sort, ironically, that had earlier typified the left. In terms of basic concerns, both left and right in the early 1930s came to have more and more in common: both were ultimately concerned with the fate of the nation. It was within this context of left-right ambiguity created by the resurgence of nationalist sentiment that another important phenomenon, the mass *tenkō* (apos-

27. These groups and their activities are described in detail in *ibid.*, and in Kōan chōsachō, *Senzen ni okeru uyoku dantai no jōkyō*.

28. For sketches of the Tokyo Imperial students in the group, see Tōkyō teikoku daigaku, Gakuseika, *Shōwa shichinenjū ni okeru hongakunai no gakusei shisō undō no gaikyō* (February 1933), appendix, pp. 1–2. For details on the incident, see Kinoshita, *Nihon fashizumu shi*, I, 169–178. The eighth student was from Kokugakuin University.

tasy) of the communist movement, occurred. Some of the underlying reasons for the ease which Japanese communists renounced their ideological creed will be touched on in the next chapter. Suffice it to stress at this point that *tenkō* resulted both from certain inherent weaknesses in the organization and ideology of the communist movement in Japan and from the sophisticated use of techniques of persuasion by the government authorities, especially the Ministry of Justice. These techniques were on the whole psychological rather than physical and were aimed at encouraging a spontaneous reintegration of the jailed thought criminals with the mainstream of Japanese social and political values.

Under such pressures, which were developed systematically by justice officials from mid-1931, jailed communists began gradually to recant, normally in return for suspended sentences. The real turning point came in June 1933 with the spectacular *tenkō* of Sano Manabu and Nabeyama Sadachika, who in a lengthy statement denounced the Japanese Communist Party's error of subservience to the Comintern. The defection of this highly respected worker-intellectual combination obliterated much of the already declining moral authority of the Communist Party and led to the apostasy of hundreds of other imprisoned leftists. Radical students, who had read and studied the six-volume *Sano Manabu Anthology* (*Sano Manabu shū*; Kibōkaku, 1930) as a paragon of Japanese communist theory, were profoundly shaken. This blow was compounded the following winter with the revelation of a series of "lynch" incidents in which party leaders, driven to paranoid extremes under intense suppression, had brutally turned against some comrades suspected of being government spies. With this, communism as a political movement in prewar Japan came to an effective end.

It was thus in a setting of mounting nationalism and the progressive defection of high communist leaders that the student left gradually declined in the early 1930s. The decline was not as rapid as one might suspect, however, given the great pressures under which the students labored. The case of Tokyo Imperial again serves as a useful reference point for describing some of the major trends which occurred on the student left in this period of decline.

The left-wing leadership in the early 1930s was wholly clandestine and lived in constant fear of arrest. Individual identities were concealed by aliases, not only in ties with the outside but often even among the students themselves. Official surveillance reports often admitted confusion as to the true identity of leaders whose appearance and general activities were known in detail. The extreme secrecy forced by suppression tended to discourage the emergence of colorful or charismatic leaders, lending the student movement a certain faceless monotony. Since arrests of the core leadership were frequent, both on and off campus, little continuity was possible, and most activists were removed from the scene before developing any expertise in organization and agitation. Such discontinuity worked gradually to decrease the quality of the leadership.

Discontinuity and difficulties of communication led the underground student leaders to devote much of their time to elaborate organizational schemes which would ensure survival of the movement even if key leaders were arrested. In January 1932, thus, the student supervisor's annual report at Tokyo Imperial detailed the activities of eight different underground front groups exclusive of the central cell leadership.[29] Within each group, furthermore, complex organizational schemes and chains of command were painstakingly devised. Special attention was devoted to recruiting first-year students entering from the higher schools, who were approached and wooed from the moment they arrived in Tokyo to take the entrance examinations.[30] The preoccupation in the student movement of the early 1930s with organization amounted often to an obsession, taking total precedence over long-range strategy. Government officials carefully reconstructed many of the schemes in schools throughout the country on the basis of testimony by arrested students. Close inspection of these charts, which are conscientiously reproduced in government reports, shows single individuals holding myriad positions, suggesting that many of the organizations were little more than shadowy fantasies of the increasingly frustrated student left.[31]

On-campus surveillance at Tokyo Imperial, as elsewhere, was intensified in this period, with central direction through the student supervisors' office. The supervisors had control over all campus events,

29. Tōkyō teikoku daigaku, Gakuseika, *Saikin ni okeru hongakunai no sayoku gakusei soshiki to sono undō no gaiyō* (January 1932), pp. 7–59.

30. *Ibid.*, pp. 2–3.

31. Many such charts may be found in Naimushō, *Shakai undō no jōkyō*, in the sections on the student movement; see especially the 1930 edition.

and maintained a large force of campus patrolmen to watch for potential disturbances, not only at extracurricular events but even in classroom lectures.[32] The intensity of campus surveillance forced the radicals to turn to off-campus bases. One of these was the Teidai Settlement, which remained active throughout this period but which was inconvenient because of its rather distant location from the campus. Far more important was the Tokyo Imperial University branch of the Tokyo Student Consumers Union, which had been established off campus in 1928 when university recognition was denied. This merchandising cooperative, which sold a wide variety of student supplies, was of great value for its financial reserves and physical facilities. The Tokyo Imperial radicals took over leadership of the cooperative, filling the shelves with elaborate assortments of left-wing literature for sale, using the back rooms for secret meetings, and running off thousands of illegal handbills on the office mimeographs. Both the settlement and the cooperative survived much longer than other radical bases because of their valid social and economic functions and their independent off-campus status, but even they were eventually crushed: the Teidai Settlement was closed in February 1938 and the Tokyo Student Consumers Union two years later, both following the arrests of leaders for left-wing activities.[33]

As in the past, the left-wing students devoted themselves both to the off-campus "proletarian movement" and to the on-campus "student movement." The primary function of students in the off-campus movement in this period other than as a personal reservoir, as described above, was as a constant source of funds. Students had given relatively little money to the communist movement before 1928, but the continuous suppression and the large number of needy comrades in jail made new sources of revenue imperative. Much attention was lavished on setting up student "support groups" for national communist fronts

32. It is not clear when the system of campus patrolmen was begun, but it was doubtless in the wake of the March 1928 arrests. An article in the *Teikoku daigaku shimbun* in early 1930 mentions an increase in the police force from thirty-five to forty-five men. See no. 336 (April 21, 1930), p. 2.

33. Details on the activities of left-wing students in these organizations may be found in Naimushō, *Shakai undō no jōkyō;* for the case of Tokyo Imperial, see the annual reports of the university Gakuseika. The role of the student cooperatives in the left-wing movement is also discussed in Nose, *Saikin gakusei sayoku undō hiroku*, pp. 33–45, and in Hasegawa Akira, pp. 309–321.

or "readership groups" for their publications. Thus one finds at Tokyo Imperial, for example, such groups as the "Zenkyō Support Group," "Friends of the *Proletarian News*," and "Tokyo Imperial Red Aid." In most cases, membership was awarded less for ideological commitment than for payment of dues which would be channeled to the underground leaders off campus. One government report estimates that in 1931 Tokyo Imperial alone supplied off-campus communist groups with five hundred yen ($250) a month, a huge sum in time of depression.[34]

In their campus-oriented activities, the Shinjinkai successors in the early 1930s pursued most of the techniques that had been developed during the previous decade, although now in the face of far greater hostility from the university authorities. The study group network continued to be organized through the reading societies, the only university-recognized format for the study of Marxist texts. Attempts to create a more unified and rational study-group system met with considerable resistance from the university. At the same time, the student left attempted, as in the past, to win popular support by sponsoring campus-wide campaigns in defense of student interests. The issues were for the most part familiar and made possible a series of major upheavals on the campus in this period. In the spring of 1929 a proposed tuition raise (from 100 to 120 yen a year) provoked vehement student resistance, leading to the organization of a protest rally on May 15, in which one of the campus patrolmen was injured.[35] A year later, the student left engineered a movement to revive the various faculty clubs, especially the Midorikai, which had been languishing since the Gakuyūkai dissolution.[36]

The most prolonged student-interest battle came in the spring of 1931, however, over the old issue of dining hall management. Back in the hands of commercial purveyors after the difficulties encountered by student management in the mid-1920s, the dining hall was attacked

34. Tōkyō teikoku daigaku, Gakuseika, *Shōwa shichinenjū ni okeru hongakunai no gakusei shisō undō no gaikyō*, p. 6.

35. For an account of the incident and a list of those disciplined, see Naimushō, *Shakai undō no jōkyō* (1929), pp. 326–327. A similar incident occurred simultaneously at Waseda, and the two received front-page coverage in the *Tōkyō asahi shimbun*, May 18, 1929, evening ed.

36. *Teikoku daigaku shimbun*, no. 341 (May 26, 1930), p. 7.

as being too expensive and inefficiently run. The result was a series of protest demonstrations in June, which the administration countered over summer vacation with severe disciplinary measures to twenty-five students (one expelled, the rest suspended). This in turn, in the usual spiral of protest, led to an animated movement in the fall urging the waiving of the disciplinary actions, to which the university turned a deaf ear.[37] The result of this and similar campaigns tended to be occasional short-run victory (the management of the dining hall was changed for the better, for example) but long-run disadvantage to the student left in terms of activists arrested and disciplined.

The activities of the student left in this period centered to a great extent around the mimeograph machine, that indispensable tool of the campus revolutionary. Virtually every campus in Japan was deluged by an endless stream of handbills and irregular periodicals, poorly reproduced on cheap paper and most commonly cast from the tops of school buildings to combine maximum distribution with minimum detection. The educational authorities made concerted efforts to control this activity—over half of the left-wing "incidents" counted by the Ministry of Education in 1930, for example, consisted of handbill distribution—but the flood persisted.[38] Many were single handbills commemorating a particular day or agitating for a specific issue, with a peak in numbers coming in the three "demonstration season" months of November, February, and June. Many others were in the form of a periodical organ of a specific underground organization, typically called a *nyūsu* (news) and highly erratic in frequency.

The actual amount of mimeographed material cast over the Tokyo Imperial campus in this period is difficult to calculate, but the visibility of handbills must have been constant. The student supervisors' office counted fifty-six different handbills in a six-month period in 1931 and listed in addition a number of mimeographed periodicals.[39] Most of these, such as the *Anti-Imp News,* the *Tokyo University Proletarian News Bulletin,* or the *Akamon Daily News,* were erratic and ephemeral, but the focal publication of the underground cell, *Akamon senshi*

37. This movement was covered in almost every issue of the *Teikoku daigaku shimbun* from June through November 1931.
38. Hasegawa Akira, p. 239.
39. Tōkyō teikoku daigaku, Gakuseika, *Saikin ni okeru . . . undō no gaiyō,* p. 18.

(Red gate fighter), founded on June 1, 1931, proved extremely durable. It was to continue as a weekly mimeographed sheet of two to four pages for 123 issues until June 1934, never suffering an interruption of more than two weeks—an admirable record in a time of constant leadership arrests.[40] Hastily prepared and filled with crude cartoons, *Akamon senshi* was illegal, cheaply and hastily done, largely propagandistic in tone, and free. It was in strong contrast with *Democracy* and the other organs of the early Shinjinkai, which were professionally printed, legal, and sold by subscription. The difference in the magazines suggests the great change in the quality of the student movement after a decade of suppression.

The peak in these last years of the prewar student movement on the Tokyo Imperial campus came in the academic year 1931–32. The dining hall incident and the ensuing disciplinary issue provided cause for a number of substantial demonstrations, and the rate of handbill distribution reached a new peak. The Manchurian Incident in September had an initial effect of stirring the left-wing to new protests against militarism and fascism. But by the spring of 1932, the tide was clearly turning, as radical groups grew strangely quiescent. The Ketsumeidan Incident and the May 15 assassination of Prime Minister Inukai stunned the nation with the virulence of right-wing radicalism. On campus, the new term in April 1932 saw a burst of activity from the old Shichiseisha and from some new nationalist groups formed in the wake of the Manchurian Incident. By this time, the depression was beginning to relax its hold, and the problems of student poverty and unemployment began to show signs of relief, undercutting the generalized discontent upon which the left thrived.

The student movement at Tokyo Imperial and throughout Japan was given a fortuitous reprieve in May 1933, just as it stood on the verge of total collapse, by the outbreak of the "Kyoto University Incident," in which Takigawa Yukitoki, a professor of law at that university, was forced to resign for allegedly left-wing pronouncements and writings. This undisguised violation of academic freedom provoked a burst of protest both among faculty and students, particularly

40. Lists of the contents of *Akamon senshi* are included in the 1932 and 1934 editions of the Tōkyō teikoku daigaku, Gakuseika reports. Scattered copies of the original may be found in Naimushō, "Banned newspapers, pamphlets, and handbills, 1928–1940."

at imperial universities. The basically liberal character of the protest encouraged many moderates to participate, and in this way the radical core was given a new lease on life. The protests tapered off in the fall, however, and the vitality of the left wing continued to wane, especially under the shock of the Sano–Nabeyama *tenkō* and the lynch incidents which came within a few months after the Takigawa incident. The student underground at Tokyo Imperial was the longest to survive, always managing to reorganize after each series of arrests. The final reorganization attempt came in the spring of 1934 but by summer had been broken by arrests. The last issue of *Akamon senshi* on June 28 may be taken as the terminus of all continuity in the prewar student movement.[41] One revealing sign of the change on the university campus wrought by the annihilation of a central radical core was the virtual absence of any organized protest among Tokyo Imperial students in 1935 when law professor Minobe Tatsukichi was indicted for lese majesty in his interpretation of the emperor as an "organ" of the state. The situation had dramatically changed since barely two years before, when the similar persecution of Takigawa had led to protests on almost every campus in Japan.[42]

The death of the student left as a coordinated and activist movement, however, by no means meant that left-wing ideas disappeared from the university campus. On the contrary, it would appear that those passions which had previously been vented in protests, handbills, and organizing activities were now merely turned inward to the more docile modes of scholarly research and cultural activity. This tendency was manifested outside the campus as well in the activities of senior Marxist intellectuals, who throughout the 1930s devoted all their energies to impassioned debates over the proper interpretation of the historical development of Japanese capitalism. Similarly among students, from about 1932, the left had turned its attention to the organization and manipulation of small "circles" devoted to innocuous

41. Tōkyō teikoku daigaku, Gakuseika, *Shōwa kunenjū ni okeru . . . undō no gaikyō,* p. 13, mentions an issue no. 124 of *Akamon senshi,* dated September 15, 1934, which however is described as "not published" (*mihakkō*).

42. This point is made in Matsumura Sadahiko, *Saikin ni okeru sayoku gakusei undō—Shu toshite Gakusei gurūpu kankei,* Shihōshō, Shisō kenkyū shiryō tokushū, no. 85 (May 1941), pp. 115–118. It should be mentioned, however, that Minobe had recently retired as a Tokyo Imperial professor at the time of the incident, thus weakening his ties with the campus.

cultural pursuits such as the study of drama, cinema, or dance. Other groups were formed on the older pattern of the reading society, along the lines of hometown, higher school, or departmental affiliation. But whatever the formal title, these groups served to channel political passions into obscure corners and constituted the only mode of left-wing student activity to survive the collapse of the central radical core. Having no overall coordination and indulging in no overt activities, these "circles" were tolerated but closely watched by the control authorities. The annual Ministry of Interior report on the left-wing movement for 1935, thus, listed over sixty "campus left-wing groups," the majority of which were small literary magazines, Esperanto clubs, drama and cinema study groups, and history reading circles.[43]

On sporadic occasions throughout the 1930s, these small circles turned to activist attempts at organization, but were inevitably arrested before any extensive contacts could be made. One of the most widespread of such efforts was an attempt in 1938 to set up a coordinated student movement through the Materialist Study Group (Yuibutsuron Kenkyūkai), an organization of Marxist scholars (and itself a channel for the passive expenditure of political energies). This "intercollege" network, however, which drew its strength from cultural clubs on several campuses, collapsed under arrests beginning in late 1938. Again in 1939–40 a new network of clandestine student activists emerged at Tokyo Imperial University and made contact with off-campus communists in a scheme to reorganize the Japanese Communist Party. The activities of this student "leadership group" were abruptly terminated in the familiar pattern of mass arrests.[44]

But if attempts at coordination and action in the left-wing student movement in the early war years were few and unsuccessful, the memories of a more dynamic past remained strong. In the quiet isolation of the study groups and cultural circles, students continued—at least until 1941—to read and study Marxist texts, which remained widely available in spite of strengthened censorship procedures. Communist ideology survived on the Japanese campuses in the form of pure theory, a quiescent underground stream ready to surface once again should

43. Naimushō, *Shakai undō no jōkyō*, 1935, pp. 146–151.
44. A detailed secondary account of the student movement in the middle and late 1930s, based on government sources, may be found in Matsumura, *Saikin ni okeru sayoku gakusei undō*.

the adverse circumstances of war and suppression be reversed. The lingering tone of suppressed revolt among Japanese students was suggested by an October 1938 entry in the diary of Ishigami Takaaki, a third-year student at Tokyo Imperial University who was to die in central China in 1942: "There is something really despicable and hateful about the indifference and callousness of Imperial University students. They are no more than a flock of thorough-going opportunists. Eager pawns of the capitalists, whose dictates they meekly obey, they are self-protecting to the end. Where now is the spirit of the former age of the Shinjinkai? Reactionary slaves!" [45]

45. Nihon sembotsu gakusei shuki henshū iinkai, ed., *Kike wadatsumi no koe* (Tōkyō daigaku shuppankai, 1952), p. 4.

9 | The Shinjinkai Membership, Before and After

In commemoration of the fiftieth anniversary of the founding of the Shinjinkai, a reunion of the surviving members was held on January 18, 1969—the first and probably the last such gathering ever to take place. As part of the intensive preparations for the reunion, which was directed by a committee representing the various generations in the group's eleven-year history, a membership list of the Shinjinkai was prepared for the first time.[1] This list, compiled on the basis of my research and substantially expanded through extensive correspondence by Ishidō Kiyotomo (a member of the class of 1927), remains incomplete owing to difficulties in ascertaining actual membership. During the years that the Shinjinkai was active, only a single membership list is thought to have been prepared—in the period shortly after the Kanto earthquake—and this has yet to be unearthed.[2] Despite the lack

1. Tsurumi Shunsuke has listed 54 Shinjinkai members in his article on the early Shinjinkai in Shisō no kagaku kenkyūkai, ed., Tenkō, 3 vols. (Heibonsha, 1959–62), I, 117. Of these, however, 15 (over one fourth) were in fact *not* Shinjinkai members. Kitazawa Shinjirō, Murobuse Kōshin, Honjō Kasō, Kamei Kan'ichirō, and Imanaka Tsugimaro had all left the university before the Shinjinkai was formed (the first two did not even attend Tokyo Imperial); Takano Minoru, Hemmi Shigeo, Ishida Eiichirō, Matsukata Saburō, Utsunomiya Tokuma, and Takayama Gizō were all active in the student movement, but not at Tokyo Imperial (Takano was at Waseda, the rest at Kyoto Imperial); Sakisaka Itsurō, Fukumoto Kazuo, Tezuka Tomio, and Murayama Tomoyoshi were all at Tokyo Imperial while the Shinjinkai was active, but none of them joined the group, as confirmed by numerous former members.

2. The Shinjinkai kaihō, no. 1 (December 1923), which carries a membership list of the kaiyū (honorary alumni members), mentions on p. 28 that "we have omitted the list of [regular] members this time," suggesting that such a list did exist. Mention of a "membership list" (meibo) is also made in Shinjinkai kaihō, no. 3 (July 1, 1924), p. 45; this may, however, be a figurative usage of the term.

of such official records, however, it may be presumed, on the basis of various estimates of the size of the Shinjinkai at its peak, that the present membership list is about 80 per cent complete, with the greatest gaps existing in the final years.[3]

Of the 343 members on the present list (slightly revised since the reunion version),[4] 221 were known to be alive as of the time of the reunion, while 120 had died (roughly the same number before the war as after) and two were obscure. Of the survivors, fifty-nine attended the anniversary reunion, an impressive number in view of their advanced years, ranging from Tanahashi Kotora, the eldest at eighty, to one or two still under sixty. Thanks to the high rate of survival and the overall prominence which the members have achieved, it is possible to give a fairly accurate account of the fate of the membership as a whole in the period of over four decades since graduation, as well as a rough assessment of the types of persons who were initially led to enter the group. The Shinjinkai membership, by virtue of its large size and the wealth of biographical information available, offers an exceptional opportunity to view an important modern student movement in long perspective. It may be argued that much of the significance of student radicalism lies not in the influence exerted as students—which, even if momentarily large, is unsustained—but rather in the life-long attitudes, radical or otherwise, which are molded by the student experience. In this sense, it is of importance as well as interest to investigate the lives of the Shinjinkai members beyond the limits of the 1920s.

One might first demand to know how "representative" the Shinjinkai was of the entire prewar student left in Japan. One important

3. The problem in the final period, from the 3.15 arrests until dissolution, lies in the absence of any clear distinction between the membership of the Shinjinkai proper and of the reading societies (*dokushokai*) which it controlled.

4. See Appendix for complete list. For the anniversary reunion list, see Tōdai Shinjinkai gojusshūnen kinen gyōji hokkininkai, ed., *Tōdai Shinjinkai kaiin meibo* (editor, 1968). On the grounds of insufficient confirmation, I have omitted the following five names which appear on the reunion list: Kanai Mitsuru (p. 5), Nakano Masato (p. 21), Yamaguchi Hisatarō (p. 23), Kawada Hiroshi (p. 24), and Ohara Kōsuke (p. 24). I have at the same time added thirteen who do not appear on the reunion list, but who have since been confirmed as members: Ch'en I-sung, Hirao Ujirō, Kiyatake Yasumasa, Kunitani Yōzō, Murai Yasuo, Nishimura Nobuo, Okazaki Kazuo, Ōuchi Masami, Tashiro Shirō, Tomonaga Shigeo, Tsuji Tsunehiko, Uchimura Tomoichi, and Yoshio Yoshimitsu.

qualification was their presence at Tokyo Imperial University, which assured both that they were exceptionally capable students to begin with and that they would be assured positions of high status after graduation—no matter what their profession.[5] Over half the Shinjinkai members have appeared in *Jinji kōshinroku* (the major *Who's Who* in Japan), but the proportion would be somewhat less for a university such as Waseda and dramatically less for one such as Nihon. A further limitation on the typicality of the group was its position as the *most* left-wing group on the Tokyo Imperial campus, excluding the large number of "liberals" of the sort that predominated in the Esperanto Club, the Debating Society, the Tōdai Shaken, the League of Nations Club, and so forth. The term "left-wing," in other words, must be here taken to exclude a number of moderate elements that it might encompass in conventional usage.

A warning should also be put forth against viewing the Shinjinkai membership as a homogenous unit. At any given time, the degree of commitment among the members would vary widely, from those who had become dedicated communists in their midteens to those who joined the group with great reluctance and only at a friend's urging.[6] Some were members for three solid years of frenzied activity, others for only a few months of hesitant participation. Even more important, one must bear in mind the variety of changes undergone by the group in its existence of over a decade, in size and composition, in ideology and tactics, and in style of life. The variable which most influenced career patterns, for example, was simply the faculty to which a student belonged, since Japanese university faculties are basically professional

5. Only two Shinjinkai members did not actually enter Tokyo Imperial University; these were Nosaka Sanzō, a Keiō graduate, and Ōkōchi (now Isono) Nobutake, a member of the Urawa Higher literary group within the Shinjinkai even though he was not actually enrolled in the university.

6. Pressures on the less committed to join were evident in the cases of certain small cliques from single higher schools, which typically consisted of a single charismatic leader and a number of personal followers. In the largest two such cliques, which had ten members each, at least two or three joined for reasons of personal loyalty rather than political commitment, as their later careers in business suggest. One of these cliques was from the Third Higher (Kyoto) and consisted of the ten alumni of that school in the class of 1925, plus Ariizumi Shigeru of the class of 1924; all in this group except Suzuki Takeo had been organized as a group called the Jūninkai (Club of Ten) while at higher school under the leadership of Ōya Soichi. The other group was from Second Higher (Sendai), in the class of 1929, and was led by Shimano Takeshi.

schools which offer a rather narrow range of employment options. Hence the tendency for the Shinjinkai after 1923 to expand from its exclusive Law Faculty base into all the other liberal faculties,[7] and even into a few technical ones, as seen in Table 2, meant a wider range of career patterns. The unusually large number in the four departments of literature in the middle years has naturally meant that a greater proportion of the membership of that era later became writers and critics. So also the increasing number from the Faculty of Economics in the later years forced relatively more of the members into careers in business.

Table 2. Departmental distribution of later Shinjinkai membership [a]

Subject	Graduating Classes				
	1925–26	1927–28	1929–30	1931–32	Total
Law [b]	23 (42)	24 (32)	17 (19)	10 (17)	74 (26)
Economics [b]	7 (13)	19 (25)	39 (43)	27 (46)	92 (33)
Sociology [c]	14 (25)	5 (7)	5 (5)	1 (2)	25 (9)
Esthetics [c]	0 (0)	3 (4)	9 (10)	9 (15)	21 (8)
Literature [d]	7 (13)	13 (17)	7 (8)	3 (5)	30 (11)
Other [e]	4 (7)	9 (12)	11 (12)	7 (12)	31 (11)
Unclear	0 (0)	2 (3)	3 (3)	2 (3)	7 (2)
Total	55	75	91	59	280

[a] Percentage of total graduating class in parentheses.

[b] Law includes both departments (Law and Politics) in the Faculty of Law; Economics includes both departments (Economics and Commerce) in the Faculty of Economics.

[c] Sociology and Esthetics are both departments within the Faculty of Letters.

[d] "Literature" includes the departments of Japanese Literature, French Literature, German Literature, and English Literature (all in the Faculty of Letters).

[e] "Other" includes students in the faculties of Medicine (12), Engineering (4), Science (1), and in departments of the Faculty of Letters other than the above (Philosophy 7, Education 3, Japanese History 2, Ethics 1, Western History 1).

7. It should be mentioned that there were a few non-Law Faculty members of the early Shinjinkai: Kawai Hideo in agriculture, Okabe Kansuke and Sakamoto Masaru in economics, and Machino Shigeyuki in commerce. These four were so minor, however, as to permit the generalization that the Faculty of Law did indeed monopolize the membership; the minor role of the non-law members may in fact have been related to their outsider status.

Another important variable within the Shinjinkai stemming from historical changes, although almost impossible to identify statistically, is an evolution of personality as the student movement became ever more extreme, more suppressed, and more clandestine. My own subjective impression on the basis of interviews and biographical studies is that the earlier members tend to be relatively tolerant and easygoing in personality, and the later members seem more rigid in outlook and less personable in approach. It may be that this shift, if it indeed exists, stems from fundamentally different personality patterns in the students attracted at different periods. But it may equally well relate to the influence of the student movement experience on basically *similar* personalities. Those from the later Shinjinkai, in other words, were forced to participate in a student movement dominated by secrecy, dogmatism, and the constant fear of suppression. It would scarcely be surprising that those living through such a period would tend to be less sanguine and relaxed than their predecessors who were blessed with an age of general openness and freedom.

SOCIAL ORIGINS

In geographical origins, the Shinjinkai members came from every corner of Japan, representing *all* the forty-seven prewar prefectures and including at least one Taiwanese and two Koreans.[8] Although certain influential regional factions existed within the Shinjinkai —the Kyushu group entering in 1923 is the best example—the overall tendency was to wide geographical distribution, as seen in Table 3, which compares regional percentages for 315 Shinjinkai members with a random selection of Law Faculty graduates and with the national population. In view of the unbalancing effect of certain higher school cliques, the ratios are remarkably similar and suggest that regional influences were on the whole of little relevance.

Statistics on the family background of the Shinjinkai members are impossible to compile without more information than is currently available, but rough generalizations may be made on the basis of a

8. The Taiwanese was Ch'en I-sung, and the Koreans were Kim Chun-yŏn and Kim Tu-yong; none appear to have participated regularly in Shinjinkai activities.

Table 3. Geographical distribution of Shinjinkai membership [a]

Location	Shinjinkai	Law Faculty [b]	National [c]
Hokkaido	2	1	4
Tohoku	10	10	10
Kanto	16	26	20
Hokuriku	13	6	7
Tozan	6	3	6
Tokai	7	10	10
Kinki	14	12	13
Chugoku	13	10	9
Shikoku	3	6	6
Kyushu	17	16	15

[a] In percentages, for 315 Shinjinkai members whose geographical origins (*shusshinchi*) can be ascertained.

[b] Based on a random selection of 315 graduates of the Tokyo Imperial University Faculty of Law in 1928. *Source:* Tōkyō daigaku, *Tōkyō daigaku sotsugyōsei shimei roku* (1950).

[c] Calculated from the 1920 census. *Source:* Naikaku tōkeikyoku, ed., *Nihon teikoku tōkei nenkan,* 40 (1921), 26–27.

minority of the group, corroborated by government reports.[9] Probably over one third of the total membership came from rural agricultural families, with status ranging widely and evenly from impoverished tenant farmer to large landlord. Another third were the sons of petty provincial bureaucrats and small-to-middle merchant families. The remaining one third would cover an extremely varied range from the very poor to the extremely wealthy, stretching in social class from the outcast eta (a single such case is known) to the nobility (of whom there were at least three),[10] and in profession from sake brewers and school-teachers to fishermen and carpenters. The social origins of the Shin-jinkai members were so varied that they might best be described by exclusion. Very few, for example, were the sons of the urban prole-tariat, which had available neither the independent means nor the

9. One good sampling of such information is for the defendants in the Kyoto Gakuren arrests, which may be found in Shihōshō, *Gakusei chian iji hō ihan jiken kōgai,* pp. 111–164.

10. Ishiwatari Haruo was of eta origin, while Yamana Yoshitsuru, Ōkōchi Nobutake, and Kuroda Takao were all from the nobility.

system of provincial subsidies to send its children to the university. At the same time, very few came from urban intelligentsia, like university professors, politicians, or high-level national bureaucrats.

In fact, it would appear that *provincial origin* was the most critical common denominator in the backgrounds of the Shinjinkai members. Certainly it was more important than wealth, which could work either to discourage or to encourage radicalism and was frequently irrelevant. It is perhaps significant that the Kanto (Tokyo area) proportion of the Shinjinkai was 4 per cent lower than the national level and 10 per cent lower than the university average. To be sure, a large minority of the Shinjinkai came from distinctly urban backgrounds: yet on the basis of limited evidence it would seem that those of urban (or, more specifically, metropolitan) upbringing, with their greater tolerance of the tensions of modern life and higher degree of political sophistication, tended on the whole to be more moderate and less enthusiastic than the members with provincial and rural backgrounds. To cite a single comparison, one thinks of the sophisticated apoliticism of Ōya Sōichi, who was reared in Osaka, in contrast to the intense moralism of Nakano Shigeharu, whose upbringing in a small village in Fukui prefecture is constantly mirrored in his novels.

Family stability appears to have been high in the childhood experiences of Shinjinkai members. Most came from families of over four children, and, although documentation is scarce, there is no reason to suspect traumatic sibling rivalries as a radicalizing force; in fact, one may find a number of relatives in the membership, including two pairs of brothers and one uncle-nephew combination.[11] It is commonly observed that first sons in Japan tend to be conservative, responsible, and inhibited, and yet 42 out of 100 Shinjinkai members whose sibling rank is known were first sons (while 26 were second sons, 14 third sons, and the remaining 18 fourth sons or lower): such a distribution was probably about average for all students, suggesting the irrelevance of such considerations.

11. The brothers were Shimano Takeshi and Kadoya Hiroshi (Kadoya is an adopted name), and Ōmura Hiroshi and Einosuke; Sano Manabu was the uncle of Sano Seki. A number of other Shinjinkai members have since become related through marriage to each other's sisters.

On the whole, Shinjinkai members were respectful of their parents, sensing an indebtedness for the privilege of attending an imperial university; mention is seldom made of divisive personal or ideological antagonisms. Since the majority of the parents of Shinjinkai members were uneducated and ignorant of the Western political jargon which their sons bandied about, articulated conflict was minimal. Contempt for or disappointment in the behavior of one's parents was far less common than a feeling of pity for their unwitting preoccupation with traditional ways. It was this very sympathy for one's parents that was to prove critical in leading many Shinjinkai members later to renounce communism.

GROWING UP

Evidence on the early childhood of Shinjinkai members is too scarce and unreliable to allow any special observations. It should simply be noted that all were of the post-Russo-Japanese War generation; of the few who did remember the war, it was only a distant memory and not part of their generational experience. The glories of Meiji were to the generation of the Shinjinkai much what the Depression and World War II have been to American youth since the 1960s: awesome events that one hears and reads of constantly but productive of no immediate personal reaction. All Shinjinkai members attended primary school after the introduction in 1903 of the standardized textbooks which marked the full institution of nationalistic indoctrination in the educational system. Primary school for most members seems to have been a normal, uneventful passage of time, in an era of relative prosperity, little social unrest, and no international disaster.

The doubting of established social priorities, in time to lead to left-wing activism, began generally in middle school, in the early teens. Most reminiscences of this period focus on certain special personal experiences which awakened a latent sensitivity to social injustice. In some cases, these were personal privations, with a resulting resentment over unequal distribution of wealth. In other cases, family misfortune, such as bankruptcy, led young minds to doubt the justice of the economic and social order. One later activist recalls that the sad plight of two divorced women in his family led to a feeling of anger at social injustice.[12] For those in comfortable and stable surroundings, observation of less fortunate classmates or of working people in their own town was often the stimulus. Thus Kisamori Kichitarō recalls how the sight of the oppressed dock workers in Yokohama as a child stirred his sense of justice.[13] Guilt over one's own privileged position often reinforced these feelings. Such early sense impressions seem on the whole to have been dictated less by peculiar environments than a native sensitivity to social dislocation.

In the next phase, these initial unsettling experiences, which were often latent and unarticulated, began to find concrete reinforcement through the reading of literature, normally late in middle school or early in higher school. Russian novels were the most common, and many Shinjinkai members still recall their emotional reactions upon reading Tolstoy, Dostoyevsky, and Turgenev. Novels with specific social content such as Hugo's *Les Misérables* or Shimazaki Tōson's *Broken Commandment (Hakai)* were likewise popular, offering the young readers a framework in which to locate their own personal experiences. This period of reading novels tended soon to progress to a stage of intense interest in philosophy and religion, in a confused adolescent search for meaningful explanations of the injustice and cruelty which they had first witnessed and then vicariously experienced through novels. Kant and Abe Jirō, Nietzsche and Nishida Kitarō, the combinations varied, but all suggested a preoccupation with ultimate answers to immediate problems. The religious excursion was typically a brief but impassioned flirtation with Christianity, which was widely popular among Taishō youth; in rarer instances, the searching led to Buddhism.

But finally all this literary absorption, philosophical meditation, and religious mysticism reached a frustrated impasse with the conviction that literature provided only powerful descriptions with no solutions, while religion and philosophy tended only to personalize and internalize problems that were basically social. The breaking through of this dead end, commonly described as an "enlightenment,"

---

12. Miyahara Seiichi in Ōkōchi Kazuo and Shimizu Ikutarō, eds., *Waga gakusei no koro* (Sanga shobō, 1957), p. 62. Miyahara was involved in the student movement at Tokyo Imperial in the early 1930s, after the dissolution of the Shinjinkai.
13. Kisamori interview.

was almost inevitably provoked by the reading of certain books, typically in the second or third year of higher school. It bears emphasis that it was via the printed page that the actual conversion took place, even though the reading matter may have been suggested by a close friend: conversion by direct persuasion and argument was rare.

The specific readings which provided the breakthrough varied a great deal from one individual to another, but the sense of sudden enlightenment was common to many. Katayama Satoshi recalls reading Stalin's *The Fundamentals of Leninism* in his last year at Matsue Higher: "I was so moved I could not stand still. I thought I now understood how to make a revolution, I really did. My eyes seemed newly opened. My pilgrimage was ended." [14] Or again, the same student who had been disturbed by the maltreatment of divorced women turned to reading on the problem of women and after some six months suddenly hit upon Yamakawa Kikue's translation of Bebel's *Die Frau und der Sozialismus:* "This is the real thing, the real thing, I exclaimed, entranced." [15] More common examples of the crucial turning-point books were Kawakami Hajime's *Tales of the Poor* (*Bimbō monogatari*), Kropotkin's *An Appeal to the Young*, Yamakawa Hitoshi's *The Scheme of Socialism* (*Shakai shugi no karakuri*), or of course any of the standard assortment of classical Marxist literature.

The change provoked by this reading is most commonly described as a shift from "self to society." The tremendous appeal of socialism was that it went beyond a mere description of society to an analysis of *why* certain problems existed and, most important, explained *how* they might be solved. It was above all the claim of Marxism to scientific accuracy which lured the students, an appeal which was all the greater for their disappointment with the "unscientific" solutions of religion and philosophy. It would appear, in fact, that the more extreme the period of philosophic anguish, the more intense the commitment to Marxism as an antidote, and ultimately, the more thor-

14. Shimane daigaku shimbun bu, ed., "Shimane no gakusei undō shi," pp. 29–30.
15. Miyahara in Ōkōchi and Shimizu, eds., p. 62.

ough the usual rejection of Marxism. One might also argue, from a rather different perspective, that it was less the overt claim of Marxism to pragmatic, scientific accuracy than its underlying philosophical idealism and its tendency to a high degree of intellectual abstraction that provided a natural link for students whose preoccupations were basically intellectual and philosophical.

The details and the precise timing of this course of intellectual development varied with the individual, but the broad pattern is remarkably constant for all those Shinjinkai members (and other student radicals of their era) who have left accounts. From this standard progression, it is possible to suggest some of the character traits most common to the prewar student leftist. One notes first an innately strong sense of justice, combined with a certain selflessness. This is further reflected in the general tendency to moral rigidity in the Shinjinkai members throughout their lives. Self-seeking, power-conscious, and morally lax personalities were on the whole rare in the Shinjinkai and are often mentioned by former members as exceptional. The tendency to highly developed reading habits and a preference for intellectual pursuits are also characteristic of Shinjinkai members, although one does find a conspicuous minority of highly gregarious, personable, emotional individuals, especially among the top leaders like Akamatsu Katsumaro, Ōya Sōichi, or Tanaka Seigen. The frequency of the philosophical-religious stage suggests a basic preference for spiritual solutions which often later reappeared in the form of *tenkō*.

This estimate of the basic Shinjinkai character as formed during the period before entering the student movement accords generally with the conclusions reached by Okada Tsunesuke, chief of the Research Section in the Thought Bureau of the Ministry of Education, in his classic 1935 study of left-wing students. On the basis of personality descriptions of over three thousand student radicals, he concluded that while the character of left-wing students shows wide variety, those judged "amiable and gentle" were the most numerous. He found that radical students were in no way prey to specific character defects or traumas that might explain their Marxist tendencies. He also found that the grades of the students before entrance to the university (after which the neglect of classes inevitably brought a decline) indicated a scholastic ability that was average or above.[16] This was all the more true in the case of the Shinjinkai, both because the standards of Tokyo Imperial guaranteed intellectual ability and because radical activity seems to have attracted the brightest. Many Shinjinkai members have been consistently described as "geniuses" (*shūsai*) and often ranked at the top of their higher school classes. The usual decline in grades while active in the student movement hints at the amount of high-quality cerebral energy which went into the study of Marxism.

AFTER GRADUATION

The Shinjinkai members on the whole examined career possibilities in the light of their political commitments. Activity in the student movement was not for them, as it would appear to be among a number of postwar student radicals, a stimulating extracurricular pastime, but a matter of enduring dedication. The group held meetings prior to graduation to discuss the prospective employment of each member; [17] the aim was not to force the members into inherently left-wing areas such as labor unions or socialist political parties but rather to encourage them to maintain a progressive attitude no matter what profession they might select. They sought, in other words, to *deploy* the membership throughout Japanese society. This conception even had a geographical dimension; among the early Shinjinkai members, for example, several decided to find jobs in the Kansai area in order to supplement what they saw to be a lack of radical talent there.[18]

A certain number of Shinjinkai members dedicated themselves immediately and exclusively to the left-wing movement on a professional basis, as labor union leaders, tenant movement organizers, and socialist politicians. The early Shinjinkai members, who began their activity when legitimate leadership positions were easily available for intellectuals, went on to form the core of much of the moderate labor and socialist party movement. Of the three major wings within

16. Okada, *Shisō sakei no gen'in oyobi sono keiro*, pp. 125–128, 139.
17. For a description of such a meeting, see Nakano, *Muragimo*, pp. 387–390.
18. Yamazaki Kazuo interview.

the social-democratic movement before the war, Shinjinkai members were most conspicuous in the centrist Japan–Labor (Nichirōtō) lineage under the leadership of Asō Hisashi, but the group was also represented on the left (Hososako Kanemitsu, Kuroda Hisao) and right (Miyazaki Ryūsuke, Akamatsu Katsumarò).

The members of the later Shinjinkai, by contrast, tended to turn to the underground communist movement, less because they were innately more extreme than because it was the only organized channel of political activity open to them. Of the entire Shinjinkai membership, at least one out of four was at some time arrested under the Peace Preservation Law, most often as a Communist Party member and full-time underground leader. These men considered themselves, in Lenin's phrase, "professional revolutionaries" and engaged in minor nonpolitical jobs only for income or as a front. This type of activity in the communist underground in the period from about 1926 to 1935 was not a student pastime but rather a profession after leaving the university.

For most Shinjinkai members after graduation, however, contribution to the left-wing movement was through technical and professional assistance, or, more passively, through financial contributions and support at the ballot box. Several who became lawyers thus aided in the defense of those arrested for left-wing activities, and some joined the Civil Liberties Legal Group (Jiyū Hōsōdan), which since its founding in 1922 has provided most of the legal defense for radical causes.[19] The many Shinjinkai members who went into university teaching also tended to retain strong sympathies with the left-wing movement and did much to encourage the spread of Marxism in the academic world. In particular, the career professors from the early Shinjinkai, who were able to rise quickly to prominent academic posts, had a strong influence in the scholarly world and were noted for their encouragement and defense of Gakuren radicals in the mid-1920s. Typical of these were Ishihama Tomoyuki and Sassa Hiroo, who were both dismissed as professors at Kyushu Imperial University in 1928 for their left-wing persuasions.

19. Most notable among the Shinjinkai members in this group have been Koiwai Jō, Okazaki Kazuo (the president of the organization since the early 1960s), and Moriya Fumio. For their activities, see Jiyū hōsōdan, ed., *Jiyū hōsōdan monogatari* (Rōdō jumpōsha, 1966).

To claim that Shinjinkai members have made important "contributions" to the prewar left wing is in a way deceptive, for in most cases they—and former student activists like them from other universities—*were* the left. Shinjinkai members seized the initiative and leadership in all of the many areas into which the left-wing movement spread before the war, and for this reason one may find at least one member in almost any of the numerous left-wing arrests throughout the 1930s, including even the most exotic. Thus, to give a single example, five Shinjinkai members were among the thirty-six arrested for left-wing activities in the South Manchurian Railway's Research Department in 1942–43.[20] Whether in the government, in the universities, or in the underground communist movement, Shinjinkai members could inevitably be found among the ranks of the subversive.

By no means all the Shinjinkai members, of course, sought out professions which would specifically enable them to contribute to the left-wing movement. A number soon abandoned radical commitment and pursued their careers in a tone of political disinterest or even of a positive opposition to the left wing. Conspicuous in this group were those who entered business and the state bureaucracy, most of whom, however, had been relatively inactive as Shinjinkai members or had even left the group before graduating. On the whole, both business and bureaucracy were anathema to the Shinjinkai; thus of the early members, whose Law Faculty affiliations naturally prepared them for the bureaucracy, not one entered government service. In the later Shinjinkai, however, the proportion to enter the bureaucracy was considerably greater. Most infamous were Mizuike Akira, who entered the Ministry of the Interior and rose to become one of the most powerful wartime police officials, and Yoshikawa Mitsusada, who joined the Ministry of Justice and in 1964 became the director of the Public Security Investigation Agency (the rough equivalent of the American FBI). Both, however, were active in the student movement primarily in higher school and had terminated all such ties by university graduation, being minor Shinjinkai members. The same on

20. These were Edayoshi Isamu, Ishidō Kiyotomo, Itō Takeo, Shuzui Hajime, and Tanaka Kyūichi. See John Young, *The Research Activities of the South Manchurian Railway Company, 1907–1945* (New York, 1966), pp. 26–32. Itō relates that he and Tanaka were arrested specifically because of their Shinjinkai ties; Itō Takeo, *Mantetsu ni ikite* (Keisō shobō, 1964), pp. 243–245.

the whole was true of those who went into business immediately after graduation.

To detail the responses of the Shinjinkai members to the crises after 1930 which led Japan into the "dark valley" of war would be to write a history of the national conscience in those years, with its staggering range of tension and elation, remorse and pride, fear and confidence. In the following section, specific case studies will detail some of the individual responses; here it is possible merely to suggest some of the broad patterns of change which were effected in the lives of many of the members. For perhaps half the total membership, that half which was engaged in routine professional matters, no overt response was either demanded or given. They continued to hold their jobs, whether as doctors, reporters, teachers, or businessmen, perhaps questioning the wisdom of the course which the nation was taking, but in the end accepting it with the same resignation as the nation as a whole.

The other half of the membership was faced with the necessity of a more positive response: these were the men who, either by profession or by personal commitment, were somehow involved in the political life of the nation. Here it is possible to distinguish a variety of categories. One such would be the small group, scarcely more than a dozen, who were professionally involved in the legal left, whether as leaders of the proletarian parties or as officials of above-ground peasant and labor organizations. Almost all these men remained with the legal left-wing movement throughout the 1930s as it moved ever closer into total integration with the war effort. These men, almost all of them from the early years of the Shinjinkai, retained their basic commitment to social reform and were able, although not without anguish, to find this goal basically compatible with Japan's military expansion abroad. With the formation in 1940 of the Imperial Rule Assistance Association, a unitary government support group which replaced the political parties, most of these men left the movement and found jobs elsewhere. Thus Kikukawa Tadao in 1941 was purged from the Industrial Patriotic Association (Sangyō Hōkokukai, the unitary organization under which all labor unions were subsumed) as a "red element" and went to work for a labor organization in Manchuria, switching in 1943 to a job in a friend's aircraft manufacturing company. These prewar professional left-wing organizers generally entered the Japan Socialist Party after the war.

A similar group, also small and predominantly from the early Shinjinkai, entered the bureaucracy and took an active role in trying to lead Japan into what they saw as an alternative to the increasing domination of policy by the military. Some of these, like Sassa Hiroo and Taira Teizō, were conspicuous in the "brain trust" of Prince Konoe.[21] Still another group, mostly economists, entered the Planning Bureau (Kikakuin) and were among those arrested in 1941 on charges of plotting to socialize the Japanese economy.[22] All these men seemed willing to admit a special mission of Japan in East Asia and turned their efforts to making that mission a progressive one by focusing on reform at home and striving to limit the policy-making power of the military.

A much broader and less homogeneous group included the intellectuals and professors who encountered pressures for their left-wing views. A number were purged from universities, sometimes finding jobs at other schools, sometimes living by writing for progressive magazines, and often in a final pinch working for a company. Most continued to hold their positions but increasingly confined their political activity to scholarly Marxist analyses which had only indirect implications for the contemporary situation; many were active in the debates which raged among Marxist scholars in the 1930s over the interpretation of the Meiji Restoration. Most of these men never accepted the war as just but were forced into silence both by the heavy censorship of the times and by their own ambivalent feelings about the applicability of Marxism to the immediate crisis.

A further group consisted of the literary men, the novelists, poets, and dramatists who composed an important part of the middle and later Shinjinkai. Most of them were involved in the organized proletarian literature movement but, as that movement collapsed, were

21. For details on the Konoe brain trust, see Johnson, *An Instance of Treason,* pp. 114–122.
22. Masaki Chifuyu and Sata Tadataka were the two Shinjinkai members arrested in the Kikakuin Incident. Two other Shinjinkai members, Okuyama Teijirō and Ozawa Masamoto, had earlier served in the Kikakuin. See Masaki Chifuyu, *Chian iji hō ihan Kikakuin sayoku gurūpu jiken: Jōshinsho (Hikokunin Masaki Chifuyu)* (mimeo., 1944), p. 61.

faced with the dilemma of how to pursue their political ideals. The moral agony of apostasy (*tenkō*) was the most dramatic and has been best documented in the case of the writers, perhaps because their basic emotionalism tended to make them much more sensitive than the more hard-headed scholars and politicians to the lure of Japan's unique esthetic and religious traditions. This group thus produced some of the most notable traditionalist *tenkōsha* (one who commits *tenkō*), like Kamei Katsuichirō and Hayashi Fusao, both of whom turned to writing apolitical works, the former with strongly religious overtones and the latter with a much lighter, more popular orientation.

By far the largest group faced with a clear crisis of conscience in the 1930s consisted of those arrested and jailed as communist activists under the Peace Preservation Law; these were for the most part members of the latest period of the Shinjinkai. It was only in such cases that a clear declaration renouncing communist ideology was demanded, and the clarity of the act makes the case of *tenkō* an acute one here. Only a handful did not recant: a number died in jail, while one—Shiga Yoshio—stayed in prison until the end of the war, wholly unrepentant. But the rest wrote *tenkōsho*, formal statements renouncing communism in return for release. Of these, perhaps one third felt acute remorse which led them back to the Communist Party after the war: Nakano Shigeharu and Moriya Fumio are perhaps the two most dramatic examples of the extreme moral anguish which *tenkō* produced. A larger number merely renounced political activity of every sort, with a variety of rationalizations, and retreated into professional endeavors. A very few became true converts to the right-wing movement, Ōyama Iwao, a dedicated anti-communist and advocate of remilitarization after the war, being perhaps the best known. Some, like Mizuno Shigeo and Tanaka Seigen, became big businessmen with a clearly conservative orientation but scarcely right-wing ideologues.

The phenomenon of the *tenkō* of these jailed intellectuals has been the object of much recriminatory polemic in the postwar period and has even been made the subject of a substantial collection of scholarly essays by intellectual historians in the Institute for the Science of Thought (Shisō no Kagaku Kenkyūkai).[23] Even the most academic writers, however, have found it difficult to extricate themselves from

23. Shisō no kagaku kenkyūkai, ed., *Tenkō*.

the praise-and-blame matrix, and the topic remains a sensitive one. The problem must at least be mentioned on its own terms here if only because the prewar student movement produced some of the most illustrious *tenkōsha,* men like Mizuno Shigeo, Sano Manabu, and Kamei Katsuichirō. Such prominence is of course not necessarily because ex-student intellectuals were more prone than others to renounce communism—indeed, the proportion of laborers was of the same magnitude—but merely because they were on the whole the most articulate and well-known communist spokesmen in prewar Japan.

Dispensing with any discussion of how (or indeed whether) the problem of *tenkō* should be approached, I would merely like to mention what I conceive to be the major factors in explaining the relative ease with which most imprisoned Shinjinkai members renounced communist ideology.[24] Perhaps the *least* persuasive explanation is overt police pressure in the form of torture and threats; this existed, of course, but appears to have been small in scale and of very little efficiency compared with other techniques. The *most* persuasive explanation for *tenkō* is also the most commonsensical and hence most easily overlooked: this is simply that the situation of Japan in the world changed very rapidly in the 1930s. The young intellectuals who committed *tenkō* so readily had forged their political ideals in the era from the Treaty of Portsmouth until the London Naval Conference, a period in which Japan felt on the whole very little threatened by other powers. Their attention had been riveted on internal reform; international relations had been interpreted only in the metaphor of the class conflict which was their primary concern at home. This easy preoccupation with internal conflict was simply no longer possible after 1931, and many of the left-wing intellectuals came to the realization, sometimes inspiring and sometimes embarrassing, that they were Japanese and that this meant something special.

Beyond this broad context of a changing balance between domestic and foreign concerns was a general intellectual weakness of Marxism within Japan. It was of course the thoroughness of Marxism which appealed to the students of the 1920s, its promise to include every

24. For an interesting and detailed treatment of the phenomenon of *tenkō* from a sociological standpoint, see Patricia Golden Steinhoff, "*Tenkō:* Ideology and Societal Integration in Prewar Japan," Ph.D. diss., Harvard University, 1969.

area of human endeavor in a simple interpretive framework, its "scientific" accuracy. But this very appeal was by the same token a major weakness in that a single doubt pulled the entire structure of Marxism into question. Like a fine timepiece, it worked with great precision when all the pieces fitted. But with a single faulty component, the viability of the ideology as an organic unity collapsed, and its separate parts became suddenly vulnerable to a far more critical analysis than before. In the process of such analysis, many basic elements could and did survive, including the general commitment to a class analysis of society or to the desirability of a socialist state. But at the same time, weaknesses which had previously been but dimly perceived now became painfully apparent. The truly fatal weakness, many of the jailed communists came to feel, was the failure of Marxism–Leninism to allow for any uniqueness in the Japanese case and to demand subservience to what were merely the national interests of the Soviet Union. It was this central weakness that led so many Japanese Marxists to a formal renunciation of communism, even though they continued to believe many of the basic tenets of Marxism.

The ease with which the communists reconsidered their allegiance also had an important social dimension. All Japanese, as sociologists often point out, work most effectively in small groups and submerge themselves wholly in the life of the group, which carries on all value and meaning. This was equally true of the communist movement in Japan, which functioned in tight cell units and depended very heavily on the coherence and sustaining power of the close group of comrades, the *dōshi* or "like-minded." When isolated from the group, the ideology which it had carried was deprived of much of its meaning, and the individual communist alone in a jail cell had little reason to sustain his allegiance. Severed from the supportive warmth of small group solidarity, the prisoner's loyalty was easily transferred to another small group, the family. The police authorities took great pains to play on feelings of filial duty and family solidarity of the prisoners, by encouraging family visits and by talking frequently of the grief and shame which a communist was causing his parents. Few could or did resist such pressures. A related explanation of *tenkō* would stress the particularism of Japanese religious values. Marxism being a highly universalistic ideology, it might be argued, it could simply not be sustained by those nurtured in a tradition which encouraged religious tolerance and the tailoring of behavior to specific situations rather than absolute moral maxims. In these terms, *tenkō* is simply a natural manifestation of the Japanese value system and no great occasion for surprise. Certainly in the case of the many Shinjinkai members who committed *tenkō,* there is little reason to suspect that it represents either a basic moral failing or behavior in any sense abnormal.

The end of the war brought major changes to the careers of as many as half of the former Shinjinkai members. A number were purged by the American occupation, largely for positions in the Imperial Rule Assistance Association and the wartime Diet. A few were released from jail and overnight became communist heroes. Others returned from abroad in search of new jobs, while some former academics found themselves restored to teaching posts from which they had been purged before the war. Their activity in the student movement before the war was a source of pride and prestige for some, especially those in academic life, journalism, and politics, while it was a well-hidden embarrassment for a number of businessmen. On the whole, the far more liberal climate of postwar Japan, combined with the prestige which naturally accrues to Tokyo University graduates, has allowed many Shinjinkai members to become very prominent in their respective professions. The range of professional activity into which the members have progressed is very wide and can scarcely be capsulized except to suggest that it is probably similar to that of any random group of university graduates of their generation. The following percentage breakdown is rough but gives some idea of the professional distribution of the Shinjinkai membership after the war:

Businessmen	18
Scholars	17
Journalists	12
Writers and critics	12
Politicians	11
Bureaucrats	10
Lawyers	7
Physicians	5
Miscellaneous	8

By the time of the anniversary reunion, almost twenty-five years after the end of the war, many Shinjinkai members, most of them in their sixties, had retired from professional posts, but most remained intensely active with political pursuits, hobbies, and the writing of books, articles, and memoirs. Many retained considerable power as elder statesmen in their respective fields.

TEN CASE STUDIES

The fascination of the Shinjinkai membership lies not in any generalizations as to "what became of them," for they became too many things. Rather the group must be thought of as a revealing assortment of individuals, individually fascinating, who happened to come together with similar interests for one brief period in their lives. To give some idea of the specific flavor of these lives and of the wide variety they offer, I have chosen ten former Shinjinkai members for brief case studies of careers and personalities. The selection has been both on the basis of available information and with an eye to giving as wide a cross-section as possible in terms of generation, personality, and career. No claim is made as to statistical representativeness. Listing is in order of year of graduation.[25]

25. Many sources have been used for compiling biographical information on the Shinjinkai members, but the most useful have been: personal interviews; Jinji kōshinjo, ed., *Jinji kōshinroku* (postwar editions); *Kaihō no ishizue;* Gakushi-kai, *Kaiin shimeiroku* (annual, 1925–1942); alumni directories for the prewar higher schools; Noguchi, *Musan undō sō-tōshi den;* and personal correspondence with Ishidō Kiyotomo, 1968–69. The specific sources used in the ten case studies are as follows:

Tanahashi: Interview; Noguchi, *Musan undō sō-tōshi den,* pp. 174–176.

Kadota: Interview.

Koiwai: Koiwai Jō tsuitōgō henshū iinkai, ed., "Koiwai Jō tsuitō tokushūgō", *Aichi daigaku shimbun,* no. 112 (April 10, 1960); Jiyū hōsōdan, ed., *Jiyū hōsōdan monogatari,* pp. 333–350; Noguchi, *Musan undō sō-tōshi den,* pp. 117–118.

Hattori: Shimonaka Kunihiko, ed., *Dai jimmei jiten,* 10 vols. (Heibonsha, 1958), IX, 549; Shisō no kagaku kenkyūkai, *Tenkō,* III, 484; Matsushima Eiichi, "Kaisetsu," in Hattori Shisō, *Kurofune zengo—Hattori Shisō zuihitsushū* (Chikuma shobō, 1966), pp. 363–385.

Hayashi: Interview; Hayashi Fusao, *Bungakuteki kaisō;* Mishima Yukio, *Hayashi Fusao ron* (Shinchōsha, 1963), pp. 110–126; Hisamatsu *et al.,* eds., *Gendai Nihon bungaku daijiten,* pp. 898–902.

Katsuki: Interview.

Tanaka Toshio: Interview.

Moriya: Interview; Jiyū hōsōdan, ed., *Jiyū hōsōdan monogatari,* pp. 367–383.

Tanaka Seigen: Ino Kenji, "Zengakuren o sōjū suru hankyō no Tanaka Seigen,"

Tanahashi Kotora (1889–   ) was born in the old castle town of Matsumoto in the Japan Alps, the youngest of ten children of a former samurai who after the Restoration worked alternately as a policeman and a schoolteacher. The poverty and pride of this heritage, Tanahashi feels, bred in him a natural spirit of rebellion. After middle school in Matsumoto, he entered Third Higher in Kyoto, where with Asō and Yamana he organized a progressive debating group, the Jūōkai. Graduating from Tokyo Imperial in 1917, he worked for over a year in the Ministry of Justice—to fathom the operations of the opposition, he claims—before joining the Yūaikai. After five years of hectic activity in the labor movement, he took a trip to Europe on the profits of a volume of essays written by leading socialists, which Asō edited on his behalf.[26] After his return via the Soviet Union, he opened a law practice and became involved in the budding proletarian party movement. He participated in the founding of the centrist Japan Labor–Farmer Party (Nichirōtō) and was president of its affiliated Federation of Japanese Labor Unions (Nihon Rōdō Kumiai Dōmei). Throughout the 1930s, he served on the central committee of the major proletarian party and ran (unsuccessfully) in the Diet elections of 1930 and 1937. After the war, in 1946, he was elected to the lower house of the Diet from the new Japan Socialist Party but was forced to withdraw his candidacy for reelection shortly before the 1947 election under the purge directive for his brief wartime involvement in the East Asia League (Tōa Remmei) in his native Nagano prefecture. He was depurged on appeal and was elected to the upper house of the Diet in 1950, serving two terms until 1962. After retirement from active political life, he devoted himself to travel (including a trip to the Soviet Union in 1967 at age 72) and to writing his autobiography. Gentle-spoken and personable, Tanahashi displays little of the intellectualism that characterizes many other Shinjinkai members. Undogmatic on issues of ideology, he is known as a man of strong and honest character.

Kadota Takeo (1895–   ) was raised in Matsuyama on the island

---

Hōseki, 3.11 (November 1967), 102–108; Kusayanagi Daizō, " 'Tōkyō taiga' Tanaka Seigen," *Bungei shunjū*, 47.11 (October 1969), 220–234.

Kisamori: Interview; Sugiura, ed., *Aru seishun no kiroku*, pp. 16–66.

26. Asō Hisashi, ed., *Shin shakaiteki chitsujo e* (Dōjinsha shoten, 1922).

of Shikoku and attended Seventh Higher in Kagoshima, an area known for its nurture of tough and independent men. At higher school, he was converted to Christianity, and thus came naturally to lodge in the Hongō YMCA when he entered Tokyo Imperial in 1918. There he met Yoshino Sakuzō, then president of the YMCA, and took a quick interest in his exciting ideas. He attended the famous Yoshino–Rōninkai debate and shortly after joined the Shinjinkai along with several other YMCA members. Preferring street activity to intellectual pursuits, Kadota was a key member of the "activist" faction in the early Shinjinkai, speaking frequently at labor rallies and winning a reputation for fiery agitation which forced him out of the YMCA dormitory. He entered the *Tōkyō nichinichi shimbun* on graduation through Asō's introduction. He had initially planned to gain experience for eventual work on a labor newspaper but ended up staying with the commercial press, switching to the *Yomiuri shimbun* in 1933 and specializing in the purely technical task of make-up editing. In 1943, pessimistic over the outcome of the war, he quit his newspaper job. With the surrender, he took a series of jobs, first with the official newspaper of the Japan Socialist Party and later with the *Sankei shimbun* (Japan's *Wall Street Journal*) in the early 1950s. In about 1963, he was given a position as "adviser" at Yomiuriland, an amusement park in the Tokyo suburbs; the post was arranged by *Yomiuri shimbun* president Shōriki Matsutarō to give his former employee a tranquil place (a tiny room not far from the Yomiuriland swimming pool) to sit and meditate. Kadota's self-image as a small-but-tough type in his youth and his administrative career in journalism belie a deeply mystical strain in his character, which has led him on an unbroken religious quest throughout his life. From the Christianity of his student days, he went on to study Shintō extensively and then to take an interest in animism. He claims that he occasionally receives spiritual messages and once even aspired to be a full-time prophet. When I interviewed him in 1967, he was deeply involved in learning about Judaism.

Koiwai Jō (1897–1959) was born in a farm village in the outskirts of Matsumoto (also the birthplace of Tanahashi, suggesting the influence of the traditional liberalism of that district). His father left for America while he was a child, leaving him with his mother and two older sisters in a life that was economically tolerable and generally pleasant. Taking an early interest in literature, he even edited his own magazine in elementary school and was an avid reader of Natsume Sōseki, Tokutomi Roka, and Tolstoy. One summer he is said to have composed thirty tanka a day, modeling his verse after Ishikawa Takuboku. He soon turned in more political directions, however, and was expelled from middle school in his last year for leading a strike in opposition to the principal's suppression of a student meeting. He managed nevertheless to enter First Higher by special examination, an extremely unusual feat. In the summer of 1918, he joined a group traveling to Shanghai and was reportedly shocked by the activities of the foreign imperialists there. Entering Tokyo Imperial in 1919, he immediately joined the Shinjinkai, soon taking a special interest in syndicalism, then a dominant force in the labor movement. After three active years, he graduated and took a job as professor of law at Kansai University in Osaka but resigned after a year to open a labor-oriented law practice. For a full decade he was deeply involved in the Osaka labor movement, providing critical leadership in a formative period. He was briefly involved in the First Communist Party in 1922, but his later political affiliations were with the Labor–Farmer Party (Rōnōtō), and he was elected to the Osaka City Council in 1929. He moved to Tokyo in 1933 and opened the Japan Research Institute in Politics and Economics (Nihon Seiji Keizai Kenkyūjo), in which he was active until he moved to Shanghai in 1940 to head a research center there. During the war, he became a lecturer and then professor at Tōa Dōbun Shoin, a school with a tradition of providing Japan's "China hands." After the war, Koiwai headed a large group from Tōa Dōbun Shoin which became the core of the faculty for the new Aichi University in Nagoya. First a professor of political science, he became president of the university from 1955 until his death four years later. He was the author of a number of books on political science and many articles on politics and economics.

Hattori Shisō (1901–1956) was born in Shimane prefecture, the eldest son of a Shin Buddhist priest, and attended Third Higher in Kyoto, where he was a member of the progressive "Jūninkai" (Club of Ten) organized under Ōya Sōichi. By this time he was already, according to one classmate, a dedicated Marxist. Joining the Shinjinkai upon entering the Tokyo Imperial Department of Sociology, he was active primarily in the Teidai Settlement and played a leading role in founding it. After graduation in 1925, he held such positions as lecturer at Tōyō University and director of the Chūō Kōronsha Publishing Division, but his real base was within the professional research groups of the left-wing movement, notably the Proletarian Science Institute (Puroretaria Kagaku Kenkyūjo) and the Society for the Study of Materialism (Yuibutsuron Kenkyūkai). He was one of the leading members of the orthodox Kōza School of interpretation of Japanese capitalism and wrote two essays for the famous *Nihon shihonshugi hattatsu shi kōza* (Symposium on the Historical Development of Japanese Capitalism) of 1932–33, which gave the group its name. His major contribution to Kōza theory lay in his study of the development of manufacture before the Meiji Restoration. As a member of the Kōza School, he was arrested in the 1936 "Communist Academy Incident" and presumably released for a declaration of *tenkō*. The following year he joined the Kaō Soap Company, becoming head of the publicity section, and continued his scholarly efforts in the compilation of the impressive *Fifty-Year History of Kaō Soap* (*Kaō Sekken gojūnenshi*) in 1940. Free at the end of the war to continue his research in Japanese history, Hattori held teaching positions at Hōsei University and at a private school in Kamakura while writing many books and articles. As before the war, his base was more journalistic than academic, as reflected in his literate and popular style, but the underlying framework of analysis remained strictly Marxist. Among his postwar writings were several books on medieval Buddhism which sought to apply a class analysis to religious development. He was briefly a member of the postwar Japanese Communist Party but soon withdrew.

Hayashi Fusao (1903–   ) was born as Gotō Toshio in the town of Ōita in northeast Kyushu, the son of a moderately well-to-do innkeeper whose fortunes declined so rapidly that by his teens Hayashi was peddling sandals made by his father. Ever more impoverished, he was forced to rely on the patronage of a local banker to continue his education beyond elementary school. In middle school he was interested largely in literature but showed political promise by leading a school strike. Entering Fifth Higher in Kumamoto, he joined with some classmates to form a Marxist study group, the R.F. Kai. A Fifth Higher representative in the High School League, he immediately joined the Shinjinkai upon entering the Department of Politics at Tokyo Imperial in 1923. For the next two years, Hayashi was a central and charismatic leader of the group, but from about 1924 his interests began to revert to literature as he took the pen name Hayashi Fusao and started writing short stories, the first of which was published in April 1926. He was one of four Shinjinkai members involved in the 1926 Gakuren arrests, and during his five months in jail in Kyoto he betrayed slightly more hesitation over his commitment to communism than did his resolute comrades. His arrest forced him to withdraw from Tokyo Imperial, after which he began an active career in the proletarian literature movement. In July 1930, however, he began a two-year jail term for the earlier Gakuren conviction, which had been upheld after lengthy appeals. After his release in 1932, Hayashi's literary interests became gradually more conservative, although he still considered himself a "proletarian" writer. He joined with such unproletarian writers as Kobayashi Hideo and Kawabata Yasunari in 1933 to form the Bungakkai, and by 1935 he had clearly turned in the direction of apolitical romanticism with a strong interest in the Japanese past. After the February 26 rebellion in 1936, Hayashi expressed his strong sympathy for the romantic impulsiveness of the young officers. He continue to move to the right in the late 1930s, and shortly before the beginning of the war wrote "Tenkō ni tsuite" (Concerning *tenkō*), a pamphlet in which he argued that *tenkō* should be not merely a negative renunciation of communism but rather a positive spiritual commitment to the emperor system. He maintained such an attitude himself during the war by writing a number of pieces in support of Japan's "holy war." After the defeat, he turned to writing popular, bright, humorous novels which earned him a wide middle-class readership. He has continued to write prolifically throughout the postwar period, although his conservative views have earned him the antipathy of much of the literary world, as well as the dedicated support of a few (notably Mishima Yukio). One of his most criticized works has been *A Positive View of the Greater East Asian War (Daitōa sensō kōteiron)*, in which he sees the whole of

Japan's modern history as a continuous struggle against the Western threat. Hayashi represents a type of personality within the Shinjinkai whose basically romantic preferences led him naturally from the student movement into literary conservatism.

Katsuki Shinji (1903–) was born the son of a Kanazawa doctor. Although influenced by Kawakami Hajime's *Tales of the Poor* while a student at Third Higher, it was not until he entered Tokyo Imperial in 1923 that he was persuaded to join the student movement by classmate Kikukawa Tadao. A serious medical student, he was active in the Social Medicine Study Group of the Tōdai Shaken and occasionally worked at the clinic of the Teidai Settlement. In his third year he was chosen as secretary-general of the Shinjinkai, probably because of his safe respectability. Following graduation in 1927, he spent two years recuperating from an illness before taking a job in Kurashiki (Okayama prefecture) in the Social Hygiene Research Division of the Ōhara Social Problems Research Institute. He remained with the institute for over three decades, as it was set up independently as the Kurashiki Institute of Labor Science and then moved to Tokyo in 1937, where it remains today in the suburbs of Zoshigaya. Katsuki was director of the institute for seven years after the war until his retirement in 1962. His research has centered on the problems of labor hygiene, much of which was contracted by the Japanese government and hence involved few direct ties with the left-wing movement. After leaving the Institute of Labor Science, Katsuki became director of the Meiji Life Insurance Social Work Foundation's Physical Capability Research Institute. An earnest and courteous man, Katsuki is typical of the Shinjinkai medical students in his dedication to the social aspects of medicine.

Tanaka Toshio (1902–) was a native of Fukuoka and, like many of the Kyushu members of the Shinjinkai, won a reputation as an outgoing activist. Graduating from Fifth Higher two years after Hayashi Fusao, he quickly became a central Shinjinkai leader and served at one point as secretary-general. In 1927 he became involved with the Japanese Communist Party as a member of the "Student Fraction" and was arrested in the spring of 1928 while attempting to reorganize the party in the wake of the 3.15 roundup (although it is not clear that he was ever a formal party member). After *tenkō* and release in 1930, he worked for a time in a private research institute in Tokyo, a position arranged for him by his former teacher Yoshino Sakuzō. After this, he earned a living by doing translation work and writing free-lance articles on politics and economics for a variety of magazines. For a brief time he worked as an official of the Japan Social Masses Party and in 1939 finally found a steady job as an official in the Tokyo city government. In 1943 he left this for a position with Nihon Steel and was sent to Borneo in 1944 to work at one of the company mills there. He returned after the war in 1946 and the following year was elected to the lower house of the Diet as a Socialist. During his long Diet tenure until his upset defeat in the 1967 election, he became known as an expert on foreign affairs, and his sympathy with the communist bloc took him on many trips abroad, including seven to Communist China and two to the Soviet Union. His wife Sumiko is also prominent on the Japanese left, first as a writer on women's problems and since 1965 as a member of the House of Councilors. Tanaka, as a member of the left wing of the postwar Japanese Socialist Party, stands at the political center of gravity of the Shinjinkai membership in the postwar period.

Moriya Fumio (1907–   ) was born in Okayama, where he attended Sixth Higher and was active in the debating club. He participated briefly in the Shinjinkai upon entering Tokyo Imperial in 1926 but soon decided, with a seriousness of purpose which has characterized his entire life, to devote himself to his studies of law and withdrew from the student movement. By chance, however, he was in Okayama in March 1928 when the 3.15 arrests struck a group of students at Sixth Higher, and was appalled by the summary manner in which the arrestees were treated. Disillusioned over the value of the law which he had been studying, he rejoined the Shinjinkai and has ever since been a dedicated communist. Falling ill shortly after graduation in 1929, he returned to Okayama to recuperate but managed to set up a communist labor union from his hospital bed and was forced by the police to leave town. He returned to Tokyo, found a job in a respectable law office to please his father, and was active underground as a communist organizer, formally joining the party in mid-1932. Arrested in 1933, he was released from prison late the following year after writing a *tenkō* statement which his acute conscience led him to regret for many years after. Through a relative he found a job with the Kurashiki Rayon Company in Osaka, working as legal adviser and then as economic researcher. In this period, he began to earn fame as a Marxist economist of the Kōza School, writing in a number of journals under the pen name Noguchi Hachirō. He was again arrested in 1938 for certain of his writings but was released in early 1940 with a suspended sentence. During the war, he worked for the government in the economic control organization for textiles. After the war, Moriya immediately joined the revived Japanese Communist Party, of which he has remained a totally dedicated member. By profession he remains a lawyer, active in the Civil Liberties Legal Group and at the same time is a productive scholar of Marxist economics. Among his several books are an economic analysis of the textile industry and a highly rated introduction to Marxist economics. Moriya is almost extreme in his seriousness and his dedication to the causes which he came to espouse as a Shinjinkai member, being one of the very few to have remained loyal to the Japanese Communist Party throughout the postwar period.

Tanaka Seigen (Kiyoharu) (1906–   ) is the most curious and colorful personality to emerge from the Shinjinkai. Raised in Hakodate on Hokkaido—whence, some argue, comes his rough-and-tumble spirit—Tanaka was raised by his widowed mother and eventually entered Hirosaki Higher School. There he joined the school *shaken* and participated in some local labor strikes. Entering the Esthetics Department of Tokyo Imperial in 1927 with not the slightest intention of studying, Tanaka immediately joined the Shinjinkai and became renowned for his belligerent style, most notably in his formation of a self-defense group against the Shichiseisha (he was a third *dan* karate expert at the time). With the gradual decimation of the Communist Party leadership after March 1928, Tanaka gradually emerged as a defiant and elusive organizer, and by late 1929, at the age of 23, he became the chairman of the party's Central Committee. His tenure was brief and he was arrested in July 1930 after leading the party through its "armed era" of terrorist attacks on the police. He spent the next eleven years in jail, despite a *tenkō* statement in 1933 (commonly ascribed to his mother's suicide but doubtless also influenced by Sano and Nabeyama). He became known as the "emperor of Kosuge Penitentiary" for his defiant prison behavior, occasionally pummeling guards who dared to touch him. In these years he also made the acquaintance of a number of right-wing extremists jailed after the February 1936 rebellion, some of whom were later to become his business partners. Released by an amnesty in 1941 before serving his full term, he then spent two years undergoing Zen training at a temple in Shizuoka before launching into a business career. During the war he set up a construction company which did contract work for the navy and which at the end of the war expanded rapidly as the Shin-chūgumi, involved largely in reparations-related construction in Southeast Asia and in the building of American bases on Okinawa. Tanaka has since created a number of further companies, but his fame rests not on his business acumen—which some claim is only modest—but upon his constant involvement in a great variety of incidents and scandals. Tanaka has a natural talent for working behind the scenes, for ferreting out information, and manipulating people on a personal basis. He has been reputed to have close ties with the American Central Intelligence Agency, to have played a role in the fall of Sukarno in 1966, to have given some $15,000 to the radical Zengakuren student leadership in 1960, and to have set up a personal intelligence apparatus in Europe. A dapper dresser and a man of seemingly inexhaustible energy, Tanaka represents a boss-like personality of a sort rare in the Shinjinkai. In striking contrast to such earnest types as Moriya Fumio, Tanaka feels no guilt whatsoever over his *tenkō*. His ideology might be described as libertarian, a wild dedication to freedom and fear of any kind of binding system—hence the frequent confusion in the press as to whether he is "left-wing" or "right-wing."

Kisamori Kichitarō (1906–   ) was born in Yokohama, the son of a freight agent for the shipyards there. A number of his school classmates were sons of shipyard workers, and he was from an early age sensitized to the hardships of the urban working class: he claims to have been particularly stirred by a strike at the shipyards when he was a middle school student in 1922. He was further influenced by the Christian socialism of one of the teachers at the mission school he was then attending. In 1926 he entered Mito Higher School, where he quickly became involved in the embryonic school *shaken* through the influence of such charismatic students as Chiba Shigeo (later Shinjinkai secretary-general) and Utsunomiya Tokuma (later a central leader of the Kyoto Imperial Shaken). After working diligently in the Mito Shaken (largely through the debating club), Kisamori naturally joined the Shinjinkai when he entered Tokyo Imperial in 1928, just at the time of the formal suppression of the group. Like many others, Kisamori had entered the low-powered Department of Esthetics to leave time for agitation and rarely set foot on the Tokyo Imperial campus. He emerged as a key Gakuren leader in the winter of 1928–29 but was arrested for participation in a demonstration on the Tokyo Imperial campus in May 1929 and suspended from the university. He shortly thereafter withdrew from the movement, in part from family financial problems, and was expelled from the university for failure to pay his tuition. In 1930, he went to work for the Tokyo Stock Exchange, thus terminating all ties with the left-wing movement. He entered Nomura Securities in 1940, shortly after which his left-wing past led to his arrest in connection with the infamous Yokohama Incident (in which many journalists, academics, and researchers were arrested), but he was released after two months through the influence of friends. He continued his career in the stock brokerage business in the postwar period, switching in 1955 to Kakumaru Securities, of which he became a director. He has written several books on investment and stocks, such as *An Introduction to Investing in Securities* (*Shōken tōshi nyūmon*). An affable man, he looks back with nostalgia on his days in the student movement and was an eager participant in the 1969 anniversary celebrations.

10 | The Shinjinkai in Historical Perspective

One former student activist of the 1920s has compared the rebirth of the communist student movement in 1945 to the sudden reappearance of submerged Christian groups in late Tokugawa Japan when the ban on their religion was lifted. Just as the Japanese Christians in the early seventeenth century had been forced to renounce their beliefs through *fumie* (treading on an image of the crucifix) and yet managed to perpetuate an underground tradition for two hundred years, so the communists in spite of *tenkō* retained their faith in a foreign creed, reemerging at the end of the Pacific War with energy seemingly undiminished after two decades. The left-wing student tradition, he writes, "was carried on, never extinguished, like an underground stream in student society. Only by understanding this can one comprehend the confidence and fearlessness of the postwar student movement." [1]

One obvious dimension of continuity in the student movement has been the personal influence in the postwar period of the men who were themselves student activists in the 1920s and 1930s. Many of the Shinjinkai members have gone into professions such as journalism, academic life, and socialist politics, where they and other ex-student radicals like them have helped to provide a comfortable environment for the postwar student movement. The progressive tone of national journalism has encouraged both wide and sympathetic coverage of student protest. Similarly, the constant postwar expansion of the left-

1. Takatsu Seidō, "Hata o mamorite," pt. 2, pp. 135–136.

wing publishing empire, much of which is written and edited by the older left, has created a plethora of available materials to guide the thinking of student radicals today and to maintain a high degree of continuity with prewar ideology.

Probably the most important sphere of the personal influence of the "old left" is in the university itself, where almost all tenured positions during the first two postwar decades have been held by men with some firsthand acquaintance with—and often participation in—the prewar student movement. These memories have instilled in postwar professors less an enthusiastic urge to support their radical students (although a vocal minority do so) than a paralyzing sense of guilt over the failures of their own student generation. Those who *were* active in the student movement before the war feel guilty because, with few exceptions, they were arrested and forced to recant; those who were *not* active anguish simply because they were not. One striking example is the case of Tōyama Shigeki, a noted historian of the Meiji Restoration who attended Tokyo Imperial from 1935 to 1939 and was there attracted, by way of the study group network, to Marxism as a tool of historical analysis. His commitment, however, like that of all left-wing students in those years, remained passive, as he confessed to postwar students in a tone of deep remorse in a *Tokyo University News* article in 1952, berating himself as "cowardly and commonplace."[2] This quasi-masochistic attitude of many Japanese academics educated before the war has in effect served as a major source of encouragement to the postwar student movement.

The degree to which the prewar student activists have encouraged or at least condoned their postwar successors was suggested by the reactions of the sexagenarian Shinjinkai members, as they gathered for the fiftieth anniversary reunion in January 1969, to the tactics of the younger generation which was then battling the riot police within earshot. Without exception, the older men carefully refrained from any overt criticism of the contemporary student movement, even though the techniques of violent confrontation now employed are clearly against the basic principles of the Shinjinkai in its heyday (one recalls the strong Shinjinkai denunciation of Shichiseisha violence in 1928).

2. Tōyama Shigeki, "Honemi ni shimiru kaikon—Okubyō de heibon na ichi gakusei no omoide," *Tōkyō daigaku shimbun;* no. 137 (October 30, 1952), p. 3.

Some, like Tanaka Seigen, offered positive praise of the armed ultra-radicals.[3]

Far more important than direct personal influence of the prewar student leaders, however, has been the institutional legacy to the postwar movement, the precedents set in terms of ideology, organization, and techniques. Before considering such institutional continuity, however, it would be well to pause and recapitulate the role of the student movement in the 1920s in terms of the general evolution of the entire left-wing movement in modern Japan.

The Intellectualization of the Japanese Left

It was scarcely a surprise, looking back, that an organized and articulate student movement should have appeared in Japan in 1918–19. The prestige and concomitant responsibility which the new Japanese universities of the Meiji period promised to their graduates, given the context of a long Confucian tradition which imposed upon educated men the moral obligation of social and political criticism, made the students naturally sensitive to a wide variety of political stimuli. The rural origins of much of the studentry and the idyllic experience in the higher schools set the stage for an unsettling reaction in the politicized urban atmosphere of the university. The preponderance of Western-style learning in the university curriculum was in itself highly radical in the context of a nation which had by no means cast off its deep and unique cultural traditions. Precedents for student rebellion were also ample, in the traditions of student rowdiness and the *gakkō sōdō*.

To this institutional setting was added towards the end of World War I an intoxicating array of external stimuli: the journalistic activity of the Taishō democrats, the escalation of mass protest in the rice riots, the sudden growth of organized labor, the news of revolution in Russia and elsewhere, and the visionary idealism of Woodrow Wilson. But if the student movement of the 1920s was precipitated by such influences outside the university, it was sustained through the decade and especially into the early 1930s by the pervasive changes then occurring in the character of the student population. The ex-

3. Tape recordings of the proceedings of the Shinjinkai anniversary reunion are in the possession of the author and of Mr. Ishidō Kiyotomo.

plosive growth in numbers together with the decline in available prestige jobs for university graduates led students increasingly to think of themselves as a distinctive social grouping with its own peculiar problems, demanding the same attention as any other interest group. This growth of a quasi-class-consciousness among university students in the 1920s was clearly reflected in the rapid spread of student newspapers, cooperatives, mutual aid societies, and co-ordinated extra-curricular associations (*gakuyūkai*), all of which were nonexistent in Meiji and had become almost universal by the 1930s. The insecurity of the future for many students in this period also led them, far more than their Meiji predecessors, to question the aims and means of university education, providing fertile ground for political manipulation.

The rapid transition of student movement ideology from the cries of "Democracy" and "Humanism" in 1918 to the orthodox Marxism–Leninism of the mid-1920s seems understandable in terms both of the times and of the inherent appeal of Marxism in Japan. The intense idealism of the students led them easily to frustration with the slow pace of gradualist reform and with the lethargy of the working class to waken to their call, so that the activist mainstream became progressively more revolutionary in its ideology. Marxism of itself was appealing both for its easy accommodation with the Confucian legacy that equated the search for truth ("social science" in Marxist jargon) with moral virtue, and for its intelligibility within the framework of German academism which dominated the modern Japanese university. A further appeal was offered by the Bolshevik techniques of organization introduced in the mid-1920s, which provided not only the "shivering thrill of intrigue" but also a highly efficient defense against increasing suppression by police and educational authorities.

A further strength—and the ultimate weakness—of Marxism–Leninism in the 1920s lay in its international thrust, a source of great appeal to students whose Western-style education made them yearn to view their own country as part of a universal pattern. Such internationalism was viable only to the degree that students centered their concerns on domestic rather than foreign policy issues, but such a focus proved on the whole tenable until 1930. It is revealing that the student movement of the 1920s rarely if ever addressed itself to issues of foreign policy, being able in good conscience to leave matters of Japanese national interest to the discretion of the Comintern. In this sense, it is hardly surprising that the perceived threats to Japanese national interest which emerged successively in the early 1930s should have seriously undercut the appeal of the left-wing student movement, relying as totally as it did on Comintern-defined policy.

The lasting significance of the prewar student movement lay not in any immediate political changes which it influenced, which were negligible if any, but in the underlying changes which it effected in the personnel and modes of operation of the entire left-wing movement. These changes must be seen in terms of the role of the student movement in serving to create a totally new type of intelligentsia in Japan, an intelligentsia which has in fact come to dominate the intellectual life of the nation in the period since the 1920s. It is an intelligentsia which is characterized first by the necessity of a university education for qualification and second by a political quality known most broadly as "progressive" (as in the postwar derogatory expression, *shimpoteki bunkajin,* or "progressive men of culture") and more narrowly as Marxist.

While such left-wing intellectuals are by no means the entirety of the Japanese "intelligentsia," they do by and large set the tone of the whole, and here again the influence of student radicalism is central: so great has been the impact of the student movement that it is impossible to pass through a Japanese university without acquiring some passing acquaintance with Marxism. It is certainly true that the majority of Japanese students would never have called themselves "Marxists," and yet few would have had any trouble describing the fundamentals of Marxist theory. Thus Japanese intellectuals since the 1920s, whether or not they consider themselves in any sense Marxist, have been forced to define their position *relative to* Marxism. One is reminded of Mishima Yukio, an intellectual who was by no definition left-wing, engaging in an animated public debate with Tokyo University radicals in 1969 and showing a perfect understanding of (and even some sympathy for) the students' ideology.[4]

The importance of the student movement in providing the seedbed of this new intelligentsia is best understood in terms of the contrast

4. Mishima Yukio and Tōdai zengaku kyōtō kaigi Komaba kyōtō funsai iinkai, *Tōron: Mishima Yukio vs. Tōdai zenkyōtō* (Shinchōsha, 1969).

between the Shinjinkai members and the generation of left-wing intellectuals which immediately preceded them—the Meiji socialists. The
first and most fundamental difference lay in the area of *respectability*.
The Meiji socialists were wholly outside the political power structure,
both in terms of their education—which was almost entirely in private
schools strong in "outsider spirit" [5]—and in terms of their social
origins, which were so confused and variegated as to defy categoriza-
tion. They were treated by the Meiji state as the outlaws they were,
being kept under very strict surveillance and shown no mercy when
punished—as in the Kōtoku Incident which, by the execution of thirteen socialists for an alleged plot against the emperor, put an end to
the Meiji socialist movement in 1911.

The sharp break with this Meiji outlaw-socialist tradition was dramatically articulated by the Shinjinkai in the very first line of the
group's statement of purpose, which pointed out that the formation of
a socialist group in the Tokyo Imperial Faculty of Law—the pillar of
burcaucratic orthodoxy—was "truly thunder in a clear sky." From this
point on, the mainstream of the Japanese intellectual left was produced from within the universities and primarily from the state universities which were the most closely integrated with the political
establishment. Private universities of course also produced their share
of radicals, but they were no longer imbued with the kind of "outsider
spirit" which had earlier been imparted to a number of the Meiji
socialists. By the 1920s, private universities, with the partial exception
of Waseda and Dōshisha, had lost all sense of independence and had
fallen neatly into the hierarchy determined by the imperial university
system.

It is perhaps the greatest paradox of this new generation of left-wing
intellectuals that they have tended to accept the prestige and preferment accorded them as university graduates at the same time that they
have vowed to overthrow the very political system which allows them
such prestige. This contradiction was perceived at an early point by
Ōsugi Sakae, one of the last and greatest of the Meiji radicals, in his
insistence in 1921 that "it is wrong that these Shinjinkai types should
enter the Yūaikai and right away become leaders and members of the

5. Matsuda Michio, *Nihon chishikijin no shisō* (Chikuma shobō, 1965), p. 42,
lists the educational background of the leading Meiji socialists.

top executive. They should enter as the rank and file." [6] Yet the Shin-jinkai members and others from the student movement have by and large risen quickly and surely to the very top, by virtue of their ascribed prestige as university (and especially Tokyo Imperial) graduates, no matter whether in the state bureaucracy or in the Japanese Communist Party.

One result of this fundamental respectability of the new generation of radicals was a new approach to the problem of control by the government. The university, with its prestige and with a tradition of autonomy well-established by the end of the Meiji period, offered an effective extra-territorial base which the government found difficult to attack. Suppression in the manner of Kōtoku was clearly out of the question: it was one thing when the children throwing stones at the windows of the establishment were urchins from the other side of the tracks, but a wholly different problem when they were one's own children, destined to take over the family business. Thus evolved the peculiar mode of suppression of the student left—and hence of the left as a whole—which combined the approach of the educator with that of the police. It is doubtful that the policy of *tenkō* would have been pursued as assiduously—and so successfully—if all those arrested as communists had been lower-class workers and Meiji-style renegade intellectuals.

The student movement imparted to the left wing as a whole a far greater respectability and a decidedly more cerebral tone than in the past. This was a reflection of the academic setting in which the student movement was located, but beyond that of a wholly different approach to radical commitment. The Meiji socialists had on the whole arrived at their convictions through direct personal experiences, as seen in the generally eclectic nature of their ideology, which was posterior to the commitment to socialism and which they hence saw no need to systematize. The Meiji socialists on the whole were journalists and publicists rather than theorists and scholars, and this was reflected in the intensely human, direct quality of their prose.

The student radicals of the 1920s, as the prototypes of the new left-wing intelligentsia, came to their beliefs rather *through* ideology. It is true that some personal experiences commonly sparked the initial

6. Quoted in *ibid.*, p. 45.

interest in socialism, but the actual conversion was typically via theory on the printed page. Compared to the Meiji socialists, they were driven less by an emotional sense of urgency than by the intellectual persuasiveness of theoretical arguments. This fundamentally different approach to advocacy of radical ideas has colored the entire left-wing movement since the 1920s, giving it a highly scholarly and theoretical tone. It would be no exaggeration to suggest that the primary institution for effecting this change was the left-wing student *kenkyūkai*, the small study group aimed at the mastery of theoretical texts which was repeated hundreds of times on dozens of campuses in the prewar period. These study groups, the "trenches" of the student warriors, served as the major vehicle for the injection of a heavy dose of Marxism into the intellectual life of the Japanese nation.

One rather specific way in which the student movement has been responsible for leading the left wing as a whole in more scholarly and theoretical directions has been through their demand for theoretical works for use in study-group sessions, a demand which has been a basic factor in the emergence of a commercial left-wing publishing establishment. In the era of the early Shinjinkai, the students themselves were among the translators and publishers, but for primarily ideological reasons. It was only when the student movement began to expand rapidly on a national scale in the mid-1920s that a critical mass of demand was reached which enabled left-wing publishing to become economically profitable. The result has been the availability of a very wide variety of theoretical works, largely translations of Western originals, which has naturally tended to encourage disputation throughout the left wing. The left-wing publishing empire has also helped provide a much greater element of continuity within the left-wing intelligentsia than the sustaining power of the student movement alone could allow. Thus when the campus left began to revive after 1945, many volumes of socialist literature survived as primers for a new generation. One leader of the postwar Zengakuren claims that close ties developed between the students and the Japanese Communist Party *not* because of Party efforts but because students understood the meaning of communism through the prewar books available to them.[7]

7. Ōno Akio, *Zengakuren keppūroku* (Nijusseiki sha, 1967), p. 24.

One of the most conspicuous traits of the new left-wing intelligentsia which was born with the Shinjinkai has been a highly ambiguous attitude towards the "people." One finds on the one hand a recurrent tendency towards a romantic populist urge to enter "into the people" of the sort articulated most clearly in the early Shinjinkai but never entirely absent thereafter. Even where there has been an unwillingness among left-wing intellectuals to enter *physically* into the people, the "people" have nevertheless played a central part in the rhetoric of the left, given the dictates of Marxist class theory. Against this has always been an acute perception of the difficulty (indeed even the impropriety) of attempts by university graduates actually to sustain communication with the Japanese masses, not only because of the gap in educational background but also because of the rigid social hierarchy which both sides are bound by long training to maintain. One feels that this sense of distance was rarely present among the Meiji socialists, who, despite a certain tendency to sermonize from afar, were by virtue of being outsiders much closer in spirit to the masses than their university-bred successors.

The long-term impact of the student movement of the 1920s might thus be understood as a process of the "intellectualization" of the Japanese left, by which intellectuals themselves come to play a more conspicuous role in left-wing leadership and by which the less educated elements in the movement are subjected to a pressure to become more "intellectual," to devote more concern to theoretical purity than pragmatic success. One might also suggest that the element of respectability which the student movement has given to the left-wing movement as a whole has been instrumental in the postwar period in creating a virtual "left-wing establishment," in which the basic criterion of prestige—the type of education received—is precisely that of the more conventional Establishment.

THE LEGACY TO THE POSTWAR STUDENT MOVEMENT

Any comparison of the postwar student movement in Japan with its predecessor in the 1920s and early 1930s must first take account of a political environment so dramatically changed as to make *any* basic similarities between the two rather surprising. The overnight dissolution of the vast apparatus of thought suppression left students with a degree of political freedom which had not been known for at least twenty years—if ever. The Japanese Communist Party for the first time since its founding became legal, developing an established system of professional party workers and putting up candidates for election to the Diet in its own name. Students were given almost unlimited freedom of political activity, not only on the campus but in the streets as well. The lowering of the voting age by five years to twenty meant that a number of students even had a direct voice in the political process. Gone were the student directors, police spies, the Peace Preservation Law, censors, and the thrill of underground intrigue. While the postwar period has undeniably seen periodic crackdowns on student radicals, such moves are little more than gentle harassment in comparison with the blanket suppression of the 1930s.

Gone also, although the left wing did not view it in such a light, were many of the issues that students had previously made the focus of their energies. Suppression was scarcely an appealing target with the new political freedom. The military establishment had been completely dismantled, so that students were no longer faced with either the draft or with on-campus military education. The plundering landlords who had been the target of student activities in the farm tenant movement were largely eliminated in the land reform. Labor unions became free to organize and found little need to rely on students and the extra-territoriality of their campus bases as the only link to legality.

The collapse of the suppression apparatus freed not only the students but the press as well, thus serving indirectly to encourage student activism still further. Whereas before the war radical student activities were allowed only the most perfunctory coverage in the press, they have become big business for postwar journalism. The advent and near-universal proliferation of television in Japan has brought student demonstrations into every home, greatly magnifying their influence. When riot police drove the diehard ultra-radicals from the Tokyo University campus in January 1969, thirty-odd hours of pitched battle were covered in vivid detail on live television by cameras which had been built into fortified positions weeks before the event. The mutually reinforcing relationship of radical student histrionics and journalistic attention which had emerged by the late 1960s was inconceivable under the strict censorship controls of the 1930s.

Apart from the increase in political freedom, the most striking changes in the environment of student protest since 1945 have been in the university itself. Three aspects of educational change in particular —the structural reforms of the occupation period, the tremendous quantitative growth of higher education, and the mounting crisis of the private university—have exerted critical influences on the context of student radicalism.

Under the encouragement of the American occupation authorities, the structure of the Japanese system of education was revised to conform to the American model (see Chart 4). The old five-year middle school became a six-year high school (three years each of junior high and senior high), while the higher school–university course of six years was compressed into a single four-year program. Among the consequences of this structural reform was an intensification of the "examination hell" and its deleterious effects (which had been serious enough before the war). In the first place, the examination was taken a year later than before, prolonging the agony of preparation another precious year of adolescence. Worse still, the practice of the *rōnin* ("masterless samurai," students who spend extra years practicing for entrance examinations in order to enter a prestige school), which was virtually unknown before the war, became so common that by 1956 over 40 per cent of all students entering universities had spent at least one extra year.[8] The number of man-years sacrificed to the "examination hell" has thus already run into the millions, representing a substantial increase in the tension and frustration to which Japanese youth are subjected.

Not only was the examination delayed, but the time spent in school after entrance was reduced by two years through the virtual annihilation of the tradition of the old higher school. The facilities of the schools were either converted into a two-year program of "general education" (*kyōyō gakubu* or *kyōyōbu*) in the new university or upgraded to a full four-year university (the latter not without some dilution of quality). Gone, however, was the spirit of the old higher

8. Mombushō, *Wagakuni no kōtō kyōiku* (1964), p. 158.

school, the blissful three years of irresponsible freedom and meditation which had been so critical in the intellectual development of Japan's prewar elite. The postwar Japanese student has been denied the chance to unwind in provincial idleness following the entrance examinations, being thrust immediately into the urban university, with graduation

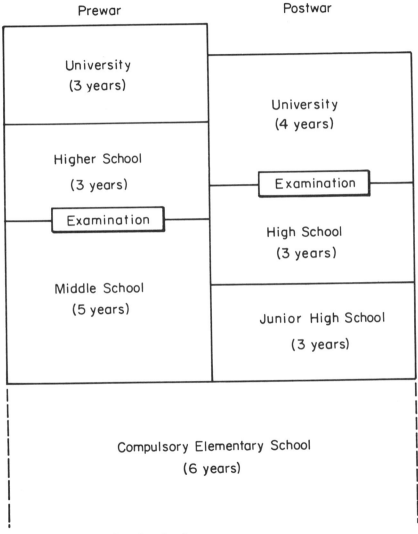

Chart 4. Postwar educational reforms

and the cruel world a scant four years off. The "examination hell" is thus aggravated both before and after by the new educational structure and has become one of the most critical factors in producing the alienation, frustration, and despair which lie behind much of postwar student radicalism.

A further change in the educational setting has been the tremendous growth of higher education in postwar Japan, at a rate of expansion not unlike that of the 1920s, the setting for the prewar student movement. In the first decade after the end of the war, the number of male students in higher education doubled and by 1967 had reached a level four times that of 1934.[9] Since the rate of growth has been even greater in private than in state education, the tendency to a high degree of concentration of university students in the great urban centers has become even more pronounced. The student population of Tokyo in particular has swelled to a size which creates a potential for radical disruption far greater than in the prewar years. Female education has expanded at a rate even more rapid than that of men, making women for the first time a calculable influence in the student movement. This growth in the sheer bulk of the Japanese studentry has greatly magnified the numbers of the student movement while leaving the quality largely unaffected.

Finally, the crisis in private education, which bulks ever larger within the whole of higher education (especially in the urban areas where the student movement is based) has conditioned the setting. The crisis is, in the simplest terms, a financial one and is in this sense an extension of precedents set before the war. The discrimination against private education continued into the postwar period, perpetuated by the traditional hierarchical ranking of universities, which consistently places state above private, and by institutional mechanisms which deprive private universities of the funds which they desperately need for quality education. Certain postwar educational reforms have even exacerbated this trend, the evils of which were clear enough in the 1920s; most serious was the drastic reduction of tuition in national universities, which before the war had been on a par with private education. In 1935 both Waseda and Tokyo Imperial had identical tuition of 120

9. Based on statistics in Mombushō, *Gakusei kyūjūnen shi* (1964), pp. 617, 621, 629, 653; and *Mainichi nenkan* (1967), p. 795.

yen ($35) per year; in 1968 Tokyo University was 12,000 yen ($33) and Waseda 185,000 yen ($554).[10]

The tuition reform, intended to allow for equal opportunity regardless of financial resources, has ironically worked in the long run in undemocratic ways, since only students whose parents can afford to finance tuition at the most prestigious high schools (tuition being free only for students lucky enough to live in the districts of these schools) and extra years as *rōnin* in cram schools will have a decent chance of the high powered preparation necessary to enter the narrow gate of a first-rate state university. At the same time, the prestige—and elitism— of the state universities has become even more deeply rooted, since the tremendous tuition gap encourages few to apply to a private institution if it is possible to enter a state one. Meanwhile, private universities must do their best to keep down tuition while receiving only meager support from government subsidies and alumni giving. The result has been a continuing resort to mass production education, skimping on facilities and faculty salaries, and in a vicious circle providing more and more causes for student discontent and issues for student protest.

Given the tremendous changes in the postwar environment of student radicalism, one might have expected a distinctly new sort of student movement to appear. In fact, however, the degree of continuity with the prewar movement is quite remarkable, especially in terms of ideology, organization, and technique. This continuity, it must be emphasized, has been instinctive but seldom conscious. Japanese student radicals since the late 1940s have been precluded by generational self-consciousness from open recognition of any history to student protest, preferring to consider themselves the first true revolutionaries. Those in the early postwar period had some vague knowledge of the prewar movement (one finds, for example, some postwar groups named the "Shinjinkai" [11]), but more recent activists have been largely igno-

10. Teikoku daigaku shimbun sha, ed., *Teikoku daigaku nenkan* (editor, 1935), pp. 220, 400; and Okumura Kaichi, ed., *Gakkō annai—Daigaku hen* (Okumura shoten, 1967), pp. 7, 141. These are the fees for comparable liberal faculties.

11. The most notable postwar "Shinjinkai" was founded at Tokyo University in 1947 in opposition to the Communist Party cell which controlled the campus left at the time. This group consciously resurrected the memory of the prewar (actually, pre-1922) Shinjinkai in support of its moderate, "humanistic" ideology, although

rant of its very existence. Even if apprised of the activities of the old Gakuren, postwar students tend to express skepticism, for the memory of the intermediate student generation decimated in the Pacific War has been sufficient to disqualify the prewar movement as a respectable model. Yet neither ignorance nor open rejection of the prewar legacy can obscure its significance, for the heritage of long-established patterns of radical student thought and behavior was too deep-rooted to be discarded.

The legacy of the prewar student movement may be most easily understood through a comparison with the postwar movement in the following five respects: motivation, ideology, organization, areas of activity, and mode of protest.[12]

Motivation. Two separate statistical studies of Japanese left-wing students in the early 1960s, made by sociologists Suzuki Hiroo and Tsurumi Kazuko, enable a tentative comparison with the prewar period in respect to *which* students enter the movement and with what motives.[13] In terms of birthplace, Tsurumi finds that the proportion of

----

there was no actual organizational linkage with the old Shinjinkai. See Nihon gakusei undō kenkyūkai, ed., *Gakusei undō no kenkyū* (Nikkan rōdō tsūshin sha, 1966), pp. 6, 302. For the founding statement, see San'ichi shobō henshūbu, ed., *Shiryō sengo gakusei undō*, I, 157–159. The postwar Shinjinkai survived into the early 1950s, although its ultimate fate is not clear; Allan B. Cole, *et al., Socialist Parties in Postwar Japan* (New Haven, 1966), states that it was active after 1955 but gives no documentation. A different postwar "Shinjinkai" was apparently founded at Hokkaido University in the late 1940s; see *Kaihō no ishizue*, p. 50, under Aramata Misao (the founder of the group); no ties with the prewar Shinjinkai are evident.

12. In addition to the Japanese works cited, two books in English are available dealing with the postwar student movement. Lawrence H. Battistini, *The Postwar Student Struggle in Japan* (Tokyo and Rutland, Vt., 1956), deals with the period until 1955 and is of doubtful reliability. More adequate is Stuart Dowsey, ed., *Zengakuren: Japan's Revolutionary Students* (Berkeley, 1970), which however focuses only on the period of the late 1960s.

13. Suzuki Hiroo, *Gakusei undō—Daigaku no kaikaku ka, shakai no henkaku ka* (Fukumura shuppan, 1968), chap. 6, and Kazuko Tsurumi, *Social Change and the Individual: Japan Before and After Defeat in World War II* (Princeton, 1970), pt. 3. These two studies are contradictory and difficult to compare at many points, largely because of the contrasting backgrounds and interests of the authors. Suzuki is a relatively conservative male educational sociologist from the Tokyo University of Education and tends to stress the Japanese student movement as a symptom of flaws in the system of higher education. Tsurumi, on the other hand, is a "progressive" (but non-Marxist) female sociologist of a far more theoretical bent, trained in the United States, who analyzes the student movement within a broad conceptual framework of socialization patterns in Japan before and after World War II. It

student activists from small towns is higher than that among apathetic students, suggesting a continuation of the prewar tendency to rural origins on the student left and a lack of urban sophistication as a motivating factor in student movement participation.[14] As for class origins, Suzuki has attempted to categorize a sample of 125 activists according to family income and finds that substantially more than average are from middle and upper-middle class families, and fewer from upper, lower-middle, and lower class families.[15] Tsurumi, however, concludes from indirect evidence that student radicals tend to come from families which are *less* wealthy than average.[16] In terms of a comparison with prewar student activists, one can only conclude tentatively that in neither case does family wealth seem to diverge so far from the average as to have made a decisive influence on motivation.

Both Suzuki and Tsurumi analyze the "generation gap," but in seemingly contradictory ways. Tsurumi mobilizes a complex methodology to prove that student activists have more "communication" with their parents than the politically less committed, whereas Suzuki detects a definite "sense of separation" (*danzetsukan*) between the generations.[17] I would tentatively suggest that both explanations are in fact plausible and combine to indicate a contrast with prewar radicals. Students participating in the movement of the 1960s were the children of parents who by all odds were far more highly educated than the parents of the prewar student radicals, given the tremendous expansion of higher education in the intervening decades.[18] This would mean that postwar students are more able to discuss with their parents, in a generally Western framework, problems of politics and ideology—hence more "communication"—but that the generational difference at the same time produces more perceived conflict or "sense of separation." Whereas prewar radicals were on the whole so differently edu-

---

should also be stressed that both studies analyze the student movement *only* for the early 1960s and hence do not enable any consideration of variations *during* the postwar period, which may well be substantial.

14. Tsurumi, p. 314.

15. Suzuki Hiroo, p. 232.

16. Tsurumi, pp. 315–317.

17. *Ibid.*, pp. 318–322, and Suzuki Hiroo, pp. 236–241.

18. Tsurumi, p. 317, further finds that activists tend to have more highly educated fathers than nonactivists.

cated from their parents that little common ground for conflict was possible, their postwar heirs are ironically more at odds with their elders precisely because they share more basic intellectual assumptions by way of comparable educational backgrounds.

Suzuki has analyzed the personality of student leftists and compared his findings with those of Okada Tsunesuke's prewar study, concluding that little has changed: left-wing students are still driven on the whole by strong humanitarian urges, with extroverts, nihilists, and blind followers in a definite minority.[19] In terms of intelligence, both Suzuki and Tsurumi conclude that postwar activists closely resemble their prewar predecessors in being among the brightest in their high school classes but then falling off academically when they enter the student movement and divert their intellectual energies to political activity.[20] Both Suzuki and Tsurumi also investigate the motivation of students entering the left-wing movement, but their classification schemes differ so much that no simple message is evident.[21] In terms of a comparison with the prewar period, the one provocative finding is a suggestion by Tsurumi that postwar students tend to be relatively less moved by reading books than those before the war. In comparison with a prewar Ministry of Education study which shows almost half of all student leftists stirred to political activity by reading books, Tsurumi has calculated only 32 per cent for her sample and concludes that postwar students are more moved by *events* than by the printed page.[22] This would suggest on the whole a slightly more emotional, less intellectual pattern in the motivation of postwar students, although it must be emphasized that, as Suzuki points out, postwar activists continue to be far more avid readers than average students, suggesting that the book orientation of the Japanese student movement is still very strong.[23]

Limited evidence suggests, then, that the postwar student movement draws on roughly the same type of student as that in the 1920s: they tend to come from slightly more rural, slightly more well-to-do background than average and are of good and selfless character and high intelligence. Slight postwar differences may be detected in a higher

19. Suzuki Hiroo, pp. 241–251.
20. *Ibid.*, pp. 261–263, and Tsurumi, pp. 327–328.
21. Suzuki Hiroo, pp. 259–260, and Tsurumi, pp. 350–362.
22. Tsurumi, pp. 354–355.
23. Suzuki Hiroo, pp. 266–269.

level of parent-child communication *and* antagonism, as well as a slightly less intellectual thrust in motivational patterns.

Ideology. Any comparison of the student movement before and after the war must begin with one fundamental similarity: the Japanese student movement remains totally Marxist in basic ideology. In both periods, a social democratic student movement has been nonexistent, while anarchist groups have been small and transient. Right-wing student radicals have continued to constitute an interesting variant which nevertheless has consistently failed to rival the numbers and influence of the student left. Within the basically Marxist orientation of the Japanese student movement, however, some conspicuous changes are apparent in the postwar period, the most notable of which has been the fragmentation of the ideological uniformity imposed by the Comintern before the war. This tendency emerged only gradually after 1945, however, and the early years of the postwar student movement saw a conformity under Japanese Communist Party domination which was very similar to that before the war. It was only from the mid-1950s that fundamental changes in the political environment began to affect the ideology of the student left. At home, the legalization of the communist movement relaxed the need for strict ideological discipline and students gradually became critical of the Japanese Communist Party for its moderation. International pressures led in the same direction: as monolithic international communism crumbled after the death of Stalin, so did a monolithic approach to ideology in communist movements throughout the world. The student movement of the late 1950s in Japan thus underwent a critical split, with part of the Zengakuren (then known as the "Mainstream faction") taking a stand in opposition to the Japanese Communist Party. This was a decisive break with the student movement since the 1920s, which had been characterized by absolute submission to the will of the party.

Ever since the emergence of an anti-Communist Party position, the student movement in Japan has been characterized by intensive factionalism, which by the late 1960s had become so complex as to require elaborate charts to trace ideological lineages.[24] It bears emphasis, however, that this differs from the student movement of the 1920s less in a

24. See, for example, Ōno Akio, *Zengakuren—Sono kōdō to riron* (Kōdansha, 1968), p. 308.

fundamentally changed ideological posture than simply in an *orga-nizational* tendency to factionalism. The various factions of course differ in their programs, but less on any fundamental issues, for all are basically Marxist, than on tactical matters.

It might also be possible to suggest a contrast with prewar ideology in terms of the generational concerns which were outlined in the Preface, where it was suggested that students in the 1920s were on the whole more concerned with "society" than with "nation" or with "self." In the postwar student movement, one may detect from an early point a conspicuously greater preoccupation with the role of the individual than ever existed before the war. This reemphasis on the "self" has emerged in the form of a continuous debate over *shutaisei,* a word which Robert J. Lifton has interpreted as a combination of "selfhood" and "social commitment." [25] This view would suggest an attempt by postwar students to *integrate* their concerns with "self" and "society." At any rate, it is obvious that concern for self-identity bulks far larger in the ideology of postwar radicals than in the 1920s; this is reflected, for example, in the great popularity of existentialism among many postwar student leftists.[26]

The "nation" as well has reemerged as a focus of student ideological concern, although to a less explicit degree than the "self." Student radicals in contemporary Japan would of course reject outright any suggestion that they are "nationalistic," but in fact the heavy emphasis on opposition to American imperialism in the postwar student ideology appeals indirectly to nationalistic sentiment. They are certainly concerned with foreign policy issues to a degree unimaginable in the 1920s and tend on the whole to appeal much more to specifically *Japanese* sentiment than to universal class sentiment as in prewar ideology.[27] In a very general way, then, the postwar student movement seems more psychologically balanced in terms of ideology in its ability

25. Robert J. Lifton, "Youth and History: Individual Change in Postwar Japan," in Erik H. Erikson, ed., *The Challenge of Youth* (New York, 1963), p. 274.

26. Suzuki Hiroo, p. 269, suggests that postwar students fall into two distinct groups in terms of ideology, those interested in Marxist economics and philosophy and those of more literary inclination who turn to existentialism from an emotional sense of alienation.

27. This point is emphatically made with respect to the Japanese Communist Party itself by Robert A. Scalapino, *The Japanese Communist Movement, 1920–1966* (Berkeley, 1967), pp. 44, 53.

to deal with youthful concerns both for "self" and "nation" while maintaining the fundamental Marxist focus on "society."

Mention should be made of the concept of the student movement itself in the ideology of postwar radicals, and here it may be suggested that there is little change from the prewar era, given the basic domination of a Marxist framework of analysis. In virtually all postwar theories of the student movement, the starting point is the same as that in the 1920s: students are basically petty bourgeois, and the task of the student movement is to elevate them to a "proletarian consciousness." [28] Beyond such a class interpretation of the student movement, theories of course differ greatly on priorities, especially on the problem of on-campus versus off-campus activity. Yet fundamentally, student movement ideology sees student radicals as only one part of a much larger class movement to which it is subservient.

On the whole, then, ideology has shown a general continuity with the prewar period, the major differences emerging only *during* the postwar era, especially in the pluralization of communist ideology since the middle 1950s. In general, the continuities are rather striking in view of the very different political environment and suggest that the prewar heritage was of considerable importance in sustaining the enormous prestige of Marxist orthodoxy in the postwar student movement.

Organization. The premise to any discussion of organization is that the *scale* of the postwar student movement is far greater than before the war, so that by comparison the Gakuren of the 1920s may seem almost negligible. In one sense, however, this contrast is less than it appears, since the relative proportion of student radicals has probably changed very little. In the early 1930s, as we have seen, some six thousand students were arrested over a five-year period, or about 2 per cent of the college and university level population per year. One reliable estimate of the radical core of the Zengakuren in the late 1960s was 15,000, or just under 2 per cent of the total male university population.[29] But while the *relative* scale of student radicalism, although showing considerable variation from year to year, is of a level com-

---

28. For an extended analysis of postwar theories of the student movement, see Nihon gakusei undō kenkyūkai, ed., pp. 173–210.

29. Ōno Akio, *Zengakuren Sono kōdō to riron*, p. 263.

parable to that before the war, the *absolute* increase is considerable. This change, however, simply reflects the greatly expanded scale of higher education itself: postwar students are in no way more radical, there are simply more of them. The impact on society of the postwar movement has of course been greatly enhanced, both by the larger scale and by the far greater attention given to student radicals by the press, although it might be suggested that left-wing influence on the university campus itself is not very much greater on the whole than in the prewar period.

The basic organizational concept of the student movement remains the same as before the war, that of a small, dedicated core working through various camouflages to exert an influence far beyond its numbers on the "belt theory" by which a tiny, rapidly revolving pulley can mobilize a much larger inert one. The formal organizational unit, however, has undergone an important change. Before the war, the *shaken* or "social science study group" was the basic unit of organization, existing where possible as recognized extra-curricular campus groups and federated nationally in the Gakuren. After 1929 the core unit was changed to a campus cell of the Communist Youth League (or, in a few instances, of the Japanese Communist Party). In both cases, a core group attempted to infiltrate and manipulate various front groups, such as school newspapers, debating clubs, "reading societies," student cooperatives, and so forth.

In the early postwar period, there did exist for a time Communist Party cells on the campus which functioned as formal units of organization in much the same way as the Communist Youth League cells in the early 1930s. Shortly, however, a very different and much more desirable organizational form presented itself, that of the student "self-governing association" or *jichikai*. Before the war, it will be recalled, the Shinjinkai had pioneered the concept of an overall extra-curricular association with compulsory membership and dues for all students but had eventually failed in its efforts to control the Tokyo Imperial Gakuyūkai because of right wing and athletic club opposition. At the end of the war, however, certain critical reforms were enacted which made the *gakuyūkai* a much more manageable target for student radicals. In the first place, all faculty supervision, nominal or actual, was eliminated in the interests of student democracy, in accord with the ideology of the American occupation, and in most schools the organization was renamed a *jichikai* (although in some cases the term *gakuyūkai* has been preserved). Second, *jichikai* activities were now limited to the nebulous realm of "student self-government," and all sports and cultural clubs were set up independently in the "circle" format—thus removing the threat of opposition from conservative athletic elements. All that remained of the old *gakuyūkai*, in fact, was the critical tradition of compulsory membership and dues for all students. These changes were ideally suited to student radicals, since control of the *jichikai*—an easy matter given general student apathy and the absence of specific club interests—assured both substantial funds and a legitimate platform which conveniently claimed to represent *all* students.[30]

The student radicals thus found themselves in the late 1940s organizing through control of the *jichikai*, formalized in 1948 with the creation of the All-Japan Federation of Student Self-Governing Associations (Zen-Nihon Gakusei Jichikai Sōrengō), or "Zengakuren." Despite the new title, however, this was not substantially different from the All-Japan Student Federation of Social Science, the prewar Gakuren.[31] The federation remained, as before, an alliance of small campus cliques of left-wing activists, the postwar facade of all-student representation being a patent fiction in the face of pervasive student apathy towards the *jichikai* (even though all are obliged to pay the dues which finance the left-wing activists). The factionalism which has appeared in the Japanese student movement since the mid-1950s has split the national Zengakuren, so that a number of competing federations claiming the title of "Zengakuren" had emerged by the late 1960s. The actual *jichikai* participating in a particular federation were determined simply by which faction controlled the *jichikai* on a particular campus or in a particular faculty.

On a national scale, one finds that the postwar student movement has been dominated largely by the same three universities as before

30. For an analysis of the *jichikai* and their problems, see Nishida Kikuo, "Gakusei no jichi katsudō," in Rōyama Masamichi, ed., *Daigaku seido no saikentō* (Fukumura shoten, 1962), pp. 123–134.

31. The prefix "All-Japan" (Zen-Nihon) was added to the Gakuren title in July 1925, making the abbreviation "Zengakuren" possible; the usage "Gakuren" persisted, however.

the war: Tokyo, Waseda, and Kyoto. Thus, for example, the chairmanship of the Zengakuren was monopolized for all but three months in the first decade of the federation's history by leaders from Tokyo and Kyoto, the former imperial universities.[32] This pattern has been modified to some degree since 1960, with a number of less prestigious schools emerging in a position of dominance. This tendency is related in part to the increasing factionalism within the student movement, which has upset old patterns of authority and hierarchy, and in part to the shift to tactics of armed confrontation with the police. Since physical prowess is more crucial in hand-to-hand combat than theoretical brilliance, the superior brains of students at prestige schools like Tokyo and Waseda have become largely irrelevant.

On the whole, then, the postwar student movement has continued the basic pattern of small campus cores, federated nationally, attempting to manipulate on-campus organizations. The emergence of the *jichikai* as a new organizational unit is a critical innovation which however depended on the prewar precedent of compulsory *gakuyūkai* membership and dues. The one great difference in the postwar student movement in terms of organization, as in ideology, has been the intense factionalism which has appeared, especially the polarization into pro- and anti-Japanese Communist Party forces which by the late 1960s were actually engaged in physical combat with each other. There were of course strong tendencies to factionalism in the prewar student movement, but these rarely took concrete organizational form, less because of the types of disputes involved, which were serious, than because solidarity was of prime importance in the face of heavy police suppression. In this sense, the factionalism of the postwar student movement is simply an expression of the changed political environment.

Areas of activity. In the first place, *study* is still, as before the war, the core activity of the student movement. Suzuki's study shows that student radicals tend to be far more avid readers than the average, and long hours of theoretical disputation remain essential to the Japanese student movement, although outside observers often tend to overlook quiet study for the more dramatic street activities.[33] This funda-

32. See list of Zengakuren officers in Nihon gakusei undō kenkyūkai, ed., pp. 290–292.
33. Suzuki Hiroo, p. 266.

mental focus on the reading of accepted texts has helped sustain the high intellectual content of the student movement which was a pre-war tradition. The actual texts studied by postwar students have undergone remarkably few changes since the era of the Gakuren, with the Marxist classics continuing to play a crucial role.[34]

On-campus activity in defense of mass student interests has been a major stream of postwar student movement activity, comparable in the prewar period perhaps only to the "era of chronic student dis-turbances" of the early 1930s. The numbers of postwar students are far greater, and their complaints continue to be numerous. Since stu-dent poverty remains a major problem, economic issues such as tuition raises and dining facilities arise quite frequently. One also finds, however, virtually all the other campus-related issues which were prevalent in the early 1930s, such as the suppression of the student left, low-quality education, disputed disciplinary actions, student con-trol over facilities related to student life, and curriculum reform. The philosophy, techniques, and issues of the "student self-government movement" in the prewar period have continued with little change; the manifesto in *Student Movement* in late 1926 (see page 197) would serve, with few revisions, as a catalog of campus-related issues cham-pioned by the student left over thirty years later.

The student movement has also carried on the prewar tradition of manipulating extracurricular groups for political advantage. The campus "circles," which encompass study groups, drama and literary clubs, sports teams, and so forth, have been systematically infiltrated by the student left and are of considerable use as channels for massing demonstrations. It is revealing that the very term "circle" (*saakuru*) was initiated by the communist movement in the early 1930s to refer to the organizational units of its cultural endeavors both on and off campus.

It is only in the off-campus political arena that one finds a very distinctive postwar change in the activity of the student movement, away from work in support of proletarian organization (in labor unions and farm tenant unions) in the direction of mass demonstra-tions to exert direct political pressure on the government. This change has come about both because working-class organizations have little

34. *Ibid.* and Tsurumi, pp. 355–359; see also Ikeda Shin'ichi, "Sengo gakusei katsudōka ni yomareta hon," *Shuppan nyūsu* (mid-February 1969), pp. 6–9.

need for students and because the changed political situation has made street demonstrations legal. The increase in student numbers has further made it possible to stage massive street demonstrations of a scale inconceivable before the war. In the relative freedom of the years of the early Shinjinkai, prewar students did participate in street demonstrations, such as those in support of universal suffrage, but such activity soon faded as students themselves became more extreme and the police more watchful. It is only in the postwar period that left-wing students have carefully developed the techniques of mass demonstration, even pioneering such novelties as the snake-dance, which has become a kind of symbol of student protest in contemporary Japan.

In general, postwar students have thus engaged in all of the same types of activity as prewar radicals, placing considerably more emphasis, however, on campus-related agitation and street demonstrations and much less on direct contact with the working class. Both before and after the war, of course, a great amount of debate and concern have been devoted to the question of priorities of activities, and the answers have varied widely depending on the period and the group.

Mode of protest. I have suggested that one long-term effect of the prewar student movement on the Japanese left was to intellectualize it, to impose a strong bias in favor of theory and intellectual acuity. In terms of the evolution of the student movement itself, it is possible to see this same tendency continuing into the postwar period, but with a gradual shift away from a verbal-intellectual mode towards a more physical-emotional mode. The entire postwar student movement has been, like that in the 1920s, strongly verbal; anyone who has been in the midst of a postwar student "struggle" in Japan has doubtless found it hard to avoid an overwhelming impression of *words:* words in the cacophony of the portable loudspeakers, words in the huddling groups of arguing students, words in the hundreds of handbills handed out at the school gates, words in the eight-foot signboards that line the campus avenues.

In the prewar student movement, the verbal mode was predominant, and left-wing leaders on the whole were contemptuous of anyone who suggested the use of physical force to accomplish their ends. In the postwar era, physical violence has likewise been a minor element in student protest until the dramatic appearance of the so-called *Gewalt*

(German for "force," pronounced *gebaruto* in Japanese and popularly abbreviated *geba*) technique in the two "Haneda Incidents" of late 1967.[35] This new mode focused on armed confrontations with riot police, with the students donning helmets, wielding staves, and hurling stones and firebombs. There had previously been brief periods of armed tactics, as in the so-called "Molotov cocktail era" of the early 1950s, but these had been short-lived and soon discredited. With the *geba* technique, the Japanese student movement took a decisive turn away from its fifty-year history in directions which are not yet entirely clear. It must be noted, however, that even in the *geba* the basic preference is for a controlled *show* of force, while imposing strict restraints on its actual use. A tiny faction within the student movement has gone beyond this in the direction of underground terrorism and guerilla warfare in the so-called Red Army Faction (Sekigun-ha), but it remains to be seen whether such tactics will spread beyond the lunatic fringe.

Taken as a whole, the continuity between the prewar and postwar student movements is striking, suggesting that the legacy of the era of the Shinjinkai was critical in determining many of the forms and techniques of student protest after 1945. In the early postwar period, this legacy was an advantage, since it made available to the students an arsenal of precedents which enabled the rapid expansion of a well-organized national student movement. In the long run, however, the prewar legacy may have been more of a hindrance, precisely because it was forged under circumstances of political suppression and monolithic ideology which have been radically altered in postwar Japan. One result of this perpetuation of old attitudes in a new environment has been the persistent fear of any kind of authority, a fear which often verges on paranoia. In the early 1930s, it was completely understandable that students should treat any proposals by the government or educational authorities with suspicion; this style of intransigent opposition in postwar Japan, however, merely makes for an inflexible dogmatism which is highly unproductive in terms of real political change.

35. These incidents involved student attempts to prevent Premier Satō Eisaku's departure from Haneda International Airport on trips first to Southeast Asia and then to the United States. For a description, see Dowsey, ed., pp. 125–130.

288 | CHAPTER TEN

The major changes in the postwar student movement have occurred since the Security Treaty crisis of 1960, with a crucial turning point coming in the introduction of the *geba* style of armed confrontation in 1967. Seen in the perspective of nearly half a century, the most profound changes in the ideology, organization, and style of the student movement seem to have come not during the Pacific War, which appears more as a passive lull, but rather in the 1960s. In this sense, the era which began with the founding of the Shinjinkai at Tokyo Imperial University in 1918 is a coherent period in the history of social and intellectual protest in modern Japan, corresponding almost exactly to the second half-century after the Meiji Restoration and signaling the shift from the strains of modernization to the tensions of modernity. This study has suggested that Japan's first student radicals were perhaps more fickle idealists than effective reformers. But at the very least they have served as a warning sign of deeper tensions in the Japanese body politic, and their vigor has been as much a mark of healthy growing pains in a rapidly changing nation as their enforced silence has been a cause for despair.

Appendix
Bibliography
Glossary
Index

Appendix

This list has been compiled by Ishidō Kiyotomo and myself from Shinjinkai publications, government documents, and the recollections (both published and through personal inquiry) of the surviving members. All those appearing on the list have been definitely confirmed as Shinjinkai members. For the differences between this list and the list prepared for the fiftieth anniversary reunion of the Shinjinkai, see Chapter 9, note 4. Biographical details for many of the members are available but have been omitted for reasons of space and problems of documentation; I would be happy to respond to direct requests for information on any of the individuals appearing on the list. For reference works useful in tracing the careers of Shinjinkai members, see Chapter 9, note 25. Readings of names have in most cases been verified directly by the individual or indirectly by those who knew him.

The following information is given for each member: name, later adopted name in parentheses, literary penname in brackets; higher school; Tokyo Imperial University department (the abbreviations E, F, G, and J stand for English, French, German, and Japanese) and year of graduation (parentheses indicate failure to graduate); and dates (d. indicates that date of death is unclear).

Abe Makoto 阿部眞琴, 2nd, J. Hist. '31, 1908–
Adachi Tsurutarō 安達鶴太郎, 1st, Econ. '31, 1906–
Akamatsu Katsumaro 赤松克麿, 3rd, Pol. '19, 1894–1955
Akine Masayuki 秋根昌之, 5th, Pol. '30, ?–
Andō Seiichi 安藤誠一, Niigata, Med. '42, 1905–53
Andō Toshio 安藤敏夫, 8th, Pol. '28, 1904–
Aoki Fumio 青木文雄, Urawa, Econ. '30, ?–1958
Aoyama Mitsuo 青山三雄, 4th, ? ('30), 1907–
Ariizumi Shigeru 有泉茂, 3rd, G. Law '24, 1900–
Asada Shinji 淺田眞二, Mito, Com. '31, ?–1945
Asano Akira 淺野晃, 3rd, F. Law '25, 1901–
Asanuma Yoshimi 淺沼嘉實, 3rd, Pol. '28, 1906–
Asari Kazuyoshi 淺利和吉, 5th, Pol. '26, 1902–

Asō Hisashi 麻生久, 3rd, F. Law '17, 1891–1940

Asō Yoshiteru 麻生義輝, 7th, Esth. '27, 1903–38

Azuma Toshihisa 東利久, 5th, Com. '27, 1902–

Ch'en I-sung 陳逸松, 6th, Pol. '31, 1906–

Chiba Shigeo 千葉成夫, Mito, Econ. ('30), 1906–62

Chiba Yūjirō 千葉雄次郎, lst, Pol. '22, 1898–

Doi Kikuo 土井喜久雄, 7th, F. Lit. '28, 1904–67

Edayoshi Isamu 枝吉勇, Matsumoto, Econ. '27, 1904–

Endō Kikuo 遠藤喜久郎, Fukuoka, F. Lit. ('29), 1905–32

Enomoto Kingo 榎本謹吾, lst, Pol. '29, 1905–

Fugono Shinzō 畚野信藏, 7th, Soc. ('25), 1902–

Fujii Shin 藤井信, Mito, J. Hist. '33, 1906–

Fujiki Tatsuo 藤木龍郎, 5th, Law '35, 1907–d.

Fujisawa Kenzō 藤澤健三, 2nd, Applied Chem. '29, 1902–

Fujisawa Takeo 藤澤桓夫, Osaka, J. Lit. '30, 1904–

Fukuma Toshio 福間敏男 [Ihara Roku] 井原六, 3rd, F. Law '25, 1902–36

Furukawa Shigeru 古川苞, Yamagata, Soc. ('29), 1906 35

Furusue Ken'ichi 古末憲一, lst, Esth. ('31), 1907–

Fuyuno Takeo 冬野猛夫, lst, Soc. ('24), 1899–c. 1931

Gotō Hiroshi 後藤浩, 8th, G. Law '27, 1902–

Gotō Toshio 後藤壽夫 [Hayashi Fusao] 林房雄, 5th, Pol. ('26), 1903–

Hamashima Masakane 濱島正金, Niigata, Phil. ('27), 1904–

Hanamura Nihachirō 花村仁八郎, Yamaguchi, Econ. '32, 1908–

Han'ya Takao 半谷高雄, 8th, Econ. '29, 1906–

Hasegawa Hiroshi 長谷川浩, lst, Law ('31), 1907–

Hashimoto (Kaiguchi) Morizō 橋本（海口）守三, 3rd, Econ. '25, 1901–

Hatano Kanae 波多野鼎, 8th, E. Law '20, 1896–

Hattori Eitarō 服部英太郎, 3rd, Pol. '23, 1899–1965

Hattori Shigeru 服部藹, Mito, Econ. ('31), 1905–

Hattori Shisō 服部之總, 3rd, Soc. '25, 1901–56

Hayasaka Fumio 早坂文雄, 2nd, Esth. ('31), 1907–c. 33

Hayasaka Jirō 早坂二郎, 2nd, Pol. '21, 1897–1943

Hayashi Hirotsugu 林廣次 [Akita Minoru] 秋田實, Osaka, Phil. '31, 1905–

Hayashi Kaname 林要, lst, G. Law '20, 1894–

Hayashi Mutsuo 林睦夫, lst, Econ. '31, 1909–

Hayashi Susumu 林進, Hirosaki, Esth. ('31), 1906–

Hirao Ujirō 平尾卯二郎, 3rd, Econ. '31, 1908–

Hirata (Hikosaka) Takeo 平田（彦阪）竹男, Shizuoka, Econ. '29, 1905–

Hirose Zenshirō 廣瀬善四郎, Mito, ? ('30), 1906–

Hisaita Eijirō 久板榮二郎, 2nd, J. Lit. '27, 1898–

Hoashi Kei 帆足計, Osaka, Econ. '31, 1905–

Hompu Ichiro 本富一郎, lst, E. Lit. '27, 1904–

Horikawa Katsuji 堀川克治, Mito, Com. '32, ?–

Hōshaku Hajime 寶積一, lst, Econ. '27, 1902–66

Hosono Michio 細野三千雄, 8th, G. Law '20, 1897–1955

Hososako Kanemitsu 細迫兼光, 3rd, E. Law '22, 1896–1972

Iguchi Masao 井口昌雄, lst, Med. '29, 1904–

Ikeda Teitarō 池田貞太郎, 2nd, ? ('28), ?–d.

Imaoka Takeshi 今岡雄, Matsue, Econ. '29, 1904–61

Imura (Shiho) Kiyoshi 井村（志甫）幾與之, 4th, Pol. '27, ?–

Inabuchi Keitarō 飯淵敬太郎, 2nd, Econ. '29, ?–1948

Inamura Junzō 稲村順三, Hokkaido Imperial preparatory course, Soc. ('25), 1900–55

Irie Shōji 入江正二, 8th, Pol. '27, 1903–d.

Irokawa Kōtarō 色川幸太郎, 2nd, G. Law '27, 1903–

Ishida Tomoichi 石田外茂一, 4th, E. Lit. '26, 1903–

Ishidō Kiyotomo 石堂清倫, 4th, E. Lit. '27, 1904–

Ishihama Tomoyuki 石濱知行, 2nd, Pol. '20, 1895–1950

Ishimaru Sueo 石丸季雄, lst, Econ. '30, ?–d.

Ishiwatari Haruo 石渡春雄, 7th, E. Law '19, 1892–1966

Itō Kōdō 伊藤好道, lst, Pol. '25, 1900–56

Itō Sadayuki 伊藤貞幸, Yamaguchi, Econ. '30, ?–

Itō Takeo 伊藤武雄, lst, Pol. '20, 1895–

Iuchi Isamu 井内勇, 4th, Com. '27, 1903–

Izawa Shimpei 伊澤信平, 2nd, Econ. '31, 1907–

Izumi Hiroshi 泉廣, Hirosaki, Econ. '29, 1904–

Kadota Takeo 門田武雄, 7th, Pol. '21, 1895–

Kaji Ryuichi 嘉治隆一, lst, G. Law '20, 1896–

Kajinishi Mitsuhaya 楫西光速, Osaka, Econ. '29, 1906–64

Kamei Katsuichirō 龜井勝一郎, Yamagata, Esth. ('29), 1907–66

Kamihira Shōzō 上平正三, 8th, Mining Eng. '30, 1900–42

Kanazawa (Miyazaki) Susumu 金澤（宮崎）達, 3rd, Med. '30, 1905–

Kaneda Jirō 金田二郎, Mito, Com. '36, 1911–

Kanki Hiroshi 神吉洋士, Fukuoka, G. Lit. ('31), 1907–33

Kanzaki Kiyoshi 神崎清, Osaka, J. Lit. '28, 1904–

Kasahara Hideyoshi 笠原英節, 4th, Law '27, 1903–46

Kashimura Minoru 樫村實, 4th, Esth. '29, 1903–

Katayama Satoshi 片山睿, Matsue, Econ. ('29), 1906–

Katō Teikichi 加藤定吉, Urawa, ? ('28), 1904–45

Katsuki Shinji 勝木新次, 3rd, Med. '27, 1903–

Kawahara Jikichirō 川原次吉郎, lst, Pol. '22, 1896–1959

Kawai Atsushi 河合篤, 6th, Pol. '31, 1906–45

Kawai Hideo 河合秀夫, 8th, Agric. '21, 1898–

Kawai Yūkichi 河合勇吉, 4th, Educ. ('30), 1905–

Kawamura Matasuke 河村又介, 7th, Pol. '19, 1894–

Kawanishi Taichirō 河西太一郎, lst, Pol. '20, 1895–

Kazahaya Yasoji 風早八十二, 3rd, F. Law '22, 1899–

Kiire Toratarō 喜入虎太郎, 7th, Pol. '26, 1902–40

Kikukawa Tadao 菊川忠雄, lst, Econ. '26, 1901–54
Kim Chun-yŏn 金俊淵, 6th, G. Law '20, 1894–
Kim Tu-yong 金斗鎔, 3rd, Esth. ('29), 1905–
Kinoshita Hanji 木下半治, lst, F. Law '24, 1900–
Kisamori Kichitarō 木佐森吉太郎, Mito, Esth. ('31), 1906–
Kishii Jurō 岸井壽郎, 3rd, E. Law '17, 1891–1971
Kishimoto Naoyuki 岸本直行, 6th, Econ. '29, 1905–46
Kitano Seiichi 喜多野清一, 3rd, Soc. '25, 1900–
Kiyatake Yasumasa 喜屋武保昌, Urawa, Econ. '28, 1902–39
Kiyose Saburō 清瀬三郎, 3rd, Educ. '25, 1902–
Kobayashi Shigejirō 小林繁次郎, Mito, Econ. '29, 1906–
Koga Kensuke 古閑健介, 5th, Soc. ('30), 1905–
Koiwai Jō 小岩井淨, lst, F. Law '22, 1897–1959
Kojima Kenji 兒島健爾, 8th, G. Law '20, 1894–1966
Komiya Yoshitaka 小宮義孝, lst, Med. '25, 1900–
Komiyama Shin'ichi 小宮山新一, Matsumoto, Med. '37, 1905–67
Kondō Tadao 近藤忠雄, 3rd, Med. '27, 1904–45
Kōno Mitsu 河野密, lst, G. Law '22, 1897–
Koreeda Kyōji 是枝恭二, 7th, Soc. ('26), 1904–34
Koshimizu Minoru 輿水實, Tokyo, Phil. '31, 1908–
Kubo Azusa 久保梓, Matsumoto, Com. ('31), 1904–
Kubo Kenji 久保健治, 2nd, Econ. '29, ?–1944
Kubota Teisaburō 窪田貞三郎, 6th, Pol. '31, 1908–45
Kudō Eizō 工藤永藏, Hirosaki, Fac. of Sci. ('30), 1906–
Kunitani Yōzō 國谷要藏, 3rd, Law '30, 1903–
Kurahashi Tōru 倉橋亨, lst, F. Law '23, 1895–1964
Kurazono Kiyoichi 倉園清市, 7th, Econ. '30, 1907–70
Kuroda Hisao 黑田壽男, 6th, G. Law '23 1899–
Kuroda Takao 黑田孝雄, Gakushūin, Com. '24, ?–?
Kurokawa (Kanai) Nobuo 黑川（金井）信雄, Hirosaki, Soc. '35, 1907–51
Kuroki Yoshiyuki 黑木美之, 7th, J. Lit. '26, ?–
Kurokōchi Hideomi 黑河内秀臣, Mito, Elec. Eng. '29, 1905–60
Kurokōchi Tōru 黑河内透, lst, Law '28, 1904–
Kurokōchi Yasutaka 黑河内康孝, Mito, Law '33, 1906–
Kuruma Kyō 來間恭, 3rd, E. Law '22, 1897–1947
Machino Shigeyuki 町野重之, 7th, Com. '21, ?–1959
Maejima Masamichi 前島正道, Mito, Econ. '28, ?–d. in war
Maejima Tadao 前島忠夫, 8th, Med. '26, 1901–
Masaki Chifuyu 正木千冬, lst, Econ. '26, 1903–
Matsukawa Shichirō 松川七郎, 2nd, Econ. '37, 1906–
Matsumoto Hiroji 松本廣治, Osaka, Pol. '28, 1904–
Matsumoto Seiji 松本征二, Shizuoka, Pol. '29, 1905–
Matsumoto (Noma) Shinkichi 松本（野間）新吉, 7th, Pol. '27, 1902–
Matsumoto Tokuichi 松本篤一, 7th, Soc. ('27), 1903–

Matsunobu Shichirō 松延七郎, 5th, Soc. '28, 1903–63
Matsunoo Shigeo 松野尾繁雄, 2nd, G. Law '26, 1903–
Matsuo Takeo 松尾武夫, 6th, Pol. ('30), 1906–
Matsuoka Hatayo 松岡二十世, 2nd, Pol. '25, 1901–c. 48
Matsutani Kyō 松谷彊, Niigata, Esth. '30, 1908–
Matsuura Nagahiko 松浦長彦, Fukuoka, Econ. ('31), 1907–
Matsuzawa Kenjin 松澤兼人, 7th, Pol. '21, 1898–
Mitsuoka Tadanari 滿岡忠成, Himeji, Esth. '30, 1907–
Miura Jirō 三浦次郎, 5th, Pol. '32, 1907–71
Miwa Jusō 三輪壽壯, lst, G. Law '20, 1894–1956
Miyakawa Ken'ichi 宮川謙一, 4th, Esth. '31, 1908–
Miyanoshita Fumio 宮之下文雄, 7th, Econ. '29, 1907–39
Miyazaki Ryūsuke 宮崎龍介, lst, F. Law '20, 1892–1971
Mizuike Akira 水池亮, lst, Pol. '26, 1900–
Mizuno Shigeo 水野成夫, lst, F. Law '24, 1899–1972
Mochizuki Morikazu 望月守一, Matsue, Com. '30, 1907–45
Mori Shizuo 森靜夫, 3rd, Econ. '28, 1900–1971
Morimatsu Keiji 森松慶治 [Moriyama Kei] 森山啓, 4th, ? ('28), 1904–
Moritani Katsumi 森谷克巳, 6th, G. Law '27, 1904–64
Moriya Fumio 守屋典郎, 6th, Law '29, 1907–
Murai Yasuo 村井康男, lst, J. Lit. '25, 1901–
Murakami Takashi 村上堯, lst, ? ('21), 1898–1920
Murao Satsuo 村尾薩男, 7th, Soc. ('26), 1902–70
Murata Fukutarō 村田福太郎, 5th, Educ. ('30), 1906–
Murayama Tōshirō 村山藤四郎, lst, E. Law '24, 1899–1954
Nagahama Yoshiyuki 長濱義之, Niigata, E. Lit. ('25), ?–c. 1928
Nagai (Nakai) Naoji 長井（中居）直二, Niigata, Econ. '29, 1906–
Nagao Masayoshi 長尾正良, Osaka, Econ. ('29), 1906–
Nagao Takio 長尾他喜雄, 4th, Econ. '26, ?–
Nagaoki Makoto 長沖一, Osaka, Esth. '29, 1904–
Nagasaka Keiichi 長坂慶一, 3rd, Pol. '27, 1901–57
Nagaya Hajime 長屋肇, 5th, Econ. '31, ?–1940
Nakahira Satoru 中平解, lst, F. Lit. '27, 1904–
Nakai Seiichi 中井精一, lst, Western Hist. '29, 1903–
Nakamura Jūichi 中村重一, 2nd, Law '29, 1903–1971
Nakanishi Fumio 中西文雄, Mito, Com. '34, ?–1970
Nakano Hisao 中野尚夫, Niigata, Pol. ('26), 1901–
Nakano Shigeharu 中野重治, 4th, G. Lit. '27, 1902–
Nakao Shōhei 中尾正平, Osaka, Pol. '32, 1907–
Nakata Chōshirō 中田長四郎, lst, Econ. '31, 1907–
Narazaki Akira 楢崎輝, 5th, Pol. '23, ?–1931
Nasu Tatsuzō 那須辰造, Fukuoka, F. Lit. '29, 1904–
Negishi Shinroku 根岸眞六, 6th, Law '32, 1907–
Nibu Yoshitaka 丹生義孝, Fukuoka, Law '30, 1906–

Nishida Nobuharu 西田信春, lst, Ethics '27, 1903–33

Nishigori Hikoshichi 錦織彦七, Matsue, Esth. ('31), 1905–34

Nishimoto Takashi 西本喬, 3rd, Soc. ('27), 1902–

Nishimura Nobuo 西村信雄, 3rd, F. Law '25, 1900–

Nishio Toshizō 西尾十四三, Matsue, J. Hist. '31, 1907–50

Niwa Michio 丹羽道雄, Osaka, Econ. ('31), ?–

Niwa (Suzuki) Tomojirō 丹羽（鈴木）知治郎, Osaka, Pol. '31, 1907–

Noda Takayoshi 野田萬穀, 7th, Law '28, 1903–d.

Noda Yasaburō 野田彌三郎, Kōnan, Econ. '30, 1905–

Nomura Jirō 野村二郎, 4th, Pol. '27, 1902–

Nosaka Sanzō 野坂參三, Keiō '17, 1892–

Nozawa Ryūichi 野澤隆一, 2nd, Com. '27, 1902–

Obase Takuzō 小場瀨卓三, Kōnan, F. Lit. '30, 1906–

Oda Tadao 小田忠夫, 2nd, Econ. '25, 1901–

Odabe Keijirō 小田部啓次郎, Fukuoka, Econ. '30, 1906–

Odakura Hajime 小田倉一, lst, Med. '27, 1903–

Ogata Wataru 緒方渉, 5th, Soc. ('28), ?–1945

Ogawa Haruo 小川治雄, Mito, Econ. ('30), 1905–38

Ogawa Tarō 小川太郎, Shizuoka, Econ. '29, 1904–

Ogura Shirō 小倉司郎, 7th, Econ. '28, 1906–33

Okabe Ichirō 岡部一郎, 7th, Soc. '26, 1900–

Okabe Kansuke 岡部完介, lst, Econ. '22, 1895–

Okada Sōji 岡田宗司, Matsumoto, Econ. '26, 1902–

Okai Yoshio 岡井美夫, Mito, Esth. ('32), ?–d.

Okanoe Morimichi 岡上守道 [Kuroda Reiji] 黒田禮二, lst, Econ. '16, c. 1890–
    c. 1945

Okazaki Kazuo 岡崎一夫, 2nd, G. Law '22, 1899–

Ōkōchi (Isono) Nobutake 大河內（磯野）信威 [Ogawa Shin'ichi] 小川信一,
    Urawa, did not enter university, 1902–

Okuyama Teijirō 奥山貞二郎, 2nd, Econ. '29, 1905–39

Ōmachi Tokuzō 大間知篤三, 4th, G. Lit. '27, 1900–70

Ōmori Harushi 大森春四, 5th, Econ. '31, ?–1946

Ōmura Einosuke 大村英之助, 2nd, Econ. '29, 1905–

Ōmura Hiroshi 大村博, 2nd, G. Law '27, 1903–

Ōmura Takeo 大村武男, 4th, E. Lit. '26, 1902–

Orimoto Toshi (Gan) 織本利(侃), lst, Pol. '25, 1900–54

Ōsawa Mamoru 大澤衞, 4th, E. Lit. '27, 1904–

Ōshima Hideo 大島英夫, 4th, Pol. ('25), 1900–30

Ōta Keitarō 太田慶太郎 [Tani Hajime] 谷一, Urawa, Law ('28), 1906–

Ōtake Heishirō 大竹平四郎, 2nd, Econ. '29, ?–1937

Ōtsuka Torao 大塚虎雄, Saga, Soc. '26, 1901–c. 37

Ōuchi Masami 大內正巳, Mito, Econ. '31, ?–1949

Ōya Sōichi 大宅壯一, 3rd, Soc. ('25), 1900–70

Ōyama Hikoichi 大山彥一, 7th, Soc. '25, 1900–65

Ōyama Iwao 大山岩雄, 5th, Soc. '29, 1906–67
Ozawa Masamoto 小澤正元, 2nd, G. Law '25, 1899–
Ozawa Tsunehisa 小澤恒久, lst, Econ. '31, 1906–35
Rōyama Masamichi 蠟山政道, lst, Pol. '20, 1895–
Sakamoto Hikotarō 坂元彦太郎, 5th, Soc. '26, 1904–
Sakamoto Masaru 阪本勝, 2nd, Econ. '23, 1899–
Sakamoto Yoshiaki 坂本喜亮, 7th, Soc. '27, 1902–
Sakata Seiichi 坂田精一, 4th, Esth. '29, 1903–
Sano Manabu 佐野學, 7th, Pol. '17, 1894–1953
Sano Seki 佐野碩, Urawa, Law ('28), 1905–66
Sassa Hiroo 佐々弘雄, 5th, Pol. '20, 1896–1949
Sata Tadataka 佐多忠隆, 7th, Econ. '28, 1904–
Satō Masayuki 佐藤昌之, Niigata, Law '33, 1909–
Satō Shirō 佐藤四郎, 6th, Pol. '33, 1907–43
Sawada (Hirao) Saburō 澤田（平尾）三郎, 6th, ? ('29), 1905–39
Sawada Seibei 澤田清兵衞, 4th, G. Law '22, 1898–c. 1930
Sawai Tetsuji 澤井哲二, lst, Econ. ('31), 1909–
Sayama Reiichi 佐山勵一, lst, Pol. '25, 1901–
Seguchi Mitsugi 瀬口貢 [Kaji Wataru] 鹿地亘, 7th, J. Lit. '27, 1903–
Senge Tsunemaro 千家恒麿, Matsue, Econ. '30, 1905–
Shibata Kentarō 柴田健太郎, lst, G. Law '20, 1896–1966
Shida (Suita) Hidezō 信田（吹田）秀三, 2nd, Econ. ('31), 1907–
Shiga Hidetoshi 滋賀秀俊, lst, Med. '27, 1902–
Shiga Yoshio 志賀義雄, lst, Soc. '25, 1901–
Shima (Nagamatsu) Masao 島（永松）正夫, Kōnan, ? ('31), 1909–
Shimano (Kadoya) Hiroshi 島野（門屋）博, 2nd, Soc. '26, 1901–
Shimano Takeshi 島野武, 2nd, Econ. ('29), 1905–
Shimmei Masamichi 新明正道, 4th, Pol. '21, 1898–
Shinohara Kyōsuke 篠原恭弼, Matsue, Econ. '30, 1907–
Shionoya Suekichi 鹽谷末吉, lst, Pol. '29, 1904–
Shōbara Tōru 莊原達, 2nd, Pol. '23, 1893–
Shōji Hikaru 庄司光, lst, Med. ('29), 1905–
Shuzui Hajime 守隨一, Urawa, Econ. '28, ?–1944
Soda Takemune 曾田長宗, lst, Med. '26, 1902–
Sogi Katsuhiko 曾木克彦, 2nd, Econ. '29, 1905–37
Sonobe Shin'ichi 園部眞一, lst, Pol. '25, 1899–1935
Sugi Toshio 杉捷夫, 3rd, F. Lit. '26, 1904–
Sugino Tadao 杉野忠夫, 3rd, Pol. '25, 1901–65
Sugita Yōtarō 杉田揚太郎, 7th, Econ. '29, 1906–
Sumiya Etsuji 住谷悅治, 2nd, Pol. '22, 1895–
Sunaga Masao 須永正雄, Mito, Pol. '30, 1906–
Sunama Ichirō 砂間一良, lst, Econ. '28, 1903–
Suzuki Kohei 鈴木小兵衞, 7th, Law ('25), 1900–1950
Suzuki Seiichi 鈴木精一, 7th, Pol. '20, 1893–c. 1954

Suzuki Takeo 鈴木武雄, 3rd, Pol. '25, 1901–

Tachibana Kyōsuke 立花強助, 5th, Pol. '23, 1896–c. 1924

Taira Teizō 平貞藏, 3rd, Pol. '20, 1894–

Takabatake Haruji 高畠春二, 4th, Law '27, 1898–1970

Takahashi Makoto 高橋信, 4th, Phil. '32, 1906–

Takaishi Shigekatsu 高石重勝, 5th, Econ. '31, ?–1934

Takano Makoto 高野信, 2nd, Econ. '29, 1903–

Takashima (Noda) Senzō 高島（野田）宣三, lst, Econ. ('31), 1908–d. in war.

Takashima Shiyō 高島志容, 8th, G. Law '20, 1895–1948

Takayama Yōkichi 高山洋吉, Matsumoto, Econ. '26, 1901–

Takeda Rintarō 武田麟太郎, 3rd, F. Lit. ('29), 1904–46

Takei Kazuo 武井一雄, Mito, Econ. '29, 1905–

Takei Reisuke 武井禮介, Mito, Econ. '29, 1904–48

Takeishi Tsutomu 武石勉, Matsue, Econ. '30, 1905–

Tanahashi Kotora 棚橋小虎, 3rd, G. Law '17, 1889–

Tanaka Kyūichi 田中九一, 8th, G. Law '21, 1896–

Tanaka Seigen (Kiyoharu) 田中淸玄, Hirosaki, Esth. ('30), 1906–

Tanaka Sōtarō 田中宋太郎, 5th, Pol. '30, 1904–d.

Tanaka Toshio (Seibun) 田中稔男(正文), 5th, Pol. '28, 1902–

Tanaka Toyonobu 田中豐稔, Saga, Econ. '31, 1907–

Tanigawa Iwao 谷川巖, Osaka, Pol. '28, 1906–

Tankei Yoshizō 丹慶與四造, Shizuoka, Econ. ('30), 1908–

Tashiro Shirō 田代四郎, 5th, G. Lit. '28, 1903–

Tateyama Toshitada 堅山利忠, 7th, Econ. ('29), 1907–

Toda Kyōji 戶田京次, 8th, Econ. '28, 1903–

Tobishima Sadashiro 飛島定城, Hirosaki, Law '28, 1904–

Togashi (Saitō) Tomitarō 富樫（齋藤）富太郎, lst, Econ. '27, 1902–d.

Tominaga Osamu 富永理, 7th, Phil. '28, 1902–

Tomonaga Shigeo 友永重雄, 5th, Pol. '28, 1904–

Tomooka Hisao 友岡久雄, 5th, Pol. '23, 1899–1966

Tono Kenji 戶野憲二, 2nd, Phil. '33, 1909–

Toriumi Tokusuke 鳥海篤助, lst, G. Law '26, 1901–

Toyoda (Hirai) Sunao 豐田（平井）直, lst, Fac. of Eng. ('24), 1900–

Tsugane Tsunetomo 津金常知, Matsumoto, Econ. '30, 1907–

Tsuji Kōshichi 辻幸七, 4th, Soc. '30, 1903–

Tsuji Tsunehiko 辻恒彦, 5th, Pol. '25, 1899–

Tsujibe Masatarō 辻部政太郎, Osaka, Esth. '29, 1905–

Tsukamoto Masato 塚本正人, Shizuoka, Com. '32, 1908–44

Tsunoda Morihei (Giheiji) 角田守平(儀平治), 2nd, Pol. '31, 1906–

Tsuru Kazuo 鶴和夫, 5th, G. Law '26, 1903–65

Uchida Gembei 內田源兵衞, 3rd, Pol. '25, 1899–

Uchida Sakurō 內田佐久郎, 4th, Arch. '27, 1905–

Uchigaki Yasuzō 內垣安造, lst, Econ. ('28), 1903–36

Uchikata Shinnojō 打方新之丞, 4th, J. Lit. ('27), ?–c. 1926

Uchimura (Ishijima) Harushi 内村（石島）治志, 7th, Soc. '25, 1899–
Uchimura Tomoichi 内村奉一, 5th, Law '28, 1905–65
Uchino Sōji 内野壯兒, lst, Esth. ('31), 1908–
Uenaka Tatsuo 上中龍男, 3rd, Pol. '28, 1904–
Wakiyama Yasunosuke 脇山康之助, 4th, J. Lit. '27, 1907–
Watanabe Kiyoyoshi 渡部清吉, Niigata, G. Lit. ('30), 1906–64
Watanabe Takeshi 渡邊武, 5th, Econ. '29, 1906–c. 29
Watanabe Tamotsu 渡邊保, 6th, Fac. of Letters ('31), 1907–30
Yamaguchi Tadayuki 山口忠幸 [Kawaguchi Hiroshi] 川口浩, Urawa, G. Lit. '29, 1905–
Yamamoto Gen'ichirō 山本源一郎, 2nd, Econ. '28, 1904–36
Yamana Yoshitsuru 山名義鶴, 3rd, Pol. '17, 1891–1967
Yamane Ginji 山根銀二, lst, Esth. '28, 1906–
Yamauchi Tadayoshi 山内忠吉, Yamaguchi, Econ. '32, 1909–
Yamauchi Toshio 山内俊雄 [Uchiyama Tsutomu] 内山敏, 2nd, Phil. '32, 1909–
Yamazaki Kazuo 山崎一雄, 4th, Pol. '21, 1896–
Yamazaki Shinjirō 山崎新次郎, Niigata, Econ. '31, 1908–
Yamazoe Naoshi 山添直, Niigata, Econ. '28, 1905–
Yodono Ryūzō 淀野隆三, 3rd, F. Lit. '28, 1904–67
Yokota Rihei 横田利平, 6th, Esth. '31, 1908–
Yosano Yuzuru 與謝野讓, lst, Econ. '27, ?–c. 1930
Yoshikawa Mitsusada 吉河光貞, lst, Law '30, 1907–
Yoshikawa Saneharu 吉川實治, 3rd, Soc. '29, 1904–
Yoshizawa Manji 吉澤萬二, 8th, Econ. '31, ?–d.
Yoshino Jō 吉野城, 5th, Pol. '30, 1908–
Yoshio Yoshimitsu 吉尾義光, 3rd, F. Law '26, 1904–28

INDEX OF ADOPTED NAMES AND PENNAMES

Bibliography

Materials for the history of the prewar student left in Japan are so motley as to demand some indication of the more useful and reliable. For the period of the early Shinjinkai, 1918–1923, the most valuable source is the Shinjinkai magazine itself, now conveniently reprinted with an excellent index and commentary in Ōhara shakai mondai kenkyūjo, ed., *Shinjinkai kikanshi: Demokurashii, Senku, Dōhō, Narōdo*. Asō Hisashi's celebrated "autobiographical novel" *Reimei* (1924) is useful for the events and especially the mood around the time of the founding of the Shinjinkai but must be handled with great care for the author's tendency to distort the factual narrative for dramatic effect. Biographical and autobiographical materials relevant to this period are numerous, but I would single out the recollections of Hayashi Kaname ("Shinjinkai no koro") and the biographies of Asō and Miwa (Miwa Jusō denki kankōkai, *Miwa Jusō no shōgai*, and Asō Hisashi denki kankō iinkai, *Asō Hisashi den*) as the most thorough, although by no means wholly accurate.

For the middle period of the Shinjinkai, from the Kanto earthquake until 1928, the single most useful work is Kikukawa Tadao's *Gakusei shakai undō shi* (1931). Since Kikukawa was himself a leading Shinjinkai member, the chapters covering the period from the 1923 earthquake until his graduation in 1926 are of special use, presenting much personal information as well as documentary evidence. After his graduation, Kikukawa remained in touch with the student movement, but his own position as a leader of the social democratic left denied him access to materials on the communist underground activities in the student movement. For the period after 1928, he drew largely upon such above-ground contemporary materials as the daily press, the Ōhara shakai mondai kenkyūjo's *Nihon rōdō nenkan*, and the *Teikoku daigaku shimbun*, and one will do better to go directly to those primary sources than to rely on Kikukawa's selection. For the Shinjinkai in particular, the campus newspaper, the *Teikoku daigaku shimbun*, is invaluable for its description of the student radicals' on-campus activities after 1923.

Only for the last years of the Shinjinkai, after the Kyoto Gakuren arrests of 1926, do government materials become particularly valuable, beginning with the voluminous records of the preliminary investigation of the Gakuren arrestees (Shihōshō, "Taishō jūgonen Kyōto o chūshin to suru gakusei jiken chōsho kiroku," 21 vols.). For regular accounts of developments in the student movement after 1927, the annual Ministry of the Interior reports on the left-wing movement (Naimusho, *Shakai [shugi] undō no jōkyō*) are the most useful. In addition, survey histories of the student movement were compiled by both the Ministry of Justice (Hasegawa Akira, "Gakusei no shisō undō ni tsuite") and the Ministry of Education (Mombushō, *Gakusei shisō undō no gaiyō*), both of which are handy reference works for the period until 1931. For a survey of the 1930's, see Matsumura Sadahiko, *Saikin ni okeru sayoku gakusei undō*. Kawamura Tadao, *Shisō mondai nempyō*, is a very detailed and useful government-sponsored chronology for the period until 1935.

For the entire period of the prewar student movement, the most provocative and colorful material is to be found in the mountains of biographical and auto-biographical writings by and about the participants, of which many examples will be found in the bibliography below. A sense of the range of materials available may be gained by looking through Kokuritsu kokkai toshokan, Sankō shoshibu, *Nihon shakai, rōdō undōka denki mokuroku*, a bibliography of biographical materials on prominent left-wing leaders. Most such items are published as separate books and isolated magazine articles, but some may be found in the convenient form of anthologies of reminiscences dealing specifically with the student movement, such as the three-volume series *Watakushi no gakusei no koro*, edited by Gakusei shobō henshūbu in the late 1940s. Many such materials were written at a date much later than the events described, so that errors of fact (in particular chronology) and distortions of interpretation are common, and wherever possible I have sought to find corroboration in other sources. The interviews which I conducted were subject to similar limitations and were primarily of use for biographical information on the individual members of the Shinjinkai.

For tracing the careers of the individual members of the student left, three reference works in addition to standard biographical dictionaries have been of special use. Noguchi Toshiaki's *Musan undō sō-tōshi den* is a colorful and surprisingly reliable directory of major left-wing leaders in the 1920s. More cursory but more numerous are the entries in Kaihō no ishizue kankō iinkai, *Kaihō no ishizue*, a list of those who had died in the service of the left-wing movement as of 1956. Finally, the alumni directories of the old higher schools, while troublesome to assemble, are of great help in locating graduates of the imperial universities in the absence of any such directories for the universities themselves.

Several excellent bibliographies are available for those wishing to do further research on the prewar student left. For the left-wing movement as a whole, Cecil Uyehara, *Leftwing Social Movements in Japan: An Annotated Bibliography*, is the basic starting point, especially for American scholars because of its extensive coverage of the rich collections on the Japanese left in the Hoover Institute and the Library of Congress. For the student movement and student affairs in general, see Shimbori Michiya, "Gakusei undō ni kansuru bunken." On the history of Japanese higher education, Terasaki Masao, "Daigakushi bunken mokuroku" is excellent. Good introductory bibliographies to the baffling jungle of government materials on the left wing are Omori Megumu, "Teikoku kempōka ni okeru shakai, shisō kankei shiryō," for Ministry of Justice and Ministry of the Interior documents and Okamoto Yōzō, "Mombushō kankei no kaikyū undō chōsa shiryō ni tsuite" for the Ministry of Education.

INTERVIEWS

Interviews were conducted on the dates indicated. In a few cases, additional meetings were held, but only the date of the initial interview has been given.

Asano Akira	3/19/67	Miyazaki Ryūsuke	1/27/67
Dan Tokusaburō	12/1/67	Moriya Fumio	3/27/67
Fukumoto Kazuo	11/19/67	Nakano Shigeharu	12/1/67
Hatano Kanae	11/16/67	Nishiyama Yūji	11/13/67
Hayashi Fusao	1/25/67	Ōta Keitarō	1/24/69
Hayashi Kaname	9/8/64	Sata Tadataka	2/15/67
Hoshishima Nirō	3/17/67	Shiga Yoshio	9/13/67
Ishidō Kiyotomo	10/30/67	Shimmei Masamichi	10/31/67
Kadota Takeo	9/8/67	Sumiya Etsuji	6/9/67
Kadoya Hiroshi	11/25/67	Taira Teizō	2/26/67
Kaji Ryūichi	7/11/64	Takayama Gizō	6/10/67
Katsuki Shinji	11/1/67	Takei Kazuo	6/9/67
Kawanishi Taichirō	10/29/67	Tanahashi Kotora	4/7/67
Kazahaya Yasoji	11/2/67	Tanaka Toshio	9/19/67
Kinoshita Hanji	11/28/67	Tateyama Toshitada	9/20/67
Kisamori Kichitarō	10/28/67	Uchida Sakurō	9/30/67
Kishii Jurō	3/16/67	Uchino Sōji	10/3/67
Matsukata Saburō	5/15/67	Yamazaki Kazuo	11/22/67
Matsuzawa Kenjin	11/24/67		

WORKS CITED

For all books published in Japan, the place of publication is Tokyo unless otherwise indicated.

Akamatsu Katsumaro 赤松克麿. "Shinjinkai no rekishiteki ashiato" 新人會の歴的足跡 (The historical mark left by the Shinjinkai), *Kaizō* 改造, 10.6 (June 1928), 68–74.

Almond, Gabriel. *The Appeals of Communism.* Princeton: Princeton University Press, 1954.

Altbach, Philip G. *A Select Bibliography on Students, Politics, and Higher Education.*

Rev. ed. St. Louis and Cambridge, Mass.: United Ministries in Higher Education and Center for International Affairs, Harvard University, 1970.

Alumni directories, prewar higher schools. Miscellaneous editions.

Amakusa Rintarō 天草麟太郎. *Nihon kyōsantō daikenkyo shi* 日本共產黨大檢擧史 (A history of the mass Japanese Communist Party arrests). Bukyōsha, 1929.

Andō Katsuichirō 安藤勝一郎, ed. *Daisan kōtō gakkō benrombu bushi* 第三高等學校辯論部部史 (A history of the Third Higher School Debating Club). Daisan kōtō gakkō benrombu, 1935.

Aoki Kōji 青木虹二, comp. *Nihon rōdō undō shi nempyō* 日本勞働運動史年表 (A chronology of the Japanese labor movement). 4 vols. Shinseisha, 1968–.

Asahi jānaru 朝日ジャーナル, ed. *Daigaku no niwa* 大學の庭 (University campuses). 2 vols. Kōbunsha, 1964.

Asahi shimbun, Ōsaka honsha, Shashi henshūshitsu 朝日新聞大阪本社社史編修室, ed. *Murayama Ryūhei den* 村山龍平傳 (The life of Murayama Ryūhei). Asahi shimbun sha, 1953.

Asano Akira 淺野晃. *Izumu ni ugoku mono* 主義にうごく者 (Those moved by ideology). Nihon kyōbunsha, 1955.

——— "Tōdai jidai no Kikukawa-kun" 東大時代の菊川君 (Kikukawa at Tokyo University), in Kikukawa Tadao tsuitō shuppan iinkai 菊川忠雄追悼出版委員會, ed., *Kikukawa Tadao—Sono shisō to jissen* 菊川忠雄—その思想と實踐 (Kikukawa Tadao—His thought and deeds). Editor, 1956, pp. 4–6.

Asayama Kaisuke 麻山改介 [Asō Hisashi 麻生久], Kuroda Reiji 黒田禮二 [Okanoe Morimichi 岡上守道], and Katashima Shin 片島新 [Sano Manabu 佐野學]. *Kagekiha* 過激派 (The bolsheviks). Min'yūsha, 1919.

Asō Hisashi 麻生久, ed. *Shin shakaiteki chitsujo e* 新社會的秩序へ (Towards a new social order). Dōjinsha shoten, 1922.

——— *Dakuryū ni oyogu* 濁流に泳ぐ (Swimming in muddy waters). Shinkōsha, 1923.

——— *Reimei* 黎明 (The dawn). Shinkōsha, 1924. Postwar ed., Kaiguchi shoten, 1947.

Asō Hisashi denki kankō iinkai 麻生久傳記刊行委員會, ed. *Asō Hisashi den* 麻生久傳 (The life of Asō Hisashi). Editor, 1958.

Battistini, Lawrence H. *The Postwar Student Struggle in Japan*. Rutland, Vt.: Charles E. Tuttle, 1956.

Beckmann, George M., and Okubo Genji. *The Japanese Communist Party, 1922–1945*. Stanford: Stanford University Press, 1969.

Bownas, Geoffrey, and Thwaite, Anthony, trans. *The Penguin Book of Japanese Verse*. Baltimore: Penguin Books, 1964.

Chow Tse-tsung. *The May Fourth Movement: Intellectual Revolution in Modern China*. Cambridge, Mass.: Harvard University Press, 1960.

Cole, Allan B., et al. *Socialist Parties in Postwar Japan*. New Haven: Yale University Press, 1966.

Dazai Osamu. *No Longer Human*. Trans. Donald Keene. Norfolk, Conn.: New Directions, 1958.

Dowsey, Stuart, ed. *Zengakuren: Japan's Revolutionary Students*. Berkeley: Ishi Press, 1970.

Ebihara Haruyoshi 海老原治善. *Zoku gendai Nihon kyōiku seisaku shi* 續現代日本教育政策史 (A history of educational policy in modern Japan—Sequel). San'ichi shobō, 1967.

Fisher, H. H. *The Famine in Soviet Russia, 1919–1923*. New York: Macmillan, 1927.

Fujimura Kazuo 藤村一雄. *Gakusei shisō mondai zatsuwa* 學生思想問題雜話 (Miscellaneous talk about the student thought problem). Nihon hyōronsha, 1930.

Fukumoto Kazuo 福本和夫. "Hōkō tenkan wa ikanaru sho-katei o toru ka, wareware wa ima sore no ikanaru katei o katei shitsutsu aru ka" 「方向轉換」はいかなる諸過程をとるか，われわれはいまそれのいかなる過程を過程しつつあるか (Through what stages will the "change of direction" pass, and which stage are we staging now?), *Marukishizumu* マルキシズム, 3.4 (October 1925). Reprinted in Takeuchi Yoshitomo 竹內良知, ed. *Marukishizumu II* マルキシズム II (Marxism, II), Gendai Nihon shisō taikei 現代日本思想大系 (An anthology of modern Japanese thought). Chikuma shobō, 1965. XXI, 61–87.

——— *Shakai no kōsei narabi ni henkaku no katei* 社會の構成並に變革の過程 (The structure of society and the process of social change). Hakuyōsha, 1926.

——— *Kakumei undō razō* 革命運動裸像 (A candid portrait of the revolutionary movement). San'ichi shobō, 1962.

Gakusei shakai kagaku rengōkai kaihō 學生社會科學連合會會報 (Student Federation of Social Science bulletin). No. 1 (November 25, 1924; the word "*gakusei*" is omitted in the nameplate) and no. 3 (October 20, 1925).

"Gakusei shakai kagaku rengōkai no soshiki oyobi kaiinsū" 學生社會科學連合會の組織及び會員數 (Organization and membership of the Gakuren). Mimeo. (July 1927). Located in Yoshino Bunko, Tokyo University.

Gakusei shobō henshūbu 學生書房編集部, ed. *Watakushi no gakusei no koro* 私の學生の頃 (My student days). 3 vols. Gakusei shobō, 1948–49.

Gakusei undō 學生運動 (Student movement). Nos. 1–2 (October-November 1926).

Gakushikai 學士會. *Kaiin shimeiroku* 會員氏名錄 (Gakushikai membership list). Annual, 1925–42.

Hall, John W. "The Confucian Teacher in Tokugawa Japan," in David S. Nivison and Arthur F. Wright, eds. *Confucianism in Action*. Stanford: Stanford University Press, 1959. Pp. 268–301.

Hasegawa Akira 長谷川明. "Gakusei no shisō undō ni tsuite" 學生の思想運動に就いて (The student thought movement), *Shihō kenkyū* 司法研究, vol. 15, pt. 4 (March 1932).

Hasegawa Nyozekan 長谷川如是閑 et al. *Shinshakai e no sho-shisō—Dainikai Shinjinkai gakujutsu kōenshū* 新社會への諸思想—第二回新人會學術講演集 (Concepts for a new society—Second Shinjinkai academic lecture collection). Shūeikaku, 1921.

Hayashi Fusao 林房雄. "Robin fuddo jiken" ロビンフッド事件 (The Robin Hood incident), *Shinchō* 新潮, 26.9 (September 1929), 2–16.

—— *Bungakuteki kaisō* 文學的回想 (Literary reminiscences). Shinchōsha, 1955.

Hayashi Kaname 林要. "Shinjinkai no koro" 新人會のころ (Shinjinkai days), in Tōkyō daigaku kyōdō kumiai shuppan bu 東京大學協同組合出版部, ed. *Rekishi o tsukuru gakusei-tachi* 歴史をつくる學生たち (Students who make history). 2nd ed. Editor, 1948. Pp. 135–188.

High, Stanley, ed. *The Revolt of Youth*. New York: Abingdon Press, 1923.

Hisamatsu Sen'ichi 久松潜一 et al., eds. *Gendai Nihon bungaku daijiten* 現代日本文學大事典 (Dictionary of modern Japanese literature). Meiji shoin, 1965.

"Honshi no ayumi—Sōkan kara konnichi made" 本紙の歩み—創刊から今日迄 (The progress of the *Imperial University News*, from founding to the present), *Teikoku daigaku shimbun* 帝国大学新聞, no. 250 (April 30, 1928), pp. 3–5.

"Honshi no jūgonen" 本紙の十五年 (The first fifteen years of the *Imperial University News*), *Teikoku daigaku shimbun* 帝国大學新聞, no. 602 (December 4, 1935), pp. 57–58.

Horie Muraichi 堀江邑一, ed. *Kaisō no Kawakami Hajime* 回想の河上肇 (Kawakami Hajime remembered). Sekai hyōron sha, 1948.

Ichō kurabu 銀杏クラブ, ed. *Ichō kurabu kaiin meibo* 銀杏クラブ會員名簿 (Membership list of the Gingko Club). Editor, 1967.

Ikazaki Akio 伊ヶ崎暁生 and Usuda Noboru 碓田登. *Shigaku no rekishi* 私學の歴史 (A history of private universities). Shin Nihon shuppan sha, 1967.

Ikeda Katsu 池田克. "Nihon kyōsantō jiken no tōkeiteki kōsatsu" 日本共産黨事件の統計的考察 (Statistical considerations of the Japanese Communist Party incidents), *Keisatsu kenkyū* 警察研究, 1.5 (May 1930), 55–82 and 1.6 (June 1930), 65–86.

Ikeda Shin'ichi 池田信一. "Sengo gakusei katsudōka ni yomareta hon" 戰後學生活動家に讀まれた本 (Books read by postwar student activists), *Shuppan nyūsu* 出版ニュース (Mid-February 1969), pp. 6–9.

Ikeda Susumu 池田進. "Nihon no nyūgaku shiken seido no enkaku" 日本の入學試驗制度の沿革 (A history of the Japanese entrance examination system), *Kyōto daigaku kyōiku gakubu kiyō* 京都大學教育學部紀要, vol. 4 (1958), pp. 96–124.

Ino Kenji 猪野健治. "Zengakuren o sōjū suru hankyō no Tanaka Seigen" 全學連を操縦する反共の田中清玄 (Tanaka Seigen, anti-communist manipulator of the Zengakuren), *Hōseki* 寶石, 3.11 (November 1967), 102–108.

Ishidō Kiyotomo 石堂清倫. "Kōki no Shinjinkai" 後期の新人會 (The later Shinjinkai), *Rōdō undō shi kenkyū* 勞働運動史研究, no. 16 (July 1959), pp. 35–39.

—— "Sono koro no Fukumoto shugi" そのころの福本主義 (Fukumotoism in those days), *Gendaishi shiryō geppō* 現代史資料月報, supp. to Misuzu shobō みすず書房, ed., Gendaishi shiryō 現代史資料, vol. XX. Editor, 1968. Pp. 1–4.

—— personal correspondence with author, 1968–69.

Itō Takeo 伊藤武雄. *Mantetsu ni ikite* 滿鐵に生きて (Life in the South Manchurian Railway Company). Keisō shobō, 1964.

Jansen, Marius B. *The Japanese and Sun Yat-sen.* Cambridge, Mass.: Harvard University Press, 1954.

—————, ed. *Changing Japanese Attitudes Toward Modernization.* Princeton: Princeton University Press, 1965.

Jinji kōshinjo 人事興信所, ed. *Jinji kōshinroku* 人事興信録 (Who's who). Postwar editions.

Jiyū hōsōdan 自由法曹團, ed. *Jiyū hōsōdan monogatari* 自由法曹團物語 (Tales of the Civil Liberties Legal Group). Rōdō jumpōsha, 1966.

Johnson, Chalmers. *An Instance of Treason: Ozaki Hotsumi and the Sorge Spy Ring.* Stanford: Stanford University Press, 1964.

K. T. [Kiire Toratarō? 喜入虎太郎]. "Gakusei undō to kojin no nimmu" 學生運動と個人の任務 (The student movement and the individual's responsibility), *Shinjinkai kaihō* 新人會會報, no. 3 (July 1, 1924), pp. 34-39.

Kaigo Tokiomi 海後宗臣, ed. *Inoue Kowashi no kyōiku seisaku* 井上毅の教育政策 (The educational policies of Inoue Kowashi). Tōkyō daigaku shuppankai, 1968.

Kaihō no ishizue kankō iinkai 解放のいしずえ刊行委員會, ed. *Kaihō no ishizue* 解放のいしずえ (Cornerstones of liberation). Kaihō undō giseisha gassō tsuitōkai sewaninkai, 1956.

Kaji Ryūichi 嘉治隆一. *Rekishi o tsukuru hitobito* 歴史を創る人々 (People who make history). Ōyaesu shuppan K. K., 1948.

————— "Mimponshugi zengo" 民本主義前後 (The era of 'mimponshugi'), in Ōkōchi Kazuo 大河内一男 and Takahashi Seiichirō 高橋誠一郎, eds., *Rōdō seisaku to sono haikei* 勞働政策とその背景 (Labor policy and its background). Nihon keizai shimbunsha, 1949. Pp. 41-58.

————— "Sano Manabu to sono jidai" 佐野學と其時代 (Sano Manabu and his times), *Kokoro* 心, 6.8 (August 1953), 46-54.

————— "Mimponshugi to Daigaku fukyūkai" 民本主義と大學普及會 ('Mimponshugi' and the University Extension Society), *Kōsen rempō* 公選連報, no. 14 (January 1, 1967), p. 3.

Kanda Bunjin 神田文人. "Gakusei no shakai shugi undō kikanshi" 學生の社會主義運動機關誌 (Magazines of the student socialist movement), *Shisō* 思想, no. 264 (February 1963), pp. 117-128.

—————, comp. "Kensetsusha dōmei kikanshi *Kensetsusha, Seinen undō, Musan kaikyū, Musan nōmin* sōmokuji" 建設者同盟機關誌「建設者」「青年運動」「無産階級」「無産農民」總目次 (Contents of the Kensetsusha Dōmei organs), *Rōdō undō shi kenkyū* 勞働運動史研究, no. 36 (May 1963), pp. 28-34.

Karasawa Tomitarō 唐澤富太郎. *Gakusei no rekishi—Gakusei seikatsu no shakaishi-teki kōsatsu* 學生の歴史——學生生活の社會史的考察 (A history of students—A study of the social history of student life). Sōbunsha, 1955.

Katayama Tetsu 片山哲. *Kaiko to tembō* 回顧と展望 (Prospect and retrospect). Fukumura shuppan, 1967.

Kawai Eijirō 河合榮治郎 and Rōyama Masamichi 蠟山政道. *Gakusei shisō mondai* 學生思想問題 (The student thought problem). Iwanami shoten, 1932.

Kawamura Tadao 河村只雄, comp. *Shisō mondai nempyō* 思想問題年表 (A chronology of the thought problem). Seinen kyōiku fukyūkai, 1936.

Keiō Gijuku 慶應義塾, ed. *Keiō Gijuku hyakunen shi* 慶應義塾百年史 (A hundred-year history of Keiō Gijuku). 5 vols. Editor, 1962.

Kikukawa Tadao 菊川忠雄. "Wakaki gakuto wa tatakau—Gakusei shakai kagaku undō no yokogao" 若き學徒は戰ふ—學生社會科學運動の横顔 (Young students are fighting—A profile of the student social science movement), *Chūō kōron* 中央公論, 44.10 (October 1930), 161–178.

———— *Gakusei shakai undō shi* 學生社會運動史 (A history of the left-wing student movement). Chūō kōronsha, 1931; rev. ed., Kaiguchi shoten, 1947. Footnote citations are from the uncensored (but otherwise unrevised) postwar edition.

———— unpublished manuscript notes used in preparation of *Gakusei shakai undō shi*, undated, now in possession of Mr. Uchida Sakurō.

Kim Chun-yŏn 金俊淵. *Na ŭi kil* 나의길 (My road). 2nd ed. Seoul: author, 1967.

Kinoshita Hanji 木下半治. *Nihon fashizumu shi* 日本ファシズム史 (A history of Japanese fascism). 2 vols. Iwasaki shoten, 1949.

Kishi Yamaji 貴司山治. "Watamasa den" 渡政傳 (The life of Watanabe Masanosuke), *Kaizō* 改造, 13.4 (April 1931), 132–143.

Kōan chōsachō 公安調査廳. *Nihon kyōsantō shi (senzen)* 日本共産黨史（戰前） (A history of the prewar Japanese Communist Party). Reprint ed. Gendai-shi kenkyūkai, 1962.

———— *Senzen ni okeru uyoku dantai no jōkyō* 戰前における右翼團體の狀況 (The state of right-wing groups before the war). 3 vols. 1964.

Kobayashi Kōzō 小林浩三. "Gakusei no jiyū kakutoku undō" 學生の自由獲得運動 (The student movement to win freedom), *Gakusei undō* 學生運動, no. 2 (November 1926), pp. 2–8.

Koiwai Jō tsuitōgō henshū iinkai 小岩井淨追悼號編集委員會, ed. "Koiwai Jō tsuitō tokushūgō" 小岩井淨追悼特集号 (Special Koiwai Jō memorial issue), *Aichi daigaku shimbun* 愛知大學新聞, no. 112 (April 10, 1960).

Kokuritsu kokkai toshokan, Rippō kōsakyoku 國立國會圖書館立法考査局, comp. *Daigaku no jiyū ni kansuru bunken mokuroku* 大學の自由に關する文獻目錄 (A bibliography on academic freedom). Compiler, 1952.

Kokuritsu kokkai toshokan, Sankō shoshibu 國立國會圖書館参考書誌部, comp. *Nihon shakai, rōdō undōka denki mokuroku* 日本社會・勞働運動家傳記目錄 (Bibliography of biographies of Japanese social and labor movement leaders). Compiler, 1966.

Kondō Eizō 近藤榮藏. *Komuminterun no misshi* コムミンテルンの密使 (Secret emissary for the Comintern). Bunka hyōron sha, 1949.

Konno Washichi 昆野和七. "Nihon saisho no gakusei sutoraiki" 日本最初の學生ストライキ (Japan's first student strike), *Jimbutsu ōrai* 人物往來, 10.4 (April 1965), 42–49.

Koyama Hirotake 小山弘健 et al. *Nihon no hi-kyōsantō marukusu shugisha—Yamakawa*

Hitoshi no shōgai to shisō 日本の非共産黨マルクス主義者―山川均の生涯と思想 (Japan's non-Communist Party Marxist—The life and thought of Yamakawa Hitoshi). San'ichi shobō, 1962.

Kubota Shun 久保田唆. Personal correspondence to author, September 28, 1970.

Kurahara Korehito 藏原惟人 and Tezuka Hidetaka 手塚英孝, eds. *Monogatari puroretaria bungaku undō* 物語プロレタリア文學運動 (Tales of the proletarian literature movement). 2 vols. Shin Nihon shuppansha, 1967.

Kusayanagi Daizō 草柳大藏. " 'Tōkyō taigā' Tanaka Seigen" "東京タイガー" 田中淸玄 (Tanaka Seigen, the "Tokyo Tiger"), *Bungei shunjū* 文藝春秋, 47.11 (October 1969), 220–234.

Kushida Tamizō 櫛田民藏 et al. *Minshū bunka no kichō—Daiikkai Shinjinkai gakujutsu kōenshū* 民衆文化の基調―第一回新人會學術講演集 (The keynote of a popular culture—First Shinjinkai academic lecture series). Shūeikaku, 1920.

Kyōikushi hensankai 教育史編纂會, ed. *Meiji ikō kyōiku seido hattatsu shi* 明治以降教育制度發達史 (A history of the development of the educational system since Meiji). 12 vols. Ryūginsha, 1938–39.

Kyūshū daigaku sōritsu gojusshūnen kinenkai 九州大學創立五十周年記念會, ed. *Kyūshū daigaku gojūnen shi—Tsūshi* 九州大學五十年史―通史 (A fifty-year history of Kyūshū University—General outline). Editor, 1967.

Lifton, Robert J. "Youth and History: Individual Change in Postwar Japan," in Erik H. Erikson, ed., *The Challenge of Youth*. New York: Anchor Books, 1963. Pp. 260–290.

Mainichi nenkan 毎日年鑑 (Mainichi annual), 1967.

Masaki Chifuyu 正木千冬. "Chian iji hō ihan Kikakuin sayoku gurūpu jiken: Jōshinsho (Hikokunin Masaki Chifuyu)" 〔治安維持法違反企畫院左翼グループ事件〕上申書（被告人正木千冬） (Statement of defendant Masaki Chifuyu in the Kikakuin Incident). Mimeo. 1944.

Matsuda Michio 松田道雄. *Nihon chishikijin no shisō* 日本知識人の思想 (The thought of Japanese intellectuals). Chikuma shobō, 1965.

Matsumura Sadahiko 松村禎彦. *Saikin ni okeru sayoku gakusei undō—Shu toshite Gakusei gurūpu kankei* 最近における左翼學生運動―主として學生グループ關係 (The recent left-wing student movement, with emphasis on the "Student Group"), Shihōshō 司法省, *Shisō kenkyū shiryō tokushū* 思想研究資料特輯, no. 85 (May 1941).

Matsuo Takayoshi 松尾尊兊. *Taishō demokurashii no kenkyū* 大正デモクラシーの研究 (Studies on Taishō Democracy). Aoki shoten, 1966.

Matsushima Eiichi 松島榮一. "Kaisetsu" 解説 (Commentary), in Hattori Shisō 服部之總, *Kurofune zengo—Hattori Shisō zuihitsushū* 黑船前後―服部之總隨筆集 (The era of the Black Ships—Collected essays of Hattori Shisō). Chikuma shobō, 1966. Pp. 363–385.

Matsuzawa Kenjin 松澤兼人. *Watakushi no gendai jūsō* 私の現代縦走 (My journey through the modern era). Author, 1964.

Matsuzawa Kōyō 松澤弘陽. "Marukusu shugi ni okeru shisō to shūdan" マルクス主義における思想と集團 (Ideology and the group in Marxism), in Chikuma shobō 筑摩書房, ed., *Kindai Nihon shisō shi kōza* 近代日本思想史講座 (Symposium on modern Japanese intellectual history). 8 vols. Editor, 1959–61. V: 218–273.

Meiji hennen shi hensankai 明治編年史編纂會, ed. *Shimbun shūsei Meiji hennen shi* 新聞集成明治編年史 (A newspaper chronicle of the Meiji era). 15 vols. Limited second ed. Rinsensha, 1940–41.

Midoro Masaichi 美土路昌一, ed. *Meiji Taishō shi 1: Genron hen* 明治大正史 1 — 言論篇 (A history of Meiji and Taisho, 1: Public expression). Asahi shimbun sha, 1930.

Miller, Frank O. *Minobe Tatsukichi: Interpreter of Constitutionalism in Japan.* Berkeley: University of California Press, 1965.

Minobe Ryōkichi 美濃部亮吉. *Kumon suru demokurashii* 苦悶するデモクラシー (Democracy in agony). Bungei shunjū sha, 1959.

Mishima Yukio 三島由紀夫. *Hayashi Fusao ron* 林房雄論 (On Hayashi Fusao). Shinchōsha, 1963.

———— and Tōdai zengaku kyōtō kaigi Komaba kyōtō funsai iinkai 東大全學共鬪會議駒場共鬪焚祭委員會. *Tōron: Mishima Yukio vs. Tōdai Zenkyōtō* 討論— 三島由紀夫 vs. 東大全共鬪 (A debate between Mishima Yukio and the Tokyo University All-Campus Joint Struggle Council). Shinchōsha, 1969.

Misuzu shobō みすず書房, ed. *Zoruge jiken* ゾルゲ事件 (The Sorge Incident). Gendaishi shiryō 現代史資料 (Materials on modern history), I–III. Editor, 1962.

————, ed. *Shakai shugi undō* 社會主義運動 (The socialist movement). Gendaishi shiryō 現代史資料 (Materials on modern history), XIV–XX. Editor, 1964–68.

Mitamura Takeo 三田村武夫. *Sensō to kyōsan shugi* 戰爭と共產主義 (War and communism). Minsei seido fukyūkai, 1950.

Miwa Jusō denki kankōkai 三輪壽壯傳記刊行會, ed. *Miwa Jusō no shōgai* 三輪壽壯の生涯 (The life of Miwa Jusō). Editor, 1966.

Miyake Shōichi 三宅正一. *Iku sanga o koete* 幾山河を越えて (Crossing many mountains and streams). Kōbunsha, 1966.

Miyazaka Tetsubumi 宮坂哲文. "Meiji jidai ni okeru kagai enzetsu tōron katsudō ni tsuite no ichi kōsatsu" 明治時代における課外演說討論活動についての一考察 (Reflections on extracurricular speech and debating activity in the Meiji era), in Ishikawa Ken hakushi kanreki kinen rombunshū hensan iinkai 石川謙博士還暦記念論文集編纂委員會, ed., *Kyōiku no shiteki tenkai* 教育の史的展開 (The historical development of education). Kōdansha, 1952. Pp. 409–427.

Miyazaki Ryūsuke 宮崎龍介. "Shinjinkai to wakaki hi no Katsumaro-kun" 新人會と若き日の克麿君 (The Shinjinkai and the young Katsumaro), *Nihon oyobi Nihonjin* 日本及日本人, 7.2 (March 1956), 42–49.

———— "Yanagihara Byakuren to no hanseiki" 柳原白蓮との半世紀 (My fifty years with Yanagihara Byakuren), *Bungei shunjū* 文藝春秋, 45.6 (June 1967), 220–230.

Mizuno Shigeo 水野成夫. "Kukyō no aji" 苦境の味 (A taste of hard times), *Chūō kōron* 中央公論, 47.3 (March 1952), 148–152.

Mombushō 文部省, ed. *Nihon teikoku Mombushō nempō* 日本帝國文部省年報 (Annual report of the Japanese Ministry of Education). Vols. 46–63 (1918–1935).

———, ed. *Gakusei hachijūnen shi* 學制八十年史 (An eighty-year history of the school system). 1954.

———, ed. *Gakusei kyūjūnen shi* 學制九十年史 (A ninety-year history of the school system). 1964.

——— *Wagakuni no kōtō kyōiku* わが國の高等教育 (Higher education in Japan). 1964.

Mombushō, Gakuseibu 文部省學生部. *Gakusei shisō undō no keika gaiyō* 學生思想運動の經過概要 (An outline of the course of the student thought movement). 1930.

——— *Gakusei shisō undō no enkaku* 學生思想運動の沿革 (History of the student thought movement). March 1931.

——— *Gakusei shisō undō zukai* 學生思想運動圖解 (An illustrated explanation of the student thought movement). September 1932.

——— *Kokka shugi teki tachiba o hyōbō suru gakusei dantai* 國家主義的立場を標榜する學生團體 (Nationalistic student groups). February 1934.

——— *Sakei gakusei seito no shuki* 左傾學生生徒の手記 (Confessions of leftist students). 3 vols. 1934–35.

——— *Shisō chōsa sankō shiryō* 思想調査參考資料 (Thought investigation reference materials). Nos. 1–4 (1928–29).

——— *Shisō chōsa shiryō* 思想調査資料 (Thought investigation materials). Nos. 5–36 (1928–36). Issued after 1934 by the Mombushō, Shisōkyoku.

Mombushō, Shisōkyoku 文部省思想局. *Shisōkyoku yōkō* 思想局要項 (An outline of the Thought Bureau). 1934.

——— *Gakusei seito no fukuri shisetsu* 學生生徒の福利施設 (Student welfare facilities). 1935.

Morito Tatsuo 森戸辰男. "Kuropotokin no shakai shisō no kenkyū" クロポトキンの社會思想の研究 (Studies in Kropotkin's social thought), *Keizaigaku kenkyū* 經濟學研究, 1.1 (January 1920), 57–122.

——— *Seinen gakuto ni uttou* 青年学徒に訴う (An appeal to young students). Kaizōsha, 1925.

——— *Gakusei to seiji* 學生と政治 (Students and politics). Kaizōsha, 1926.

Moriya Fumio 守屋典郎. *Nihon marukusu shugi riron no keisei to hatten* 日本マルクス主義理論の形成と發展 (The formation and development of Japanese Marxist theory). Aoki shoten, 1967.

Morooka Sukeyuki 師岡佑行. "Meiji nijūnendai no shakai undō nempyō" 明治二十年代の社會運動年表 (A chronology of the left-wing movement in the Meiji twenties), *Nihonshi kenkyū* 日本史研究, no. 25 (September 1955), Pp. 40–60.

Nagai Michio 永井道雄. *Nihon no daigaku* 日本の大學 (Japanese universities). Chūō kōron sha, 1965.

Nagasue Eiichi 永末英一, ed. *Mizutani Chōzaburō den* 水谷長三郎傳 (The life of Mizutani Chōzaburō). Minshu shakaitō hombu kyōsenkyoku, 1963.

Naikaku tōkeikyoku 内閣統計局, ed. *Nihon teikoku tōkei nenkan* 日本帝国統計年鑑 (Statistical annual of Imperial Japan). Vols. 40–57 (1921–38).

Naimushō, Keihokyoku 内務省警保局. *Tokubetsu yō-shisatsunin jōsei ippan* 特別要視察人状勢一斑 (A survey of the state of persons requiring special surveillance), 9 (November 1, 1919). Reprinted in Kindai Nihon shiryō kenkyūkai 近代日本史料研究會, ed., *Nihon shakai undō shiryō* 日本社會運動史料 (Historical documents of the Japanese left-wing movement), series 2, supp. vol. III, Meiji bunken shiryō kankōkai, 1962.

——— "Shisō yō-chūinin meibo 思想要注意人名簿 (List of persons requiring thought surveillance). Mimeo. Undated, c. 1921.

——— *Shakai shugi undō no jōkyō* 社會主義運動の状況 (The state of the socialist movement). 2 vols. 1927–28.

——— *Shakai undō no jōkyō* 社會運動の状況 (The state of the left-wing movement). 12 vols. 1929–40.

——— "Banned newspapers, pamphlets, and handbills, 1928–1940." Microfilm no. MJ–143, U.S. Library of Congress.

——— *Tokubetsu kōtō keisatsu shiryō* 特別高等警察資料 (Special Higher Police materials), 2.4 (August 1929).

Naka Arata 仲新. *Meiji no kyōiku* 明治の教育 (Meiji education). Shibundō, 1967.

Nakahira Satoru 中平解 et al. "Shōsetsu *Muragimo* to Shinjinkai jidai" 小説『むらぎも』と新人會時代 (The novel *Muragimo* and the Shinjinkai days), *Chūō hyōron* 中央評論, no. 36 (December 1954), Pp. 76–86.

Nakamura Hideo 中村英雄, ed. *Saikin no shakai undō* 最近の社會運動 (The recent left-wing movement). Kyōchōkai, 1929.

Nakano Shigeharu 中野重治. *Muragimo* むらぎも (The heart of youth), Nihon no bungaku 日本の文學 (Japanese literature), XLI. Chūō kōron sha, 1967. 183–410.

Nakano-Han no otoko 中野班の男 [Koreeda Kyōji 是枝恭二]. "Wareware wa kaku susumu" 我々は斯く進む (Thus we proceed), *Shinjinkai kaihō* 新人會會報, no. 4 (May 1925), pp. 2–6.

Natsume Sōseki. *Botchan* (Master darling). Mori Yasotarō, trans. Kinshōdō, 1948.

Nihon gakusei undō kenkyūkai 日本學生運動研究會, ed. *Gakusei undō no kenkyū* 學生運動の研究 (Studies on the student movement). Nikkan rōdō tsūshinsha, 1966.

Nihon sembotsu gakusei shuki henshū iinkai 日本戰歿學生手記編集委員會, ed. *Kike wadatsumi no koe* きけわだつみのこえ (Hark to the voice of the sea). Tōkyō daigaku shuppankai, 1952.

Nijō Einosuke 二城英之輔. "Gakusei jiyū yōgo dōmei no seiritsu oyobi sono nimmu" 學生自由擁護同盟の成立及び其の任務 (The founding of the Student League for the Defense of Liberty and its tasks), *Gakusei undō* 學生運動, no. 1 (October 1926), pp. 15–20.

Nishida Kikuo 西田龜久夫. "Gakusei no jichi katsudō" 學生の自治活動 (Student self-governing activities), in Rōyama Masamichi 蠟山政道, ed., *Daigaku seido no saikentō* 大學制度の再檢討 (A reexamination of the university system). Fukumura shoten, 1962. Pp. 123–134.

Noguchi Yoshiaki 野口義明. *Musan undō sō-tōshi den* 無產運動總鬭士傳 (Biographies of fighters in the proletarian movement). Shakai shisō kenkyūjo, 1931.

Noma, Seiji. *Noma of Japan: The Nine Magazines of Kodansha.* New York: Vanguard Press, 1934.

Nōmin kumiai shi kankōkai 農民組合史刊行會, ed. *Nōmin kumiai undō shi* 農民組合運動史 (A history of the tenant union movement). Nihon minsei chōsakai, 1960.

Nomura Masao 野村正男. *Hōsō fūunroku* 法窓風雲錄 (Tales of the judiciary). 2 vols. Asahi shimbun sha, 1966.

Nosaka Sanzō 野坂參三. Personal correspondence to author, October 18, 1967.

Nose Iwakichi 能勢岩吉. *Saikin gakusei sayoku undō hiroku* 最近学生左翼運動祕錄 (A secret account of the recent left-wing student movement). Banrikaku, 1931.

Odagiri Hideo 小田切秀雄 and Fukuoka Iyoshi 福岡井吉, eds. *Shōwa shoseki, shimbun, zasshi hakkin nempyō* 昭和書籍・新聞・雜誌發禁年表 (A chronology of books, newspapers, and magazines banned in the Shōwa era). 4 vols. Meiji bunken, 1965–67.

Ōgiya Shōzō 扇谷正造, ed. Ā *gyokuhai ni hana ukete—Waga kyūsei kōkō jidai* あゝ玉杯に花うけて—わが舊制高校時代 ("Sipping wine beneath the cherry tree . . ."—Our days in the prewar higher schools). Yūki shobō, 1967.

Ōhara shakai mondai kenkyūjo 大原社會問題研究所. *Nihon rōdō nenkan* 日本勞働年鑑 (Japan labor annual). Vols. 1–21 (1920–40).

[Hōsei daigaku] Ōhara shakai mondai kenkyūjo 法政大學大原社會問題研究所, ed. *Ōhara shakai mondai kenkyūjo sanjūnen shi* 大原社會問題研究所三十年史 (A thirty-year history of the Ōhara Social Problems Research Institute). Editor, 1954.

———, ed. *Shinjinkai kikanshi: Demokurashii, Senku, Dōhō, Narōdo* 新人會機關誌—デモクラシー・先驅・同胞・ナロオド (The Shinjinkai magazines: *Democracy, Senku, Dōhō, Narod*). Hōsei daigaku shuppankyoku, 1969.

Okada Sōji 岡田宗司. "Inamura Junzō no ashiato" 稻村順三の足跡 (The mark left by Inamura Junzō), *Shakai shugi* 社會主義, no. 45 (April 1955), pp. 2–6.

Okada Tsunesuke 岡田恒輔. *Shisō sakei no gen'in oyobi sono keiro* 思想左傾の原因及び其の經路 (The causes and course of leftism). Kokumin seishin bunka kenkyūjo, 1935.

Okamoto Kōji 岡本功司. *Nagatomi Ryūken to iu otoko—Kyosetsu Mizuno Shigeo den* 永福柳軒という男—虛說・水野成夫傳 (A man called Nagatomi Ryūken—An unsubstantiated biography of Mizuno Shigeo). Dōmei tsūshinsha, 1965.

Okamoto Yōzō 岡本洋三. "Mombushō kankei no kaikyū undō chōsa shiryō ni tsuite" 文部省關係の階級運動調査資料について (Ministry of Education research materials on the class movement), *Rōdō undō shi kenkyū* 勞働運動史研究, no. 33 (September 1962), pp. 38–45.

Ōkōchi Kazuo 大河内一男 and Shimizu Ikutarō 清水幾太郎, eds. *Waga gakusei no koro* わが學生の頃 (Our student days). Sanga shobō, 1957.

Ōkubo Toshiaki 大久保利謙. *Nihon no daigaku* 日本の大學 (The Japanese university). Sōgensha, 1943.

Okumura Ka'ichi 奥村嘉一, ed. *Gakkō annai—Daigaku hen* 學校案内—大學編 (A guide to schools: Universities). Okumura shoten, 1967.

Omori Megumu 小森惠. "Teikoku kempōka ni okeru shakai, shisō kankei shiryō" 帝國憲法下における社會・思想關係資料 (Materials related to socialism and thought under the imperial constitution), 8 parts, *Misuzu* みすず, nos. 20–26 (November 1960—May 1961) and no. 28 (July 1961).

Ōmori Toshio 大森俊雄, ed. *Tokyo teikoku daigaku setsurumento jūninenshi* 東京帝國大學セツルメント十二年史 (A twelve-year history of the Tokyo Imperial University Settlement). Tōkyō teikoku daigaku setsurumento, 1937.

Ōno Akio 大野明男. *Zengakuren keppūroku* 全學連血風録 (The Zengakuren saga). Nijusseiki sha, 1967.

———— *Zengakuren—Sono kōdō to riron* 全學連—その行動と理論 (Zengakuren, theory and action). Kōdansha, 1968.

Ōta Masao 太田雅夫. "Hoshishima Nirō to *Daigaku hyōron*" 星島二郎と『大學評論』 (Hoshishima Nirō and *Daigaku hyōron*), *Kirisutokyō shakai mondai kenkyū* キリスト教社會問題研究, no. 11 (March 1967), pp. 116–168.

———— "Taishō demokurashii undō to Daigaku hyōron sha gurūpu" 大正デモクラシー運動と大學評論社グループ (The Taishō Democracy movement and the Daigaku hyōron sha group), *Dōshisha hōgaku* 同志社法學, no. 102 (October 1967), pp. 21–51.

———— "Taishōki ni okeru demokurashii yakugo kō" 大正期に於けるデモクラシー譯語考 (Thoughts on terms used to translate 'democracy' in the Taishō period), *Kirisutokyō shakai mondai kenkyū* キリスト教社會問題研究, no. 13 (March 1968), pp. 34–68.

Ōya Sōichi 大宅壯一. *Ōya Sōichi no hon 4: Nihonteki chūseishin* 大宅壯一の本4—日本的忠誠心 (The writings of Ōya Sōichi 4: The Japanese spirit of loyalty). Sankei shimbun shuppankyoku, 1967.

Ozaki Shirō 尾崎士郎. *Waseda daigaku* 早稻田大學 (Waseda University). Bungei shunjū sha, 1953.

Passin, Herbert. *Society and Education in Japan*. New York: Teachers College, Columbia University, 1965.

Paul, Eden and Cedar. *Proletcult (Proletarian Culture)*. New York: Thomas Seltzer, 1921.

Pyle, Kenneth B. *The New Generation in Meiji Japan—Problems of Cultural Identity, 1885–1895*. Stanford: Stanford University Press, 1969.

"Resolution of the Young Communist International on Japan (Extract)," *International Press Correspondence*, 9.4 (January 18, 1929), 69.

Rōdō undō shi kenkyūkai 勞働運動史研究會, ed. *Shūkan Heimin shimbun* 週刊平民新聞 (The weekly *Commoners' News*). Meiji shakai shugi shiryōshū 明治社

會主義資料集 (An anthology of documents on Meiji socialism), 20 vols. Meiji bunken shiryō kankōkai, 1962. Supp. vols. III–IV.

Sakai Toshihiko 堺利彥. *Nihon shakai shugi undō shi* 日本社會主義運動史 (A history of the Japanese socialist movement). Kawade shobō, 1954.

Sakisaka Itsurō 向坂逸郎, ed. *Arashi no naka no hyakunen* 嵐のなかの百年 (A stormy century). Keisō shobō, 1952.

———— *Nagare ni kōshite* 流れに抗して (Moving against the current). Kōdansha, 1964.

San'ichi shobō henshūbu 三一書房編集部, ed. *Shiryō sengo gakusei undō* 資料戰後學生運動 (Documents on the postwar student movement). 8 vols. San'ichi shobō, 1968–70.

Sasaki Mitsugu 佐々城貢. "Gunji kenkyūdan jiken no shinsō" 軍事研究團事件の眞相 (The truth about the Military Study Group incident), in Asanuma tsuitō shuppan henshū iinkai 淺沼追悼出版編集委員會, ed., *Bakushin— Ningen kikansha Numa-san no kiroku* 驀進—人間機關車ヌマさんの記錄 (Dashing forward—A chronicle of 'Numa, the human locomotive). Nihon shakaitō kikanshikyoku, 1962. P. 110.

Scalapino, Robert A. *The Japanese Communist Movement, 1920–1966.* Berkeley: University of California Press, 1967.

Seiji hihan 政治批判 (Political criticism), nos. 1–13 (February 1927–February 1929).

Sekki 赤旗 (Red flag), no. 15 (May 1923).

Shakai bunko 社會文庫, ed. *Shōwaki kanken shisō chōsa hōkoku* 昭和期官憲思想調查報告 (Police investigative reports in the Shōwa era). Kashiwa shobō, 1965.

————, ed. *Taishōki shisō dantai shisatsunin hōkoku* 大正期思想團體視察人報告 (Surveillance reports on thought groups in the Taishō period). Kashiwa shobō, 1965.

Shiga Yoshio 志賀義雄. *Nihon kakumei undō no gunzō* 日本革命運動の群像 (A group portrait of the Japanese revolutionary movement). 4th ed. Shin Nihon shuppansha, 1963.

Shihōshō, Keijikyoku 司法省刑事局. *Gakusei chian iji hō ihan jiken kōgai* 學生治安維治法違反事件梗槪 (An outline of the student incident in violation of the Peace Preservation Law), Shisō kenkyū shiryō 思想研究資料 (Thought research materials), no. 7 (June 1928).

———— *Gakusei shakai undō shinsō* 學生社會運動眞相 (A true picture of the left-wing student movement). Undated, c. 1926.

———— "Taishō jūgonen Kyōto o chūshin to suru gakusei jiken chōsho kiroku" 大正十五年京都を中心とする學生事件調書記錄 (Interrogation records of the 1926 Kyoto student incident). 21 vols. Mimeo. 1926.

Shimane daigaku shimbun bu 島根大學新聞部, ed. "Shimane no gakusei undō shi" 島根の學生運動史 (A history of the Shimane student movement), *Kyōdo* 鄉土, no. 11 (November 1960), pp. 25–33.

Shimbori Michiya 新堀通也. "Gakusei undō ni kansuru bunken" 學生運動に
關する文獻 (Bibliography on the student movement), *Hiroshima daigaku kyōiku gakubu kiyō* 廣島大學教育學部紀要, 1.11 (January 1963), 93–141.

Shimizu Hideo 清水英夫. *Tōkyō daigaku hōgakubu* 東京大學法學部 (The Tokyo University Faculty of Law). Kōdansha, 1965.

Shimonaka Kunihiko 下中邦彦, ed. *Dai jimmei jiten* 大人名事典 (Dictionary of biography). 10 vols. Heibonsha, 1958.

Shinjinkai kaihō 新人會會報 (Shinjinkai bulletin), no. 1 (December 1923), no. 3 (July 1, 1924), no. 4 (May 1925), and no. 5 (December 1925).

Shinjinkai kikanshi: see under Ōhara shakai mondai kenkyūjo.

Shisō no kagaku kenkyūkai 思想の科學研究會, ed. *Tenkō* 轉向 (Tenkō). 3 vols. Heibonsha, 1959–62.

Sōdōmei gojūnen shi kankō iinkai 總同盟五十年史刊行委員會, ed. *Sōdōmei gojūnen shi* 總同盟五十年史 (A fifty-year history of the Sōdōmei). 3 vols. Editor, 1964–68.

Steinhoff, Patricia Golden. "*Tenkō*: Ideology and Societal Integration in Prewar Japan." Ph. D. diss. Harvard University, 1969.

Sugi Michio 杉道夫 [Nakano Hisao 中野尚夫]. "Gakusei shakai kagaku undō no hōkō tenkan" 學生社會科學運動の方向轉換 (A change of direction in the student social science movement), *Seiji hihan* 政治批判, no. 1 (February 1927), pp. 51–67.

Sugiura Katsuo 杉浦勝郎, ed. *Aru seishun no kiroku—Kaisō no Suikō gakusei undō to Ogawa Haruo, Chiba Shigeo gokuchū shokanshū* ある青春の記錄—回想の水高學生運動と小川治雄, 千葉成夫獄中書翰集 (A chronicle of youth—Reminiscences of the Mito Higher student movement and prison correspondence of Ogawa Haruo and Chiba Shigeo). Wagatsuma shoin, 1969.

Sugiyama Kenji 杉山謙治. *Nihon gakusei shisō undō shi* 日本學生思想運動史 (A history of the student thought movement). Nihon kirisutokyō seinenkai dōmei gakusei undō shuppan bu, 1930.

Sumiya Etsuji 住谷悅治. *Kenkyūshitsu uchisoto* 研究室うちそと (Miscellaneous tales of university life). Kyoto: Ōsaka fukushi jigyō zaidan Kyōto hodōsho, 1957.

———, Takakuwa Suehide 高桑末秀, and Ogura Jōji 小倉襄二. *Nihon gakusei shakai undō shi* 日本學生社會運動史 (A history of the Japanese left-wing student movement). Kyoto: Dōshisha daigaku shuppan bu, 1953.

Suzuki Hiroo 鈴木博雄. *Gakusei undō—Daigaku no kaikaku ka, shakai no henkaku ka* 學生運動—大學の改革か, 社會の變革か (Student movements—University reform or social revolution?). Fukumura shuppan, 1968.

Suzuki Tōmin 鈴木東民. "Demokurashii no reimei" デモクラシーの黎明 (The dawn of democracy), in Gakusei shobō henshūbu 學生書房編集部, ed., *Watakushi no gakusei no koro* 私の學生の頃 (My student days). 3 vols. Gakusei shobō, 1948. III, 62–77.

Tadokoro Teruaki 田所輝明. "Zenki gakusei undō" 前期學生運動 (The early student movement), *Shakai kagaku* 社會科學, 4.1 (February 1928), 136–148.

Takakuwa Suehide 高桑末秀. *Nihon gakusei shakai undō shi* 日本學生社會運動史 (A history of the Japanese left-wing student movement). Aoki shoten, 1955.

Takano Iwasaburō 高野岩三郎. "Shakai seisaku gakkai sōritsu no koro" 社會政策學會創立の頃 (The era of the founding of the Social Policy Association), *Teikoku daigaku shimbun* 帝國大學新聞, no. 607 (November 4, 1935), pp. 6–11.

Takano Minoru 高野實. "Zengakuren no dekiru koro" 全學連のできるころ (The era of the Zengakuren founding), *Daigaku ronsō* 大學論叢, 2.3 (May 1964), 85–88.

Takase Kiyoshi 高瀨淸. "Kakumei Sobieto senkōki" 革命ソビエト潜行記 (An account of clandestine travel in revolutionary Russia), *Jiyū* 自由, 5.2 (February 1963), 127–133.

Takatsu Seidō 高津正道. "Hata o mamorite" 旗を守りて (Defending the flag), 8 parts, *Gekkan shakaitō* 月刊社會黨, nos. 55–62 (January-August, 1962).

Takayama Shūgetsu 高山秋月. *Kōtō gakkō to sakei mondai* 高等學校と左傾問題 (The higher schools and the problem of leftism). Nihon hyōronsha, 1932.

Tamaki Motoi 玉城素. *Nihon gakusei shi* 日本學生史 (A history of Japanese students). San'ichi shobō, 1961.

Tanaka Sōgorō 田中惣五郎. *Shiryō Nihon shakai undō shi* 資料日本社會運動史 (A documentary history of the left-wing movement in Japan). 2 vols. Tōzai shuppan sha, 1947–48.

—— *Yoshino Sakuzō* 吉野作造 (Yoshino Sakuzō). Miraisha, 1958.

Tateyama Takaaki 立山隆章. *Nihon kyōsantō kenkyo hishi* 日本共産黨檢擧祕史 (A secret history of the Japanese Communist Party arrests). Bukyōsha, 1929.

Tateyama Toshitada 堅山利忠. "Nihon Gakki daisōgi to watakushi" 日本樂器大爭議と私 (My experience in the Japan Musical Instrument strike), *Kikan rōdō* 季刊勞働, no. 2 (January 1967), pp. 18–23.

Teikoku daigaku shimbun 帝國大學新聞 (Imperial University News), 1923–34.

Teikoku daigaku shimbun sha 帝國大学新聞社, ed. *Teikoku daigaku nenkan* 帝國大學年鑑 (Imperial University annual). Editor, 1935.

Terasaki Masao 寺崎昌男. "Daigakushi bunken mokuroku—Nihon no bu" 大學史文獻目錄—日本の部 (A bibliography on the history of universities—Japan), *Kyōikugaku kenkyū* 教育學研究, 32.2–3 (September 1965), 62–90.

Tōdai Arubamu, Keiyūkai, Midorikai iin yūshi konshinkai 東大アルバム・經友會・綠會委員有志懇親會, ed. *Tōdai Arubamu, Midorikai, Keiyūkai iin meibo* 東大アルバム・綠會・經友會委員名簿 (List of officers of the Tokyo University Yearbook, the Midorikai, and the Keiyūkai). Yamagata Sahei shōten, 1967.

Tōdai Shinjinkai gojusshūnen kinen gyōji hokkininkai 東大新人会五十周年記念行事發起人會, ed. *Tōdai Shinjinkai kaiin meibo* 東大新人會會員名簿 (Membership list of the Tokyo University Shinjinkai). Editor, 1968.

Tokuda Kyūichi 德田球一 and Shiga Yoshio 志賀義雄. *Gokuchū jūhachinen* 獄中十八年 (Eighteen years in jail). Jiji tsūshinsha, 1947.

Tokutomi Iichirō (Sohō) 德富猪一郎(蘇峰). *Taishō no seinen to teikoku no zento* 大正の青年と帝國の前途 (Taishō youth and the future of the empire). Min'yūsha, 1916.

Tōkyō asahi shimbun 東京朝日新聞, 1924–40.

Tōkyō daigaku 東京大學. *Tōkyō daigaku sotsugyōsei shimei roku* 東京大學卒業生氏名錄 (Tokyo University alumni directory). 1950.

Tōkyō daigaku shimbun sha henshūbu 東京大學新聞社編集部, ed. *Haiiro no seishun* 灰色の青春 (Our cheerless youth). Editor, 1948.

Tōkyō teikoku daigaku 東京帝國大學, ed. *Tōkyō teikoku daigaku gojūnen shi* 東京帝國大學五十年史 (A fifty-year history of Tokyo Imperial University), 2 vols. Editor, 1932.

———, Gakuseika 學生課. *Saikin ni okeru hongakunai no sayoku gakusei soshiki to sono undō no gaiyō* 最近に於ける本學內の左翼學生組織と其運動の概要 (An outline of the recent activities and organization of left-wing students on this campus). January 1932.

——— *Shōwa shichinenjū ni okeru hongakunai no gakusei shisō undō no gaikyō* 昭和七年中に於ける本學內の學生思想運動の概況 (The condition of the student thought movement on this campus in 1932). February 1933.

——— *Shōwa kunenjū ni okeru hongakunai no gakusei shisō undō no gaikyō* 昭和九年中に於ける本學內の學生思想運動の概況 (The condition of the student thought movement on this campus in 1934). February 1935.

Totten, George O., III. *The Social Democratic Movement in Prewar Japan*. New Haven: Yale University Press, 1966.

Tōyama Shigeki 遠山茂樹. "Honemi ni shimiru kaikon—Okubyō de heibon na ichi gakusei no omoide" 骨身にしみる悔恨—臆病で平凡な一學生の想出 (Remorse which pierces to the marrow: Recollections of one cowardly and commonplace student), *Tōkyō daigaku shimbun* 東京大學新聞, no. 137 (October 30, 1952), p. 3.

Tsukada Taigan 塚田大願. *Kyōsan seinen dōmei no rekishi* 共產青年同盟の歷史 (A history of the Communist Youth League). Nihon seinen shuppansha, 1968.

Tsurumi, Kazuko. *Social Change and the Individual: Japan Before and After Defeat in World War II*. Princeton: Princeton University Press, 1970.

Uchida Yoshihiko 內田義彦 and Shiota Shōbei 鹽田庄兵衞. "Chishiki seinen no sho-ruikei" 知識青年の諸類型 (A typology of intellectual youth), in Chikuma shobō 筑摩書房, ed., *Kindai Nihon shisō shi kōza* 近代日本思想史講座 (A symposium on modern Japanese intellectual history). 8 vols. Editor, 1959–61. IV, 235–282.

Uyehara, Cecil H. *Leftwing Social Movements in Japan—An Annotated Bibliography*. Tokyo and Rutland, Vt.: Charles E. Tuttle, 1959.

Waseda daigaku arubamu kankōkai 早稻田大學アルバム刊行會, ed. *Waseda daigaku arubamu* 早稻田大學アルバム (Waseda University album). Editor, 1963.

Watanabe Tōru 渡部徹, ed. *Kyōto chihō rōdō undō shi* 京都地方勞働運動史 (A history of the labor movement in the Kyoto region). Rev. ed. Kyoto: Kyoto chihō rōdō undō shi hensankai, 1968.

Watanabe Yoshimichi 渡部義通 and Shiota Shōbei 鹽田庄兵衞, eds. *Nihon shakai shugi bunken kaisetsu* 日本社會主義文獻解說 (A bibliographical guide to Japanese socialism). Ōtsuki shoten, 1958.

Yoshino Sakuzō 吉野作造. *Futsū senkyo ron* 普通選擧論 (On universal suffrage). Banda shobō, 1919.

Young, John. *The Research Activities of the South Manchurian Railway Company, 1907–1945*. New York: East Asian Institute, Columbia University, 1966.

Zen'ei 前衞 (Vanguard), no. 13 (March 1923).

Glossary

Major geographical names and foreign loan-words have been omitted. The names of Shinjinkai members will be found in the appendix.

Abe Jirō 阿部次郎
Abe Ken'ichi 阿部研一
Akamatsu Akiko 赤松明子
Akamatsu Iomaro 赤松五百麿
Akamatsu Tsuneko 赤松常子
Akamon-de 赤門出
Akamon senshi 『赤門戰士』
Akiyama Jirō 秋山次郎
Akizeki Naoji 秋關直二
Aono Suekichi 靑野季吉
Aoyama Gakuin (Univ.) 靑山學院大學
Arahata Kanson 荒畑寒村
Aramata Misao 荒又操
Arishima Takeo 有島武郎
Asanuma Inejirō 淺沼稻次郎
Ashio 足尾
Azuma Ryōtarō 東龍太郎

Bimbō monogatari 『貧乏物語』
buchō kaigi 部長會議
bu-iinkai 部委員會
Bungakkai 文學會
Bungeibu 文藝部
bungei-ha 文藝派
Bunka dōmei 文化同盟
Bunka gakkai 文化學會
Bunka kagaku bu 文化科學部

Bunkakai 文化會

Chian keisatsu hō 治安警察法
chihōbu 地方部
chihō rengōkai 地方聯合會
chindeki seinen 沈溺靑年
Chūgai 『中外』
Chūō (Univ.) 中央大學
chūōbu 中央部
Chūō kōron 『中央公論』

Daigaku fukyūkai 大學普及會
Daigaku hyōron 『大學評論』
Daigaku nankō 大學南校
Daigaku tōkō 大學東校
Daitōa sensō kōteiron『大東亞戰爭肯定論』
Daitōkaku 大鐙閣
Dan Tokusaburō 淡德三郎
danzetsukan 斷絶感
daraku seru gense 墮落せる現世
Dazai Osamu 太宰治
Dōhō 『同胞』
dōjinkai 同人會
Dōjinsha 同人社
dōjin zasshi 同人雜誌
dokushokai 讀書會
dokushoyoku 讀書欲

319

dōmei higyō 同盟罷業
dōmei kyūkō 同盟休校
dōshi 同志
dōshi no kai 同志の會
Dōshisha (Univ.) 同志社大學

Ebina Danjō 海老名彈正
enzetsu 演說

Fujimura Misao 藤村操
Fukuda Keijirō 福田啓二郎
Fukuda Tokuzō 福田德三
Fukumoto Kazuo 福本和夫
Fukuzawa Yukichi 福澤諭吉
fumie 踏み繪
Furuichi Haruhiko 古市春彦
Fushinkai 扶信會
Futatsugi Takeshi 二木猛
futsū senkyo kenkyūkai 普通選舉研究會

gakkō sōdō 學校騒動
gakkō-teki kannen 學校的觀念
gakubatsu 學閥
gakugyō fushin 學業不進
Gakuseibu 學生部
Gakusei han-higōhō iinkai 學生牛非合法委員會
gakusei iin 學生委員
gakusei iinkai 學生委員會
gakusei jichi undō 學生自治運動
Gakuseika 學生課
Gakuseikai 學生會
gakuseikan 學生監
Gakusei rengōkai 學生聯合會
Gakusei shakai kagaku rengōkai 學生社會科學聯合會
Gakusei shisō mondai chōsakai 學生思想問題調査會
gakusei shuji 學生主事
gakusei sōdō mansei jidai 學生騒動慢性時代
"Gakusei to wa ikanaru shakaigun de aru ka" 「學生とはいかなる社會群であるか」

Gakusei undō 『學生運動』
Gakuren 學聯
gakuyūkai 學友會
gasshuku 合宿
Goshiki (Spa) 五色溫泉
Gotō Hideko 後藤秀子
Gunji kenkyūkai 軍事研究會
Gyōminkai 曉民會
Gyōmin kyōsan shugi dan 曉民共產主義團

Hachinoki 鉢の木
Hakai 『破戒』
Hakuyōsha 白揚社
han-iinkai 班委員會
hammon seinen 煩悶青年
Hara Kei 原敬
Hasegawa Nyozekan 長谷川如是閑
Hatano Misao 波多野操
hattenteki kaishō 發展的解消
Hayashi Utako 林歌子
Heimin shimbun 『平民新聞』
Hemmi Shigeo 逸見重雄
hi-kambu-ha 非幹部派
Hirano Yoshitarō 平野義太郎
Hisatome Kōzō 久留弘三
Hitotsubashi (Univ.) 一橋大學
Hōjō Kazuo 北條一雄
hombu 本部
Hongō 本郷
Honjo 本所
Honjō Kasō 本莊可宗
honka 本科
Hōsei (Univ.) 法政大學
Hoshishima Nirō 星島二郎
Hozumi Shigetō 穗積重遠
Hsueh-sheng lien-ho-hui 學生聯合會
Huang Hsing 黃興
Hyōgikai 評議會

Ichikawa Shōichi 市川正一
ichi kōsei bunshi 一構成分子
ichi nōto sanjūnen 一ノート三十年
ichiyoku 一翼

Ijūin 伊集院
Ikeda Takashi 池田隆
ikueikai 育英會
Imanaka Tsugimaro 今中次麿
Inamura Ryūichi 稲村隆一
Inokuchi Masao 井之口政雄
Inomata Tsunao 猪俣津南雄
Inoue Kowashi 井上毅
Inukai Tsuyoshi 犬養毅
Iryō no shakaika 『醫療の社會化』
Ishida Eiichirō 石田英一郎
Ishigami Takaaki 石神高明
Ishikawa Sanshirō 石川三四郎
Ishikawa Takuboku 石川啄木
Isshinkai 一新會
Isukurakaku イスクラ閣
Itagaki Taisuke 板垣退助
Itō Byakuren 伊藤白蓮
Itō Denzaemon 伊藤傳左衞門
Itō Hirobumi 伊藤博文
Itō Masanosuke 伊藤政之助
Itō Ushinosuke 伊藤丑之助
itoku shugi 遺德主義
Iwauchi Zensaku 岩内善作

jichi 自治
jichikai 自治會
jikyoku kōkyūkai 時局講究會
jissai-ha 實際派
jissen-ha 實踐派
Jiyū hōsōdan 自由法曹團
jiyū minken undō 自由民權運動
jōjun 上旬
jōmu iinkai 常務委員會
Jūninkai 十人會
Jūōkai 縦横會
Jūō (Club) 縦横倶樂部
jusha 儒者

Kagawa Toyohiko 賀川豊彦
Kaihō 『解放』
kaihō 會報
Kaisei gakkō 開成學校
Kaiseijo 開成所

Kaishintō 改進黨
kaiyū 會友
Kaizo 『改造』
Kaizōsha 改造社
kakumei 革命
Kakumeikai 鶴鳴会
kakumei zen'ya shugi 革命前夜主義
Kamada Eikichi 鎌田榮吉
kambu-ha 幹部派
Kamei Kan'ichirō 龜井貫一郎
Kameido 龜戸
Kami-Fujimae-chō 上富士前町
Kamihira Shōzō 上平正三
Kanai Mitsuru 金井滿
Kanda 神田
kanemochi no wakadanna 金持の若旦那
kanji 幹事
kanjichō 幹事長
Kansai (Univ.) 關西大學
Kansai Gakuin (Univ.) 關西學院大學
kanshō taiji 奸商退治
kan'yū 勸誘
Kao Sekken gojūnen shi 『花王石鹼五十
  年史』
Katagiri Michiya 片桐道宇
Katayama Tetsu 片山哲
Kawabata Yasunari 川端康成
Kawada Hiroshi 河田廣
Kawai Eijirō 河合榮治郎
Kawai Etsuzō 河合悦三
Kawakami Hajime 河上肇
Kazama Tetsuji 風間徹二
Keiō (Univ.) 慶應大學
Keiyūkai 經友會
keizai shugi 經濟主義
kenkyū-ha 研究派
kenkyūkai 研究會
Kensetsusha dōmei 建設者同盟
ketsugi 決議
Ketsumeidan 血盟團
Kibōkaku 希望閣
kibunteki itchi 氣分的一致
Kigensetsu 紀元節
Kikakuin 企畫院

Kikufuji (Hotel) 菊富士ホテル
Kindai shisō 『近代思想』
Kitazawa Shinjirō 北澤新次郎
Kobayashi Hideo 小林秀雄
Kobayashi Kōzō 小林浩三
Kōdansha 講談社
kōdō-ha 行動派
kōenkai 講演會
kōgaku-ha 好學派
Kōjinkai 行人會
Kōkoku dōshikai 興國同志會
Kokumin kōdan 『國民講壇』
Kokumin seishin bunka kenkyūjo 國民
　精神文化研究所
Kokuryūkai 黑龍會
kokutai 國體
Komagome 駒込
Kondō Kenji 近藤憲二
kōtō gakkō 高等學校
Kōtō gakkō remmei 高等學校聯盟
Kōtoku Shūsui 幸德秋水
kōza 講座
Kōza (School) 講座派
Kubo Kanzaburō 久保勘三郎
Kubota Shun 久保田畯
Kumagai Takao 熊谷孝雄
kunji 訓示
Kushida Tamizō 櫛田民藏
Kusunoki Masashige 楠木正成
Kuroda Reiji 黑田禮二
Kyōchōkai 協調會
Kyōgakukyoku 教學局
Kyōmeisha 教明社
Kyōsan seinen dōmei 共產青年同盟
Kyōseikaku 共生閣
kyōyōbu 教養部
kyōyō gakubu 教養學部

Mainichi shimbun 『毎日新聞』
makanai seibatsu 賄征伐
Marukishizumu kenkyūjo マルキシズ
　ム研究所
Marukusu-Engerusu zenshū 『マルクス・
　エンゲルス全集』

Marukusu shugi geijutsu kenkyūkai マ
　ルクス主義藝術研究會
Maruzen 丸善
Matsukata Saburō 松方三郎
Matsukawa Ryōichi 松川亮一
Matsumoto Kaoru 松本馨
Matsuo Shigeki 松尾茂樹
Matsuura Kenzō 松浦健三
meibo 名簿
Meiji (Univ.) 明治大學
Meiji Gakuin (Univ.) 明治學院大學
Mejiro 目白
Midorikai 綠會
mihakkō 未發行
mimponshugi 民本主義
Minjin dōmeikai 民人同盟會
Minobe Tatsukichi 美濃部達吉
Min'yūsha 民友社
Mishima Yukio 三島由紀夫
Miyahara Seiichi 宮原誠一
Miyake Setsurei 三宅雪嶺
Miyake Shōichi 三宅正一
Miyamoto Kenji 宮本顯治
Miyazaki Shinsaku 宮崎震作
Miyazaki Tamizō 宮崎民藏
Miyazaki Tōten (Torazō) 宮崎滔天
　(寅藏)
Mizobuchi Shimma 溝淵進馬
Mizuno Hideo 水野秀夫
Mizuno Rentarō 水野錬太郎
mohan seinen 模範青年
Mokuyōkai 木曜會
Morikawa-chō 森川町
Morito Tatsuo 森戸辰男
Murayama Tomoyoshi 村山知義
Murobuse Kōshin 室伏高信
Musan seinen dōmei 無產青年同盟
Musansha 無產社
mushoku seinen 無色青年

Nabeyama Sadachika 鍋山貞親
Nagai Ryōkichi 永井了吉
Nagamine (Celluloid Co.) 永峰セルロ
　イド會社

Nagase 長瀬
Nagashima Matao 長島又男
naikun 內訓
Nakagawa Hanako 中川ハナ子
Nakagawa Minoru 中川實
Nakamura Yoshiaki 中村義明
Nakano Masato 中野正人
Nakao Katsuo 中尾勝男
Nammei (Club) 南明俱樂部
Nankatsu rōdōkai 南葛勞働會
Narushima Ryūhoku 成島柳北
Natsume Sōseki 夏目漱石
nenkō joretsu 年功序列
Nichirōtō 日勞黨
Nihon (Univ.) 日本大學
Nihon rōdō kumiai dōmei 日本勞働組
　合同盟
Nihon seiji keizai kenkyūjo 日本政治經
　濟研究所
Nihon shakai shugi dōmei 日本社會主
　義同盟
Nihon shakaitō 日本社會黨
Nippori 日暮里
Nishida Kitarō 西田幾太郎
Nishijin 西陣
Nishi Masao 西雅雄
Nishi Seiho 西成甫
Nobusada Takitarō 信定瀧太郎
Noguchi Hachirō 野口八郎
Noma Seiji 野間清治
Nonaka Tetsuya 野中徹也
Noro Eitarō 野呂榮太郎

Ōba Kakō 大庭柯公
Ohara Kōsuke 小原公助
Ōhara shakai mondai kenkyūjo 大原社
　會問題研究所
Oiwake-chō 追分町
Okada Ryōhei 岡田良平
Ōkōchi Masatoshi 大河內正敏
Ōkuma Shigenobu 大隈重信
Ōmori Yoshitarō 大森義太郎
omoshiroi おもしろい
Omoya Sōkichi 面家莊佶

Ono Azusa 小野梓
Ōsaka asahi shimbun 『大阪朝日新聞』
Ōsugi Sakae 大杉榮
Ōtani (Univ.) 大谷大學
Ōtokai 鷗渡會
Ōyama Ikuo 大山郁夫
Ozaki Hotsumi 尾崎秀實
Ozaki Yukio 尾崎行雄

Puroretaria kagaku kenkyūjo プロレタ
　リア科學研究所

R. F. Kai RF會
Rēnin chosakushū 『レーニン著作集』
Reimeikai 黎明會
Reimei kōenshū 『黎明講演集』
ribekka リベッ化
rijikai 理事會
Rikugō zasshi 『六合雜誌』
Rikkyō (Univ.) 立教大學
Rinji kyōiku kaigi 臨時教育會議
Riron tōsō 『理論鬪爭』
risshin shusse 立身出世
Ritsumeikan (Univ.) 立命館大學
Rōdōsha-ha 勞働者派
Rōgakkai 勞學會
rōnin 浪人
Rōninkai 浪人會
Rōnōtō 勞農黨
ryōsho 良書
Ryūkoku (Univ.) 龍谷大學

Saeki Tetsuo 佐伯哲夫
Sakai Kisaku 酒井龜作
Sakai Magara 堺眞柄
Sakai Toshihiko 堺利彥
Sakisaka Itsurō 向坂逸郎
Sakuragi-chō 櫻木町
san'akuhō hantai undō 三惡法反對運動
Sangyō hōkokukai 產業報國會
Sangyō rōdō chōsajo 產業勞働調査所
Sankei shimbun 『產經新聞』
Sano Fumio 佐野文夫
Sano Hiroshi 佐野博

Sano Manabu shū 『佐野學集』
Sasaki Sōichi 佐々木惣一
Satō Eisaku 佐藤榮作
Seiji hihan 『政治批判』
Seiji kenkyūkai 政治研究會
seikō seinen 成功青年
Seikyōsha 政教社
Seinen bunka dōmei 青年文化同盟
Seinen jiyūto 青年自由黨
Seinenkai-ha 青年會派
seishun 青春
Sekigun-ha 赤軍派
Sekirankai 赤瀾會
semmonbu 專門部
semmon gakkō 專門學校
senden enzetsukai 宣傳演說會
Senku 『先驅』
setchūshugi 折衷主義
Shakai mondai kenkyū 『社會問題研究』
Shakai mondai kenkyūkai 社會問題研究會
Shakai seisaku gakkai 社會政策學會
shakai shisō kenkyūkai 社會思想研究會
Shakai shisōsha 社會思想社
Shakai shugi kenkyū 『社會主義研究』
Shakai shugi no karakuri 『社會主義のからくり』
shaken 社研
shibu 支部
Shichiseisha 七生社
Shichiseisha-in bōkō jiken taisaku kaku-dantai kyōgikai 七生社員暴行事件對策各團體協議會
shijuku 私塾
shikkō iinkai 執行委員會
Shimada Seijirō 島田清次郎
Shimizu-chō 清水町
Shimizu Heikurō 清水平九郎
shimpoteki bunkajin 進步的文化人
Shinchūgumi 神中組
Shindō Kyūzō 神道久三
Shinjin 『新人』
Shinjinkai 新人會

Shinjinkai gakujutsu kōenkai 新人會學術講演會
Shinjinkai sōsho 新人會叢書
Shirokiya 白木屋
shi-seikatsu hihankai 私生活批判會
Shisō kenkyū 『思想研究』
Shisōkyoku 思想局
shisō yō-chūinin 思想要注意人
shisō zendō 思想善導
"Shisō zendō no shushi tettei kata"「思想善導ノ趣旨徹定方」
shitamachi 下町
Shiyūkai 紫友會
shōben-zeme 小便攻め
Shōheikō 昌平黌
Shōken tōshi nyūmon 『証券投資入門』
Shōriki Matsutarō 正力松太郎
shosai-ha 書齋派
shosekibu 書籍部
Shūeikaku 聚英閣
Shūkai jōrei 集會條例
Shūkai oyobi seisha hō 集會及び政社法
shūsai 秀才
shusshinchi 出身地
shutaisei 主體性
Soda Hidemune 曾田英宗
Sōdōmei 總同盟
Soejima Tane 副島種
Sōrengō 總連合
Suehiro Izutarō 末弘嚴太郎
Suenobu Hifumi 末延一二三
Sugi Michio 杉道夫
Suiheisha 水平社
Suiyōkai 水曜會
sūmei 數名
Sumida Haruo 隅田春雄
Sutārin-Buhārin chosakushū 『スターリン・ブハーリン著作集』
Suzuki Bunji 鈴木文治
Suzuki Tōmin 鈴木東民
Suzuki Yasuzō 鈴木安藏
Suzuki Yoshio 鈴木義男

Tadokoro Teruaki 田所輝明
Takabatake Motoyuki 高畠素之
Takada-mura 高田村
Takada Sanae 高田早苗
Takahashi Seigo 高橋清吾
Takano Minoru 高野實
Takase Kiyoshi 高瀨清
Takatsu Seidō 高津正道
Takatsu Wataru 高津渡
Takayama Gizō 高山義三
Takeuchi Yoshimi 竹内好
Takigawa Yukitoki 瀧川幸辰
Tamaki Hajime 玉城肇
Taman Kiyoomi 田万清臣
Tanaka Sumiko 田中壽美子
Tanemaku hito 『種蒔く人』
Teiyūkai 丁友會
Teikoku daigaku shimbun 『帝國大學新聞』
tenkō 轉向
"Tenkō ni tsuite" 「轉向について」
tenkōsha 轉向者
tenkōsho 轉向書
Terasaki Masao 寺崎昌男
Tetsumon (Club) 鐵門クラブ
Tezuka Tomio 手塚富雄
Tōa dōbun shoin 東亞同文書院
Tōa keizai chōsa kyoku 東亞經濟調査局
Tōa remmei 東亞連盟
Tōdai 東大
Tōdai shaken 東大社研
Tokano Takeshi 戸叶武
tokubetsu yō-shisatsunin 特別要視察人
Tokuda Kyūichi 德田球一
Tokunaga Sunao 德永直
tokushu na mibun no de 特殊な身分の出
Tokutomi Roka 德富蘆化
Tokutomi Sohō 德富蘇峰
Tōkyō daigaku 東京大學
Tōkyō kaisei gakkō 東京開成學校
Tōkyō nichinichi shimbun 『東京日日新聞』
Tōkyō semmon gakkō 東京專門學校

Tōkyō teikoku daigaku setsurumento 東京帝國大學セツルメント
tōron 討論
Toshimaen 豊島園
toshobu 圖書部
Tōyama Shigeki 遠山茂樹
Tsukishima 月島
Tsurumi Shunsuke 鶴見俊輔
tsūtatsu 通達

Uchimura Kanzō 內村鑑三
Uesugi Shinkichi 上杉愼吉
Ugaki Kazushige 宇垣一成
Undōkai 運動會
Utsunomiya Tokuma 宇都宮德馬

Wada Iwao 和田巖
Wadagaki Kenzō 和田垣謙三
Wakayama Kenji 若山健二
Warera 『我等』
Waseda (Univ.) 早稻田大學
Waseda shakai gakkai 早稻田社會學會
Watanabe Masanosuke 渡邊政之輔
Watanabe Taeko 渡邊多惠子

Yamada Moritarō 山田盛太郎
Yamaguchi Hisatarō 山口久太郎
Yamakawa Hitoshi 山川均
Yamakawa Kikue 山川菊榮
Yamamoto Kenzō 山本懸藏
Yamazaki (Nishiyama) Yūji 山崎（西山）雄次
Yanagihara Byakuren 柳原白蓮
Yanagishima 柳島
Yanaihara Tadao 矢內原忠雄
Yasukichi 安吉
Yōgakusho 洋學所
yoka 豫科
Yomiuri shimbun 『讀賣新聞』
Yoshikawa Morikuni 吉川守邦
Yoshino Sakuzō 吉野作造
Yūaikai 友愛會
Yūben 『雄辯』

Yūbenkai 雄辯會
Yūben remmei roshiya kikin kyūsaikai 雄辯聯盟露西亞飢饉救濟會
Yuibutsuron kenkyūkai 唯物論研究會
yūzei 遊説

"Zakki" 「雜記」
Zen'ei 『前衞』
Zengakuren 全學連
Zenkoku gakusei gunji kyōiku hantai dōmei 全國學生軍事教育反對同盟

Zenkoku seruroido shokkō kumiai 全国セルロイド職工組合
Zenkokuteki kyōtei 全國的教程
Zenkyō 全協
Zen-Nihon gakusei jichikai sōrengō 全日本學生自治會總連合
Zen-Nihon gakusei jiyū yōgo dōmei 全日本學生自由擁護同盟
Zen-Nihon gakusei shakai kagaku rengōkai 全日本學生社會科學聯合會

Index

For Shinjinkai members not appearing in the text, see the Appendix.

Harvard East Asian Series

32. *The Chinese World Order: Traditional China's Foreign Relations*. Edited by John K. Fairbank.
33. *The Buddhist Revival in China*. By Holmes Welch.
34. *Traditional Medicine in Modern China: Science, Nationalism, and the Tensions of Cultural Change*. By Ralph C. Croizier.
35. *Party Rivalry and Political Change in Taishō Japan*. By Peter Duus.
36. *The Rhetoric of Empire: American China Policy, 1895–1901*. By Marilyn B. Young.
37. *Radical Nationalist in Japan: Kita Ikki, 1883–1937*. By George M. Wilson.
38. *While China Faced West: American Reformers in Nationalist China, 1928–1937*. By James C. Thomson Jr.
39. *The Failure of Freedom: A Portrait of Modern Japanese Intellectuals*. By Tatsuo Arima.
40. *Asian Ideas of East and West: Tagore and His Critics in Japan, China, and India*. By Stephen N. Hay.
41. *Canton under Communism: Programs and Politics in a Provincial Capital, 1949–1968*. By Ezra F. Vogel.
42. *Ting Wen-chiang: Science and China's New Culture*. By Charlotte Furth.
43. *The Manchurian Frontier in Ch'ing History*. By Robert H. G. Lee.
44. *Motoori Norinaga, 1730–1801*. By Shigeru Matsumoto.
45. *The Comprador in Nineteenth Century China: Bridge between East and West*. By Yen-p'ing Hao.
46. *Hu Shih and the Chinese Renaissance: Liberalism in the Chinese Revolution, 1917–1937*. By Jerome B. Grieder.
47. *The Chinese Peasant Economy: Agricultural Development in Hopei and Shantung, 1890–1949*. By Ramon H. Myers.
48. *Japanese Tradition and Western Law: Emperor, State, and Law in the Thought of Hozumi Yatsuka*. By Richard H. Minear.
49. *Rebellion and Its Enemies in Late Imperial China: Militarization and Social Structure, 1796–1864*. By Philip A. Kuhn.
50. *Early Chinese Revolutionaries: Radical Intellectuals in Shanghai and Chekiang, 1902–1911*. By Mary Backus Rankin.
51. *Communication and Imperial Control in China: Evolution of the Palace Memorial System, 1693–1735*. By Silas H. L. Wu.
52. *Vietnam and the Chinese Model: A Comparative Study of Nguyễn and Ch'ing Civil Government in the First Half of the Nineteenth Century*. By Alexander Barton Woodside.
53. *The Modernization of the Chinese Salt Administration, 1900–1920*. By S. A. M. Adshead.
54. *Chang Chih-tung and Educational Reform in China*. By William Ayers.
55. *Kuo Mo-jo: The Early Years*. By David Tod Roy.
56. *Social Reformers in Urban China: The Chinese Y.M.C.A., 1895–1926*. By Shirley S. Garrett.
57. *Biographic Dictionary of Chinese Communism, 1921–1965*. By Donald W. Klein and Anne B. Clark.
58. *Imperialism and Chinese Nationalism: Germany in Shantung*. By John E. Shrecker.
59. *Monarchy in the Emperor's Eyes: Image and Reality in the Ch'ien-lung Reign*. By Harold L. Kahn.
60. *Yamagata Aritomo in the Rise of Modern Japan, 1838–1922*. By Roger F. Hackett.
61. *Russia and China: Their Diplomatic Relations to 1728*. By Mark Mancall.
62. *The Yenan Way in Revolutionary China*. By Mark Selden.

63. *The Mississippi Chinese: Between Black and White.* By James W. Loewen.
64. *Liang Ch'i-ch'ao and Intellectual Transition in China, 1890–1907.* By Hao Chang.
65. *A Korean Village: Between Farm and Sea.* By Vincent S. R. Brandt.
66. *Agricultural Change and the Peasant Economy of South China.* By Evelyn S. Rawski.
67. *The Peace Conspiracy: Wang Ching-wei and the China War, 1937–1941.* By Gerald Bunker.
68. *Mori Arinori.* By Ivan Hall.
69. *Buddhism under Mao.* By Holmes Welch.
70. *Student Radicals in Prewar Japan.* By Henry Smith.